Codes of the Underworld

Codes of the Underworld

How Criminals Communicate

Diego Gambetta

PRINCETON UNIVERSITY PRESS   *Princeton & Oxford*

Copyright © 2009 by Princeton University Press
Requests for permission to reproduce material from this work should be sent
  to Permissions, Princeton University Press

Published by Princeton University Press, 41 William Street, Princeton,
  New Jersey 08540
In the United Kingdom: Princeton University Press, 6 Oxford Street,
  Woodstock, Oxfordshire OX20 1TW

LIBRARY OF CONGRESS CATALOGING-IN-PUBLICATION DATA
Gambetta, Diego, 1952–
    Codes of the underworld : how criminals communicate / Diego Gambetta.
    p.   cm.
    Includes bibliographical references and index.
    ISBN 978-0-691-11937-3 (hardcover : alk.
paper) 1. Criminals. 2. Communication. 3. Criminals—Social
conditions. I. Title.
    HV6085.G36 2009
    364.301'4--dc22
    2009006822

British Library Cataloging-in-Publication Data is available

This book has been composed in Bembo and Frutiger

Printed on acid-free paper. ∞

press.princeton.edu

Printed in the United States of America

10 9 8 7 6 5 4 3 2 1

Contents

Acknowledgments

I have been at this book on and off for nearly ten years. I was able to take a major step forward thanks to a British Academy Research Readership, which gave me two blissful years of leave in 2000–2002. Then new projects intruded, especially on suicide attacks, and completing the last 10 percent took me as long as writing the first 90 percent—one more thing you can blame on 9/11.

Another cause of my delay was a rather more fortunate one—and I am not referring only to my two children. Unlike the protagonists of this book, whose world is laced with mistrust, violence, and fraudulent communications, I am lucky to inhabit one that enjoys quite extraordinary levels of cooperation, in which what matters is getting an argument or fact right, and in which people are very generous with their ideas. Don't get me wrong; there is no shortage of bad apples in the academic world too—a few of whom earn an honorable mention in the book—but that isn't surprising. What is surprising is to be able to count on so many kindred spirits. I owe a great debt of gratitude to Michael Biggs, Avinash Dixit, Jon Elster, Peter Hill, Marek Kaminski, Gerry Mackie, Thomas Schelling, Federico Varese, an anonymous reviewer for Princeton University Press, and last but most emphatically not least my wife Valeria Pizzini-Gambetta. They all read the whole manuscript and showered me with stories, sources, comments, *and* criticisms that made me embark on some thorough rethinking and lengthy revisions. Together they produced a total of forty single-spaced pages, plus myriad e-mails and a countless number of words scribbled by hand on the copies I had given some of them to read. Had they given me fewer and shallower comments, you would not have been deprived of this book for so long!

The list of events and people, young and old, we should blame for my procrastination, while it should definitely exclude me, should include several other sharp friends and colleagues who helped me with individual chapters. On "Information as Hostage" (chapter 3), I benefited greatly from the comments of Abigail Barr, Ernesto dal Bò, Robert Gibbons, Alena Ledeneva, and the participants at three presentations: at the Department of Political Science, Columbia University, in September 1998; at MIT in November 1999; and at a workshop at the Centre for the Development of African Economies in Oxford in 2004. Lucia Zedner gave me very good advice on "Why Prisoners Fight (and Signal)" (chapter 4); also on the same chapter, I benefited from the lively discussions at two criminology seminars that I gave, in 2003, at All Souls College, Oxford, and at the London School of Economics. Rakesh Kurana valiantly helped me with "Why (Low) Life Imitates Art" (chapter 10), which also profits from the comments of the participants at a seminar I gave at the Sociology Department at Harvard University in 1999. Rakesh and Peter Rutland also called many articles to my attention. Heather Hamill and Marina Tzvetkova gave me interesting comments on "Self-harm as a Signal" (chapter 5), and Marina also helped me with bibliographic searches and editing the manuscript. Finally, many more people sent me stories and suggestions—Scott Atran, Robert Ford, Wolfgang Herbert, Stephen Holmes, Velisarios Kattoulas, Chu Yiu Kong, Dan Sperber, Laura Stoker, and Clinton Watson Taylor are those whom I can remember.

My good fortune grew even larger thanks to Ian Malcolm, the editor of this book for the Press. Ian, who is gifted with patience worthy of Job, edited and commented on all the chapters in the book, just as the editors of a bygone era used to do—*rarae aves* now, whom authors are more likely to encounter in their dreams.

Introduction

Not much is known, let alone understood, about how criminals communicate with one another. This is not just because the evidence is hard to gather. The storytellers of the underworld collect tales of crime and marvel at the variety of rituals, styles, and languages that criminals use, but seldom go beyond descriptive accounts. Criminologists focus on deviant actions, but they rarely seem to appreciate in full the information that actions themselves can convey in the underworld. Sociologists, who have given us fine ethnographies of gangs and racketeers, have not been interested in developing explicit theories linking the seemingly extravagant displays of their subjects with rational pursuits. To gather evidence, even to understand that certain events *are* evidence of something interesting, one needs to be guided by theoretical expectations. Yet economists, who have developed sophisticated theoretical means to model information, have enough troubles collecting data on the world of ordinary business to bother with the underworld.

The study of criminal communications has also fallen between the stools of two common views, which reinforce each other. One pertains to how communication is understood in general. It is still all too frequent, even among scholars, to think of communication as symbolic communication or, more narrowly still, as linguistic communication. Words are set in opposition to actions, thereby inserting a bogus demarcation, as if actions could be undertaken only for tangible purposes rather than for communicative ends. In fact, a primary goal of communication, namely to modify people's beliefs about a situation or a person, is often better achieved by deeds than by words. Actions send signals and are often meant to.[1] The other view concerns the fact that criminals are perceived as the quintessential men of action, thus lacking in the skills required for handling the subtleties of communication. The association between criminal behavior and the use of violence further strengthens the inference that criminals are too busy beating people up to care about communication. Yet, even violent acts, as I hope to show, often have a communicative purpose.

Because of the nature of their business, criminals have a lot to lose by misreading signs or by emitting signals that are misread (unless they want them to be misread). They are thus driven to draw from a large repertoire of communicative options, some of which will come as a surprise to law-abiding readers. For instance, an insurance salesman who wishes to know whether a certain establishment is already insured can just ask. But a mafioso who wants to discover whether a certain bar or restaurant is already "mobbed up"—under someone's protection, that is—cannot risk asking directly. He must look for subtle signs. FBI agent Joe Pistone, who infiltrated the mob under the name Donnie Brasco, wrote that Benjamin "Lefty Guns" Ruggiero "would size the place up, look for little things":

> He pointed out to me things he was seeing. Maybe there's a guy hanging around the cash register not doing anything. See who talks to him. See if there's a guy sitting at a certain table all the time, no meal in front of him, like he is just waiting to talk to people. And people go over one at a time and sit down and have conversation with him and leave. Watch how people treat him. See how the waitresses treat the guy. An ordinary citizen could look at this and not see anything. A wiseguy sees things if there are wiseguy things to see: how a person acts, carries himself, talks; what deference is paid to him.[2]

Criminals face severe constraints on communication imposed by the action of the law, and, unlike the rest of us, cannot easily develop institutions aimed at circumventing them. This central feature of criminal lives makes communication and above all *reliable* communication exceptionally hard to sustain. For instance, the same secrecy that protects criminals from the law hinders their opportunities to advertise their goods and qualities. And the very fact of being a criminal makes one less trustworthy in the eyes of other criminals. In the underworld, moreover, punishments for mistakes and irrational behavior are harsher than they are elsewhere. In the world of regular business, failures of communication can lead to a loss of business, but in the underworld they can result in years behind bars, or worse. At the same time, to dupe their victims criminals need to work hard on the quality of their deceptive signals, which are vital to their predatory activities. The decisiveness and brutality of many criminal actions do not numb the cognitive skills required for emitting and reading signs. On the contrary, the paramount role that both rapacious and defensive motives take in the underworld confers an intensity and subtlety to criminal communications that those who lead law-abiding lives seldom experience. The rarity of institutional solutions, combined with the formidable pressure of the incentives and constraints that criminals face, makes underworld communications a remarkable test case that allows us to see human interactions at their rawest, to lift the veil that civilizing mores and institutions spread over our daily lives.

THE ESSAYS

Two forces drive the chapters in this book. Five chapters are concerned with making sense of puzzling empirical questions. Some such questions are known in the literature—for instance, why criminals use nicknames more frequently than law-abiding citizens do (chapter 9), or why prisoners very often fight violently with one another (chapter 4)—but are here revisited with new eyes. Other questions concern facts that are not as well known: why mafiosi imitate gangster movies (chapter 10), why they believe that the word *mafia* will "never die" (chapter 8), and why inmates often engage in deliberate self-harm (chapter 5). All the empirically driven chapters seek to identify the theoretical models that can best account for these practices and offer data to test whether the models are at least plausible. The word *criminal* in this group of essays refers to serious practitioners, such as mafiosi, prison inmates, gang members, and career criminals generally.

The other five chapters deal with some of the dilemmas faced by criminals. In these chapters the word *criminal* is used in a generic fashion, as these questions are encountered both by career criminals and by those who simply want to commit one crime. The meaning of *criminal* here also extends to encompass white-collar crime, such as academic corruption or shady politics. In these chapters I investigate how criminals signal and screen their villainous credentials, how in other words they guard themselves against undercover agents and informants who try to pass themselves off as criminals (chapter 1). Next I explore how they find out whom to trust and how they manage to persuade others of their trustworthiness. I do not so much ask the age-old question of whether there is honor among thieves as I ask what thieves do when they know, as they often do, that there is none. I consider in particular two peculiar ways through which criminals reassure each other of their reliability, one by displaying their limits and constraints, including even incompetence, and the other by mutually disclosing their misdeeds, a strategy that acts as an exchange of information hostages (chapters 2 and 3). Third, I consider how criminals communicate, identify each other, and advertise the goods they trade while at the same time maintaining secrecy vis-à-vis rivals and law enforcers (chapter 6). Finally, I investigate how criminals manage to protect the conventional signals they use among themselves from impostors and mimics who would copy the signals to exploit the advantages that they confer (chapter 7). Rather than testing hypotheses or providing systematic evidence, this set of chapters takes on these dilemmas in theoretical terms, trying to identify the theory that could best predict what a rational criminal would do. My aim is to establish a new way of thinking about criminal practices, and the empirical evidence I use in these chapters illustrates the real-life plausibility of my theoretical points.

The sources of evidence I use in the book are various, and, when relevant, their reliability will be discussed case by case. A sizable part of the evidence comes from studies of mafia-like groups, including my own study of the Sicilian mafia. Another part comes from criminals' biographies; yet another reinterprets evidence from the many studies carried out on various criminals, young and old, petty and grand, occasional and die-hard. Finally, many episodes, comprising an assortment of criminal vicissitudes, are taken from the press.

I make no claim to cover all that is interesting or important about criminal communications. I do not for instance discuss gossip among mafiosi or their initiation ritual, on both of which I wrote elsewhere,[3] or how fraudsters con their victims—the strategies of con men would require a whole other book. I also do not deal with the logic of threats and the relations between fear and surprise attacks, for these are well understood, thanks largely to Thomas Schelling's work. Still, the reasoning here proposed lends itself to other empirical phenomena that I merely touch on, such as the use of graffiti by gang members or the effects of new information technology on crime.

A few themes run through both the empirical and the theoretical chapters. The most important one concerns what makes signals credible when agents have an interest in misrepresenting their identity, trustworthiness, or toughness. (The main elements of the theory I use are described below.) Two other important themes lie in the forms taken by the empirical answers to that question, searching for which has led me to explore odd and unexpected quarters. One such form suggests that actions which in ordinary circumstances are harmful to those who carry them out do in fact assist criminals in establishing the credibility of their claims. Another suggests that criminals benefit from a perverse exploitation of the actions of the law and of the social norms that sanction what they do. While the threat of conviction and imprisonment does indeed deter crime, being in prison also helps criminals, and not just in the well-known sense of being in a "school of crime"; it helps them to establish their credentials both cheaply and credibly. In a vein inspired by Thomas Schelling's classic *The Strategy of Conflict*, I show many instances in which there are unexpected strategic advantages in having or even in imposing limits on oneself, in behaving badly or even irrationally, and in letting others know. Yet another theme that runs through several chapters is that of the relations between criminals and the world outside theirs. In particular, the ways that the media describe and interpret criminals' lives, fictional or real, feeds back on the underworld.

The book is divided into two parts, each of which contains both empirical and theoretical chapters. The first part, "Costly Signals," deals with communicative *actions* designed at once to inform and to give credibility to the information being conveyed. The signals discussed here typically consist of such costly actions as killing, fighting, self-harming, taking risks, "burning bridges," or disclosing incriminating information about the self. The second part of the book, "Conventional Signals," deals with linguistic and symbolic communications: ordinary language claims, nicknames, code words, or more exotic devices, such as colored handkerchiefs, which convey information understood by convention rather than by an intrinsic link with the message. The theoretical texture that runs through both parts, which I developed elsewhere and for different research purposes,[4] is quite rich and needs to be briefly presented in general terms at the onset of this book, beginning with a description of what, exactly, communication means.[5]

COMMUNICATIVE ACTION

Communication refers to more than the transmission of linguistic messages.[6] It includes any kind of act undertaken by an agent, the signaler, with the intention of conveying information to another agent, the receiver. Many such acts are undertaken with no intent to modify the receiver's behavior—as when we idly tell a friend how we feel about something. But many communicative acts are designed instrumentally. They aim to make the receiver respond to the new information by behaving differently than he would otherwise have done. Sometimes this can be driven by altruistic motives, as when we warn a fellow pedestrian to watch out for an approaching vehicle. Other times it is in our self-interest to modify other people's beliefs. For example, we want to persuade others that we are trustworthy so that they will agree to deal with us, or that we are fearsome so that they will refrain from cheating or attacking us. Words alone rarely suffice to achieve these aims, and the notion of communication must also cover the transmission of convincing nonlinguistic evidence as to the veracity of one's claims, especially when one has an interest to misrepresent.

Communicative acts are quintessentially social affairs. They differ from other acts in that a communicative act is always "a feature of an interaction" between a signaler and a receiver. It is never a game played with nature but only with other humans. Furthermore, it is "not an abstraction that can be discussed in the absence of some specific context,"[7] since the same act can be communicative in one context and not in another. Or it can communicate two different things, depending on the context. Moreover, many of our acts are multipurpose. We may do something aimed to achieve both communicative as well as other goals. Other times we may do something for one reason but later, realizing that what we did has communicative value, also take steps to advertise that act.

SIGNALS AND SIGNS

Signals are the stuff of purposive communication.[8] Signals are any observable features of an agent that are *intentionally displayed* for the purpose of altering the probability the receiver assigns to a certain state of affairs or "event." This event can be anything. And the "features" of an agent that make up a signal can be anything too: they include parts or aspects of his body, his behavior, and his appurtenances.

Signs are different from signals. They can be anything in the environment that is perceptible and that by being perceived modifies our beliefs about something or someone. They do not require a purposive agent. But signs are also dormant or potential signals. They are the raw material of signals. A sign typically becomes a signal when a signaler takes steps to display it. We cannot take for granted that signs are noticed. A dueling scar may not appear on the face but on the thigh or chest. The crowded tables of a restaurant may be invisible from the street. One way of signaling is to make such signs apparent: to bare the chest to display a scar or tattoo, to glaze the restaurant facade to reveal the crowds inside. One trigger of this transformation is the bearer's realization of the meaning of certain signs in the eyes of an observer. I may be unaware that my accent reveals something about me, until some observer acts in a way that makes me aware. The production of signs can take place for any number of reasons, and only sometimes that reason is to produce a signal deliberately. I may choose to go to college because I like studying, but later realize that a degree is something employers value as a sign of my ability to learn rather than of my eagerness to learn for its own sake. I may end up in prison entirely against my will, but I may then be all too happy to inform other villains about my sojourn, knowing that it is a good signal of my bona fide criminal credentials. As we shall see, especially in chapter 5, even doing crazy things because one is genuinely crazy does not prevent one from displaying one's mad acts or their results when being deemed crazy can bring advantages.

The transformation goes also in the opposite direction, and yesterday's signal can become today's sign. Consider a tattoo I might have on my wrist, one that induces in others the belief that I am a sailor. Once I have had the tattoo made, in each subsequent encounter with someone it is a fait accompli and so a sign. I am not thinking about its effects every time someone sees it. But, on the day I chose to have it done, the action was a signal. Moreover, from the perspective of that day, on which I foresaw and intended an endless string of tattoo-induced beliefs in my nautical quality, it was intended to be a signal on all these future occasions too.

Much of Erving Goffman's vivid ethnographic work on communication treads the fine line between signs and signals, between the messages that we intend to give and the signs that we inadvertently give away. Here, by contrast, I focus only on acts that are intended to be signals in the broad sense just defined. I assume that agents are tentatively trying to attain their goals as cheaply and effectively as they can by displaying their signals. The constraints and punishments that criminals face focus their minds and push them to calculate every move they make. They can afford no slack. Needless to say, criminals' communication ploys do fail sometimes, at least as often as ours do, but they certainly try hard.

THE THREAT OF MIMICRY

In part 1, I use two theories. One theory concerns signals intended to show either that it is in the best interest of the signaler to be truthful or that even if the signaler wanted to deceive, he could not to do so because of his constraints, or both. This strategy, which is dealt with in chapters 2 and 3, is important among criminals, for it is compatible with bad character: the signaler does not need to be truly trustworthy to behave in a trustworthy manner if doing so is for him the best or the only possible course of action. However, even if a signaler is forced to be trustworthy, he still needs to demonstrate that this is the case. This is not always easy. Can we trust a fellow criminal not to run away with the loot because he says he needs to remain near his ailing mother? How do we know he has an ailing mother? Perhaps he shows us his mother in a hospital. But how do we know she really is his mother? And even if she is, how do we know he really cares about her?

The problem is that signals can be fraudulently manipulated. By lying, imitating, forging, or stealing certain signs, a signaler can mimic the state of affairs one associates with those signs. What is ultimately being mimicked is a certain unobservable property, k, that the mimic does not really possess. What is being lied about, imitated, copied, or forged along the way are the signs associated with k, which leave the impression of possessing k.

The threat of mimicry is ubiquitous in the underworld. Criminals are constantly afraid of being duped, while at the same time they are busy duping others. They worry not only about the real identity, trustworthiness, or loyalty of their partners but also about whether their partners are truthful when claiming to have interests and constraints aligned with theirs. To understand how in unfavorable conditions honest signalers and receivers can still hope to communicate while screening out mimics, we need to consider in some detail the second and by far the most important theory I use, signaling theory.

SIGNALING THEORY

Signaling theory, which also runs through some of the essays in part 2, emerged from both economics and biology in the 1970s.[9] The question the theory addresses is: under what conditions can a signal be rationally believed by the receiver when the signaler has an interest in merely pretending that something is true, which in the underworld is of course often?

The theory is indifferent to the message being conveyed and the truth that is uncertain; it can apply to signals aimed at conveying any number of qualities, including most importantly those of the signaler, such as his identity, trustworthiness, and potential for violence. The main condition that the theory posits is that among the possible signals there is at least one that is cheap to emit relative to the benefit for signalers who have the quality, but is costly to emit relative to the benefit for would-be mimics. If the cost relationships are such that all and only those with the true quality can afford to emit a particular signal, the equilibrium in which they do so is called, alternatively, "discriminating," "separating," or "sorting." In this equilibrium signals are unambiguous, and the receiver is perfectly informed. No poisoner seeks to demonstrate his honesty by drinking from the poisoned chalice. Drinking from a chalice is a reliable signal that the drink is clean. When signals have such a perfect discriminating property, mimicry cannot occur, for no mimic can afford the signal. (In biology this condition has been called "the handicap principle," and in economics the "costly-to-fake principle.")[10] At the opposite extreme of separating signals, there are so-called "pooling" ones, namely signals that both true and false signalers can afford to emit—for instance statements such as "of course your drink is not poisoned, dear!" If we are worried that someone is trying to poison us, such a signal should be discounted.

The trouble is that in real life most signals are neither clearly pooling nor clearly sorting, but only semi-sorting. There is hardly such thing as a fully mimic-proof signal. Virtually everybody who boards a plane, for instance, gives a sign in doing so, most times unthinkingly, that he does not intend it to crash. And almost always this is true. But, as we know only too well, some suicide terrorists may intend just that and can afford to mimic a normal passenger by boarding. Some people can drink from the poisoned chalice. In a semi-sorting equilibrium there is a signal emitted by all those who are truthful about something but not only by them. A certain proportion of mimics can just about afford to emit it too. Here, the signal is not conclusive evidence; it makes it more likely that the signaler is genuine but does not guarantee it. No one appreciates the ever-present possibility of deception more than a criminal does, whether his intent is to deceive or to avoid deception.

CONVENTIONAL AND OTHER SYMBOLIC SIGNALS

As I said, in part 2 the attention shifts from communication that employs costly actions to communication that uses language and other symbolic signals. Just like anyone else, criminals use these signals to communicate with others they know, to identify each other when they have not met, and to advertise their wares. In chapter 6, I describe the properties that signals used for these aims require to succeed. I do this in terms of a simple cognitive theory, which postulates that in order to work conventional signals must be adapted to the receivers' psychology and be distinct, memorable, and easy to discriminate from similar signals. I also mention how conventional and other symbolic signals come to be produced in a way that ensures coordination, so that everyone will understand that signal s means k. This can occur through bilateral agreements, through natural evolution—as is the case of nicknames, which come about spontaneously and can then be used as code names (chapter 9)— or occasionally through a central authority, in the rare instances in which criminals have one. In chapter 10, I focus on yet another way in which conventions take hold in the underworld, namely by using styles, utterances, ploys, and even music that appear in fictional accounts of criminal lives, notably movies. When popular works of fiction guarantee that everyone will correctly understand a signal if it appears in real life, they provide at no cost the "common knowledge" that a given s means k.[11]

Unlike most of us most of the time, criminals are heavily constrained in the use of conventional signals by their need to keep information secret from rivals and law enforcers, or at least to make sure that if intercepted it is not understood, or if understood does not suffice to incriminate them. How criminals meet this constraint is the subject of chapter 6 and, with respect to nicknames, that of chapter 9.

A good thing about conventional signals is that they are often cheap to devise and transmit. This is a mixed blessing, however; for the same reason, they can be cheap for mimics to reproduce. The threat posed by the fraudulent use of signals in the world of ordinary business is contained with the help of the law, but criminals who cannot count on the law use a whole set of strategies to protect their signals from mimics. These strategies, which are the subject of chapters 7 and 8, can be understood once again by employing signaling theory, for they share a common trait, namely that they are designed or arranged in such a way as to increase the cost of mimicry.

CONCLUSION

There are reasons to study criminal communications other than their thrilling allure or because to understand them better is to know more about how to fight crime (or, if we are so inclined, to engage in it successfully). Some of my questions are of a kind that we are all likely to encounter at lower levels of intensity or in situations seemingly distant from crime. For instance, the strategies used to communicate in such a way that if questioned one can always claim that something perceived as a signal was not meant to signal anything—allusions, iconic gestures, or metaphors—come in handy during courtship preliminaries. Strategies for screening out undercover agents use the same principles employed, say, by taxi drivers, prostitutes, or bouncers to turn away muggers, perverts, and troublemakers. As Thomas Schelling pointed out, "we may wish to solicit advice from the underworld or from ancient despotism, on how to make agreements that work when trust and good faith are lacking and there is no legal recourse for breach of contract. The ancients exchanged hostages, drank wine from the same glass to demonstrate the absence of poison, met in public places to inhibit the massacre of one by the other, and even deliberately exchanged spies to facilitate the transmittal of authentic information."[12] Studying criminal communication problems, precisely because they are the magnified and extreme versions of problems that we normally solve by means of institutions, can teach us something about how *we* might communicate, or even should communicate, when we find ourselves in difficult situations, when, say, we desperately want to be believed or keep our messages secrets. A sizable part of the field of economics has devoted the last quarter century to understanding the problem of dealing with information under conditions of uncertainty over what game one is really playing and what the other players are really like. Joseph Stiglitz wrote that "perhaps the most important break with the past—one that leaves open huge areas of future work—lies in the economics of information."[13] Well, there is hardly any domain in which information is as highly valued and as flawed and uncertain as in the underworld. "At the beginning of every new science"—two biologists wrote—"information is densest at the boundaries. Darwin, for example, went to the Galápagos where every species is on the margin."[14] Criminals operate at the boundaries; they are my Galápagos.

Abbreviations

Copies of the sources marked with an asterisk (⋆) are deposited at the Cambridge University Library. Volumes and pages in these copies do not always coincide with those in the copies held in the archives of the Tribunale of Palermo.

PARLIAMENTARY AND JUDICIAL SOURCES

CPM — Commissione Parlamentare d'inchiesta sul fenomeno della Mafia: VII–IX legislatures, Documentazione allegata alla Relazione conclusiva, vols. 1, 2, 3 (tomi ii), 4 (tomi xxviii), 5, Roma 1985.

OSAG(⋆) — Ordinanza Sentenza per Corte di Assise di Agrigento contro Ferro Antonio+55, Agrigento maggio 1986.

OSAG Arnone — Arnone G. (ed.) 1988, *Mafia. Il processo di Agrigento.* Monreale: Edizioni La Zisa (this book contains files attached to OSAG).

OSPA(⋆) — Ordinanza Sentenza per Corte di Assise di Palermo contro Abbate Giovanni+706, Palermo 8/11/1985, 40 vols.

OSPA Stajano — Stajano C. (ed.) 1986, *Mafia. L'atto di accusa dei giudici di Palermo.* Roma: Editori Riuniti (this book contains a few sections from OSPA).

OSPA-ii(⋆) — Ordinanza Sentenza della Corte di Assise di Palermo contro Abdel Azizi Afifi+91, Palermo 16/8/1986, 5 vols.

SSPA 17/1/86 — Sentenza della Corte di Assise di Appello Palermo contro Pravatà Michelangelo + 7.

SSPA 26/1/85   Sentenza della Corte di Assise di Palermo contro Pra-
                vatà Michelangelo + 7.

TESTIMONIES OF MAFIOSI WHO TURNED
STATE WITNESSES

AC(★)   Testimony of Antonino Calderone given to Giudice
                Istruttore of Marseilles Michel Debacq and to the
                Commissione Rogatoria Internazionale including Gi-
                udice Istruttore of Palermo Giovanni Falcone et alii,
                from 19 March 1987 to 25 June 1988, 4 vols.
FMM(★)   Testimony of Francesco Marino Mannoia given to
                Giudice Istruttore of Palermo Giovanni Falcone et alii,
                from 8 October 1989 to 19 June 1990.
FMM-A   Transcripts of the recordings of court hearings in Pro-
                cedimento Penale contro Abbate Giovanni e altri, con-
                taining the interrogation of the defendant Francesco
                Marino Mannoia, Tribunale di Palermo, 4, 5, 7 January
                1990.
LV(★)   Testimony of Leonardo Vitale given to officers from
                Procura Generale della Repubblica, Police and Cara-
                binieri of Palermo, 30 March 1973.
MA-L'Ora   Testimony of Melchiorre Allegra given to Police in
                Castelvetrano in 1937, published in *L'Ora*, 22–25 Janu-
                ary 1962.
SC(★)   Testimony of Stefano Calzetta given to Consigliere
                Istruttore della Procura di Palermo Rocco Chinnici et
                alii, from 12 March 1983 to 28 February 1985, 5 vols.
SC-GdS   Transcripts of the interrogation of the defendant Ste-
                fano Calzetta in Corte d'Assise di Palermo in the trial
                against Abbate Giovanni+706, published by *Il Giornale
                di Sicilia*, 10–21 July 1986.
TB(★)   Testimony of Tommaso Buscetta given to Giudice Is-

truttore of Palermo Giovanni Falcone et alii, July–August 1984, 3 vols.

TB-GdS   Transcripts of the interrogation of the defendant Tommaso Buscetta testimony in Corte di Assise of Palermo in the trial against Abbate Giovanni+706, published by *Il Giornale di Sicilia*, 3–18 April 1986.

TC(★)   Testimony of Salvatore Contorno given to Giudice Istruttore of Palermo Giovanni Falcone et alii, from October 1984 to June 1985.

TC-GdS   Transcripts of the interrogation of the defendant Salvatore Contorno in Corte di Assise del Tribunale di Palermo in the trial against Abbate Giovanni+706, published by *Il Giornale di Sicilia*, 12 April 1986–1 May 1986.

VM(★)   Testimony of Vincenzo Marsala given to Procuratore Generale della Repubblica of Palermo Raimondo Cerami et alii, from December 1984 to April 1985.

VM-GdS   Transcripts of the interrogation of the defendant Vincenzo Marsala in Corte d'Assise del Tribunale di Palermo during the trial against Pravat ... Angelo+7, published in *Il Giornale di Sicilia*, 16–29 May 1987.

VS(★)   Testimony of Vincenzo Sinagra given to Giudici Istruttori of Palermo Vittorio Aliquo,' Domenico Signorino et alii, from 30 November 1983 to 30 April 1985, 2 vols.

VS-GdS   Transcripts of the interrogation of the defendant Vincenzo Sinagra in the Corte d'Assise of Tribunale di Palermo during the trial against Pravat ... Angelo+7, published in *Il Giornale di Sicilia*, 15–21 June 1986.

PART 1   Costly Signals

CHAPTER 1

Criminal Credentials

Just like ordinary business, most criminal endeavors are not solo affairs. Thieves need fences; robbers rely on informants; drug dealers depend on producers and pushers; pushers and contract killers require customers; terrorists want arms dealers; and corrupt officials are lost without corrupters. Among the few economists to pay attention to criminal communications, Thomas Schelling wrote: "The bank employee who would like to rob the bank if he could only find an outside collaborator and the bank robber who would like to rob the bank if only he could find an inside accomplice may find it difficult to collaborate because they are unable to identify each other, there being severe penalties in the event that either should declare his intentions to someone who proved not to have identical interests."[1] Identifying partners and, correspondingly, advertising as bona fide denizens of the underworld are indispensable means to carrying out criminal activities. And they are much more complicated than the parallel operations are for ordinary business. Even before worrying about their partner's trustworthiness or competence as a criminal, people who want to commit a crime need first of all to identify *who* is potentially prepared to cooperate with them in breaking the law.

When contemplating straying from the lawful path, people whose main business is not criminal are even more hindered than professional criminals by the problems of identification. A building contractor once told me that he would have been delighted to pass on a brown envelope to end his long wait for a planning permission if only he knew whom to approach. Identification mistakes can cost dearly, but while the risks deter many they do not deter all. George Fallows, a property landlord of Llangernyw, near Abergele, north Wales, was determined to avoid paying his wife a large divorce settlement and tried to have her killed by a hit

man, who was supposed to crash a lorry head-on into her car as she
drove down a country lane. The contract killer he sought to hire, however, turned out to be an undercover policeman posing as a criminal.
The policeman recorded the negotiations, and in 2003 Fallows was sentenced to five years in prison, lucky to have found a lenient judge.[2]

In 2000, a member of a Sicilian gang, who was planning a monumental robbery by setting up a website imitating the online services of the
Banco di Sicilia, contacted the director of a branch of the Banco di
Roma to enlist his assistance in the fraud. He failed to realize that the
director was an undercover policeman, and his mistake led to his arrest
and to that of twenty-two others, including members of a Palermo
mafia family.[3]

The hotter the trade, the more daunting are the problems of identification. How do you go about, for instance, finding a black-market buyer
for eight bars of enriched uranium? This question taxed the brains of
eleven Italian mobsters, an unholy coalition of Sicilian mafiosi and
Roman and Calabrian organized criminals, who had the bars in their
hands for some time. These bars have a troubled history. They are
90-centimeter-long cylinders, wrapped in steel, each containing 200
grams of uranium, and designed for peaceful uses. They were produced
in the labs of General Atomics in San Diego and sent to the Congo as a
gift in February 1971, where they were to be used as nuclear fuel in the
labs of the experimental reactor Mark II, in Kinshasa. The gift program
was known, ironically, as "Atoms for Peace." However, if blown up by
means of an ordinary explosive, they can serve as "the poor man's nuclear bomb," spreading deadly nuclear radiation. In the words of Captain
Roberto Ferroni of the Italian customs police in Rome, "If they were
blown up in Villa Borghese, the center of Rome would become unin-
habitable for a century."[4] From the labs in Kinshasa the bars mysteriously disappeared. In 1997, when Mobutu's regime was overturned and
he left for France, where he died of cancer, the bars apparently traveled
with him. They surfaced once in France and were the cause of a gun-
fight between French police and a group of criminal merchants who
were trying to sell them.

A year later they reemerged in the hands of the Italian mobsters, whose telephone communications were intercepted by the Italian customs police in the course of investigating them for other crimes. The police were amazed to hear the mobsters speak of unspecified "nuclear stuff" and were initially unsure what that meant. In the spring of 1998, the mobsters finally thought they had found a buyer, an emissary of an Arab country. The buyer, who introduced himself as "the Accountant," was in reality an undercover agent for whom the police had created a whole new identity. They gave him false penal and prison records for fencing, and fabricated a nonexistent relationship between him and an Arab country and the Islamic Jihad, which the agent mentioned as the ultimate buyer. "Our sellers," says Captain Ferroni, who led the operation, "did not lose their composure. On the contrary, the credibility of the Arab world, which is always hunting for nuclear material, convinced them that [our man] was not a trap." The agent brought with him an associate, an engineer, who was allowed to test one of the bars and found that it did indeed contain uranium. The police then transferred a virtual sum of 20 billion lire on a Swiss Bank account, bargaining down the requested price that was twice as much. The brilliant operation, however, was only a partial success. As in the best crime stories, the mafiosi cheated twice over. On the agreed day for completing the transaction, they showed up with only one bar, a different one from the one that had been tested, and failed to deliver the other seven. At that point, however, the cover was blown, and the police had to arrest them. The bars' current location remains unknown. Captain Ferroni says: "The man who could have taken us to those bars, Domenico Stilitano, refuses to speak. It is not in his interest. On the 11th of October [2001] he was sentenced to 4 years and 6 months as the new antiterrorism laws are not yet applicable and the traffic of strategic material is still considered, as it were, a minor crime."[5]

The identification problem is further intensified by the fact that, contrary to a widespread belief, criminal groups are unstable. In the underworld, people have a higher rate of mobility (and mortality) than in most professions: "most adult co-offending does not arise from participation in groups. . . . the typical co-offending relationship appears to be transitory and there is a continual search for co-offenders."[6] And "the

life of most of the mobs," said a professional thief, "is comparatively
short."[7] This is partly because criminals are chased by law enforcers and
have to keep moving and hiding, and because they are more inclined to
use violence against each other than regular businessmen are. It could
also be for "*endogenous* reasons. The more lucrative the business, the more
potential entry it will attract, resulting in (literally) cutthroat competition and short expected life for an incumbent."[8]

The difficulties of identifying partners keep much potential crime at
bay. Making identification hard is arguably the most powerful deterrent
against crime that the force of the law brings about, by discouraging the
countless dormant criminals who refrain from acting unlawfully for fear
of being caught when searching or advertising. A blessing for society,
identification constraints are a serious hindrance for criminals, who
dearly wish they could use the Yellow Pages. How do they solve the
problem?

MISTAKEN IDENTIFICATION

When trying to identify partners, criminals can make two types of mistakes. First, they can miss opportunities, failing to see through the disguises that genuine potential partners adopt in order to pass themselves
off as law-abiding citizens and avoid being caught (the false-negative
mistake). In this case, both parties have the same interests but miss the
opportunity for a fruitful partnership. Notice that the failure of one to
identify reflects the failure of the other to advertise. Mimicking a law-
abiding citizen, which sometimes simply means keeping a low profile, is
something most criminals have to do. This, however, can succeed too
well, and one can fail to advertise when it would be in one's interest to
do so.

Second, searchers may approach a law-abiding citizen or, worse, an
undercover agent, mistaking them for potential partners in crime (the
false-positive mistake). Law-abiding citizens are not a cause of great
concern for criminals. True, if approached they may inform the authorities. But ordinary people do not have an interest in passing themselves

off as criminals. If anything they are careful to avoid looking like one. Only utter carelessness in approaching others or some inane misunderstandings can lead to confusing law-abiding citizens for criminals—such as that of the forty-seven-year-old Canadian woman who in 1991 did use the Yellow Pages and contacted a firm in Phoenix, Arizona, called "Guns for Hire" seeking to put a contract on her husband's life. She failed to notice that the firm specialized in putting on "Wild West theatrical shows for conventions, private parties and the like." After handing $2,000 to an undercover detective posing as a hit man, the woman was arrested and later sentenced to four and a half years in jail. Before calling Guns for Hire, the detective later explained, she had considered calling motorcycle clubs and an Italian-American association.[9] If contract killers and people seeking them really could advertise openly, one wonders how many more murders there would be.

The real worry concerns undercover agents or informers who have an active interest in pretending to be a genuine partner and deceiving the searching criminal. In this case, which I consider here, the criminal's failure to identify correctly a law-and-order agent reflects the latter's mimicking success. In particular, I consider the case of two individuals who are in asymmetrical positions. A already knows that B is a criminal (and B knows that A knows that). B, however, does not know whether A is a criminal. Regardless of whether A is truly a criminal or an undercover agent posing as one, A wants to persuade B that he is a real criminal. B, at the same time, is looking for evidence of the type that A is. The question is, what kind of evidence can satisfy B?

The probability of making identification mistakes is "frequency dependent": the higher the proportion of criminals in the search environment, the lower the risk of approaching the wrong people. Where corruption is known to be widespread, for instance, corrupting others or signaling one's willingness to accept bribes is not much of a problem. If the probability of encountering a corrupt agent is correctly believed to be high, criminals will rationally try more and bolder approaches, and will easily uncover corrupt partners. In Russia, which may have approached this state of affairs in recent times, the values of corruption "fees" for different positions of authority were openly reported in the press.[10] Identification mistakes are also less likely to occur or to be consequential wherever law enforcement is feeble. Where laws are enforced, there is always a greater probability that a criminal will make acquaintances of the wrong kind while searching for partners.

So our question is: what do criminals look for, what kind of signs do they attend to, in order to identify their kindred spirits or catch the undercover agents? The little we can find in the literature explicitly discussing the identification problem suggests that criminals claim to possess a special ability that enables them to identify other crooks by "gut feelings," "a look in the eyes," "vibrations."[11] Nowhere could I find any theory that unpacks those feelings, that predicts what criminals can be expected to look for. But, carefully scrutinized, the evidence we can gather from the many ethnographic accounts of criminals' activities strongly suggests that they do not go about it erratically. Criminals systematically look for signs that identify another agent as a genuine criminal type and, at the same time, they try just as systematically (and carefully) to advertise by sending signals that only another genuine criminal type will pick up.

"On the street"—wrote FBI special agent Joseph Pistone, who infiltrated the Colombo and later the Bonanno mafia families of New York under the name of Donnie Brasco—"everybody is suspicious of everybody else until you prove yourself."[12] If someone says, "I am ready to deal with you, pal," or sports some item of clothing that conventionally indicates he is a criminal, such as a pair of dark glasses, these signals are hardly sufficient to prove that he is a criminal. As a professional thief put it, "language is not in itself a sufficient means of determining whether a person is trustworthy, for some people in the underworld are stool pigeons and some outsiders *learn some of the language.*"[13] Proving oneself requires tougher tests than cheap talk.

COST-DISCRIMINATING SIGNALS

Just how tough should these tests be? The general property for a signal, including an identifying signal, to be persuasive is the cost-discriminating condition: a given signal, *s*, can convince a rational receiver of a signaler's criminality if, given the expected benefits, a rational mimic who could gain by posing as a criminal finds *s* too costly to produce or to display. In other words, *a convincing signal of a criminal type is that which only a true criminal can afford to produce and to send*. That does not mean that such signaling will necessarily be very costly for a real criminal. In the course of his career he may have acquired much raw material that can be displayed at little extra cost. It suffices that the signal be too costly for the mimic to afford.

Selective Environments

A good, indeed the best, sign of a criminal type consists, of course, of observing someone committing a crime. This is not likely to occur, though, for people do not normally wish to be seen engaging in villainous acts. This is a constraint that ordinary businessmen do not face, as they can show what they do to third parties without fear of the law. By contrast, criminals have to resort as much as possible to indirect methods.

A common strategy that allows criminals in search of one another to exchange signals consists of frequenting places where noncriminals are not likely to be found, which is like patronizing a "singles bar" when searching for a mate. "To search for accomplices and to dispose of illegal goods . . . adult offenders patronise the same places, make the same kinds of transactions, and often reside in the same area."[14] They hang out in bars, gambling dens, boxing gyms, and social clubs full of other men during normal working hours or late at night, at times, that is, when a common person is otherwise occupied. Or they live in rough neighborhoods for the same reason well-to-do citizens move out of them—both dread making encounters of the wrong sort. In his research on crime in New York City, Sullivan (1989) found that much recruitment occurs in neighborhoods, where people know about one another and check each other out in the natural course of their daily interactions. Environments selected for their criminality, those which "regular guys" find more costly or less attractive to patronize than criminals do, make identification and advertising easier. There is a natural sorting and mixing activity in such places that takes care of the problem of identification.

By itself, though, this strategy works only up to a point. It saves criminals from dealing by mistake with law-abiding citizens. However, if the cost of hanging around in such environments is not very high for a non-criminal, they may become very dangerous places for criminals, precisely the places where undercover agents will converge when attempting to infiltrate criminal networks. Singles bars increase the probability of meeting single people, but they do not eliminate the probability of meeting patrons who, while married, go there merely pretending to be single. In the underworld, where the stakes of mistaken identity are higher, if someone just shows up in a bar full of criminals he is not likely to go far without further credentials. To be reassured, criminals need signs the cost of which a law-enforcement agent or a spy would find harder to pay. Rather than being reliable signs in themselves, selective environments merely offer better opportunities to gather further evidence, directly and indirectly.

Referrals

"Another method [to establish someone's criminal credentials] is by finding out what people the stranger knows."[15] If C knows that A is a criminal, C may introduce A to B. Or B can simply see C with A and infer that A is one too. A gangster called Jackson in his autobiography wrote: "on the street I know hundreds and hundreds of characters, but I do not know their names. Say you are a character and I'm a character and I see you with a character that I know. I have no way of checking your credit rating or anything else, so *I judge you by whom you associate with*. If I know that this person is a good person and not a polecat, not a stool pigeon, not the man's man, then I have to give you the credit for being all right."[16] In certain criminal circles, "you'd be surprised. It's a very close-knit thing among hustlers. You meet someone you've never met before in a place you've never seen before, you find out someone they know. They may even have heard of you."[17] Interestingly, this implies that criminals have to be extra vigilant about whom they are seen with, as other criminal onlookers may interpret the association as an implicit endorsement, even if no overt guarantees are given (as we shall see below, Donnie Brasco skillfully manipulated this method to infiltrate the mob).

Prisons as Screening Devices

One way to acquire good evidence of someone's criminality, which intersects with the referral method, exploits law enforcement itself. In terms of how effectively they can mix and match kindred spirits, the hangouts that criminals freely choose cannot compete with the places they are forced to go by the agents who fight *against* crime: there is nothing like prison to mix like with like. Prisons promote crime in many obvious ways,[18] teaching criminals new skills and brutal modes of behavior, but they also do so, less obviously, by shouldering the costs of advertising and identifying who is a criminal to begin with.

Just being a prisoner is a clear and simple sign that one is criminally inclined. The hard part is paying the price of going there in the first place. But it is precisely that cost that makes a prison term such a good sign of being a real criminal. Paradoxically, the better the criminal justice system is, the safer it is to assume that the company put behind bars will be invariably villainous. Though there are surely innocent prisoners, many are guilty, the more so the better the system. One can also be reasonably sure that phonies, people who talk big about their dangerous criminal tendencies but do nothing, will not end up in prison. The interpersonal conflicts that are rife within prisons, as we shall see in chapter 4, further ensure that the phonies are quickly identified. And even though undercover policemen have certainly been sent to prison for short periods to gain criminal credentials, the longer the time prisoners spend in jail, the closer we get to prison being a perfect discriminating sign—no one chooses to spend twenty years behind bars for the sake of posing as a villain. Doing time in prison can thus be both a stigma and a badge, depending on who is looking at it. An ex-convict who wishes to return to the path of the righteous can find doing so very hard because his time spent in prison identifies him as a criminal. "Once you're marked in prison you're done for," says a delinquent boy recounting his own story.[19] But one who intends to persist in his old ways will find his path smoothed, and can display his prison credentials to further his criminal career.

One may not go as far as arranging a jail sentence for oneself for the purpose of fostering new associations with kindred spirits. But, once in prison, there is an abundance of opportunity to make villainous acquaintances who will be useful after one leaves:

> Say that there are fifty quite well established thieves in Malmö, only thirty of those have a fence. Those who don't are the younger ones around eighteen or twenty who haven't been around enough, so they'll have to ask their friends or sell to thieves. For someone who has been inside as much as me, it's no problem.[20]

Incarceration as a mark of reliability works at a remove. If two former prisoners did not actually meet in jail, they can still display evidence of having been "in the can" to advertise their credentials. So even if going to prison was not intended as a perverse form of résumé building, the revelation of the experience can be and often is an intentional signal. The "referral" method I discussed above exploits prison contacts too—for if one is embedded in a network, one is in a better position both to refer others and to be referred by them. There is even evidence that, unwittingly, unions and organizations that are supposed to help ex-inmates to reenter mainstream society also help unreformed criminals in their business.[21] Not least, these charitable organizations assist them by certifying their status as genuine ex-prisoners, thus innocently facilitating encounters with active villains.

Blumstein et al. note that incarceration can have a "crimogenic effect [that] may result from the offender's enhanced identification as 'criminal.'"[22] But apart from fleeting references such as this, the existence of this particular effect is virtually unacknowledged in criminology, even though much attention is paid to other effects of incarceration, such as the learning of criminal techniques and the formation of ties with other inmates. Although there are no precise measures, and we do not know whether and how far the enhancing of one's criminal identity offsets the attempts at rehabilitation, there is much anecdotal evidence from criminals' biographies of the enhancing effect's existence. It starts early, in young-offenders' institutions. In his autobiography, Jimmy Boyle, a Scottish gangster, reminisces that when he was sixteen,

> the Approved School surely played a vital part in my criminal development. It gave me connections that I was to find useful in my adult days. It gave me an introduction to guys from towns and cities throughout Scotland and from many areas in Glasgow, many of whom grew up to be the top thieves or fighters in their areas. There is no doubt at all that most of them gained, in a criminal sense, from their Approved School experience.[23]

He was doing his best, he writes, to avoid being caught, "but every time I went into prison I broadened my criminal horizons by making more and more connections in different areas."[24] Malcolm Braly, who spent nearly seventeen years in various U.S. prisons for burglary, wrote: "He was broke, as I was, and he suggested we try something together. It was reasonable. Who is more likely to be trustworthy than someone you have just met in jail?"[25]

Criminal and rebel organizations regard a prison record as a sign of distinction. The Russian criminal fraternity known as *vory* made having been in a prison camp a formal requirement of membership.[26] According to Marek Kaminski, at least one member of the underground Solidarity movement in Poland provoked the communist secret services to put her in prison so she could improve her reputation: "Under the well-progressing perestroika in 1987, the Polish communists essentially stopped incarcerating the opposition (so the 'incarceration' was a brief 48 hours), they started talks with selected opposition groups, and many underground politicians thought that there would be some role for them to play within the communist regime soon. Thus, the expected cost of incarceration was low and the expected benefits were high."[27]

The length of time spent in prison further provides an "objective" measure of the respect one is owed relative to other gang members. Thus

Christopher Seymour writes of taking a drive with Japanese *yakuza* (mobsters): "In the loose hierarchy of the Hara-gumi, Ken is the most senior in the automobile. He has already served time in adult prison whereas the others have only been through juvenile detention."[28] Likewise, Marek Kaminski—who, when he was a sociology sophomore in the 1980s, was arrested by the Polish communist secret police together with eleven other members of an underground Solidarność publishing house and jailed for five months—reports: "Some of the Polish *grypsmen* [inmates who are members of a prison fraternity; see chapter 4] claim that in the case of a prisoner with a sentence of 20+ years he does not have to join the *grypsmen* formally and suffer the costs of the initiation rituals. He is eligible for enjoying all the benefits of the caste membership by virtue of the sentence's length."[29] For the Russian mafia as well, "the length of time spent in prison was a source of prestige and a sign of distinction among the criminals who aspired to become *vory*."[30] In a telephone conversation secretly recorded by Italian police, the wife of Ivan Yakovlev (the names have been changed), a Russian mobster arrested in Italy in 1997,[31] uses the length of her husband's prison sentence to induce one of his associates to show due respect. Assigned to the task by her husband, she warns the Russian wife of the accomplice Mario Ferrari: "Ivan is bigger than [your husband], he has been in prison for 15 years." Ferrari did not enjoy the same prison credentials, though he had clashed with the law in the past for drug dealing. He was now misbehaving, being often drunk and disheveled, and, according to Ivan's wife, did not show enough respect to Ivan. In a subsequent conversation between the two women, Ferrari's wife apologized for her husband's behavior. She clearly took the point and repeated word for word what Ivan's wife previously told her: "[My husband] understood that it is not Ivan who must look for him, but that he, clean and well dressed, must go to Ivan in the car and ask him what needs to be done because Ivan is bigger than he is, he has been in prison for 15 years."[32]

There is also some evidence that the *type* of prison in which one is incarcerated has an effect on recidivism. Using a quasi-experimental design on U.S. data, Chen and Shapiro found that "harsher imprisonment conditions cause greater recidivism," a finding that goes against the commonly accepted view that "punishing a criminal more severely reduces that individual's subsequent probability of recidivism."[33] Since prisoners are assigned to minimum-, low-, or high-security prisons on the basis of their score on a scale from 1 to 10 points "intended to reflect [their] need for supervision,"[34] Chen and Shapiro were able to compare the rearrest rates of ex-inmates who had been on either side of the cutoff boundaries that had led them to be incarcerated in prisons with different security levels: "in essence, we argue that within a small interval around a cutoff the allocation of prisoners to different security levels amounts to a random assignment."[35] Although the results are based on a small number of cases, 948, they still enable the authors to reject strongly the hypothesis that lower levels of prison security lead to more recidivism after release; instead, they indicate in many ways that the opposite effect obtains. The authors' interpretation of this effect refers to lower labor-market opportunities for higher-security ex-inmates and to peer effects— "inmates may acquire skills, learn of new prospects, or develop criminal contacts"[36] more often in higher- than in lower-security prisons. Their results are also perfectly compatible with another interpretation: having been in prisons with a stricter regime strengthens the certifying effect on criminal credentials and gives ex-inmates from these prisons, relative to those from prisons with lower security levels, greater credibility on the *criminal* labor market.

Criminal Acts as Signals

Referrals and prison sentences are both evidence of criminality acquired indirectly through a third party. B relies on the fact that C—be C another criminal or the justice system—has evidence of A's type. B does not observe direct evidence that A is a criminal. B infers this from the fact that A is known to C as a criminal. The weight of the cost-discriminating condition shifts to the trust that B has in C. If B trusts C's competence in assessing another person's type and C's truthfulness in revealing that knowledge, B too can embrace C's claim with some degree of certainty. This "referral" method involves at least three agents, two pairs of whom must already know each other, and is parasitic on the fact that

the two pairs have solved the identification problem in the past. But
what about the elementary case in which referrals are not available or
not persuasive or safe enough—can two agents then find a direct solution to the problem?

It is hard to observe someone committing a crime in the natural
course of events, but villains can certainly ask a potential partner or recruit to give them evidence of having committed crimes, and can do so
without resorting to an intermediary. This can work if the crimes in
question leave a trace that can be known or possessed only by the real
perpetrator. One cannot just *say* that one has committed a crime—a
phony may have read about it in the paper and simply be claiming to be
the perpetrator. One has to *show* the booty as it were, as in the following
case. Police in fourteen countries, including the United States, arrested
nearly two hundred suspected members of an Internet child pornography ring, the Wonderland Club. To join the ring one had to show that
one possessed ten thousand photographs and be prepared to share them
with other members. The photographs were screened by a computer
program, which checked whether they were different from one another
and from those already available from other sources.[37] This action signaled that prospective members had committed a crime and were seriously committed to the activity of common interest, and could not thus
be undercover agents (I return to this case in chapter 3).

Ultimately, criminals can also ask a potential partner or recruit to engage in a *display* crime—an act that a noncriminal would never do—and
to commit the crime under their eyes or in such a way as to leave an
unmistakable sign of authorship. The nature of the illegal act requested
depends on the type of crime in which the agents are involved and the
laws that govern it. Divine, the Los Angeles prostitute who achieved her
fifteen minutes of fame for administering oral sex to British actor Hugh
Grant in 1995, revealed her particular kind of test. Before agreeing to
trade she asked Grant to expose himself. The reason, she said, is that an
undercover policeman would not do that, for he would be breaking the
law. Divine believed, one wonders how accurately, that exposing oneself
was a signal only real customers could afford.

The same reasoning inspires a test applied by drug dealers in New

York. Since the mid-1990s, "as police have intensified their assault, the dealers have also adopted more perilous tactics. Five or six times each month, undercover investigators are now forced to use cocaine or heroin at gunpoint, to prove to dealers that they can be trusted. At least twice a month, an officer is shot or otherwise wounded during a staged purchase, say police commanders, who spoke on condition of anonymity."[38]

These kinds of tests are common in organizations where loyalty is paramount. Before initiation, mafia novices—especially those not already members of families with a mafia tradition—are asked to commit a murder (sometimes would-be members move first and commit serious crimes before anyone asked them to do so).[39] The mafia usually does not kill anyone purely for the sake of a test—it optimizes by "whacking" someone who was meant to be whacked anyway *and* at the same time trying out the determination and bona fides of a novice. The Aryan Brotherhood in prison adopted the same test: to gain membership, candidates "had to kill whomever the Brotherhood targeted."[40] A kindred outfit known as the Aryan Warriors also required would-be members to pass a test, "usually a bloody assault or, in some instances, a drug rip-off from a person outside of the brotherhood."[41] But there are cases in which heinous crimes are committed purely as tests. In a hair-raising account of life in youth gangs in Colombia, the writer Efraim Medina Reyes claims that it is not uncommon for new gang members to be asked to murder innocent friends or members of their own family, which pushes the test to the extreme.[42] Revolutionary and resistance groups deemed to be illegal by the incumbent government have also used the same test. Being asked to commit a murder was, for instance, a common practice in the Algerian FLN. Sometimes the leaders would pick victims more or less at random, to see if prospective members would obey even meaningless orders.[43]

This method exploits the law, which restricts the law-abiding undercover agents' options, and turns it to the criminals' advantage. If, however, law-enforcement agencies give their undercover operatives greater discretion to act against the law for the sake of persuading the group they are trying to infiltrate of their bona fides, the power of these signals is weakened, for the agent can now afford at least some of them. The degrees of freedom vary from time to time and from agency to agency. Police in New York are now "instructed to avoid taking the drugs *unless their lives are in danger.*" If dealers read the *New York Times*, where this information was published, they know that forcing buyers to ingest drugs by threatening their lives is now a useless test, for it no longer distinguishes genuine buyers from undercover agents.

Before discussing this problem further, I will present the case of FBI special agent Joseph Pistone, aka Donnie Brasco, who infiltrated the New York mafia and came close to being initiated. I know of no better case for illustrating all the types of cost-discriminating signals used by criminals—and by those who try to fool them. Donnie Brasco persuaded the mobsters of his criminal credentials by employing a breathtaking range of subtle signals, and narrated his experience in a book—arguably the most vivid ethnography of the U.S. mafia from "within."[44] By learning how he fooled the mafiosi into believing that he was a real bad guy and not a cop, we can flesh out in detail how signaling strategies work in practice. We shall learn more about how signals work by knowing how they fail.

THE CASE OF SPECIAL AGENT JOSEPH PISTONE, AKA DONNIE BRASCO

Entering the mob world is, needless to say, very hard: "Associates of wiseguys don't deal with people they don't know or who somebody else doesn't vouch for."[45] Prior to Pistone's infiltration, the FBI lacked experience. During J. Edgar Hoover's reign at the bureau, undercover work was rarely used, "because it could be a dirty job that could end up tainting the agents."[46] And although it had been used since, "so far as we knew, the FBI had never planted one of its own agents in the mafia."[47] Yet the operation it was about to attempt was extraordinarily shrewd. Pistone needed to build a whole barrage of signals, which taken together could persuade the mobsters that he was a real bad guy. And that is what he and his handlers set out to do, minding that the law constrained his freedom: "The FBI wouldn't let me actually go out on hijackings and burglaries because the crew went armed," Pistone writes.[48]

Pistone needed a name: he decided it was easier to stick to Donnie Brasco, the name he had used in a previous undercover operation in Florida. He needed a plausible biography that could be checked or, better, hard to check: he posed as an orphan and a bachelor. He said he had been raised in an orphanage in Pittsburgh that burned down; there were no records left. The story needed to be simple. "The fewer [lies] you have to tell, the fewer you have to remember," he notes.[49] He said he had spent time on the West Coast and in Florida, where in fact he had been before, as "Donald Brasco" in the previous operation, and had established some contacts. He needed a "profession" and settled on jewelry theft, something one can do alone and that does not require the use of weapons—something, moreover, that allowed him to use confiscated stolen jewels to sell so he would not have to break the law to steal them.[50]

He could count on advantages that would have been hard to fake had they not been part of his real biography. His Italian ancestry provided him with the "right" ethnic background. He had grown up in the "right" neighborhood and as a youngster hung out in "joints" patronized by wiseguys: "You had to be street-smart, even cocky sometimes. Every good undercover agent I have known grew up on the street, like I did, and was a good street agent before becoming an undercover agent. On the street you learn what's what and who's who. You learn how to read situations and handle yourself. *You cannot fake the ability. It shows.*"[51] He muses that given his background it was surprising that he was accepted in the FBI.

It is also interesting to know what he chose *not* to say or do. He avoided acting in a way that could raise suspicion. "No street guy is going to throw money all over the place unless he's trying to attract attention," Pistone reveals. "Then the question is: Why is he trying to attract attention?"[52] By doing so he either becomes a target, in that people think they can rob him, or raises suspicions that he may be a cop. Donnie was parsimonious too in revealing details of his life, whether real or phony, for "you never know what part of what you do will become part of your history when people want to check on you."[53]

He was also careful not to make claims that could give him away, such as that of having been in prison.

If they [the mobsters] weren't scheming and dreaming, they were telling war stories, reminiscences about their time in various jails and prisons. Everybody did time in the can. It was part of the price of doing business. They knew all about different jails, cell blocks, guards. I had enough phony background set up to establish my credentials as a serious criminal, to show that I was tough enough to do time if I had to without turning rat. But *I never claimed to have done any prison time* because I didn't know those places, and that could have just ripped me up. If you do three to five years you get to know the guards—what guard's on what tier. You get to know the inmates, guys who are doing fifteen to twenty, guys who are still there. They knew the lingo and the slang. Everybody remembers those relationships and that time.[54]

Indirectly, Pistone's choice shows what a robust signal having been in prison is. It is not something that can be easily faked: guys who have truly been there would quickly spot an impostor.

Donnie went on for a couple of months

playing this game of being noticed without being noticed, slide into the badguy world and become accepted without drawing attention. You push a little here and there, but very gently. Brief introductions, short conversations, appearances one place and another, hints about what you're up to, casual mannerisms, demeanor and lingo that you know your way around—all these become a trail of credibility you leave behind you. Above all, you cannot hurry. You cannot seem eager to meet certain people, make certain contacts, learn about certain scores. *The quickest way to get tagged as a cop is to try to move too fast.* You have to show that you have the time to play by the rules of the street, and that includes letting people check you out and come to you.[55]

He hung around bars. He bet on the horses. "The more places I was seen, the more times I was recognised by wiseguys, the better my credentials."[56] He became friendly with the bartender of a shady hangout.

He would phone the bar leaving messages for himself just to establish that he had connections and convey the belief people knew he patronized the bar.[57] "When I went other places, I could say," Pistone writes, "'I been hanging out at that place for four or five months.' And they could check it out. The guys had been hanging around in this place would say. 'Yeah, Don Brasco has been coming in here for quite a while, and he seems all right, never tried to pull anything on us.'"[58]

We also read: "You can't go in all the time by yourself, because they think you're either a fag or a cop. And it's good to vary company so they don't see you with the same people all the time and wonder what's up."[59] So Donnie would bring an occasional female or Chuck, another undercover agent. Thanks to Chuck he was introduced to Albert, "a half-ass wiseguy," a connected-to but not a made member of the Colombo family:

It's the kind of thing that feeds on itself. [Albert] sees that people know me and acknowledge me, so he feels he can introduce me to other people who know him. It enhances my credibility to be hanging out with a connected guy whose uncle is a wiseguy in the Colombo family. For his part, Albert sees that I am accepted where I go, so it's good for him to be seen with me.[60]

All in all, "getting established is a subtle business, a matter of small impressions, little tests, quiet understandings."[61]

Donnie eventually became the protégé of a made guy, Benjamin "Lefty Guns" Ruggiero, and spent six years with the mafiosi, living their daily lives and sharing their crooked dealings—constantly exposed to the risk of being discovered and killed. In the course of the operation he was offered the opportunity not only to handle the bookmaking for the mob boss of Milwaukee, Frank Balistrieri, but also to get inside the skimming operation in Las Vegas. Balistrieri said he had a good crew, but they were "older, kind of set in their ways. I could use some younger guys that I could trust to take over a couple of my clubs and other businesses. Younger guys would be able to relate to the ways of today's business world."[62] Lefty vouched for Donnie. "I told [Balistrieri]," Donnie says, "you are my blood."[63] But accepting would have made it impossible for Donnie to see his real family, so he turned down the offer. While that decision angered Lefty, it also conferred an advantage, as it further signaled Donnie's credibility: "One thing I had in my favor, seen through any mob guy's eyes, was that *no cop would ever turn that job down.* So I would be above suspicion in that regard."[64]

Donnie came up with many other signals believed to be of a kind that a cop could not afford. He pretended to beat up someone who owed money to Lefty. He roughed up a comedian who had annoyed Lefty at the Thunderbird, a Miami restaurant.[65] Furthermore, "typically, what an undercover cop will do, in a buy-bust situation, is try to buy something from you. *Cops always buy, never sell. I was going to sell,*" Pistone reveals[66]—thanks to the fact that the FBI allowed him discretion in that regard. One very special commodity he bought, though: Lefty Ruggiero's protection. The FBI dished out a total of $40,000 for this purpose while Donnie was undercover: "They were paying him for his services as a 'wiseguy' to insure they had the protection of the Bonanno family in the event another family tried to interfere with their business."[67] While payment was ostensibly aimed at compensating Lefty, it was also, literally, a costly signal, and intentionally designed to appear to be so: "By giving him money, Conti and Rossi [two undercover agents who collaborated with Donnie] led Lefty to believe that they were willing to become involved with him, and *he trusted them as bad guys.*"[68]

Mafiosi were not taken in because they were dumb; rather, Pistone was unbelievably smart and resilient, and it just was very hard for mobsters to think that, taken together, all the things he did and did not do were not near-perfect discriminating signals. The FBI was later criticized for operating very near or even beyond the limits of the law. But this relative freedom fooled the mafiosi, because they assumed that an undercover agent would not pay the cost of breaking the law. Divine could not have banked on her neat little test if agents of the law had been allowed to expose themselves. The mobsters were cheated not just in the sense that Donnie Brasco, by faking, forging, and pretending, successfully mimicked a real bad guy but also in the sense that he did some *real* bad actions.

In a short biography of Bonanno family members—posted on the Internet for a while, then removed—Lefty was described as "the biggest idiot in the history of La Cosa Nostra. His blind greed and lack of instinct were felt hard in the American mafia." And yet Lefty was careful even years after Donnie had been accepted as a connected guy. Donnie was assisted by other undercover agents, one of whom was "Rossi." To test whether Rossi was an undercover agent, Lefty deliberately "lost" a plane ticket that Rossi had booked on his own credit card for Lefty (this was a covert way of paying protection to Lefty). "By pretending to lose the ticket, Lefty wanted to see how Rossi reacted. If he was an agent, Lefty reasoned, he would get nervous because he would probably have to account for the ticket to his office, plus he would be worried that somebody 'in the underworld business' might meanwhile find the ticket and check out the American Express number to see if it was a government number."[69]

In other cases, Donnie was subtly watchful in avoiding giveaways:

> I didn't go out of my way to learn what intelligence the FBI might have been getting about the murder [of Carmine Galante in Little Italy in 1979] from informants. I did not want to know more that I could logically know as a connected guy. It would be just as risky to know too much as to know too little. I did not want the burden of having to sort out what I should know from what I shouldn't.[70]

When it was finally revealed that Donnie was an undercover agent, the mobsters were shocked and did not believe it till Donnie actually testified in court against them. His operation managed to send many of them, mostly members of the Bonanno family, to jail.[71]

The mobsters learned their lesson and increased the price of the tests. Now not just one but "two mafiosi have to vouch for the proposed member." "They have to say they have known the proposed member if not since childhood, then at least for fifteen to twenty years."[72] According to the FBI, they also resumed a traditional practice that had been abandoned: "a proposed member must 'make his bones' or kill someone, before he can become a made guy. They have done so *because no agent*

would commit murder while posing as a bad guy.[73] Murder is really a perfectly discriminating signal of being a bad guy, a signal that no undercover agent, not even one belonging to a rather lax law-enforcement
agency, could afford.

This entry requirement—which shows how criminal acts can be perpetrated not merely for their immediate instrumental value but also for
their signaling value—had never been explicitly removed, but it was
no longer used with great determination. In truth, Dominick "Sonny
Black" Napolitano, who eventually became Donnie's main mentor and
planned to propose Donnie for membership, had asked Donnie to murder someone. "He gave me a contract so that I would have that creden-
tial when he put my name up." But the opportunity to carry it out did
not arise, for Anthony Bruno Indelicato, the intended victim, went successfully into hiding. Donnie showed that he was doing all he could to
track Indelicato down, and it was not thought to be his fault when he
failed. Thus, although he did not carry out the killing, he still managed
to show his willingness to do it, and a few months later Sonny put his
name forward for membership. At that point the FBI decided to stop the
operation, and Donnie resumed once again his real identity.

Sonny paid for his mistake with his life. He was killed in 1981, but his
decomposing body was not discovered until 1982. He had been shot, his
hands severed, and then placed in a body bag on Staten Island. Lefty got
twenty years in jail, where he died of lung cancer in 1995.

FROM THE MIMICS' PERSPECTIVE

Undercover agents—who have to persuade the group they aim to infiltrate of their criminal credentials—are a serious threat, for unlike solo
mimics they can draw on the resources of state agencies and can afford
complex mimicry acts, which involve posing, forging credentials, training, and funds. Still, it can be near impossible to infiltrate groups protected by an array of features that cannot be successfully imitated—
which, in other words, perfectly distinguish the real from the phony. For

instance, Reuel Marc Gerecht, a former CIA operative, has raised serious doubts over the feasibility of infiltrating Islamic movements.[74]

> Even a Muslim CIA officer with native-language abilities (and the Agency, according to several active-duty case officers, has very few operatives from Middle Eastern backgrounds) could do little more in this environment [Peshawar, Pakistan] than a blond, blue-eyed all-American. Case officers cannot long escape the embassies and consulates in which they serve. A U.S. official overseas, photographed and registered with the local intelligence and security services, can't travel much, particularly in a police-rich country like Pakistan, without the "host" services knowing about it. An officer who tries to go native, pretending to be a true-believing radical Muslim searching for brothers in the cause, will make a fool of himself quickly.

Undercover operations are a problematic form of anticrime activity for another reason as well. The logic of cost-discriminating signals inclines undercover agents to go beyond innocent pretensions and support initiatives of the same kind a true criminal or terrorist would undertake. Since law-enforcement agencies are under pressure to keep their agents safe, they push for discretion to be granted to them. And sometimes the undercover agents themselves, unbeknownst to their employers, choose to break the law because they worry about their credibility in the eyes of the host group and the consequences if they are discovered. The memoirs of undercover agents and spies are replete with this dilemma.

A grand case of infiltration that went well beyond the limits of the law occurred in Russia in the early 1900s. In their struggle against the terrorist bombers of the Socialist-Revolutionary Party, the tsar's agencies made ample use of infiltration.

> According to incomplete calculations, there were about 6500 agents, provocateurs, and other political investigations specialists operating in various political parties and organizations in the Rus-

sian Empire at the start of the twentieth century. . . . the police and gendarmes often set priorities themselves, at times even at the risk of the lives of high-ranking government officials and members of the imperial family. Matters concerning the security of the secret agents were of top priority, and maintaining the strong positions of agents within the terrorist organizations of the Socialist-Revolutionaries was considered more important than preventing assassinations, even against officials of the government.[75]

A famous case was that of Evno Azef, an agent who operated in revolutionary circles for about fifteen years. From 1893 on, he was a police agent. As a student in a German polytechnic school, he took the initiative of offering his services to the police department at the rate of 50 rubles per month, after which he attached himself to a foreign group calling itself the Union of Russian Socialist-Revolutionaries. He knew about the majority of terrorist acts being planned by the SRs, but he did not always report to his bosses about them. Nevertheless the police paid him well for his services.[76]

Episodes of this kind are not restricted to predemocratic societies. An illuminating case occurred in Canada. At its peak in 1993, the Heritage Front was the largest and best-organized neo-Nazi group in Canada, boasting a contact list of 1,800 names. Grant Bristow, cofounder and a leading member of this white racist group, turned out to be a paid informant of the Canadian Security Intelligence Service. "Bristow orchestrated a harassment campaign that terrorized Front enemies, harbored leading international racists in his own home in clear violation of both CSIS rules and the Immigration Act, and assisted in the Front's infiltration of the Reform Party."[77] "CSIS mole Grant Bristow, was an 'agent provocateur' who, with his spymasters, broke Canadian laws and internal CSIS regulations, a group of MPs have concluded. . . . Bristow's leadership role in the white racist Heritage Front, the report suggests, *may have led to the very events that caused CSIS to keep him in place for several more years.*"[78] An inquiry by the Security Intelligence Review Committee into the affair played down the accusations, but it is clear from the report that there were serious breaches. For instance, on the issue of harassment of antiracist militants and Jewish community members, the document concludes that "any informant who enters the Heritage Front or a similar group has to maintain his credibility with his associates otherwise he would not remain a trusted member for long. The question we were faced with was whether the CSIS source [Grant Bristow] had remained within the bounds of appropriate behaviour while trying to maintain his credibility. The answer we arrived at was that *in certain circumstances he had not* [emphasis in the original]."[79]

Even if they are only supposed to collect information on criminal or subversive activities, spies may end up producing more of such activities on their own initiative. They tend to become agents provocateurs not necessarily for the conspiratorial reasons why Joseph Conrad's protagonist in *The Secret Agent* does (Verloc was in the pay of an unnamed foreign embassy that wanted to persuade the British to take a tougher line against the anarchists and used his dim-witted nephew to stage an "anarchist" bombing attack) but, typically, only out of fear of not being credible enough and of risking their lives. The costs that make their signals credible in the eyes of their targets are after all "only" those of breaking legal constraints. They may never be caught, given the intrinsic opacity of what they do, and if caught they are not so likely to be punished, certainly not by death. And on the other side of the equation they have to consider the personal costs of failing to persuade. When one's life is threatened, the costs of breaking the law may suddenly appear smaller than those of obeying it. The set of those who are ready to risk their life, sacrifice their family, and deceive dangerous criminals for long periods of time, while at the same time remaining strictly a law-abiding citizen, must be extremely small.

This raises an interesting quandary for the criminals or terrorists who are trying to test the bona fides of others. For, by increasing the severity of the punishment meted out against undercover agents who are discovered, they encourage the latter to afford costly signals that, once displayed, may make it impossible for the bad guys to say whether the potential recruits are undercover agents in the first place.

If the punishment is kept low—and amounts, for example, just to a refusal to deal with those who will not swallow a spoonful of drug—the undercover agent may find it preferable to refrain from swallowing it even at the cost of revealing his true type, for he does not want to break the law. By contrast, the real criminal who wants to deal with the drug dealers may prefer to pay the cost of the physical illness caused by swallowing, for he is entirely at ease with breaking the law. The key extra cost that discriminates between the real criminal and the undercover agent is the cost of breaking the law, which the mimic faces while the genuine article does not. A harsher punishment, however, can reverse the equation and make it cheaper for the undercover agent to swallow rather than not swallow, even at the cost of breaking the law, and thus make him behaviorally indistinguishable from the real criminal. When administered under the threat of the harsher punishment, the test no longer separates one type from the other. By failing to appreciate this quandary and threatening death against those who refuse to swallow the drug, the dealers fail to realize that they are deactivating the very source of the reliability of their test, for under that threat the agents are now allowed (and would in any case feel inclined) to swallow the drug.

CONCLUSIONS

Once someone intent on crime identifies a potential partner as a bona fide criminal, he has solved one problem only to land in another, equally difficult, one. He now has to establish whether his partner is not just a crook but an honorable one. After Hugh Grant exposed himself, Divine knew that he was not an undercover cop, for she believed that cops do not do that. Yet she still did not know what kind of a customer he was. Prostitutes are constantly on guard against robbers or perverts who pose as ordinary customers.[80] Anyone who works outside the law is more exposed than ordinary businessmen to becoming the prey of other criminals who mimic being a criminal of the honest sort. A street-drug dealer who successfully advertises to customers may also attract robbers who pretend to be customers in order to get close to the dealers and rob them.[81] A criminal has to be on guard against both kinds of mimics, law-enforcement agents and criminals of the wrong sort.

If honesty were thought to be a trait of certain criminals and not others, in order to establish whether a potential partner is honest one could follow the same strategy one uses for identifying whether someone is a criminal to begin with. The same kind of costly signals would be required for criminals to persuade one another that they were the honest type. In certain cases the game they play is indeed one of signaling their type. However, in most circumstances criminals tend to think of each other as being of just one type, namely the dishonest one, and believe that given half a chance they will take advantage of each other. The only way in which they can come almost to "trust" each other enough to cooperate is, therefore, not by signaling their type, but either by enforcing their partners' honesty with the threat of some kind of retaliation or, more generally, by putting themselves and their partners in a condition whereby "honesty" rather than cheating is their best course of action, whatever their type. I shall explore some of the strategies they adopt in chapters 2 and 3.

CHAPTER 2

The Power of Limits

The problem of trust faced by all kinds of businesses, intensified, haunts the underworld. How does one know whether to trust others, and, conversely, how does one persuade others that one is trustworthy (whether this is true or not)? Both questions are ceaselessly pressing for criminals, and if the reader takes a mental step into a criminal's boots, it is not difficult to see why. First, criminals operate under greater *constraints* that can force them to default on their agreements even if they do not want to, simply because they end up in prison or have to go on the run. In this sense they are not so much untrustworthy as unreliable, more likely to have "accidents." Next, they have greater *opportunities* to renege on their agreements. While the secrecy in which they operate acts as a constraint, it can also be turned to their advantage, as they can vanish more easily. Cheats, furthermore, do not have to fear the law when they dupe other criminals, for the dupes have no access to legal protection. Third, they are more likely to have *motivations* to defect than most ordinary people do, as they are driven by selfish goals and disregard the property or even the lives of others. Fourth, they are more likely to have the *dispositions* to defect, for they are more prone than most to take risks. They are also less likely to feel bound by norms and be deterred by punishment than law-abiding citizens are.

Thus, by solving the problem discussed in chapter 1 and identifying each other as bona fide criminals, they also unavoidably let each other know that they have those constraints, opportunities, motivations, and dispositions, thereby landing themselves in what we may call the villain's paradox: a criminal needs partners who are also criminals, but these are typically untrustworthy people to deal with when their self-interest is at stake. To be more precise, one may be able to trust a criminal partner in certain respects—to act rationally under pressure and keep his sangfroid, for example, and to respond violently or even kill if necessary. One can trust one's partner to be a competent robber. But when it comes to sharing the booty, when interests are in conflict, it is hard to trust one criminal to show concern for another. While citizens can hope to find trustworthy-making features in other people's characters, villains typically cannot. Criminals embody *homo economicus* at his rawest, and they know it. In keeping with the evidence that people who are untrustworthy are also more likely to think that others are untrustworthy,[1] criminals are more inclined to distrust each other than ordinary people do. Åkerström's research, for instance, showed that 58 percent of inmates agreed with the statement "one cannot be too careful in one's dealing with other people," while in the control group only 28 percent agreed.[2]

Crime fiction, whether in writing or film, often exploits the tensions that arise from distrust (which may further enhance distrust among real criminals, who, as we shall see in chapter 10, are affected by fiction). In Raymond Chandler's *The Big Sleep* Harry Jones imparts his wisdom to detective Philip Marlowe: "She is a grifter, shamus. I'm a grifter. We are all grifters. So we sell each other for a nickel"—an insight that does not surprise Marlowe.[3] Only rarely is loyalty found. "Come to life dearie! You are a thief among thieves, and those who don't double-cross get crossed"—the PI utters in Dashiell Hammett's *The Big Knockover* while trying to persuade Angel Grace to inform on her accomplices. The woman, gripped by a sense of identity (we are not the type that turns people in), does not yield: "I wish to God I could!"—she replies—"but I'm Paperbox-John Cardigan's daughter. It isn't in me to turn anybody up. You are the wrong side. I can't go over. I wish I could. But there is too much Cardigan in me. I'll be hoping every minute that you nail them, and nail them dead right."[4] True to her name (and surname) in Hammett's story, Angel Grace shows that there can be honor among thieves.

The evidence for loyalty in the real underworld, however, is close to nonexistent. True, there is a bias due to the fact that when things go wrong we are more likely to hear about them than when they go smoothly. Yet the evidence of cheating and betrayal is just too large to think that the problem of untrustworthiness troubles the underworld in merely the same way as it does ordinary business. Criminals dupe each other, all too easily yielding to their raw self-interest. Among a group of big drug dealers in the Netherlands who were the object of research based on a very large documentation, "betrayal and double-crossing were habitual for many of the criminal entrepreneurs, leading to mutual distrust and returning flicks of paranoia."[5] The lives of British career criminals recounted by Dick Hobbs are replete with episodes of mistrust and cheating.[6] When offered the right incentives, even many mafiosi, allegedly the most loyal of the lot, have turned state's evidence and betrayed their former friends, both in the United States and in Italy.

Given these propensities, one wonders how criminals can ever manage to do anything together. This puzzle has long been recognized. In Plato's *Republic* Socrates asks Trasymachus, who claims that injustice is a source of strength, "please [tell me] whether you think that a city, or an army, or a band of robbers or thieves, or any other company which pursue some unjust end in common, would be able to effect anything if they were unjust to one another?" "If they had been thoroughly unjust—Socrates concludes—they could not have kept their hands off one another. Clearly they must have possessed justice of a sort, enough to keep them from exercising their injustice on each other at the same time as on their victims. . . . the thorough villains who are perfectly unjust, are also perfectly incapable of action."[7] Yet, while many have raised the issue, the explanations of what could possibly support some "justice of a sort" are not often satisfactory, and merit a fresh look.

In this chapter I do not have the ambition to cover all the ways in which criminals solve or circumvent the problem of trust. Here I discuss mostly a very odd way in which a trustee can persuade a truster that it is in the trustee's own interest to be trustworthy—by displaying his own incompetence. In the next chapter, I will explore how the same goal can be achieved by revealing information about one's own bad deeds. First, however, I approach the matter from the point of view of the truster, the criminal who is worried about his partners' trustworthiness. What can he do?

VIOLENCE AND ITS DRAWBACKS

Fear of punishment deters cheating. This belief, widespread in the underworld, underpins all legal systems. If one can ensure that the threat of punishment is credible, would-be offenders think twice. In interpersonal exchange, the threat of punishment can alter a trustee's payoffs in such a way as to make it in the trustee's interest to behave, whether or not he is of good character. His interest becomes incompatible with cheating not because he will benefit by behaving well but because he will suffer by behaving badly.

Although violence is not the only means of punishment in the underworld, it plays a central role. One reason is that villains cannot run prisons or impose fines or community service on one another, so violence becomes more attractive. If one finds oneself in business with partners not renowned for their scruples, there seems all to be gained by being tough. The ideal situation from the truster's point of view is to be at least tough enough for the trustee to worry seriously about the consequences of reneging on their agreement. When the trustee knows that the truster is prepared to resort to violence, he will be more careful before taking advantage of him. This solution is attractive, for one does not need to worry about whether the trustee is trustworthy by character but only whether he is responsive to punishment. If he is, then he will behave as if he were trustworthy. The threat of violence makes trustworthiness irrelevant.

Many criminals share this philosophy and, even if they are not full-time enforcers, cultivate and display their toughness. Moreover, even if they do not set out to handle their business by the threat of violence, a period in prison, as we shall see in chapter 4, will give them ample opportunities to hone their ability to do so and gain them a corresponding reputation. For many, resolving disputes with violence is not even so much an option as a selection effect: criminals are more likely to be violent men who end up dealing with other violent men.

I must now report a story that proves that I am not the only academic mulling over these ideas. On 24 June 1998 Italian police arrested Giuseppe Longo, chair in gastroenterology at the University of Messina, Sicily, on corruption charges and for ordering the murder of a colleague. Matteo Bottari—also a professor of medicine, and a protégé of Diego Cuzzocrea, then *rettore* of Messina University—had been shot a few months earlier with a sawed-off shotgun. Apparently Longo, whom police suspected of being connected with a Calabrese mafia family, had been maneuvering to make sure that certain firms rather than others obtained the contracts for building a new university clinic. The *rettore*, who counted among his brothers a couple of building contractors whom he had favored in the past, was not inclined to agree with Longo. The murder was apparently the clan's signal that they meant business.

In the weeks prior to his arrest Longo somehow came to know he was under investigation. What he did not know was that even his bedroom was bugged by the police. About one month before his arrest, while talking to a girlfriend, Longo said:

> Clearly I am not happy to come out in the newspaper for being suspected of the murder of Bottari. But I reckon that all considered those who do not hold me in much consideration are going to be scared. Maybe all this will be positive publicity, at least in certain Calabrese and Sicilian quarters. After all one with a repute of this kind is respected, is believed to be a "bravo figghiolu" [a wiseguy].[8]

Longo, who was in the end not prosecuted for this crime (for lack of sufficient evidence),[9] alludes to two effects that must appear surprising to law-abiding citizens. First, being suspected of murder, a stigma in polite society, can be a bonus in the underworld. Whether it is good or bad depends on the audience one aims to impress. Next, being suspected of a serious criminal offense has a peculiar by-product: it provides hard-to-fake evidence that one is "bad," and it spreads the knowledge of this trait, which is arduous to advertise both credibly and widely otherwise—another instance in which the law, as we saw in chapter 1, has a perverse effect.

Using violence, however, has drawbacks. There is, of course, a contingent one, namely that thanks to its use criminals are more likely to attract police attention and end up in prison as a result. The drawbacks, however, go deeper. First, violence and even just its threat are unbalanced solutions, for they imply that the truster-enforcer bears all the costs of solving the problem of trust, while the trustee is a passive recipient. The enforcer will incur costs whether or not the trustee proves untrustworthy and punishment needs to be meted out. To make the threat of violence credible in the first place, the truster-enforcer will have to spend resources to persuade the trustee that he is happy to bear the costs—something that gives a credibility advantage to criminals who have a reputation for gratuitous cruelty: for a psychopath the chance to use violence is a pleasure rather than a cost. All deals in which the benefits for the truster (including the effects on his future reputation) do not offset the enforcement costs—which are high because criminals are not easily deterred and live secretive lives that make them harder to catch—are disadvantageous. A rational truster in this position, who has no other way either to know whether a trustee is trustworthy or to force his trustworthiness, will not enter them. From the criminal point of view, all the times in which the trustee would have been prepared even without coercion to behave in a trustworthy manner, this choice represents a loss of business.

Resorting to violence has an even more serious downside. On the one hand, by threatening violence, one indirectly increases the credibility of the promises of the *trustee*—if he freely makes a promise, he is more likely to mean what he says, for he fears punishment. What, on the other hand, it does not do is to increase the credibility of the promises of the tough guy. Being violent does not make one *generally* credible. If anything it has the opposite effect, as people fear that someone who uses force to protect himself from cheating will also use force to protect himself when *he* cheats. Unless he also enjoys a proven reputation for fairness, a very tall order for a criminal, the tough guy will scare people who deal with him but may also scare them off. If a nonviolent dealer meets a violent one, he will behave if he plays, but he may well be reluctant to play in the first place. Professor Longo, for all we know, may have been playing to a really tough extra-academic audience concerned more with lucrative public contracts than with the white-gloved practices of academic corruption, and so, as he expects, he may on balance gain from the reputation his conviction produced. However, by gaining it Longo will be unlikely to find quietly corrupt professors clamoring to deal with him once he is released from prison. They will stay away from him as much as they can. There is a trade-off in using violence: one becomes threatening to some, with good effects, but *too* threatening to others. One may avoid being cheated by one's partners while at the same time losing other potential partners.

Tough guys are thus likely to find willing partners only among other tough guys. When one expects that part and parcel of business is relying on violent means, then either one does not get involved at all or one must be prepared to contemplate violence too. This has a further adverse effect, for criminals prepared to deal with a tough guy are themselves selected on toughness and thus harder to intimidate. The level of threat required to keep them in check must thus be higher to be effective. In conclusion, violence restricts the markets in which criminals can operate by deterring peaceful people from dealing with them and puts them at greater risk of becoming themselves the victims of it. The smart criminals must seek alternatives to violence.

There is evidence of both collective and individual attempts at avoiding violence. The Russian criminal fraternity of Vory-v-zakone had "a strong code against murder," did not allow professional killers to join, and in case any of their members did kill someone "they had to justify the act to the fraternity."[10] The solution for individuals consists in limiting one's involvement to markets in which trust and punishments are pursued, at least in the first instance, by means other than violence. A young offender interviewed by Sullivan claimed that he made a practice of avoiding violence: "He stressed that he did not trade in heroin, worked at a level where hustlers co-operated with each other, had established himself as trustworthy with both customers and business associates, paid attention to older hustlers and learned from them, and avoided violence. He referred to being a reliable businessman as 'diplomacy' and said that the lack of this quality rapidly thinned out the ranks of aspiring hustlers." He also said, "I'm a hustler not a gangster. A gangster is like Al Capone, might makes right. But like an older brother told me, 'You live by the sword, you die by the sword.' There is a lot of shooting out there. A lot of people my age are caught up in something that's not real. They go too fast and they get killed. I don't want to make money like that."[11]

However, operating in nonviolent circles is not enough, for it does not remove the problem of trust. So what can criminals do to find "justice of a sort" among themselves? Given their propensities, criminals have little hope of finding "thick" trust in each other:[12] they stand hardly any chance of finding people of good character in their line of business and can aspire, at best, to find ways to sustain the "thin" or "calculative" version of trust.[13] Some scholars would be reluctant to call this "trust" at all. Apart from this semantic point, our question is straightforward: how can criminals—both those who are prone to use violence and those who are too smart to make it their first option—reassure each other enough to cooperate?

BURNING BRIDGES

All too often the problem of trust is looked at from the point of view of the truster. In so many instances, however, matters are in the hands of trustees, who want to be trusted just as much as others may wish to trust them. So here my question will be: what can a trustee do to persuade a truster that he is not going to cheat?

The situation faced by a truster and a trustee can be understood by considering briefly the basic trust game developed by Michael Bacharach and myself.[14] If the payoffs are as in figure 2.1—the numbers are purely illustrative, and in the order of (truster payoff, trustee payoff) for each situation—the trustee gains more by cheating ($4 > 1$), so all the truster can do is refuse dealing with him ($0 > -3$). Trustees in the ordinary world of legal business can try to persuade the truster that they are of good character, that they are honest, and that their real payoffs

Trustee

		Behave	Cheat
Truster	Deal	3, 1	−3, 4
	Refuse	0, 0	0, 0

Fig. 2.1. The basic trust game with an untrustworthy trustee

are as in figure 2.2. Here the trustee prefers to behave well (1 > −2), so if the truster believes this is the case, he should agree to deal with him (3 > 0).

As we know, however, a criminal has problems persuading his partners of his good character precisely because he is a criminal. He has to find very persuasive signals to convince the truster that disloyalty would not pay off for him, that his *real* payoffs are those in figure 2.2. He can show, for instance, that he wants to stay in business for as long as he can and that cheating would have negative consequences on his prospects of doing so. So even if in any one deal his payoffs are those of figure 2.1, once one adds up the payoffs of repeated games they would be transformed into those of figure 2.2. By cheating now, the trustee would lose all future business. He can thus convince the truster that even if the truster cannot punish him violently or by some other means, the truster can still punish him simply by not doing any more business with him and instructing his friends to do the same. This would be enough to deter the trustee from cheating in any one deal. In stable markets, in which agents can contemplate being in business for long periods of time *and* in which information travels well, this may work. Consider this example:

Committee member Ali Hossain was speaking [to reporters] on behalf of the newly-formed Suganda Samity association, created by the ten thousand professional thieves who operate in the Ban-

| | Trustee | |
	Behave	Cheat
Deal	3,1	−3,−2
Refuse	0,0	0,0

Fig. 2.2. The basic trust game with a trustworthy trustee

gladesh capital. "We have already enrolled two thousands pupils in our training school, and we are teaching them how to master the [ancient and honorable art of thieving]—pick-pocketing, forgery, and breaking and entering with light violence. We also run an intelligence service, so that domestic servants can give us inside information which will help us to rob their employers. In return, *we give these informants a share of the proceeds from the burglary, because it is only right and proper that we treat them with honesty.*"[15]

Honesty may be the thieves' motive, but a view to encouraging further cooperation by the domestic servants must also be a strong consideration. The members of this association are in business to stay and need to be known to be honest by those who assist them. When I did some fieldwork in Naples in the late 1980s, where the illegal lottery run by the Camorra was very popular, several people told me with admiration how prompt the bookies were in paying their wins—showing up on their doorstep, cash in hand, within twenty-four hours of the draw. The camorristi could cheat the living daylights out of each other and everyone whenever they got a chance, but they knew full well that a minor rumor that they were not paying up would be a catastrophe for their lottery business. They had a huge interest in behaving honestly. And by doing so their standing was high, and gamblers felt safe to entrust their money to the illegal market. The best way, then, for a criminal in such situations to establish a reputation for trustworthiness is simple: *behave well* and live up to one's promises, just as a dealer does in ordinary businesses. And when interests are so well aligned to good practice, one can stop worrying about good character: the only thing trusters need to trust is the ability of trustees to look after their own interests.

Even in markets that are often unstable and violence-ridden, this strategy seems occasionally viable. Asked how he managed to become established, a drug dealer replied:

> I didn't establish myself, it's just that I have never cheated anyone, which is really uncommon in the dealing trade, where bad shit is sold and where people are charged too much and all that stuff. I have never done that, always fixed my debts immediately and seldom bought on credit. . . . your reputation spreads around quickly if you have blown someone or made a bad deal or something . . . so that's the way I got it.[16]

However, as I shall discuss in chapter 8, the conditions that make having a good reputation worthwhile and effective—easy diffusion of reliable information, easy reidentification of previous partners, stability, and long-lived firms—are not common in the underworld. What else can a trustee do when conditions do not support the logic of reputation?

A whole class of signals aims to inform the truster that defection would be not so much unprofitable as impossible. This logic stresses the presence of constraints rather than benefits. If there are no ready-made constraints to display, there is still the option of designing some, of binding oneself in some way, of burning one's bridges or tying one's hands so that one's partners know that one could not defect even if one wanted to. In terms of the basic trust game it amounts to persuading one's partners that the option "cheat" just is not there, or is so infinitely costly that it is not worth worrying about it. Untrustworthiness becomes irrelevant because it is impossible to pursue it. Sometimes, just being open about one's identity and whereabouts, generally making it more difficult for oneself or one's near and dear to vanish and thus easier for one's partners to reidentify and track one down, can do the work. In his autobiography Henry Williamson, a criminal who was involved in robberies and drug dealing, says: "I had gave [sic] a few guys my telephone number. That way a guy'll trust you more."[17]

Since participants in a criminal enterprise are often both trusters and trustees at the same time, binding needs to be reciprocal. The classic cases are to make the loot only jointly available, for instance by sharing multiple keys for the same safe, or to meet unarmed or in public places with many potential witnesses. Another case is to make an exchange simultaneous, so as to minimize both parties' exposure to opportunistic behavior. Self-binding can also take the form of self-branding as found, for instance, in South African prisons:

> Erefaan's face is covered in tattoos. "Spit on my grave" is tattooed across his forehead; "I hate you, Mum" etched on his left cheek. The tattoos are an expression of loyalty. The men cut the emblems of their allegiance into their skin. The Number [the name of the hierarchical system in Pollsmoor prison] demands not only that you pledge your oath verbally but that you are marked, indelibly, for life. Facial tattoos are the ultimate abandonment of all hope of a life outside.[18]

"Tattoos worn on the face or neck are the most visible, and thus suggest a higher level of commitment than tattoos on other less visible parts of the body."[19] According to Margo DeMello, who researched the tattoos worn by inmates at Folsom State Penitentiary, "older convicts feel that younger prisoners should not get tattooed if they don't already have any tattoos, and many tattooists in prison will simply refuse to be the first to tattoo a new prisoner. . . . An 'honorable' prison tattooist doesn't want to be responsible for helping to ruin a young prisoner's life, particularly if an individual is going to be getting out of prison any time soon. By acquiring tattoos during his incarceration, he would be making concrete his identity as a convict, and may regret his decision to become tattooed."[20]

An effect of having highly visible tattoos is to make it more difficult for anyone to renounce a life of crime or, if the tattoo is gang-specific or business-specific, to switch from gang to gang or change one's business (more on tattoos in chapter 5 and 6). Even if a criminal's previous partners do not punish him, the new partners, provided that they know the code, will realize that he has switched.

In many illegal markets, however, criminals do not want to advertise to the whole world that they are criminals, and in their normal lives they mimic law-abiding citizens. They do not want to attract the attention of the law, of course, and in any case they must present an honest facade to carry out their illicit activities, as for instance in schemes involving corruption. A corrupt judge needs to look like the same old judge when he is being corrupt. Such criminals cannot carry signs as observable as tattoos to show their loyalty. They need subtler signs.

INCOMPETENCE

One way of convincing others that one's best chance of making money lies in behaving as an "honorable thief" is by showing that one lacks better alternatives. There are several ways to do this, all of which consist in displaying some limitations, be they related to character, skills, or situation. Some such limits often exist anyway and, making a virtue out of necessity, one can choose to display rather than hide them; or limits can be self-imposed. A most peculiar instance of this strategy lies in displaying one's incompetence at doing anything else. The mobsters' henchman, often caricatured as an *énergumène*, epitomizes the extreme case of this class. If he were too clever, he would be a menace to the boss. In some respect, idiocy implies trustworthiness.

I was alerted to the importance of limits as a way of demonstrating one's trustworthiness by pondering a case of corruption, a crime often perpetrated without violence, and a particular puzzle it poses. Most academic positions in Italy are allocated through national competitions, held at irregular intervals, sometimes several years apart. The system is corrupt because academic achievement counts for little in determining promotion. Evidence of this is that the Italian government itself, on several occasions, has established special funds that could only be spent for employing Italian academics who worked in foreign universities and wanted to return to their country. No matter how internationally distinguished they were, their chances of obtaining a chair in the regular (but corrupt) competitions were zero. There is near-universal agreement that loyalty and subservience to the barons (*baroni*), as the most powerful professors are dubbed, are the currency that gains promotion for applicants. There are, to be sure, important differences in that some academic fields are more driven by merit than others—those with greater international exposure or clear standards of quality, for instance. And exceptions occur in any field, and deserving candidates do manage to slip through the net. Yet, even though niches of high-quality Italian scholarship do mercifully exist, the corrupt system seems undoubtedly predominant.[21]

This system relies on a "credit" market. Positions in the selection committees rotate. The barons serving on the committees in any one competition agree to give some of the jobs to pupils of those professors who are not on the committees, in the expectation that these professors will reciprocate in the next round. The barons operate on the basis of a pact of reciprocity, which requires a lot of trust, for credits are repaid years later. Debts and credits are even passed on from generation to generation within a professor's "lineage," and professors close to retirement are excluded from the current deals, for they will not be around long enough to return favors. Professors who have accumulated credit, therefore, even if they have an opportunity to pull the rug from under the feet of their debtors by, say, criticizing their work or that of their protégés, are afraid of doing so, for in future rounds their acolytes would suffer retaliation.[22]

Here is the puzzling fact: many among the barons who wield power in the Italian academic system display not only low academic standards but lower than the average standards of their field in Italy.[23] They have a poor publication record and show little interest in substantive academic discussion or research. They edit volumes and write introductions to volumes written by their protégés, but hardly write any of their own. If they do, their books are either reviews of the literature or paraphrase some foreign author on whose fame they hope to ride. Not only do they work less at their research, as tenured scholars may be tempted to do everywhere, but whatever little they do is of shoddy quality. Also, and this is what is most intriguing, they do not try to hide their weakness. One has the impression that they almost flaunt it in personal contacts.

The existence of an academic kakistocracy, or government by the worst, seems puzzling because we would naturally expect those who are better at their job to carry more weight in their profession.[24] One explanation could lie in the effect of comparative advantages: those who have what it takes to be good at their research choose to spend less time getting involved in academic politics, and vice versa. The pursuit of power is time-consuming, and the better one is at research, the higher are the opportunity costs of investing in power maneuvers. If this was all there is to it, however, we would not be able to explain why one should also boast about one's poor research record.

A different, though not necessarily alternative, solution to the puzzle may make sense of that too. While weakness at research can motivate agents to become more involved in power politics in the first place, it also makes them eminently *suitable* for it. There is a difference between wanting a position and having the right features to manage it effectively. Being incompetent and displaying it conveys the message *I will not run away, for I have no strong legs to run anywhere else*. In a corrupt academic market, being good at and interested in one's own research, by contrast, signal a potential for developing one's career independent of corrupt reciprocity. This makes one feared. In the Italian academic world, the kakistocrats are those who best assure others by displaying, through lack of competence and lack of interest in research, that they will comply with the pacts. They and their pupils could not make it by the mere quality of their research.

The same reasoning might be applied not only to the choice of one's partners but also to the selection of candidates for promotion. The corrupt deals are not only among peers—the barons, that is—but also between barons and candidates, who enter into a "contract" with their sponsors in the selection committee, exchanging a promotion for a promise of unswerving loyalty.

A truly incompetent agent finds it easy to persuade others of his "quality." Sometimes one does not even have to make an effort to reveal it. It shows. Those not so naturally gifted with the right kind of ineptitude may resort to playing down their qualities following Mae West's advice that "brains are an asset if you can hide them." Or at least show you are sorry to have them. (When, a long time ago, I was entertaining the prospect of joining the academia in my country of origin, an Italian sociologist once half-jokingly told me, "There is something you don't understand, Diego: when you are good at your work, you must always apologize.") Still, persons trying to exaggerate their incompetence are hampered by the cost of having to construct a front. In the end, the best strategy is truly cultivating one's incompetence, working oneself up from something to nothing.

There are, to be sure, reasons other than trust-inducing incompetence for selecting low-quality candidates. The worse the appointed individual is,

1. the less likely the appointee is to outdo his appointers;[25]
2. the more grateful he will feel for having been appointed (as Machiavelli wrote, "when one receives those honors and rewards that he believes he deserves, he feels no obligations toward those who bestow them on him");[26]
3. the more the appointer can flaunt his power (the grand example of this case must be that of Caligula, who made his horse into a senator).[27]

These reasons can motivate the promotion of less-qualified people regardless of whether there is a "contract" between appointer and appointee. They do not, however, exclude the possibility that if promotion is the object of a corrupt agreement between them, the appointer can choose less-competent appointees also because he expects them to be more likely to repay him by loyalty and subservience. Even if ungrateful and opportunistic, they would still lack better alternatives.

The perception and use of incompetence as a constraint on defection extends beyond academic corruption. Selection in the world of politics offers examples of the same logic. "People imagine," wrote the author of *Confessions of a Corrupt Mayor*, "that parties at the elections put the strongest men in their list, the candidates who can bring the most votes. But this is not so, with the exception of candidates who stand as a cover or those very great personalities who act as a facade to hide the mediocrity of the others. You get in the [electoral] list because you are powerful and tied to the nomenclature, either you belong to it or comply with its rules. Or, because you are a nobody, you carry the water and don't even cast a shadow."[28]

Credible partners or loyal employees need not be globally inept, merely selectively incompetent at the relevant brand of activity that could reward their defection. Unholy priests, cowardly soldiers, and barely literate journalists can all achieve the same result in their respective domains. Lack of interest in policy making does the same job in corrupt politics, whereas thinking seriously about issues of principle or policy signals that one plans to acquire a following in other than corrupt ways. There is no greater sin than having a brilliant idea. Agents are likely to play corrupt games with one another if they are persuaded that their partners are limited in the alternative courses of action they can pursue to advance their career.

The relative value of incompetence and the problem it poses are nothing new: "[A] sixteenth- or seventeenth-century king faced an annoying dilemma. He needed expert councillors, men with knowledge and experience who could solve problems and foresee all dangers. But the more nearly a councillor approached this ideal the more likely he was to start making his own decisions rather than defer to the king."[29]

The idea that incompetence can be reassuring to one's fellow criminals is not as extravagant as it may seem. It is only a crude version of practices commonly used in ordinary business and understood by economists, such as Oliver Williamson, in the same vein. Any investment that binds agents more closely to one kind of business or transaction—known as "asset specificity"—informs others that the agents are not planning to change their line of business or disappear overnight. Highly specific assets represent sunk costs that have relatively little value beyond their use in the context of transactions related to those assets. If one's skills are predominantly tied to one type of production and are acquired after a long period of training and effort, one's competence will be best spent on that product, and the cost of switching to something else will be higher the greater the investment in acquiring those skills. Asset specificity can be achieved over a wide range of domains, which include not just skills but location, machinery, brand name, and others. If, "instead of a general purpose building of nondescript design," Williamson points out, "the producer could construct a building with a distinctive 'signature' [t]he durable investment could be the same, but the alternative value that can be realised from the second building might be much lower. The long-term commitments that are signalled by this second design relieve customers of quality shading hazards."[30] Developing asset specificity in handling corrupt deals involves abstaining from specializing in anything else. Incompetence is just the other side of the same coin.

The power of weaknesses has been also identified by Thomas Schelling with reference to bargaining situations:

> If the term "bargaining power" implies that it is an advantage to be more intelligent or more skilled in debate, or to have more financial resources, more physical strength, more military potency, or more ability to withstand losses, then the term does a disservice. These qualities are by no means universal advantages in bargaining situations; they often have a contrary value. . . . If a man knocks at a door and says that he will stab himself on the porch unless given $10, he is more likely to get the $10 if his eyes are bloodshot. The threat to mutual destruction cannot be used to deter an adversary who is too unintelligent to comprehend it or too weak to enforce his will on those he represents.[31]

MAFIOSO INCOMPETENCE

The mafia's principal activities are settling disputes among other criminals, protecting them against each other's cheating, and organizing and overseeing illicit agreements, often involving many agents, such as illicit cartel agreements in otherwise legal industries. Mafia-like groups offer a solution of sorts to the trust problem by playing the role of a government for the underworld and supplying protection to people involved in illegal markets or deals. They may play that role poorly, sometimes veering toward extortion rather than genuine protection, but they do play it.

Mafia protection may solve the problem of making one's partners behave even if they are untrustworthy, but why should one trust mafiosi to do what *they* promise? They can beat people into fearing them but cannot beat them into believing that they are trustworthy. This is a contradiction in Hegel's sense: a master cannot be loved by his slave. This is, as I have argued, a crucial limitation of violence. To succeed and make his deliberations stick, a mafioso must be feared by all parties, but he must also be thought capable of being disinterested in his deliberations and of restraining his greed. If mafioso settlements were thought to be biased, the parties would be less likely to submit to them, increasing the enforcement costs for the mafioso. And if parties feared that a mafioso, rather than just asking for protection money, could become rapacious and take over their business altogether, they would be afraid of dealing with him. They must trust the mafioso to play his part within limits—but how?

An unexpected result of my research on the mafia was to find out that mafiosi are quite incompetent at doing anything other than their enforcement job. When they do get directly involved in business, they soon give up because they prove quite remarkably *unfit* for it, whatever "it" is.[32] "Well, they fit into their own environment very well," said Donnie Brasco.[33] "They do not fit into the straight world at all, because they cannot fathom doing anything legitimate as a first means of making any type of money." Their ineptitude can reach monumental proportions:

A lot of these wiseguys did not have the ability to move around the country. Once you got these guys out of New York City, they were like fish out of water. . . . As they schooled me in the mafia, I had to school them on how to make airline reservations. I am talking about a 49-year-old man [Benjamin "Lefty Guns" Ruggiero], telling him how to make airline reservations to three different cities, with an open return, because we did not know what date we were going to return to New York City.[34]

"They cannot run a restaurant to save their lives," the late Douglas Adams, author of *The Hitchhiker's Guide to the Galaxy*, once perceptively said on the radio.

Most mafiosi declare themselves to be employed in menial jobs, and many prominent ones do not have any occupation at all.[35] The *pentiti*, mafiosi who turned state's evidence and testified in the large Sicilian trials of the 1980s, could name the occupation of only 40 of the 114 bosses that they mentioned. Of those with an occupation, 31 percent were employed in agriculture, mostly as landowners. Most of these occupations are a facade anyway. "The consideration in which a mafioso is held within Cosa Nostra is not tied . . . to his profession or degree," said Antonino Calderone, a mafioso who turned state's evidence.[36]

Once again, as in the case of the corrupt academic market, the lack of professional competence outside one's main field could simply be the outcome of selection through comparative advantages—people do what they are best at, and do not do what they are not good at. Mafiosi are good at intimidation and stick to it. This trait, however, not only motivates their involvement but makes them suitable for it: those who deal with them know that, if nothing else, because of incompetence mafiosi can be trusted not to take over their business and run it. The smart mafiosi stay out of the businesses they protect, or if involved in a legal business they may have only a nominal affiliation with it, often as a legal front to hide protection payments. They let the professionals and the entrepreneurs take care of the actual business operations. They specialize in, say, handling drug dealers, not in drug dealing itself. If they got too closely involved in their clients' businesses, they would no longer be able to be seen as "honest brokers," and if they showed any competence at it, their clients would fear that they might just take over.

The interesting fact is that the mafiosi do not seem concerned about their incompetence. Just like the academic kakistocrats, they happily reveal it, which is evidence that they know its value, at the very least that they do not consider it a negative trait. In 1980 Sonny Black met Santo Trafficante, the main mafia man in Florida, hoping to strike a deal between the latter's family and the Bonannos and be allowed room for running some gambling operations in Florida. This is how Sonny reported his conversation with Trafficante to Donnie Brasco:

> In the car Sonny unwound. "It was a feeling-out conversation," he says, "I told [Trafficante], 'listen, I'm no sophisticated person. I'm a

street person all my life.' I says [*sic*], 'I love the streets, you know. I
don't know nothing about nothing, about gambling or anything.' I
says, 'Me, I just like to go in the street, rob who the fuck I gotta
rob.'"[37]

Japanese yakuza too display this self-deprecating attitude. "No one here's
a rocket scientist," Hara, the Hara-gumi yakuza boss, likes to say. "If anyone had half a brain, they probably wouldn't be in the yakuza in the first
place!"[38] In *Silovi grupirovki* (the name of Bulgarian organized crime
groups), according to the boss of one such group that went out of business, "thinking was not held in esteem."[39] Incompetence is one way of
telling people *You can count on me, for even if I wanted to, I would not be able
to cheat you.*

DISINTERESTEDNESS

Incompetence is reassuring but only up to a point. Mafiosi could still
prove greedy and milk their protégés dry even without taking over their
business and running it. They need to display stronger signals of disregard for pecuniary success, and so they have. Sicilian Mafiosi, contrary to
the dominant opinion among outsiders, which deems greed to be their
fundamental motivation, have been ceaselessly eager to show that they
are not in the business so much for the money as for "respect." They
have projected an image of deriving pleasure from power rather than
money, and of looking down on those driven by greed—a favorite prov-
erb in their ranks is "Cumannàri è megghiu ca fùttiri!" (better to have
power than sex). And so have yakuza: "I'm not really a businessman,"
Hara said. "I don't like working, and I don't have a money obsession like
some oyabun [bosses]. Some are more like bankers than yakuza."[40] The
vory too were expected "to show contempt towards the accumulation of
assets,"[41] and, just like their Sicilian and Japanese colleagues, considered
the acquisition of "respect" as their fundamental intangible asset, and as
antithetical to seeking or holding on to worldly possessions.

   Mafiosi also play the part of good family men, the kind of guys who could not disappear, who are rooted to their community. And they have disapproved of and sometimes punished those among them who felt bold enough to deviate from these conventions. They have forbidden any involvement with pimping and prostitution, even refused membership to those who had been involved, looking down on racketeers who exploit women.[42] Mafiosi have also restrained their style, dressing simply, sometimes shabbily, traveling in anonymous cars, and living in solid but by no means grand abodes. Still today a casual observer would mistake them for farmers. They have been renowned for their understated manner of communication: "in a world like mine," Salvatore Contorno, a mafioso who turned state's evidence, explains, "in which the less one says the better, half a sentence is enough to make oneself understood."[43] This style is all the more striking in a country where chattiness rules. "It is strange—wrote Alongi in 1887—that in that hot and colourful country where ordinary speech is so honey-sweet, hyperbolic and picturesque that of the mafiosi is curt, restrained and decisive."[44] Mafiosi also display various forms of restraint in dealing with one another. They are careful to limit what they know and make sure not to be seen to be too interested in knowing anything of relevance. If one does not know, one has nothing to reveal behind the back of an associate. All mafiosi who turned state's evidence declared that asking questions "is a sign of reckless curiosity and it may, indeed, be misinterpreted."[45] Contorno even refrained from asking further questions when someone else started talking to him about something, "in order to avoid that my curiosity could arise any suspicion."[46] The less one knows, the less there is one needs to be trusted about.

Once again, mafioso signs of disinterestedness are the underworld's cruder reflections of more refined practices that go on where the light of the law shines. For the smooth functioning of several occupations— for judges, mediators, negotiators, civil servants, accountants—it is crucial to be seen as independent from clients' interests and as constrained in such a way as not to abuse power. This image has been cultivated in a variety of formal and informal ways. Priests of many religions, for instance, need people's trust to attract them to join their church and to believe in the veracity of their teaching. They also need it to be able to act as intermediaries, dispute settlers, and peacemakers in their communities, a role many priests have traditionally performed. They achieve it by very evidently nurturing and concerning themselves with unworldly pursuits and by exercising restraints in many ways. For instance, according to Catholic writer Thomas Keneally, "the idea of priestly celibacy as a total renunciation of sex found widespread favor as a means of inspiring trust in the clergy—and as a way of filling churches. By associating himself with the purity of Christ and His mother, the celibate priest appeared to have transcended the confused squalid concerns of his flock. As my hard-bitten father used to say, 'At least, when you tell your sins to a priest, you know he's not going to blab them to his missus.'"[47] The norms on marital fidelity adopted by mafiosi, a few of whom contemplated a career in the church before opting for the Honored Society, can be interpreted as a blander version of the same trust-inducing restraint. Having an affair is thought to be a signal of a disorderly and weak character, and an occasion for a mafioso to risk dangerous pillow talk with lovers as loose with their tongues as they are with their mores. "A steady marriage and proper behaviour"—Pizzini-Gambetta writes—"were excellent ways to prove one's trustworthiness: they were not values in and of themselves. . . . To cheat on a wife showed an inability to endure difficulties in order to keep one's word."[48] Gaspare Mutolo, a mafioso who turned state's evidence, said: "We were always careful with our image, because if I scold, try to kill or force a boy to marry a woman because he was her boyfriend, I must be the best in the neighbourhood—where a mafioso is esteemed by both men and women—I must be a model."[49]

Aristocrats who performed functions similar to those of priests and mafiosi in their communities sustained their legitimacy by confining themselves to leisurely pursuits, wasteful grandeur, or charitable activities. They thus signaled their detachment from the petty family or financial matters of ordinary folks in which they intervened. Any vested interest in the business of their protégés would have jeopardized their credibility qua dispute settlers and mediators. And when those attributes did not suffice, both priests and aristocrats were, regardless of their personal dispositions, prevented from entering worldly professions by the codes and conventions of their group. The Swedish aristocracy in the seventeenth century discouraged its members from getting involved in commercial activities, as this would undermine their authority,[50] and in prerevolutionary France the nobility was legally barred from engaging in commercial activities.[51]

Imposing limits on oneself as a signal of disinterestedness and detachment was practiced not only by priests. Samuel Popkin, in his research in Vietnam, found that "the self-denial of Communist organisers, the celibacy of missionary priests, the scorn of conspicuous consumption by Hoa Hao organisers, were striking demonstrations to peasants that these men were less interested in self-aggrandisement than were the visibly less self-denying organisers from other groups. Thus, another way to raise the peasant's subjective estimate of the credibility and capability of an entrepreneur is to increase the probability that he is actually going to use the resources for common rather than selfish purposes.[52]" Nowadays there are often professional codes that take care of establishing independence and punish transgressions. Judges, arbitrators, and politicians are under an obligation to declare conflicts of interest and stay away from the people over whose business they rule or whose disputes they adjudicate. But even today informal signs are still in vogue. There are politicians—whose earthly god must be former Italian prime minister Giulio Andreotti—who specialize in brokering *any* compromise, a much-required skill especially in coalition governments. They cultivate a Sphinx-like demeanor. They never display emotions or endorse a moral or political principle for fear of suggesting that they have an ax to grind that is not perfectly orthogonal with the interests of their clients. The manner of such agents is particular to their different situations and social positions. There is a common thread, however, in that all these signs of restraint, whether natural or designed, formal or informal, are meant to reassure the truster that the trustee is not just unwilling but in fact unable to take undue advantage of his position.

CHAPTER 3

Information as Hostage

When the aim is to force people to do what they do not want to do, criminals readily resort to the threat of violence, or so most of us think. Yet, quite often, even criminals find this option undesirable and resort to blackmail instead, namely the threat to reveal compromising information. Blackmail can be used either to force people to do what they never agreed or to make them comply with their agreements, especially when these, by being illicit, are unenforceable by law. The transgressions that, when disclosed, give blackmail its power include anything illegal or contrary to conventional mores or social norms. They can also include information that sharply contradicts or ridicules the public position, whether moral or political, of the target, as in P. G. Wodehouse's memorable story in which Jeeves discovers that a character modeled on British fascist Oswald Mosley, who is giving Bertie a hard time, has secretly been making a living as a merchant of women's lingerie, an activity that, while perfectly legal and proper, does not exactly match the ideal of the fascist Übermensch. Provided that the compromising information would cause sufficient trouble if disclosed, the victim may choose to obey the blackmailer to prevent revelation. Blackmail can be as effective as violence yet less risky to perpetrate.

Whether a criminal will prefer blackmail to other options depends on a number of conditions.[1] One can expect that blackmail will be more likely in circles where secret information about others is easier to acquire *and* where disclosure would cause them serious damage. Both of these conditions obtain in politics, where many of the private agreements between the protagonists, while not always illicit, are nonetheless struck in a legal netherworld where law enforcement does not apply or is not suitable and where other enforcement options are therefore in demand. The normal contacts that many politicians have with agencies whose professional task is to acquire information about others, such as police, intelligence services, and the media, offer them the opportunity to both acquire and improperly utilize compromising information. At the same time, the public position of the targets—other politicians, judges, civil servants—makes damaging information about them potentially fatal for their career.

Since the fall of communism, this way of handling political and financial affairs has been rife in Russia.[2] Russians even have a word for compromising material, *kompromat*, which is believed to derive from 1930s secret-police jargon.[3] While much of kompromat is divulged simply to discredit opponents in electoral or business competition, it is also employed to harden one's bargaining position. Under the threat of disclosure of kompromat, prosecutors trying to indict powerful characters suddenly turn a blind eye or resign; politicians' actions mysteriously fall in line with their opponents' interests; and financiers beat their competitors when bidding for public contracts and at privatization auctions. A market for kompromat—with buyers, sellers, and varying prices—has developed, and so have imaginative ways to protect oneself from these threats, including preemptive revelations by friendly sources. Kompromat was used in the past by the Communist leadership to keep their officials loyal; after 1990, with the emergence of a free-market society, it became a private good alongside many others.

One can surmise that the conditions conducive to making the kompromat market thrive are intensely present in some postcommunist countries, especially Russia.[4] First, acquiring compromising information about others is easier there than in well-established democracies. Spying was a major activity under the Soviet regime. The spying agencies had ample freedom to snoop, they could rely on wide networks of informers, and they had access to sophisticated technical means to spy on people—an apparatus that was fragmented but not completely dismantled during the transition to democracy. A correspondingly vast amount of information was filed away, some of which remained useful, even *more* useful in fact, after the fall of communism. Next, those who need to use kompromat in their affairs are also those more able to get it: many among the new politicians, financiers, and their minions either have close links with or are themselves former members of the intelligence agencies. No longer in the service of a strong centralized authority, and often after losing their job, spies entered the free market in their own peculiar way, either selling information suitable for blackmail or entering business or politics directly. Those who chose the latter course did not even have to buy kompromat; they carried it with them, looting files to which they had access thanks to their previous position. Finally, the weakness of the free press provided opportunities for developing the self-interested manipulation of news. The financial new players, the oligarchs, purchased many of the printed and televised media, securing control over many journalists and thus over the diffusion of information, including that aimed at blackmailing.

It is not often the case that those conditions are all simultaneously present *and* as developed as they are in Russia; it is thus perhaps unlikely that one will find the kompromat phenomenon being practiced on the same scale elsewhere. Occasionally, however, in Western democracies too cases of kompromat surface into public view, at times for the simple reason that the press is one of the possible vehicles of disclosure. This is exemplified by the following British episode:

> Geoffrey Robinson has been threatened with retaliation from the Government if he presses ahead with the publication of his "revelatory" memoirs. The former Paymaster General has told friends that there have been "threatening noises" from Downing Street aides suggesting that if he stirs up further trouble for the Government, there could be equally damaging disclosures about his business affairs. Mr. Robinson believes that this is a reference to a Department of Trade and Industry inquiry into allegations that he breached company law by filing late, inaccurate or incomplete records.[5]

Mr. Robinson, however, was not to be caught off guard. "Among his circle there is talk of compromising pictures that he happens to have of a cabinet minister. Robinson will not, it is said, be using them in his book or anywhere else. But they exist, and his enemies are being made aware that they do."[6] Robinson's memoirs were published, and the pictures were not.

Politicians have been able to exploit revelations of their partners' misdeeds even without having prior access to kompromat, and exposure simply arose from the law's taking its proper course. This is possible if the punishment triggered by revelation is not automatically meted out but there is scope for negotiation. For, once the knowledge of a misdeed is in the public domain, the target has an interest in avoiding punishment, so the already revealed kompromat can still be useful to politicians or others who can help the target to avoid punishment. Consider, for example, the case of Silvio Berlusconi. A media magnate and three-time Italian prime minister, Berlusconi has had several problems with the law, some of which continue to this day, involving various charges of bribery, corruption, and false accounting.[7] Commentators were surprised to observe how, rather than being forced to resign and vanish in shame, Berlusconi garnered support from his political allies, which grew stronger with every court conviction against him. Pierferdinando Casini, leader of a small centrist party that was part of Berlusconi's coalition, said after Berlusconi was sentenced to eight years in jail (later overturned in appeal), "Berlusconi knows he can count like never before on the strong solidarity of all his allies."[8] But why? One might have naïvely expected them to disavow Berlusconi, so as not to taint their own reputation by further association with their disgraced partner. However, the political fate of these allies depended on Forza Italia, Berlusconi's party and the largest in the coalition. They knew that Berlusconi would not stand as good a chance of staying out of jail without their support and that they could therefore rely on him to repay their loyalty, more now than before those verdicts. One feels tempted to suspect that, whether explicitly or otherwise, Berlusconi's allies de facto offered him a deal: we will help you stay out of jail, and when the opportunity arises you will reward us. Not only would Berlusconi be inclined to promise them more than he would have (a price increase); he would also be more inclined to deliver whatever he promised because of the threat of imprisonment. In Berlusconi's second cabinet (2001), his loyal ally Casini was appointed to the important post of president of the Camera dei Deputati (lower house), despite the minuscule electoral clout of Casini's centrist party.

It is impossible to say how typical such episodes are in Western democracies. For obvious reasons the use of kompromat goes on unbeknownst to the public; for every instance that becomes known countless others, especially the successful ones, remain hidden from view. Or they emerge much later, the best example being that of FBI director J. Edgar Hoover, who kept secret files on most top U.S. politicians, which made it impossible for them to fire him or to restrain his exercise of power or even to criticize him. The nonchalant way that stories like these are revealed in the media does not bode well, and makes one wonder whether Russia is or simply *seems* to be more in the grip of that practice. Because of Russia's turbulent transition, more episodes of this kind may come to the surface. Moreover, in Russia there is an alternative option by which to handle political and financial controversies, not so readily available elsewhere: the use of mafioso violence. Other things being equal, this should *decrease* the use of kompromat, because people can more easily resort to violence both instead of kompromat and to defend themselves from it. In addition, the standards of public mores in Russia have declined to the point that revelations about politicians or other officials' misdeeds are greeted with increasing cynicism, with the result that the value of kompromat has been if not erased at least eroded.[9] The greater quiet on the front of Western democracies could therefore be as much a sign that the practice is infrequent as that it is functioning smoothly.

Here, however, I will not pursue blackmail further. In blackmail an agent collects or somehow acquires kompromat behind the back of another agent whose actions he aims to influence while the target would rather that the information remained secret. Acquiring compromising information in this way is akin to taking a hostage by force. By contrast, in this chapter, I discuss the seemingly odd and yet important case in which kompromat is given rather than taken, in which an agent chooses rationally to make himself *blackmailable* by another agent.

Although the nature of blackmail is well understood,[10] the case of, as it were, self-inflicted blackmail has received hardly any attention at all. Yet this practice has greater generality than standard blackmail. The reason is that while ordinary blackmail produces at best a winner and a loser, and is a cause therefore of conflict and instability, the practice I am about to describe is instrumental to making everyone a winner. When nobler sources of trust are lacking, an exchange of compromising information can still bring about cooperation.

THE EXCHANGE OF COMPROMISING INFORMATION

Consider the following situation, in which an agent is desperate to be trusted by another: "both the kidnapper who would like to release his prisoner, and the prisoner, may search desperately for a way to commit the latter against informing on his captor once released, without finding one." This is an extreme instance of the situation in which two agents would like to agree on an action that leads to an outcome they both prefer to all other outcomes, but at least one of them cannot trust the other's promises. The kidnapper fears that once freed the victim will inform on him; thus the deal falls through to both parties' detriment. Not all is lost, however. Thomas Schelling, who conceived the above example, also suggested the solution: "If the victim has committed an act whose disclosure could lead to blackmail, he may confess it [to the kidnapper]; if not, he might commit one in the presence of his captor, to create the bond that will ensure his silence."[11]

Schelling's solution pinpoints a counterintuitive situation in which it is to our advantage to reveal our misdeeds to others so that they can use them against us. In this case we would have an interest in *volunteering* negative information about ourselves. If we had no bad things to reveal, we would even have the incentive to *do* something bad. Being bad and displaying credible evidence of it can make our promises credible. While commonsense rationality inclines us to think that doing so would be foolish—misdeeds are best kept secret—cases of this sort indicate that a selective revelation of secrets can be turned to advantage. Not only do agents have an interest in seeking the skeletons hidden in their partners' closets, as in the standard blackmail case. There are instances when there is an advantage to opening up one's closet for others to see the skeletons, lifting the cost of finding out from the shoulders of partners and bearing it oneself. Worse still, agents with empty closets may have an interest in filling them with skeletons, which may come in handy. The same reason that makes it best to keep incriminating information secret is also that which gives such information its persuasive force once selectively revealed.

Vivid as it is in making the point, the example of the kidnapper is a special and, as far as I know, purely hypothetical case. The situation is asymmetric, for the victim already has negative information on the kidnapper, which he can use against him. The kidnapper did not volunteer it. That was the inevitable by-product of his crime. The problem is for the victim to produce the incriminating information about himself to persuade the kidnapper to let him go. The practical difficulties of finding the right kind of evidence to hand over to the kidnapper, one can imagine, would be considerable. The only realization of this case that I know of is fictional. In the film *Albino Alligator*,[12] Janet, one of the hostages, agrees to shoot another hostage to avoid being killed with her son by the villains, who barricaded themselves inside her bar. When the police arrive, she keeps her mouth shut and allows the only surviving villain to pass himself off as a hostage. However, once one considers less extreme cases, one finds that this strategy is by no means fictional but real indeed, and used in a range of different criminal circles.

A form it often takes is bilateral, as an *exchange* of compromising information: all participants are worried about each other's loyalty, and they all disclose compromising information about themselves to one another. Starkly put, this is how it works: "The best part about this deal," Edie Marsh says in Carl Hiaasen's *Stormy Weather*, "is that nobody's in a position to screw anyone else. You've got shit on me, I've got shit on you, and we've both plenty of shit on Snapper. That's why it's going down so clean."[13]

In *Confessions of a Corrupt Mayor*, Agatino Licandro, mayor of Reggio Calabria from 1989 until 1992 and a member of the now defunct Christian Democratic Party, gives several real-life examples that show how well-established networks of corruption work on this basis. The corrupt world he so vividly describes held itself together by the mutual threat of revelation. Many participants had a history of involvement in corrupt deals, which was known to other participants. This indicates not only that they had played the game successfully before but also that they would probably be afraid to violate the pacts lest the knowledge of their deeds be used against them. (Licandro also shows some of the pitfalls of this strategy, as information revealed in order to make oneself blackmailable for one's own purposes can end up in the wrong hands.)[14]

The bilateral case, in which what we may call the "hostage-information" is traded both ways, circumvents the risk involved in revealing negative information unilaterally. Giving compromising information about oneself to X without having at the same time compromising information about X is risky, for rather than keeping it to enforce the contract, X could use it to renege on his part of it.

In cases in which mutual disclosure is beneficial, however, those involved still have a serious concern: who is going to reveal his misdeeds to the other criminal first, making himself vulnerable should the gesture not be reciprocated? The mafia solves the problem by simultaneity: they all do a bad deed together. Murders of importance are perpetrated by groups of several individuals often drawn from more than one mafia family. The murderous parties are larger than mere efficiency calculations would dictate (in fact, they may be even less efficient and harder to arrange *because* of their size).[15] Judge Giovanni Falcone wrote that "nearly all members of the Cupola [the body that comprises all top Sicilian mafiosi] took part in the assassination of police superintendent Ninni Cassarà, on 6 August 1985."[16] Mafiosi share not merely the practical burden of the action but also the knowledge of their participation in it. Illicit acts carried out jointly create a bond among the participants, not just generically because sharing significant experiences does that, but also because each will have incriminating information on everyone else. The wider the circle that jointly perpetrates a crime, the wider will be the pressure to keep it secret.

In other cases, however, simultaneity cannot be achieved, and someone has to reveal his misdeeds first. When the prize is initiation into a group that promises high rewards, for instance, novices must agree to do just that. Mafia novices—especially those who are not already members of families with a mafia tradition—are asked, as we have seen in chapter 1, to commit a murder. This costly signal is required because would-be mafiosi need to show both that they can do such a thing and that they are not undercover agents. However, it also provides their superiors with evidence against them. In cases such as these, new members do not know much about established members' misdeeds, so the relation is asymmetrical, and therefore risky. (Sicilian mafiosi have been suspected to use this practice treacherously, by persuading hoodlums to carry out a hit as if it were a test for their admission only to inform on or kill them later. It is safer and cheaper to kill the killer than the latter's target. I have not been able to find any proven case of this, but during my fieldwork in Sicily several stories of this kind were in circulation.)

The tests designed by two pedophile cyberspace rings to screen new members also amounted to an exchange of hostage-information. In 1998 police in fourteen countries arrested nearly two hundred members of an Internet child pornography ring, the Wonderland Club. The group used a gamut of precautions to prevent identification (some of which— conventional codes, passwords, and nicknames—I discuss in other chapters). Each time members entered the Wonderland website they went through five separate security checks based on secretly agreed passwords. Members created an artificial person or "robot" to ensure that strangers did not gain access; used nicknames such as Caesar, Satan, and Hopeful; and encrypted their stores of images to hide them from police. They never e-mailed pictures but logged on remotely to each other's terminals to "leech" large numbers of pictures.[17] The club styled itself "w0nderland," with a zero instead of the letter *o*, to reduce the risk of anyone hitting on their website by mistake.[18]

The test of greatest interest to the topic of this chapter, however, was the one set up for entry into the club. In order to join, a would-be member had to possess at least ten thousand photographs and be prepared to share them with all other members. The photographs were screened by a computer program that checked whether they were both different from one another and not recycled from other sources already available. This of course meant that each new member made a sizable contribution to the common capital. But it also ensured both that prospective members were not undercover agents and that they were going to stay loyal to each other. In addition, "They could not join the club without being vetted by other members, and we have evidence that members travelled to other countries and met each other for vetting."[19] This may have been arranged in order to assess would-be members' real commitment to the common interest face-to-face—feigning pleasure at watching pictures of children being sexually abused must be pretty hard. However, it also must have had a different significance. When identification is at a premium and must be kept secret, just showing one's face is itself like giving a hostage, namely the knowledge of one's key sign of identity.

Participation strategies within the Shadowz Brotherhood, another Internet ring of pedophiles—dismantled in 2002 by police who arrested thirty-one people in several countries (Germany, Belgium, Britain, Italy, the Netherlands, Spain, and Sweden)—tell a similar story. Detective Chief Superintendent Len Hynds of Britain's National High Tech Crime Unit said the ring was set up about two years before and had a total of about a hundred members, scattered also in the United States, Canada, Denmark, Romania, and Switzerland. Members included twenty-three "systems administrators" who ran the ring's website and "monitored bulletin boards and chat rooms, ensuring people were using proper security measures and excluding people from the site if they weren't."[20] Administrators also provided advice about police tactics and techniques so members could avoid detection. They used sophisticated encryption techniques, sometimes hiding material in seemingly innocent picture files. This group used an improved version of the entry test used by the Wonderland Club. They operated a "star" system to rate members: after initial vetting, newcomers were granted one star, allowing them to join relatively tame chat groups at introductory levels. To accumulate more stars and gain deeper access to the material, members were required to upload their own pictures and videos, aptly described by a reporter as "an initiation rite of shared guilt." It was in fact a hierarchical system of hostage-information giving: the more hostages one shared with others, the more one was trusted to get more in return. The amount of material provided was the currency to move further inside what the group called the "castle." In the innermost sanctum, police said, the pedophiles watched live broadcasts of children being abused.[21]

The revelation of transgressions for bonding purposes is a device of much greater appeal than is generally realized; maybe we do not even need to think about it for we are so good at using it. It seems to come naturally to many a deviant group, even, as the following case illustrates, to certain preschool children. The children in question were forbidden to take their own toys to school but found a way around that rule and chose minute toys that they smuggled in—matchbox toy cars for the boys and little plastic animals for the girls.

> What I found interesting [said William A. Corsaro, the sociologist who researched this group] was not that the kids wanted to bring their own toys, but that when they smuggled them in they never played with them alone. They played with them collectively, they wanted others to know that they had them. They wanted to share the toys with others. They are not only sharing the toy but *sharing the fact that they are getting around the rule.*[22]

Corsaro offers a generic explanation: "I think there is a strong emotional satisfaction in sharing things, in doing things together." Maybe the emotional satisfaction is there, and this may well act as the proximate mechanism that sustains sharing among these precocious little deviants. Yet Corsaro's explanation seems unconvincing, for why is it that in so many other instances young and old people alike get their emotional satisfaction by *not* sharing? Also, from his account it seems that they were sharing the *knowledge* of having the toy rather than the toy as such. A possible explanation is that children like to display their audacity to one another. At the same time, it is conceivable that these preschool children sensed the need to build their solidarity and grasped intuitively that the sharing of forbidden toys created a bond among them.

At times, the very transgressions that must be kept secret offer, as in the case both of the pedophile rings and of Corsaro's preschool children, the opportunity to enforce secrecy. Photographs and toys were at once the goods of interest and the evidence of each other's violations. When there are laws or social norms against doing something and one does it nonetheless, one wants either no witnesses to one's misdeeds or, almost instinctively, that those present during one's misdeeds do the same, a condition enabling one to trust that they will be discreet.

In some instances, the type of contact between people presents the right binding conditions and requires no additional effort. When a prostitute and a new client meet and are surprised to discover that they know each other already, though not in their respective capacities in the sex market, they both know that they have nothing to worry from each other, for they will now share a secret.

> There have been two clients that have come here in the five years that I have worked here who I have known, who live by me. I used to go to school with their children and they are much older than me, but I do know their wives. So it is mutual really—they could not say anything and nor could I so it is a secret between the two of us (Danielle, sauna).[23]

In other instances the conditions that ensure discretion need to be constructed. Making witnesses of deviant acts engage in the same act is one way to do so, as it gives witnesses a strong reason to keep their mouths shut. On reading this chapter, Ian Malcolm, the editor of this book, reminisced:

> At the boarding school I attended breaking into the kitchen and confectionary was a standard challenge for the students, harshly punished if discovered. One night kitchen raiders entered our four-person room with many Popsicles (fruit-flavored ice) to share before they melted. Not wanting any (not least because I had recently gorged after a raid in which I participated myself), I declined, which was interpreted as refusing to share guilt and exposing them to the possibility I would inform (it was probably also an insult to their achievement). So I ate the things to dispel that impression.

Members of groups who engage in deviant actions reinforce their internal loyalty by exchanging evidence of their misdeeds, an act that commits them to mutual silence. People, for instance, seem more inclined to share "joints" or the experience of drug taking generally—they try to force each other to participate and torment or ostracize those who refuse—than to share cigarette smoking or drinking alcohol. The former activities are illegal, while the latter are not. However, when smoking or drinking contravenes the orders of parents or teachers, youngsters tend to share their cigarettes and alcohol intake too. Conversely, where, say, smoking marijuana is not considered a crime—as in the Netherlands—we should observe a lessening of the pressure to conform.

The idea that exchanging negative private information has a binding force is not new. In "How to Distinguish a Flatterer from a Friend," Plutarch makes the point that the revelation of secrets, which he sees as a typical flatterer's strategy that imitates the gestures of friendship, binds people together. "If someone has been trusted with a secret, he is more inclined to disclose a secret of his own; and once he has made such disclosure, a relationship has been formed and *there is fear of loss of trust*."[24] Plutarch subtly captures how the disclosing of secrets triggers reciprocity: if A reveals some dirt about himself to B, B feels obliged to reciprocate for fear that A may think him untrustworthy. Confiding secrets to friends is constitutive of friendship. We read the exchange as a sign that we trust them. But it may be interpreted also as a way of letting them know that *we* are trustworthy: by giving our secrets away we show at once that we trust them not to misuse the information and that we are not planning to betray them. Otherwise we would not give them ammunition to retaliate.

PREDICTIONS

The exchange of compromising information is in many ways identical to an exchange of hostages. The trustee gives a hostage to the truster, which the truster can harm if the trustee reneges on their contract. Assuming the truster believes that the damage he could do to the hostage is a cost to the trustee greater than the benefit the trustee would gain by reneging, he can rely on the trustee to comply with the contract. In the bilateral exchange both parties are at once trustee and truster of each other.[25]

The exchange of hostages was typical in antiquity; it is also, as Schelling himself noted, typical in the underworld. Mob marriages, for instance, often amount to just such an exchange. Mafia feuds were brought to an end by a cross-marriage between the feuding families: the bride is the daughter or sister of a boss who wishes to make peace with the family to which the groom belongs.[26] Another case involving women as hostages is reported by FBI agent Joseph Pistone, aka Donnie Brasco. Following a mafia internecine war in the Bonanno family in New York in 1981, two members of the losing group who lived in Miami, Joe Puma and Steve Maruca, had to be informed that now "they belonged to Sonny" Black, the boss of the winning group. Afraid that they might be killed rather than generously reassigned, they were reluctant to show up at the meeting. Salvatore "Sally Fruits" Farrugia, who was in charge of passing on the information, chose a hostage-exchange strategy to persuade the men to show up. He too was afraid that Joe and Steve could make a preemptive move and be "gunning for us." "I brought my wife so the cocksuckers would feel comfortable. Because the other guy was dodging me all night I said to him 'Come to the hotel and have coffee. My wife's here, bring your wife.'"[27] The presence of both wives was a guarantee that the participants would not resort to violence. Joe Puma fled, but Steve Maruca went to the meeting and duly brought his wife along.

While fundamentally the same, an exchange of hostages and an exchange of compromising information have some differences too. In the case of information the hostage is the trustee himself, for it is on him that the compromising information, once revealed, can unleash a punishment. That is not, however, a crucial difference, as it is conceivable that the strategy could still work if the compromising information concerned somebody else whom the trustee cared sufficiently about. The crucial difference is another: when compromising information acts as the hostage, the truster does not mete out the punishment himself but only triggers it, by revealing the damaging information, if the trustee defects. The actual punishment—and this is the beauty of the strategy— is meted out by a third party who understands certain actions as deserving castigation. Evidence of bad behavior draws a punishing response by law-enforcement agencies or elicits a social response in others bound to cause shame, ridicule, and loss of reputation. Agents fear each other, not because they are violent or in some other way able to cause harm to each other directly, but more subtly because they fear the effects of being exposed to other actors, effects that the agents can unleash on each other at virtually no extra cost to themselves. The only cost they bear is that of revealing the compromising information rather than the much greater cost of administering the punishment. Someone else takes care of that, and one can happily relax.

The dependence of this strategy on external enforcement, be it legal or social, yields several predictions (which in parts concern blackmail generally rather than just the case in which one party volunteers the compromising information).

1. The transgressions suitable as hostage-information depend on the legal and normative landscape in which the strategy is employed. Thus, changes in mores, conventions, or law affect the feasible set of information suitable to be used as hostage. One can expect variations by country. For instance, in France and Italy evidence of politicians' adulterous affairs would not have much impact, while it could (and did) ruin the career of British or American politicians. And one can expect variations over time. If, for instance, homosexuality is considered improper or unlawful, evidence of it could ruin (and has ruined) people's careers. But once homosexuality becomes accepted, such evidence will not do much damage. The same can be said of smoking cannabis. As the consumption of this substance becomes more acceptable, as for instance in Britain, evidence of politicians' smoking it should no longer be much of an embarrassment, even if they inhaled. And it can go the opposite way: actions that used to be innocent can mutate into boomerangs. In 1996 Dick Cheney, before he became American vice president, made a promotional video for the accountancy firm Arthur Andersen. It shows him

saying: "I get good advice, if you will, from their people based upon how we're doing business and how we're operating over and above the just sort of normal by-the-book auditing arrangement."[28] After the financial scandals that hit Enron and Arthur Andersen in 2002, that statement became extremely embarrassing, for everyone was wondering, rhetorically, "what's wrong with the 'normal by-the-book auditing arrangement'?" In this case the story was discovered by the press, which neutralized the value of that information for private use. But, following such dramatic changes of what is acceptable by law or by the public, some people will find themselves exposed to blackmail from other people who hold information that hitherto was innocent enough but suddenly becomes valuable. These events herald changes in the coalitions in power. Anyone who now knows of any even slightly shady case of politicians' involvement with the corporate world will have more power, those involved will lose it, and those who know of any such thing about each other will suddenly discover new bonds of "friendship."

2. The harsher the punishment and the greater the likelihood of receiving it that can be triggered by the revelation of any one piece of compromising information, the greater the binding effect of *that* information. It follows that the stricter and more effectively punitive a society is, the greater the blackmailing value of transgressions. On the other hand, the more lenient a society is, the lower the value of the skeletons in one's closet. At the same time, the more lenient a society is, the worse the transgressions are that can work as effective hostages. The only way to be credible is to have more or uglier skeletons in one's closet. This yields implications for the profile of criminal groups, as the crimes that members commit as "initiation rites" to become part of the group need to be of a worse kind.[29] But the same is also true for groups that bond internally through transgressions while operating publicly in legal domains, such as political groups. When homosexuality was considered to be either illegal or at least very improper, sharing the practice or the knowledge of it was sufficient to bond political groups, such as "old-boy networks" formed in male British public schools. Now that this is no longer the case, one wonders which other transgressions may have replaced it. Civilizing progress has unexpected costs.

3. The wider the range of possible transgressions, the greater the amount of potential information available for mutual blackmailing, whether this is driven by others or volunteered by oneself. This can explain some puzzling empirical facts. Italy is a country with a high level of corruption that has proved hard to explain. It pops up as an outlier in all the regressions that try to explain cross-country corruption rates. Italy is also a country of excessive legal norms and regulation. According to the Cassese Parliamentary Commission for the Reform of Public Administration, Italy has in excess of 100,000 (one hundred thousand!) laws and regulations, as compared to 7,000 in France and 6,000 in Germany.[30] The probability of living a life, indeed of going through the day, without incurring at least one violation must be virtually zero for Italians. This produces a large number of secrets and increases the chances that at least some of one's violations will become known to others whether one likes it or not. Everyone will at once benefit from a greater number of violations by others that he can selectively reveal and suffer from the risk of potential revelation by others of a larger number of violations he has committed. There will be, literally, more hostages to fortune. One might object that the greater the number of violations, the lower the chances of getting caught, since the law-enforcement agencies will be extremely busy. One could conclude, therefore, that the potential blackmailing effect attached to any one violation evaporates. But this is not so. For the probability of being caught and convicted for any one violation in countries where the police are overwhelmed depends to a much greater extent on whether someone will inform the authorities and force them to act rather than on the latter's independently initiated investigations. The fear of sanctions becomes ancillary to the fear of someone informing on one. It seems plausible therefore to hypothesize that the high levels of corruption in Italy could depend on the fact that everybody has some dirt on everybody else—"we are all sinners," as Catholic priests like to repeat; "no one can be the first to throw a stone." This giant web of dyadic secret-sharing could sustain that pact of mutual support against the law which seems so strong among Italians, who display an uncanny predilection to privilege loyalty to their private friends over their public duties as law-abiding citizens.

TECHNOLOGY

Technology affects opportunities for the exchange of hostage-information. In the most elementary world imaginable, in which evidence cannot be recorded and stored except in people's memory, it is harder to find evidence of misdeeds to hold on to and to transmit. The opportunities to find usable hostage-information are limited, and this could explain the greater use of real hostages in antiquity and in the oral culture of the mafia. One can witness a transgression—a killing, the smoking of cannabis, the smuggling of prohibited toys—but faces greater constraints to prove that the event occurred or that it was perpetrated by someone in particular. Any revelation must either occur as a crime is perpetrated so that the intended audience can verify this—a child could reveal to a teacher that another child has a prohibited toy—or must contain bits of information that credibly and uniquely identify someone as the culprit of a certain transgression. It follows that:

4. The use of hostage-information grows alongside the growth of technology that produces transmittable records of misdeeds. It should be more feasible in literate cultures than in oral ones and more feasible where the medium in which people write is lighter than stone, where this medium can be reproduced, and where people sign, in some form, what they write. The invention of manageable cameras, which created the opportunity to capture compromising pictures, must have had an impact on politicians' careers worthy of a whole history book. The emergence of sound or video recordings, provided they can be had in hard-to-fake realizations, further increased the set of feasible hostage-information. The recent appearance of electronic communication has given the final contribution, by lowering the cost of transmission of material in many forms—text, sound, and video. The trade of illicit goods in digital form is boosted, and possession of these very goods, such as nude photos or stolen credit card numbers, becomes potentially incriminating. As the case of pedophiles illustrates, the same material that is being traded and that needs to be kept secret can be used as a bonding device. Cheap transmission of information also increases the potential

size of the groups that can coalesce for illicit purposes and to which the incriminating information can be sent. Handling photographic material by mail would make it close to impossible to reach hundreds of people, while the likes of Wonderland Club and the Shadowz Brotherhood members can visit each other's hideous wares worldwide at the click of a button.

POLITICS

Groups and their members thrive on their ability to cooperate, and this in turn depends on their ability to keep internal loyalty high enough and competition low enough not to mar the pursuit of their common goals. Groups can achieve cohesion by different means, which depend on the groups' goals and the conditions in which they operate. Insofar as shared transgressions are one such means, a worrying prediction follows:

5. Groups whose members have transgressions to hide from public view and whose members share knowledge of these transgressions with each other will enjoy a comparative advantage in their ability to support their internal cohesion. Some groups may in fact be built on, rather than preexist, the exchange of compromising information. Once loyalty is established thanks to the shared knowledge of certain transgressions, members can maintain their cohesion and employ it effectively in other fields, which may be perfectly legal. Commenting on an earlier version of this chapter, Ernesto dal Bò wrote to me that this model provides

a sad answer to the Olson-Becker type of question regarding what kind of groups will be more effective in political influence. Answer: those involving the most crooked members! If politics is about forming groups, the groups that are more likely to form will involve dirty candidates. This holds if competition among groups is not—in some loose sense—perfect. If competition were so fierce that skeletons became exposable by members of a cleaner group, or by the media, or justice, there would be a premium for a group that could form involving only clean, trustworthy people that do not need skeletons as a group-binding technology. This is the only kind of group that could both form and survive the ruthless scrutiny implied by fierce competition.[31]

Is competition so fierce as to discourage the formation of dirty parties or party factions and promote clean ones? One can surmise that there are instances in which that is not so—the rise of Silvio Berlusconi's Forza Italia[32] and of Vladimir Putin's web of ex-KGB cronies in Russia seem plausible candidates to fit the model's predictions.

BINDING VERSUS SIGNALING

Throughout the preceding discussion the act of volunteering compromising information was understood to succeed if capable of inducing the following reasoning in the truster: If the trustee gives me compromising information about himself that I can reveal if he reneges on his promises, his payoffs are altered in such as way as to make it to his advantage to be trustworthy, even if he is not inclined to be. The following considers more closely how this works.

The payoffs that would lead the truster not to trust are exemplified as follows. The pairs of numbers in parentheses represent, first, the truster's payoff and, next, the trustee's (such numbers are a conventional way to express their ordinal preferences for each outcome). If the payoffs are as in figure 3.1, the trustee, given the chance, prefers to cheat rather than to fulfill trust $(2 > 1)$; so even if the truster would prefer to trust if the trustee fulfills $(1 > 0)$, if he knows the trustee's payoffs he knows that the trustee will cheat if trusted; hence he chooses not to trust $(0 > -1)$. This, however, causes a problem for the trustee, for if the truster does not trust him he suffers (-1). The kidnapper example is interpretable as such a case. The kidnapper would like to let his victim go free $(1 > 0)$ but believes that the victim has the payoff of the trustee in figure 3.1 and that, if freed, would violate his promise and report the kidnapper to

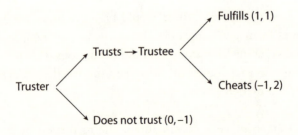

Fig. 3.1. Trust game without hostage information

the police. The victim-trustee on the other hand is under tremendous pressure to persuade the kidnapper to trust him and let him go.

If the trustee can find compromising information he can give to the truster, the payoffs could change to those in figure 3.2. The trustee, who is believed to be untrustworthy in that game, commits himself to behave as if he were trustworthy by disclosing incriminating information about himself. This amounts to giving a new option to the truster, who can reveal the compromising information if the trustee cheats, and thereby alters his own payoffs. The trustee *binds himself* to act honestly, for he knows that if he did not the consequences unleashed by the truster's revelation of the compromising information would be worse for him. So the trustee prefers 1 to x (the cheating payoff), and since the truster prefers 1 to 0, he decides to trust, and the trustee fulfills. The key condition is that the cost of disclosure should make the cheating payoff for the trustee lower than the trust-fulfilling payoff.

While it is befitting to interpret the giving of compromising information as a binding device for those who would otherwise be invariably untrustworthy, this is not the sole interpretation. One can conceive of cases in which the giving of compromising information is persuasive not because it binds the trustee ex post, but because it *signals* that the trustee is trustworthy ex ante. This latter interpretation does not fit the kidnapper's case, for in that case the kidnapper-truster believes there is only one type of victim-trustee, the untrustworthy one who would promise to keep his mouth shut but would inform on him as soon as he was freed. And it does not fit many situations involving criminal trustees, for they are believed to be always untrustworthy. But there are trust games in

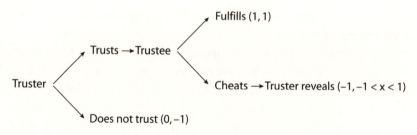

Fig. 3.2. Trust game with hostage information

which the truster believes that there are trustees of two types, those who keep their promises and those who do not, and in which the basic problem is one of screening. In this case the truster and trustee play a "basic trust game,"[33] in which the truster's primary problem consists of finding out to which of the two types the trustee belongs. The truster needs some way of screening one type from the other, and the trustee can help if he can find a signal that can persuade the truster. Compromising information could be such a signal: insofar as only the trustworthy type *can afford* to disclose a certain piece of incriminating information about himself, if he does then he should be trustworthy. Here the compromising information is a *handicap signal*: the signaler deliberately makes himself more exposed, for he knows he does not have to worry, as he will never fail to comply. If he were untrustworthy he would not do that, for he would fear the consequences.[34] This hostage-information succeeds, not because it alters the payoffs of the trustee and thereby constrains his future choices, but because it acts as a signal of his trustworthiness, which exists regardless.

That is how the pedophiles might have viewed the situation and the entry tests. They expected that a large share of would-be members were trustworthy pedophiles—trustworthy in that particular game, that is— who would not cheat on their co-offenders, for they would not gain anything by doing so. The case is quite different from that of the kidnapper, wherein the victim gains by reneging on his promises. Instead, the pedophiles worried about the possibility of an undercover agent who could mimic being a pedophile in order to get them arrested. By giving compromising pictures to the club, the trusters thought, the trustee sig-

nals that he is a bona fide pervert, for no police agent could afford to do
such a thing.

(It turns out that they were wrong. Both the Wonderland Club members and the Shadowz Brothers are now enjoying the wondrous shadows
that prisons provide. The police refused to say how they broke through
the groups' exacting screening. However, "most Internet observers," according to the *Ottawa Citizen*, "believe they must have *posed as online
paedophiles*, slowly winning trust and gaining access to the criminal archive."[35] In order to fool members into believing that they were bona
fide, they must have used photographs from a pool that was not available
to members and, if any face-to-face encounter occurred, must also have
been able to feign a genuine interest in the material. The pedophiles
thought, wrongly as it turned out, that those signals would have been
too costly for the agents to use.)

In the binding interpretation, the truster can make the following mistake: he can be persuaded by the trustee that the consequences of revealing the information would be bad enough for the trustee to desist from
cheating when the consequences would not be so bad. The trustee may
not care enough to be exposed—as, say, a homosexual—to abstain from
informing on the kidnapper. Under both the binding and the signaling
interpretation, trusters can make a different mistake: this occurs if the
trustee builds up *false* bad information about himself. This can persuade
the truster as follows: the truster, who thinks of the situation as one of
binding, believes that the trustee is vulnerable to exposure of bad deed
X—and, unlike the previous mistake, if X were truly the case, there
would be no doubt about the severity of consequences from exposure.
This ruse can also persuade the truster who believes he is in a signaling
situation, for by revealing X the trustee is believed to have given information that would be too costly for an untrustworthy type to disclose,
which again would be true if that information were true. Under both
interpretations, cheats can achieve their aims by doing the same type of
thing, namely pretending to have done a bad deed that they never did.[36]

Trusters may at times find it hard to establish which of the two interpretations applies, which of the two types of trust game they are playing.
An optimistic truster can be persuaded just by the logic of signaling,

while the pessimistic one can think that even if the dealer is not an honest type he has committed himself by giving bad information about himself in such a way that he will have to stick to his promises. Both forms of reasoning are justified a priori. The test can only come later: if the evidence is destroyed, and the trustee knows that it is. If at that point the trustee cheats, then it was a case of hostage giving, for once this is removed the trustee reveals his untrustworthiness. If he does not defect even when the weight of the hostage-information is lifted, then the trustee was of a good type. When in doubt, best to keep the evidence!

CHAPTER 4

Why Prisoners Fight (and Signal)

Although by no means common to all criminal endeavors, violence is dramatically more common in the underworld than among ordinary citizens. It is used both to enforce contracts and to defy them. It is a means of aggression and a means of defense. It redresses some wrongs and perpetrates others. Though cunning can get one a long way, success in the underworld is often decided by violence, or by the credible threat of its use.

One might expect that where *homo homini lupus* rules, aggression will obliterate communication. Brutes may well be as inarticulate as folk wisdom portrays them, yet if we do not narrowly limit ourselves to linguistic communication, it is clear that communication and violence are closely connected. First, they are inversely so, in that the more notorious an agent is for violence, the less he has to commit to prove his reputation. Even if inclined to use it, rational criminals can be expected to minimize violence whenever they can achieve the same results by merely signaling their ability to mete it out. Threatening violence persuasively is cheaper than resorting to it. Nonviolent display-acts of strength or threats are quintessentially communicative acts aimed at influencing one's opponents' beliefs and actions. Next, violence and communication are directly connected, in that the goal of much violence is to reveal one's true violent potential to others. Violence does not always flare up just for settling specific disputes; it can at the same time serve to create a useful reputation (or avoid being tarnished by a bad one), which can then be "spent" in future encounters. Violence can serve a quintessentially communicative purpose.

In this chapter I explore both the direct and the inverse connection between violence and information. I do so not for the underworld at large but within the confines of prisons. Prisons are an ideal environment in which to appreciate how important communication is even in, or rather *especially* in, extreme circumstances. There are two main features of prison life that affect the level of violence among prisoners. First, in prisons inmates lose not just their freedom[1] but many ordinary resources, which are scarce, rationed, or near impossible to obtain. An incomplete list includes goods that most of us take for granted, such as decent food, clean linen, space, privacy, silence, cigarettes, telephone use, kitchen use, porn magazines, games, drugs, money, safety from assaults, alcohol, and sex. A few of these goods are allocated under prison rules or at the discretion of prison authorities. Others are distributed via informal markets created by prisoners, and these include goods banned by prison authorities and smuggled in from the outside. At one time or another, these resources are also distributed according to the violent potential of individual prisoners or groups. "Since not all individuals can employ it with equal success, violence provides its users with a decidedly competitive advantage in securing goods and services in the institutional environment."[2] Violent fights are the order of the day in many prisons, and prisoners' safety and property are frequently under threat.

The second feature is that an inmate cannot normally select the inmates with whom to associate. A fundamental trait of prison life is that prisoners are forced to share their quarters with strangers. Sorting and mixing is not under the prisoners' control, and the restricted freedom of internal movement creates an impediment to picking one's partners the way we usually can outside prison. This creates much uncertainty about the true character of those with whom one ends up.

Prisons are a near perfect natural environment for understanding how humans communicate under those two severe constraints, the tension deriving from scarcity and the uncertainty about others' dispositions and capabilities. Army corps, gangs, fraternities, sports teams, boarding schools, and playgrounds are among the institutions that share with prisons some of the same conditions. Yet their predicaments never reach the same strictness and intensity they reach in prison. Prisons are extreme, and as such they are of particular interest for understanding human behavior. As Kaminski points out, "Scarcity and deprivation make inmates particularly alert to the immediate effects of their actions and to resulting payoffs," and put them in a firm calculating mind-set, which makes the rationale of their actions stark and transparent.[3] While not representative of the social life in most ordinary places, prisons reveal what humans are capable of under those difficult conditions. Often, some of the conditions found in prison—especially disputes over resources and lack of enforcing institutions—occur in criminal circles outside prisons. The way prisoners handle them when inside mirrors in a blunt, distilled manner the way criminals manage them outside.

VIOLENCE AND INFORMATION: HYPOTHESES

Inmates have simple preferences, uniformly recorded by all research. Like most of us they (1) prefer to have more of the goods that are scarce rather than fewer. This implies that they also (2) prefer to have their property rights and prerogatives respected by other inmates. Many of them, however, rather than doing without goods, given the chance (3) prefer to violate the rights of other prisoners. Infringing property rights is after all what many inmates are sent to prison for, and the pressures of deprivation put severely to the test their already feeble restraint.

Although familiar with violence—some of them are in prison for it—many prisoners do not enjoy fighting for the pleasure of inflicting or receiving pain. "Psychos" are an exception, and other things being equal most prisoners (4) prefer not fighting to fighting, even though they may not always want others to know that. Fighting has injury costs for weaker inmates, of course, but also for stronger ones. They may not know whether they are stronger than another particular individual before they fight, and even if they are and know it, they may still get injured. So if they can achieve the same results by means other than fighting, even stronger prisoners will prefer it. All studies of prison life concur that fighting is not undertaken lightly. The in-depth study by Edgar and Martin on violence in British prisons, for instance, makes clear that most prisoners who became involved in violent incidents did not want to fight but did so because they saw no other option.[4] In a study in the United States "a majority of the sample (69.6%) stated that they *had been forced* to 'get tough' with other inmates to avoid being victimised or exploited."[5]

On the basis of these preferences and of the two key aspects of prison life, scarcity of resources and uncertainty about one's associates, we can construct a behavioral theory from which we can derive four hypotheses predicting when interprisoner violence is likely to erupt. The theory is loosely inspired by the research on fighting and assessment in animals.[6] Generally, and somewhat trivially, we can expect that conflicts will be more frequent the scarcer and more unequally distributed are the desired commodities. We can also further expect that the probability of disputes will increase with the number of transactions in the internal black market. Here, however, I focus only on how information and violence relate. Provided that there is at least some scarcity and some uneven distribution of resources, the mechanisms described below should be triggered.

1. We can expect that prisoners will try as much as possible to establish their mutual positions in the prison "hierarchy" of violence potential by *communicative means*. They will seek both to display and to observe signals of each other's violent abilities and dispositions, especially signals that are hard to fake and thus credible but are not as costly as violence. Any condition that promotes the knowledge of each other's fighting prowess as well as of other relevant traits makes violence less likely. If we were sent to a prison inferno and could choose the circle to be in, our choice would be for that in which the knowledge of the true potential for violence of each inmate can be established by observable displays rather than by violent confrontations. In the ideal prison hell each inmate would walk in tagged by a mark that accurately reveals his disposition for and skill at violence relative to that of the other inmates.

2. If those communicative means to acquire knowledge about each other's prowess are not available or credible, we can expect that prisoners will be more likely to challenge each other and fight in order to establish their position.[7] Although there will be a certain amount of "noise" in the causes of fighting due, for instance, to psychological strain and emotional triggers, the more opaque the relative positions are, the more

fighting we expect to observe. The worst circle to be in is where one knows nothing about how everyone else ranks and inmates are driven to fight to find out and to establish the real hierarchy of force. Fighting generates information and reveals what otherwise cannot be observed.

There are two predictions that we can derive from the above hypothesis, corresponding to the two main ways in which communication can fail to dispel uncertainty and increase the pressure to fight.

2a. The first refers to the variable amount of "violence capital" any one prisoner has to display when he arrives in prison. The greater this is, the lower the reason to fight. An interesting prediction follows from this, for one can expect, contrary to a common belief, that those less versed or less experienced in using violence will have *more* reasons to fight— such as for instance younger men, women, white-collar criminals, and first timers. Not only will they have reasons to prove themselves to others (for they do not have a history to display), but also they themselves may not know how tough they really are. (Fighting dispositions are not a pure case of what is known in economics as "asymmetric information," in which one has perfect private knowledge of something about oneself—e.g., how honest one is—that others do not know.) One's readiness to use violence, whether in self-defense or to prey on others when under duress, as well as how hard one can fight, are unknown to inexperienced prisoners before the opportunity for testing arises. Even those who know that they can fight hard cannot be sure of winning all contests, as they could meet a tougher opponent. Fighting is crucial, for it generates credible information, which otherwise not only may be unavailable to display but may not even exist before the fight takes place.

2b. Communicative means may fail not for lack of displayable violence capital but for lack of means to display it or see it. The opportunities for display and observation depend on how well information that inmates may have on each other circulates in prisons. If prisoners are made to wear uniforms, some of their visible signals will be silenced. If they have no access to media, they will know less about newcomers' deeds. If they know few other inmates, they will receive less information and have less information about themselves passed on; if guards do not let them know what newcomers are like, they will have to find out by themselves. The better information circulates, the fewer reasons to fight there will be.

3. The probability of entering into fights will be directly related to the number of prisoners any one prisoner will deal with while knowing nothing about their traits. Different prison regimes will present different challenges. Where, for instance, there is a high turnover of inmates or where prisoners are frequently reallocated to new wings and cells and thus frequently meet prisoners about whom they know nothing, the hierarchy will be more unstable and will have to be reestablished at each new encounter. A round of credible displays or, failing those, of fighting may establish the hierarchy and lead to peaceful coexistence, and it often does. Once positions are clear, inmates have at least as many reasons to co-operate with each other as they have reasons to fight. Norms on the respect of property rights may emerge and be enforced informally among prisoners who consider each other as peers in terms of their "manliness." However, where internal or external turnover is higher, norms will be more precarious and cooperation less likely to emerge. Bowker, drawing also from Polsky (1962), makes a good point: "The beauty of the use of physical violence as a control technique is that once physical superiority has been established, it is not necessary to continue to attack the others physically to gain their submission."[8] This, however, obtains if one deals with others who know about one's exploits as close to firsthand as possible. Reputation can of course travel, but noise can distort it, and new inmates can challenge it. In many reports one finds that prisoners have to continue to prove themselves: "You constantly have to work on your reputation. I am not saying you got to run out every week and crack somebody's head. But you do have to be constantly aware of your dealings with other people."[9]

4. Though no prisoner will want to fight if he can get by well enough without doing so, everyone will want to know the fighting record of everyone else. Fights generate useful information not just for those involved but also for the audience, which can thus be spared some future fighting. Reliable information spares people from fighting, but fighting

provides them with reliable information. Prisoners, we can therefore expect, will tend to encourage each other to fight, and they will even cooperate with one another to strengthen their encouragement by rewarding fighters and ostracizing dodgers—at least in cases in which fights will not elicit collective punishment by guards. If the hypothesis is correct, we should observe that when there is a fight between two prisoners who are both well known to the audience, the propensity to intervene to stop it should grow.

In what follows I review the evidence available from prison research to find what confirmation we can for these hypotheses. Most of the facts reported refer to hypotheses 1, 2a, and 3, while on 2b and 4 there is a dearth of evidence.

DISPLAYING AND OBSERVING CUES

Other than resorting to violence, what options do prisoners have to sort out their disputes over the allocation of scarce goods and to decide on each other's rank in the prison hierarchy? Do they really try to find out their position while trying to avoid the cost of fighting? Virtually no research has set out to explore the nonviolent displays of violent potential that go on in prisons. Still, scattered in the ethnographic studies of prison life, we can find several fragments of evidence indicating that this activity does indeed go on.

In the natural course of their interactions prisoners observe each other with a keen eye, and the acquisition of mutual knowledge seems indeed a motivation for much of what they do and say to each other. Interest in acquiring information on others is shared by humans everywhere, as Erving Goffman notes at the outset of *The Presentation of Self in Everyday Life*.[10] But in prison this interest is much more intense and focused. Prisoners brazenly display and carefully observe signs about each other, especially signs that convey information about their fighting prowess. Body size is only one sign and not a very good one apparently. Shields and Simourd, who researched 251 young offenders in a Canadian maximum-security detention center, write: "predators and non-predators did not differ reliably with respect to weight and height. [This] tends to dispel the popular notion that the predatory relationship consists of larger residents 'picking on' smaller ones."[11] Kaminski too observed that body size is only weakly correlated with toughness.[12]

A reliable assessment takes many other observable signs into account, which include posture, fitness, and demeanor, and generally relies also on features subtler than body size. The prisoners interviewed by Toch in a New York City prison put it thus:

> "You can read fear in a man. You can smell it. It depends on what kind of life you are brought up in, and I suppose that a man who came out of Harlem would be pretty tough, and if you put another man next to him he could smell that fear of the other man." . . . "People in here know by the way you act what you're like. I can tell you just by the way people conduct themselves whether you're nervous or cool or what. If you walk around turning your head around every five minutes, it's noticeable!"[13]

Streetwise inmates may indeed be more adept at reading subtle signs, and this should make them better able to calibrate their fighting decisions; also because of this, inexperienced prisoners may end up fighting more rather than less (see below).

Prisoners also consider and display features that testify to past fighting "achievements" that leave observable traces such as scars. They also choose to cultivate activities that generally signal their fitness. In his memoirs about the time he was a prison guard at Sing Sing, Ted Conover, referring to a particular inmate, wrote: "Like many inmates, he's in excellent shape from weightlifting. And, like many inmates, he has scars: three inches long on his waist below the ribs, about one inch long on his arm, penny-size circles that look like two bullets wounds on a shoulder blade. . . . The huge quantity of scars surprises me. Half the inmates in Sing Sing seem to have been stabbed or shot at some point of their lives. Often the scars are on the face."[14] Scars are not signs that one is a loser, as Toch contends. They are rather signs that one has been through

many fights and has survived.[15] Scars on the front (not the back!) of
Roman soldiers' bodies were a testimony to their courage in battle and
loyalty to Rome.[16] Likewise, scars are an item on a criminal's CV. As one
of the prisoners in Toch's study put it: "I see all these guys walking
around here with scars, and I say to myself, 'Holy Christ, the life they led
compared to mine!'"[17]

Many criminals also mark themselves with tattoos, and not just for
the vanity of donning bodily decorations. Regardless of their symbolism
if very extensive, as in the case of yakuza members, tattoos testify to a
considerable resilience to pain. They also indicate that the bearer does
not frequent refined social circles; in this sense, tattoos work as the signals I discuss in chapter 7. They inform credibly because only true bearers of the quality being signaled dare to carry them and to violate the
prevailing social conventions that condemn their use. The symbols expressed by tattoos can further provide specific information about their
bearers. They are another way in which inmates display their CVs. For
example, they might signal membership in a particular gang—a sign that
the inmate is tough and may have friends around. As Phelan and Hunt
found in extensive research carried out in the California state prison
system, tattoos also show "rank, specialization, and personal accomplishments, which typically revolve around murder, drug-trafficking, and
other crimes."[18] Indeed tattoos have a long history among individuals in
military or pseudomilitary organizations: "both in the past and today,
they frequently use tattoos to announce their membership and/or status
in those groups, including such symbols as battle dates, crossed guns,
flags, cannons, and pyramids of bullets."[19] The content of tattoos could
denote false claims. Still, their credibility is presumably reinforced if
other inmates who know of the bearer's deeds corroborate them. Also, if
one's tattoos include the insignia of a gang and the bearer's villainous
achievements, by observing them other inmates at least know something, notably whom to ask and what to ask about to check the veracity
of the claims, a prospect that makes telling lies through tattoos a less attractive option (see chapter 7).

Prisoners, at the same time, gather information about each other that,
while not observable like the signs described above, can be verbally

communicated in ways and by sources that make it hard to fake. The crimes they are convicted of—whether they involved violence, for instance—comprise one such piece of information, sometimes supplied by third parties like prison guards or other inmates or, for notorious crimes, by the media. Another is the length of one's sentence: life without parole makes an inmate more threatening—not just because of what it signals about the seriousness of his crime but also because it removes the main incentive for the prisoner to behave well. He may be punished with, say, solitary confinement but has nothing to lose in terms of his chances of being granted parole. Yet another piece of information is of course the reputation that a prisoner acquired during a previous prison term or while outside prison. "Subjects also indicated," Connell and Farrington write, "that whether residents were bullies or victims in previous custodial facilities played a part in determining whether or not they were bullied in new facilities; that is their reputation as a bully or a victim was carried with them to new facilities."[20]

MIMICKING TOUGHNESS

Knowing that other inmates keenly monitor signs gives each inmate a powerful incentive to display those that testify to his toughness. This incentive works not only for those who are truly tough but also for the "plastic gangsters," as those who merely pretend to be tough are called in some British prisons.[21] According to Toch, some inmates "can prevent new victimisation by simulating the stigmata of manliness they observe among other inmates around them." He cites several prisoners in this regard: "I always try to make myself look like if someone would fuck with me I would kill them. . . . Just keep like a mad look. 'Don't pull any stunt,' you know?" "I have to walk like a real jerk because I don't want them to think that I am feminine. And when I talk to someone I talk really deep."[22] "I was trying to remain composed, and yet still, with all this going around in your mind, you're trying not to let them realize that you're absolutely frightened to death. Because if you let them know you're frightened they're going to make it that much worse for you."[23]

Attempts to display the signs of toughness by those who are not tough are, however, short-lived in prison. "Many [prisoners] confessed," McCorkle reveals, "that 'getting tough' often requires more than just 'tough talk.'"[24] As one prisoner said to Toch, "What kept me pretty much clear of this individual was my acting like a nut . . . everybody else knew it was an act, but he didn't. He thought that was the way I was."[25] One may fool some prisoners some of the time, but a long sequence of unavoidable encounters with a variety of inmates makes it unlikely that false displays of toughness will succeed for long. Soon one will be challenged in a way that cannot be met simply by the ruses of mimicry. "And really it's not just something that you could turn around and say, 'Get the hell away from me.' It's not something you could bluff them. It's not that kind of situation."[26] Also, according to Kaminski, "it is incredibly difficult to fake toughness. In fact, inmates develop phenomenal detection skills and can easily distinguish between, say, a genuine sociopath and a fake."[27]

One of Toch's prisoners gave a remarkably subtle account of how the only way to mask fear is by truly cultivating negative emotions, such as hatred and suspicion, which can override fear. "You can't just say that I'm afraid, but I'm going to be brave. It won't work. . . . If you can't change your emotions then you're gone. And you are going to stay weak. . . . Instead of engaging in the fear, I forced the hostility until it was a bigger point than the fear. And that is all part of forcing another emotion forward to camouflage the fear."[28] In order to survive prison, this man reconfigured his emotional space so well that when he got out of prison he found, to his apparent chagrin, that he could not revert to his meeker self—a sign that prison can indeed change one for good, though not quite for the better.

THE INCIDENCE OF VIOLENT CONFLICTS AND THEIR MOTIVES

The evidence suggests that hypothesis 1 is plausible: when enough information is available by display, prisoners do not need to fight to find out how tough they are. They know who will respond violently if attacked or challenged and who is likely to be the winner of a fight, and they act accordingly. "He's sort of a gangster, and they do not say boo to him. They sit back and watch him. They don't say boo to him. They don't pop any shit on him, because he kicks their ass."[29]

But violent confrontations are frequent in prisons, a sign that in the prison hell the best circle is not often available. The violence experienced and inflicted by prisoners on each other "lies on a continuum." It ranges, as Bottoms writes, from nonphysical acts such as verbal abuse, taunting, threats, "shouting, and 'squaring up' to acts that involve physical contacts, pushing or shoving, slapping, scratching, butting, punching, biting, elbowing, kneeing, kicking, knifing, shooting."[30] Episodes that do not escalate into physical contact are hard to measure, even though they are important for the hypotheses being discussed here, for if challenges are met with credible threats, physical conflict may not arise. I shall return to these cases below. For the moment, I review the evidence on the frequency of serious physical incidents, limiting my survey mostly to the United Kingdom.

In the National Prison Survey of 1991 in England and Wales, 9 percent of a random sample of prisoners said that they had been physically attacked in the past six months. In King and McDermott's study of 1995 of five adult prisons in the United Kingdom, 12.5 percent said that they had been assaulted during their time in prison; 33 percent said that they had been threatened with violence, and 6.8 percent claimed to have been sexually assaulted.[31] In Edgar and O'Donnell's survey of 1,566 male inmates in two adult prisons and in two young offender institutions in Britain, "30 per cent of the young offenders and 19 per cent of the adults stated that they had been assaulted at least once in the previous month." "Thirty-two per cent of young offenders and 16 per cent of adults disclosed that they had assaulted another inmate during the same period."[32] If we take longer time spans, the proportion of prisoners involved in violent confrontations grows. And, if prisoners are interviewed in depth, it also grows. In Edgar and Martin's study, which involved altogether 209 inmates (nonrepresentative sample) who were interviewed in depth, 64 percent (132) revealed that during their prison term they had used "injurious force." Eighty-nine percent of 590 inmates (representative sample) also interviewed in the same study agreed with the statement: "violence in prison is inevitable."[33]

Edgar and O'Donnell found that for both assaults and threats of violence there was a substantial element of mutuality: being a victim of assault was strongly correlated with being also a perpetrator.[34] However, those who were robbed did not rob. And they were robbed repeatedly. It looks, in other words, as if those who fight are not just victims, while there are groups of prisoners who do not fight but are only preyed on.

If hypothesis 2 is correct, namely that fighting increases as uncertainty about prisoners' violent prowess increases, the significant frequency of violent confrontations that we observe in prisons implies that not all prisoners can display enough information to be classified as either untouchable or as passive victims. There must be prisoners who for some reason do not give out any clear sign about their unobservable traits. To understand how much fighting has to do with producing and collecting information about each other, we need to consider what inmates say that they fight about.

Edgar and Martin found that "the use of force is not 'mindless'—one or both participants could always explain why the incident had occurred; nor was it 'random'—in very few cases were the participants unknown to one another." The prisoners in their study mentioned a material interest "such as drugs, personal possessions, games, food, tobacco, and phone cards" as being the principal motive of a fight only in a quarter of cases.[35] (Analyzing the data over and above what prisoners said, they found that at most a material interest was present in half of the violent incidents.) Drugs and alcohol were the most frequent source of a material dispute, appearing in over 30 percent of cases.

By contrast, "non-material interests (self-respect, honour, fairness, loyalty, personal safety and privacy) were important in *every* incident."[36] While only some violent conflicts occur for the immediate purpose of getting or keeping resources, *all of them* have to do with establishing one's reputation or correcting wrong beliefs about it. Even "a conflict that began over the disputed ownership of some item could quickly be interpreted by both parties as a test of who could exploit whom."[37] The resource considered by prisoners when deciding whether to fight is not just the resource that may be in dispute but one's reputation with the aggressor and other inmates. In the Polish prisons studied by Kaminski (on whom more below) reputation is explicitly present in established prisoners' language, and it operates as the most important asset in prison. Their fights, at least a large proportion of them, have to do with information about which type the prisoners are, which they either wish to convey about themselves or collect about others. According to Mc-Corkle, "Interviewees stated that such moves send signals to the aggressor, and to the wider audience of inmates, that the target is willing to use violence in defence of self."[38] Edgar and Martin found likewise: "Prisoners who used force to demonstrate their toughness expressed a fear that other inmates could perceive the lack of a violent response as evidence of weakness and vulnerability."[39] Fighting driven by this motive fits the definition of a communicative act, an act aimed at shaping or modifying other prisoners' beliefs. Needless to say, fighting over reputation also has material consequences, in that one who chooses to fight is possibly less likely to be victimized in future encounters. The above evidence gives credence to hypothesis 2, namely that violence produces information and that it is sought or borne with that goal in mind by prisoners themselves.

AGE AND GENDER OF OFFENDERS

Let us now consider hypothesis 2a, according to which we can expect that fights will break out when prisoners do not have enough accumulated "violence capital" to display when they arrive in prisons. If this hypothesis is correct, we should observe more violence among younger prisoners and women.

Virtually all studies that gathered data on the matter, both in the United Kingdom and the United States, found that young offenders are more likely to be involved in violent incidents than adult inmates.[40] Walters, on a large database, showed that age is inversely correlated with violence in prison.[41] The data in table 4.1 confirm the finding: institu-

TABLE 4.1
Recorded disciplinary offenses of assaults and fighting in establishments
housing male prisoners, England and Wales (yearly averages over the period
1990–96, per 1,000 inmates)

	Assaults	*Fighting*
Closed training prisons	17	54
Local prisons	36	90
Young-offenders institutions	145	451
Remand centers for under 21	187	487

SOURCE: My calculation from Bottoms 1999: 215, table 1. The data are derived from the annual volumes of *Statistics of Offences against Prison Discipline and Punishments in England and Wales.*

tions for younger male offenders (bottom two rows) recorded, by far, the
highest rates of assaults and fighting. (This pattern, incidentally, is not
just a robust finding in criminology but a universal regularity: younger
men all over the world are more likely to be victims as well perpetrators
of violent acts.)

Without invoking the larger doses of testosterone coursing through
the bodies of younger men, hypothesis 2a is consistent with this finding
and provides a plausible *social* rather than biological explanation for the
greater likelihood of fighting that younger inmates have. Young prisoners—like younger men generally—have more to prove because they
have little personal history to display to others; their CVs on fighting are
thinner than those of adults. Furthermore, they themselves may not
know how tough they really are. Equally, they may also be less skilled at
reading other prisoners' signals. They are thus fully exposed to the lack
of information and the uncertainty that causes inmates to fight.[42] Prisons, in the words of an inmate, are full of "Boys trying to become
Men. . . . They are youngsters that want to prove something—how tough
and macho and strong they are. This is their whole attitude. Very extreme
power trip and machismo. The youngsters want to prove something.
How tough they are."[43]

The data on women are even more striking. Women are significantly
less violent than men in the outside world and less lethal when they are
violent. This holds in all times and places for which relevant data exist.

TABLE 4.2
Recorded disciplinary offenses of assaults and fighting in establishments
housing male and female prisoners, England and Wales (yearly averages over
the period 1990–96, per 1,000 inmates)

	Assaults	Fighting
All-men establishments	35	95
All-women establishments	67	147

SOURCE: My calculation from Bottoms 1998: 215, tables 1 and 5. The data are derived from the annual volumes of *Statistics of Offences against Prison Discipline and Punishments in England and Wales*.

And yet in prison this universal fact is overturned: women become *at least* as violent and often more prone to violence than men are. Although women in prison rarely commit homicide, a large study of Texas prisons by Tischler and Marquart showed that there was no difference between women and men in the incidence of violent episodes.[44] Table 4.2, based on comprehensive statistics for England and Wales, shows that the gender pattern is even *reversed*: women assault each other twice as much as men do, and they fight one and half times as much as men do, a result that disconfirms the testosterone hypothesis.

Generally, women are convicted of proportionally fewer violent offenses than men are and have shorter criminal histories,[45] two circumstances that rule out some of the possible selection effects that could explain away the high rates of female prison violence. We cannot, however, rule out other selection effects. Lucia Zedner, who researched nineteenth-century prisons for British women and found that violence was endemic,[46] wrote that the explanations of why women in prison were so inclined to violence "have been mostly social-psychological. Women would suffer more at being taken away from their families (and, particularly painful, young children), suffer from greater levels of mental illness and depression inside, and seek solace in intense emotional (often lesbian) relations with other inmates and staff, all of which would lead to a greater incidence of violence."[47] Along similar lines, one could argue that since drug addiction is more frequent among jailed women than among jailed men, female prisoners are selected from a subset that is particularly prone to violence. Still, the gender differences in drug use seem to be small and thus insufficient to account for the gender differences in prison violence.[48] So, in conclusion, the evidence is consistent with hypothesis 2a, in that women, like younger males, have lower accumulated "violence capital" to display that could help them sort out their disputes without recourse to physical violence. They are also less likely, because of conventions or desire not to jeopardize their sexual attractiveness, to sport masculine tattoos or to cultivate a muscular physique. They are thus under greater pressure to generate the lacking information in prison, and more generally to settle their disputes and establish their hierarchy by violent means rather than by signaling a previously acquired reputation.

TURNOVER AND PRISON REGIME

Hypothesis 3—namely that the greater the number of unknown prisoners that any one prisoner encounters, the greater is the likelihood of fighting—can be tested by considering turnover. The higher turnover is, the higher are the chances of ending up associated to strangers, and to more of them.

The study by Edgar and Martin in two U.K. prisons found that the prisoners in the local prison, who were "a more heterogeneous group," "were more likely than others to use force in retaliation and revenge."[49] By contrast, in the dispersal prison, which was a more "settled community," episodes of violence were less frequent, and prisoners "were able to use their deeper knowledge of their peers to resolve conflicts without violence."[50] This finding is of great interest for the hypothesis of our concern. Dispersal prisons contain prisoners who have longer sentences, above four years, and who are much more likely than local prison inmates to be convicted of a *violent* crime. Consistent with this finding, Berk and de Leeuw, in a large statistical study, found that the inmates placed in higher security levels in California, who have longer sentences and are jailed for more serious crimes, engage in less in-prison misconduct. The inmates in local prisons, by contrast, have shorter jail terms and are sentenced for a wider spectrum of lesser crimes.[51]

The figures in table 4.1 confirm this finding through general prison statistics for England and Wales. In local prisons there are about twice as many fights and assaults as in "closed training prisons," which include a variety of longer-term establishments. Furthermore, there is greater violence in remand centers for prisoners under twenty-one, where inmates include those not yet convicted and thus some who will be acquitted, than in young-offenders institutions, which are only for those convicted. In the latter, the average young offender will be more likely than in the former to be violent, and yet the inmates there fight less than those in the remand centers. If violent dispositions and the "hardness" of the criminals were all that mattered, one would naturally infer the exact opposite patterns of violent occurrences.[52] The fact that this prediction is not only not borne out but reversed greatly reinforces the hypothesis that the likelihood of fights is greater the lower the amount of information prisoners have on each other.

These patterns generally reinforce hypothesis 3: a higher turnover creates more opportunities to fight, for it causes more encounters among prisoners who are strangers to each other. However, they are also consistent with hypothesis 2a, for inmates in both the local and the remand prisons have less of a reputation to display because their criminal careers are shorter and thinner. Thus they have less knowledge of their and others' proneness to violence, and a greater number of fights could erupt partly because mistaken beliefs are more likely to be formed about one another and partly just for the purpose of finding out.

Consider now two prisons with similar types of prisoners but with different regimes. The research by Sparks, Bottoms, and Hay on two British dispersal prisons, Albany and Long Lartin, yields interesting results. Long Lartin has about a quarter of the number of serious violent incidents among prisoners that Albany has (4.4 every 100 prisoners as opposed to 15.3, calculated over a two-year period).[53] Albany has also a stricter regime, while in Long Lartin prisoners are freer to roam around the prison and apply for transfer to other wings.[54] Albany, however, has also a higher proportion of inmates under twenty-five (31 percent compared with 14 percent in Long Lartin), and this, as the researchers say, could explain the higher incidence of violent confrontations between prisoners there. Yet it seems unlikely that the difference in age distribution could explain in full the difference in violent incidents. The latter is four times as high in Albany as in Long Lartin, while the proportion of younger prisoners is only twice as high. This conclusion, namely that there is something that directly relates the strictness of prison regime to violence, is reinforced by the fact that all comparative studies have found that "higher security levels are associated with higher levels of violence. It is therefore plausible, as Wright puts it, that 'more structured, more authoritarian settings may engender more disruptive behaviour.'"[55]

Hypothesis 2b, namely that communicative means can fail to establish a violence "hierarchy" for lack of ways to display or see inmates' violence capital, provides a mechanism that may just explain why this is so. A certain freedom to mix with other prisoners should decrease fighting because information circulates better when prisoners can meet, observe, and communicate with each other more. If, as in Long Lartin, they can apply for transfer, they also can pick their mates and thus are more likely to end up associating with inmates who know more about each other. Albany, by operating a stricter regime and forcibly moving prisoners from wing to wing and cell to cell, decreases the opportunities for prisoners to come to know each other by means other than direct violence. A common practice in many prisons consists of reassigning prisoners to new wings and cells after an incident occurs. While this may decrease the chances of retaliation or continued victimization, and may be put into practice with the intention of thwarting internal gang formation, it may also unintentionally generate greater levels of violence by increasing the frequency with which prisoners unknown to one another meet—and so may, overall, achieve the opposite effect from the one desired. As Kaminski found, "frequent changes of cells and jails produce Hobbesian interactions that are often 'short, nasty and brutish.'"[56] The incentives to resort to violence to uncover an inmate's "true type are especially strong when cellblocks are isolated" and "when inmates change cell frequently."[57]

A final piece of evidence consistent with hypotheses 2a and 3 is that "a number of writers have found that predatory aggression appears to peak early in the inmate's sentence, and then decline."[58] The two explanations offered for this finding (which is not, however, as well established as those above) are that the closer the potential parole date is, the stronger the incentive to behave well, or that prisoners "learn to adapt successfully to the prison setting."[59] A key aspect of adaptation may indeed consist of the acquisition of better information. When prisoners arrive in prison, they meet strangers in larger numbers and are under greater pressure to prove to others that they are tough, if indeed they are.

In conclusion, I should mention a few caveats with respect to considering the above patterns as a fully satisfactory test of the hypotheses. First, the available data do not allow us to sort out the various *relative* effects that one can attribute to each of the hypotheses—only data more focused on the relevant information and suitable for multivariate analysis could provide such a measure. Still, the patterns provide a very encouraging first test of the *overall* set of hypotheses. Next, a proper test ought to take into account the possible existence of selection biases. One could imagine, for instance, that the greater incidence of assaults and fighting among women may be due to a selection bias. Women may be more inclined to report such incidents or guards more inclined to record them, in that men may be expected to fight more and thus attract less attention when they do. Finally, each pattern could be explained by other, not necessarily alternative, mechanisms. I already mentioned biological causes for younger inmates and social-psychological mechanisms for women that could explain the higher incidence of violence in these two groups. Also, the greater incidence in prisons with higher turnover is consistent with much research on cooperation: prisons with lower turnover are also prisons in which inmates have longer sentences, and longer-term horizons increase the incentive to cooperate, for the costs of not doing so are greater. Moreover, prisons with higher turnover may also cause other effects. Some prisoners awaiting trial may be more stressed, while others may not yet be part of educational programs or be generally unaccustomed to incarceration.

All these factors may play a part. Yet the substantial size of the effects, the consistency across different sources, and the overall consistency of the different patterns with the hypotheses are encouraging. While none of the alternative mechanisms one can think of can explain all the patterns, the set of hypotheses presented here can, and passes the parsimony test remarkably well.

CHALLENGES, THREATS, AND FIGHTS

I shall now retrace my steps and try to establish in greater detail how prisoners decide to fight. At present, the evidence is insufficient to characterize all the conceivable gamelike sequences of events that could lead to fighting. In addition to being intrinsically difficult, data collection on prison violence has seldom been guided by theoretical expectations, so the best one can do is to identify a typical sequence, making do with the fragments of available evidence and filling the gaps theoretically. The outcome of this exercise is a refinement rather than a test of the hypotheses.

Some fights erupt simply because two prisoners fight over a physical resource they both covet there and then, or over something one of them owns and another tries to snatch away. If arguments and threats do not suffice to settle the dispute, a fight may ensue. This sequence of events, however, as we have seen, does not seem to be all that frequent; violence often erupts regardless of an immediate conflict over resources. These other fights may break out because new entrants who fear seeming weak—those who have no violence capital to show—may choose to attack unprovoked or respond violently at the mildest provocation rather than waiting to be challenged. They want to create a reputation and gain respect, and in order to do that they need to resort to violence rather than just challenge or threaten. But perhaps the most common prelude to a violent conflict is a challenge issued by a settled inmate and designed to test a new entrant's mettle. There is evidence that new entrants, in prison or in new cells and wings, unless overtly and credibly menacing, are soon challenged—by bullying, taunting, intimidation, insults, provocations, or overt invitations to fight. Sometimes the challenge is veiled under the mantle of a conflict over resources, including attempts to extract sexual favors. The prisoner, however, is often not "a serious target of rape but an object of manoeuvres designed to test his 'manliness' or coping competence. Aggressors and spectators seem concerned with his reactions or non-reactions to aggressive overtures. The man is on trial, and he is fatefully examined. The penalty for failure is accelerated victimisation. If a man acquits himself fully, he ensures his immunity to attack. The test is manliness. The criterion is courage. Courage is evidenced by willingness to fight and by the capacity for doing so."[60]

Whether a challenge is issued depends on a number of conditions. If the preference for not fighting over fighting is universal, why would anyone want to pick a fight? A determined new entrant may attack first to gain respect, but the action of a settled challenger begs an explanation: if the preference for not fighting were rock solid, no one would ever fight, for each prisoner would wait for someone else to do it first. A rational challenger acts only if he expects that acting will be better for him than doing nothing (all outcomes must have a payoff better than 0, including being harmed in or losing a fight). These payoffs may occur naturally for inmates who are in a special position: those who feel strong enough relative to the new entrant to risk a fight, but not so strong as to feel safe in their own position in the hierarchy; and so they aim to improve it. By challenging, they show that they can take risks, and they perform a useful task for other inmates by acting as the catalyst of an information-generating event.

When these payoffs do not naturally occur, more-established inmates may manipulate them. Generally, prisoners have an interest in combining to give one of them the right incentive to issue a challenge to a new entrant. Kaminski, during his sojourn in Polish prisons, where tests of toughness are carefully organized (see below), found out that Maniek, his own challenger, his potential rapist, "was himself subject to a test. The task assigned to him was to make a fag of a rookie [a new entrant]. . . . Maniek flunked his higher-level test, though his punishment was merely not advancing his status among the other inmates."[61] As with social norms generally, the reward and punishment that enforce them may consist of approval and disapproval, "you are one of us" as opposed to

"stay away from us." Kaminski found out that attackers even win material rewards, notably a portion of the victim's endowment.[62] Also the
"designer [of the test] is often rewarded for his role in the game in prestige and valuable prison goods that he can more or less violently extract
from a rookie."[63]

When the challenge does not begin with a physical attack but it is
verbal or provocative in some other way, the response of the target prisoner can be initially appeasing or dismissive. This will not suffice, though,
for it leaves the suspicion that the victim is just weak. One of the prisoners interviewed by Toch said:

> You try to talk some sense to them and say, "Now look, I am an
> inmate and you're an inmate." And they will say, ah—"Don't tell
> me that pussy shit." They will tell you that, you know? And so I
> figured that talking was not good with this guy, you know, there is
> only one way to handle him, and that is to fight with him. Like, he
> might say something like "Are you ready?" And I don't react to
> him. And I just say, "I despise you." And he takes it as a joke. Even if
> I'm serious, he takes it as a joke.[64]

The response to provocations and insults can be in kind and still refrain
from physical violence. Yet banter, verbal abuse, and put-downs can go
back and forth and fail to produce a clear winner. As Edgar and Martin
point out, "A verbal exchange could always lead to arguments about
who got the better of the other."[65] Thus, the target may choose to show
his willingness to respond violently to the challenge. Even if he expects
to lose, it may still be better to risk a fight than to back down, in order
to impress on the attacker and on the audience that he is not a hapless
victim. The prison hierarchy seems to sort prisoners initially into two
main types—not so much winners and losers, but fighters and passive
victims: "So I fight and get punched a few times, and I punch him a few
times, and they see that I'm a man."[66] The lives of most inmates are nasty
and brutish at some point, but the tribulations of those who fail to respond to challenges will not be short. Being known as someone who
responds ensures that the prisoner will not be victimized on a regular

basis. Responding to challenges does not identify one as either a "hawk," someone who will always attack, or a "dove," someone who never will. It will identify one as "bourgeois," the term used in animal studies to describe someone who behaves as a hawk and attacks if and only if his property or status is under threat; otherwise he behaves as a dove.[67]

When a challenge is leveled, the choice faced by the target prisoner is not simply to respond violently or to succumb. There is a third option, namely making threats, adopting behaviors that while not involving physical violence signal determination to use it. Threats are displays of a focused and specific kind, in contrast to the displays we reviewed above, which occur in the natural course of interaction and reciprocal observation, and are not directed at someone with whom one is in conflict. In order to persuade the opponent of the seriousness of the threat, menacing signals have to be credible, of a kind that a mimic could not easily afford. Targets may raise their fists, advance toward and fix their gaze on the challenger, maybe verbally describing what they are prepared to do. These gestures have a threatening effect if they work as "handicap signals," the name that biologists have chosen to designate signals that are hard to fake: "walking away from the opponent"—Zahavi writes—"is equally possible for an animal ready to fight and one which is not. Hence it is not a good threat signal. On the other hand, walking toward the opponent is less costly for an individual ready to fight and, who is not frightened of a clash, while it may be detrimental to an individual not ready to fight by decreasing its chances to escape its rival if a clash occurs. Hence of all possible threat signals by walking, walking toward the rival is the best threat display."[68]

When people make threats, they also change their tone of voice; they either shout or lower it. Zahavi and Zahavi claim that "the pitch of the voice reliably discloses the tension of the signaller's body. A tense body makes a more high-pitched sound than a relaxed one. A frightened individual is tensed to take flight or to fight back. Only one who is relaxed, not poised to take instant action, can sound a low-pitched threatening note. Such an individual discloses reliably that he does not fear its rival; it is not coiled like a tightly wound spring and thus has exposed itself to a first strike."[69] Still, following the same reasoning, a case could be made for the effectiveness of raising one's voice. By shouting, one shows that one has energy to waste and is not worried about having to spend it even if a fight is looming. Without focused empirical studies of prison contests, it is impossible to say how vocalization or credible threatening signals generally take shape.

What we know is that if the threat is credible, the challenger will have to choose whether to back down or return the threat, escalating the contest further. Also, if the threat appears to the audience, this will provide good information about the target, and the test could be fruitful even if it ends there. Whether it does depends on whether the challenger is aiming to show that he can win a fight rather than just test whether the target is of a fighting type. If the threat is not credible, presumably the challenger will come back issuing yet harder provocations. In either case, before the contest's resolution the exchange of threats can continue for several rounds evolving into a game of chicken, also referred to in game theory as "brinkmanship," in which each tries to intimidate the other by pushing himself to the brink of taking the threatened action, hoping this will be "intolerable to the other party and force his accommodation."[70] The escalation of threats raises the risk of a fight, for it increasingly commits the contenders not to desist.

Notice however that a test can fail to provide the desired information if it is recognized as a test by the target. The more a prisoner suspects that the challenge is a mere test, the more reasons he will have to respond by showing that he is spoiling for a fight, for he knows that that will suffice. As Kaminski makes clear, if the tested prisoner knows that it is just a ritual challenge, then the challenge will not reveal whether he is really tough, for even a meek but astute prisoner will have a reason to be seen to react violently.[71] The skill of the challenger lies in his ability to persuade the target that he is facing a real conflict. To pretend that the conflict is over resources could be a ploy designed to make the victim think that the fight is for real. In disorganized contests this may in fact turn out to be easier than in highly organized ones, for the target will not really know who, exactly, he is up against and why.

A circumstance that is also amply shown by research and that further proves the informational value of fights is the effects of the audience on the payoffs. First, the more public the challenge, the greater the negative consequences on the target's reputation if he chooses not to respond and, correspondingly, the greater is the incentive to respond violently, for more inmates will be informed. Next, challengers who are interested in information have an incentive to stage the attack in as public a situation as possible. Similarly, prisoners who set out to respond also have an interest in staging their fights publicly to increase the number of other inmates who will be informed. Third, insofar as this does not get them all into trouble with the prison authorities, inmates encourage each other to fight and do not back down, for they all stand to gain new knowledge. "The majority of them told me to hit this guy," an interviewee of Toch reveals, "or anybody that comes up to you, just hit them and make sure that it is in front of a bunch of people, so that they will see where you are at and that you don't mess around." "Everyone has been talking to me and telling me that I should fight, and I've tried everything else, so now I might as well fight."[72]

FIGHTS BETWEEN PEERS

In prisons the hierarchy does not consist simply of those who fight and those who do not. In Long Lartin, for instance, prisoners distinguish between "real gangsters" and "plastic gangsters," namely phony inmates who mimic real gangsters; and also between real gangsters and "ordinary cons," who are not phonies but are unable to achieve the status of a gangster. Ordinary cons represent the "bourgeois" type, who fights when his position is threatened but not otherwise. There are also "nonces," inmates sentenced for sexual crimes, "kids," namely younger and less experienced prisoners, and "psychos."[73] Nonces are a favorite target of victimization by other prisoners, and some of them, in order to be left alone, "consciously cultivated a reputation as 'psychos,' people who would meet violence with greater violence."[74]

We can expect that a certain number of fights will not concern the first question, whether or not one will fight when challenged. When gangsters fight each other or when ordinary cons aspire to gangster status, they and their audience will already know that they are of the fighting type. Being among those who fight spares one from being victimized—one's rights will be respected; but when a dispute breaks out with an equally violence-prone peer, the key question about which the participants lack clear information is not whether they fight but who is going to win, who is the top dog.

This type of conflict can be predicted to be more likely in long-term prisons than in short-term ones, for the proportion of inmates who already know who is ready to fight will be higher. It can be expected that this type of conflict will be more serious in terms of injuries, for no one will back down before the contest throws up a winner and a loser. And for this very reason, such a conflict will be less frequent than the pure testing game. It can also be expected to concern not just respect for one's property and safety but the allocation of more and better goods, which can be achieved only by being at the top of the hierarchy. Finally, in line with animal behavior research, we can expect that in humans, as in other species, the individuals who will be more likely to fight violently over resources are the ones who are similar in terms of fighting strength, who cannot establish by sheer display who the winner is going to be.[75]

Sparks, Bottoms, and Hay's research on the two long-term British dispersal prisons provides some evidence for these hypotheses. First, most prisoners are "at pains to avoid overt conflict," "because fights around here do get nasty," says one of the prisoners they interviewed. "It's no kindergarten. If you have a fight with somebody you've *got* to win or lose, and either way you've got to be friends afterwards. A lot of blokes do."[76] Whereas in the study by Edgar and Martin a large proportion of conflicts were sparked by tension over nonmaterial goods, most of the conflicts reported in this study were triggered by tension over specific resources. They occurred notably over unpaid debts (which result from the lively internal markets of goods, gambling, and money lending) or attempted extortion.[77] And if one breaks down the data from Edgar and Martin, one finds that fights due to conflict over clear and immediate interest are more frequent in the dispersal prison they considered than in the local prisons.[78]

Those who use force and threats to make themselves respected in these prisons gain "gangster" rank, which "entails achieving a certain status and recognition among the other prisoners and to some degree the staff. Achieving the status of a 'face' [or leading figure] confers certain benefits. These include being left alone, having preferable jobs, holding more material possessions, being treated with a certain consideration by the staff, perhaps to the extent of being consulted in limited ways by managers."[79]

RITUALIZED TESTS OF TOUGHNESS

In some prisons the testing of new inmates is organized and ritualized. Marek Kaminski has given us the best description of one such case, thanks to his ability to make academic use of his unplanned five-month-long sojourn in a total of thirteen cells in two Polish prisons for career criminals in the 1980s because of his anti-Communist activities as a member of Solidarność.[80] His perspective is germane to that pursued in this essay. The case he describes gives credence to the claim that many violent incidents are designed by prisoners to test other prisoners' toughness, for the good reason that this was the explicit aim that prisoners themselves attributed to their activities. Projected on the more disorganized cases, Kaminski's account strengthens the main hypotheses that violence and information are closely related. It is worth giving a brief summary of his findings.

In the two jails where Kaminski was held, prisoners were classified in the following main categories. Newcomers were either "rookies," that is, first timers, or "newbies," who may not have been first timers but were new to the prison or to a block. These were transient categories and incumbents would in time be "tested" and allocated to the three "castes." At the top we find the "grypsmen," inmates who were part of a prison fraternity and who distinguished themselves by a secret knowledge, consisting of an argot and shared norms and taboos. Next, we have the "suckers," who could not make it to the rank of grypsmen and could be exploited. Last, and least, there were the "fags." A fag was someone "who

once agreed to please sexually a grypsman or, less often, was raped."[81]
Grypsmen comprised 70 to 80 percent of the inmate population, fags
only 1 or 2 percent, and suckers the remaining part.

In terms of the theory of interprisoner violence put forward here, a
main advantage of this organization is clear: on entering the new prison
newbies were immediately questioned and asked whether they were
grypsmen. The veracity of a positive claim was easily verified by checking whether the claimant truly possessed the shared distinguishing
knowledge—sanctions for simulating membership in a higher caste were
severe. In addition, the newbie's declaration was "authenticated through
in-depth interviews and background reports collected from other cells,
cell block, or even remote prisons."[82] Testing a newbie could be a matter
of hours, and did not involve violence. The newbie was thus classified as
either a genuine grypsman, a sucker, or a fag. If someone who had been
in prison before was not a grypsman, the chances were high that he did
not make it in the previous prison and was either a fag or a sucker. The
tightly knit organization of the grypsman fraternity achieved the situation that I have called the best circle of prison-hell, namely a prison in
which the true traits of a new prisoner are credibly and cheaply on display. In this situation one's reputation travels well and clearly, from prison
to prison and block to block. The advantage for all those concerned is
significant, as it saves on information-gathering costs. Testing does not
need to be repeated. No violence is risked by anyone. Notice that this
system saves trouble even for the unfortunate inmates in the lower categories, for their rank would otherwise still have to be established by
more painful means.

Not all rookies, by contrast, had a reputation to display, and most of
them were tested and sorted through a process that could go on for
weeks. If a rookie's toughness was assessed as questionable, he would be
subjected to a fag-making ritual. A designated inmate would try to
threaten and cajole the rookie into agreeing to provide him with sexual
services. Various forms of humiliation and oppression preceded the request, and the victim was led to believe that these would stop if he accepted. Although some inmates who ended up in the fag caste reported
having been raped, in Kaminski's experience this was rarely the case.
Victims were fooled into consenting because of fear. A tough enough

rookie or an informed one who knew the ordeal was basically a test would have known that it was to his advantage to refuse even if he was not tough.

If the fag-making test was successfully passed, the rookie could request to be inducted as a grypsman. Or, more precisely, any rookie who was "not a child molester, communist party member, former prison guard, policeman, prosecutor, etc." was "eligible for grypsing candidacy."[83] "Baptism" might be the next stage. This was designed not so much to test the fighting disposition of an inmate as his ability to endure pain. Kaminski describes the ordeal:

> Rookies are blindfolded and spread on the stools. The executioner prepares a special wet towel that is supposed to break your bones and yet not leave external signs of beating. Surrounded by a circle of bloodthirsty half-naked inmates, the rookie awaits mortal blows. Just before the slaughter begins he is offered an option out of the ceremony in exchange for the privilege of joining the grypsmen. Those who accept, frightened by the performance, immediately get cursed and beaten by the executioner, and become suckers.[84]

Once again the rookie was led to believe that he was about to suffer, but this was not really so, as the "actual blows" were "symbolic."

If the inmate passed the baptism, a whole set of new tests awaited him before he could be inducted into the grypsman fraternity. A distinctive aspect of the Polish case is that these new hurdles were "little games" designed to test the rookie's cleverness as much as his toughness. Grypsmen put a high premium on cleverness, something one would not expect to find in many prisons. Kaminski explains the overall purpose: "Old inmates who learn about these characteristics form clearer expectations about the rookie's future behaviour. This allows them to optimally exploit the rookie's skills and take advantage of his weaknesses. In addition, toughness serves as a proxy for the rookie's expected loyalty in conflicts with the personnel [prison guards and authorities]."[85]

There are several advantages to such an organized process as compared to the disorganized conflicts in prisons where these matters are decided in a state of nature. "The games of fag-making and baptism exploit fundamental knowledge asymmetries between old inmates and rookies,"[86] which make it possible to avoid violence while acquiring information about the rookie's disposition to violence and endurance at the same time. The tests can be organized when it is optimal for the old inmates to acquire knowledge about the new inmate and not left to haphazard events. Everyone endures similar tests, for the procedures are standardized. The conditions under which a test occurs can be controlled: it can be held in public and when no guards are around to interrupt the ritual and punish those involved. The executioner and those who administer the test do not run any risk of becoming involved in a violent confrontation, and can be compensated for their service. If there are immediate returns in terms of resources, these can be evenly distributed. And, as mentioned above, those among the old inmates who bear the greater cost can be compensated or use their effort for furthering their position in the prison hierarchy. These various advantages enable the grypsmen to develop better cooperation with each other at the expense of the other castes. Grypsmen often encourage other grypsmen to fight with lower-caste members since this is equivalent to testing them. However, they do not look with sympathy on fighting within their group. An active encouragement of within-group fighting is extremely rare among them. Overall, the procedure is an efficient and inexpensive way to gather information, even though such a test can fail if the knowledge that it is a test somehow reaches the rookie, who will then seem to pass the test even if he is just well informed rather than tough.

In another paper Kaminski and Gibbons address the question of why this kind of tightly organized system develops only in some prisons and not in others.[87] The only other documented cases in which something similar to the Polish system has been found were in the prisons and gulag of the Soviet Union, whereas in American or British prisons no such system has been found. Kaminski and Gibbons attribute the difference to the relative weakness of administrative control that was common in Polish prisons, which gave greater autonomy to the prisoners to create and enforce their normative system. In terms of variation in the level of control, at the high end

we find Alcatraz or similar maximum security prisons, where inmates spend most of the time in one-man cells with doors made of
bars [no privacy], and, at the other end, we find Polish "barns,"
with 40–50 inmates locked in an essentially private space that
guards are usually afraid to enter and who have lots of freedom to
organize their life. These different constraints exercise strong effects on inmate incentives to create and maintain a common subculture. For instance, in Alcatraz comprehensive and routine initiation rituals would be impossible since staging tests requires long
stretches of time spent by inmates jointly and the lack of interfer-
ence from guards.[88]

Weakness of administrative control may well explain opportunities to
institutionalize the screening of new prisoners, but what about the incentives? It is plausible to surmise that these may have to do with the
peculiar mix of prisoners found predominantly in prisons of communist
countries and not so often in those of other countries. In the prisons
where Kaminski was incarcerated, career criminals with long sentences
were mixed with inmates sentenced to just a few months. In a large cell
with over forty prisoners he observed "a constant flow of five to ten
new inmates per month"—a very high turnover rate—that needed to
be tested. This made it advantageous for the older and longer-term residents to organize the testing process rather than leave it to haphazard
challenges and fights. Furthermore, as in the gulag, the long-term prisoners were part of a penitentiary system that shifted them frequently
from one prison to another, thereby raising the incentive to design ways
to avoid having to undergo painful initiation at every move. These inmates were under considerable pressure to find ways to make their reputation travel with them.

CONCLUSIONS

The brutality of one's prison experience, and the revelation of how
tough one is, carry a value that travels beyond prison walls. I argued in

chapter 1 that having been to prison is one of the best signals one can give of criminality; it is a trait that, while stigmatized in polite society, is of much value in promoting one's criminal affairs. A prison experience, however, is relevant not just for identifying bona fide criminals as opposed to undercover agents or informants. Given the kind of tests that prisoners endure, having been in prison and not having been broken by it implies that one has conducted oneself as a "real" man. Signaling one's prison credentials outside prison lets others know that one is a type to be reckoned with. "I have heard you did some time. I checked up on you. A lot of people know you; you're a tough kid, a real stand up kid," said Frank Bova to Pete Salerno, who had just completed a five-year sentence.[89] In his autobiography Malcolm Braly, a robber, makes clear that the value of serving prison time is not, as is often claimed, that prisons function as schools of crime: "Today anyone with the price of a movie ticket or access to a television can see the most elaborate criminal techniques worked out in accurate detail and presented as entertainment. . . . What one learns to want in a 'criminal school' is the respect of one's peers. This is the danger. The naïve will be drawn into competing for status in a system of values that honors and glorifies antisocial behaviour."[90]

Those who aim to develop a criminal career are proud of their time in jail and even relish it: "I was arrested and I achieved my desire—a fifteen-month prison sentence as opposed to Borstal [a juvenile prison]," says John McVicar in his autobiography.[91] This understanding of time spent in prison is not in conflict with the fact that inmates hate and fear the experience, which they do.[92] On the contrary, it is because prison is not a holiday camp that it has such value in fostering a criminal career. It makes the ex-inmates both trusted (because it testifies to their bona fide criminality) and feared—because they endured it.

CHAPTER 5

Self-harm as a Signal

As we have seen in the previous chapter, under conditions of intense competition over scarce resources, unenforceable property rights, and uncertain ranking in terms of toughness, prisoners are likely to fight with other prisoners, not just to defend themselves from immediate threat but also to establish a primitive hierarchy by signaling that they are tough enough not to be messed with. In the absence of credible alternative signals of toughness, not fighting would be taken as a license for abuse.

Fighting, however, is not the only option for those who want to deter others from attacking or preying on them. Another option, which I consider in this chapter, is resorting to deliberate physical self-harm (DSH). This may seem a rather far-fetched supposition. Head-butting a wall, biting oneself to the bleeding point, cutting one's skin, or mutilating oneself are generally regarded as impulsive and irrational actions, or as pathological manifestations of unbalanced minds. Before recoiling from the idea, however, and suspecting that I may be trying to rationalize insanity, bear with me.

DSH is common among humans, first of all in the myriad forms that are normatively regulated and have been practiced for millennia all over the globe. These are sometimes associated with religious rituals such as fire walking, self-flagellation, and ritual crucifixion. They may involve social rituals, as with the Aztec and the Maya, who held regular public ceremonies in which elites in particular bled themselves—the higher the class, the more copious the bleeding.[1] Or they may arise from social customs including bodily mutilation or deformation of various body parts: lips, cranium, nose, ears, neck, fingers, genitals, feet, or skin.[2] Among criminals there is at least one case of normatively regulated self-injury: finger cutting by yakuza members as a form of self-punishment for mistakes. While some forms of DSH leave no trace, others leave permanent marks, and these are often used as hard-to-fake identifiers of group membership or status.

Some of the normatively prescribed forms of DSH may be explained by signaling theory. For example, in the literature on public ceremonies of autosacrifice in Mesoamerican cultures this is quite apparent: "those who could best endure the sufferings of the perforators [were believed] to be best suited for the highest positions and thus most deserving of the accompanying rewards.... Time and again we are told [by the testimonies of conquistadores and priests] that demonstration of the ability to endure the pain of bloodletting was a major means to status and advancement."[3] However, the landscape of regulated DSH, the object of many anthropological studies, is too rich and varied to be dealt with here and would take us too far from the criminal world.

I will focus instead on the cases in which self-harm, rather than being prescribed by group norms, is chosen by individuals, in particular when they find themselves in a conflict. As in the previous chapter, I will take into account the patterns of DSH in prisons and explore to what extent these are compatible with the predictions of signaling theory. In confining institutions both for adult and for juvenile offenders a variety of acts of DSH—self-cutting and mutilation, burning or scraping of the skin, head banging, swallowing of objects—occur with significant frequency. One review of the literature found prevalence rates ranging from 6.5 percent to 25 percent for male prisoners.[4] In the United Kingdom in excess of 130 episodes for every 1,000 male prisoners are reported each year.[5] In Italy data from official records of the Ministry of Justice on self-harming behaviors in prisons from 1990 to 2002 show a similar incidence of over one in ten individuals engaging in such acts.[6] And, clearly, official data understate the real extent of the practice, which some evidence suggests to be actively considered as an option by many inmates. In the Polish prisons that Kaminski had to patronize, his observation was that "practically every prisoner was contemplating at some point self-harm or faking it. Discussions of self-harm, both in general and of specific cases, were held almost daily."[7]

While suicide, the most extreme form of self-harm, has attracted the attention of social scientists for well over a century, DSH has oddly been ignored. When social scientists have paid attention to it, DSH has been considered as kindred to suicide. The criminological literature, well represented by Alison Liebling's research, converges in seeing DSH on a continuum with suicide, as an act born of distress and desperation prompted by the strains of prison life—essentially as a nonrational response to "pressures of isolation, inactivity, regulation, loss of control, and unpredictability."[8] Quoting Toch's study of 1975, Liebling wrote: "Acts of self-injury, like suicide attempts and suicides, are associated with feelings of melancholy tinged with self-contempt, depression, self-doubt, and the search for relief. They are acts of 'dead-end desperation,' expressing, 'an intolerable emptiness, helplessness, tension . . . a demand for release and escape at all costs.'"[9]

The academic literature on unregulated DSH, however, does not come from the social sciences but from psychology and psychiatry. Researchers in these disciplines tend to assume that DSH is a manifestation of some syndrome. The reasoning, to quip slightly, is that we are programmed to seek pleasure and avoid pain. If we inflict pain on ourselves, there must be something wrong with us. Occasionally, instrumental motives for DSH are recognized in the literature, such as inducing pity, seeking attention, blackmailing, avoiding dangerous chores, wanting to be moved to different wards, or gaining a more comfortable hospitalization. However, most explanations are psychological, and see agents as responding to a perturbed state of mind rather than to social circumstances: uncontrollable rage, the need to relieve tension, and denumbing are the sources of DSH most often mentioned.

These explanations may account for many instances of the phenomenon. Also, as Favazza, in his comprehensive review of self-harming practices, points out, the variety of forms of DSH is so rich that it would be impossible to explain the phenomenon with one grand theory.[10] However, my impression is that many studies are trapped in a hedonistic weltanschauung that eschews self-inflicted violence and explains any departures from pain avoidance as pathological—a perspective that emerged in the last few centuries in the Western world, and which is often dubbed—with a somewhat self-congratulating expression—"the

civilizing process."[11] There is a failure to recognize that mankind's famil-
iarity with pain—the fact that countless people, whom we cannot assume were all pathological, did and do inflict self-harm in a normatively
regulated manner—suggests that even in the unregulated cases there
could be more to DSH than mental imbalance. Precisely because it so
radically violates our expectations of self-preservation, all the more so
because of the "civilizing process," DSH acquires a special significance—
only cannibals can be blasé about another cannibal. DSH can provide
hard-to-fake information on unobservable traits of those who engage in
it: it shows one's ability to resist punishment, to endure pain, and indirectly a readiness to go to "mad" extremes. It separates those who merely
claim to have those traits from those who truly have them. In ordinary
circumstances we may have milder ways to signal fortitude; we have
time to prove ourselves, build a reputation, and display it when convenient. But in extreme conflict situations in which there is no easy way
out, in which stakes are high and opponents display aggressive intentions, the ordinary options may be unavailable.

Some of the psychological literature recognizes that subjects who engage in DSH do so not only to regulate "their own internal emotional
states" but are also "trying to manage situations in their environment."[12]
Favazza describes "pathological self-mutilation" as "a morbid form of
self-help" that reduces "troublesome and painful symptoms temporarily
but also serves the deeper purposes of healing, salvation and order."[13] Yet
what, exactly, these "situations" that need to be managed are, what the
threats to order that trigger DSH are, and how DSH can help regain it,
remain loosely specified.

No one to my knowledge has systematically considered DSH as a
signaling strategy designed to deter attackers,[14] although, once again,
Thomas Schelling came close and, in *The Strategy of Conflict*, he stressed
the strategic role of irrationality, including that of self-injury, in bargaining situations (the idea that irrational acts, and cultivating a reputation
for irrationality, can have strategic advantages in politics has become
known as the "madman theory"[15]). Schelling writes: "I am told that inmates in mental hospitals often seem to cultivate, deliberately and instinctively, value systems that make them less susceptible to disciplinary

threats and more capable of exercising coercion themselves. A careless or even self-destructive attitude toward injury—'I'll cut a vein in my arm if your don't let me . . .'—can be a genuine strategic advantage."[16]

In this example Schelling has in mind the blackmailing rather than the signaling effect of DSH. An agent threatens DSH, and since he is already believed to be mad (that is why he is an inmate in a mental hospital in the first place), this threat is credible; the opponent, who wants to avert the subject's DSH, yields to his requests.

However, Schelling's reasoning can be taken a step backward to cases in which an agent does not yet have a reputation for being mad but could gain an advantage by establishing one. To make his threat credible, the agent needs to signal first that he is mad, something than he can achieve by doing rather than just threatening DSH. Subsequently, if he issues threats that require a certain dose of "madness" to be carried out, these threats will be credible.[17] Schelling's interesting point, furthermore, is that this process need not be coolly thought out, and even subjects who are pathologically prone to DSH may realize its strategic advantage and turn their weakness into a strength.

A CLASSIC EXAMPLE OF DSH

The social sciences' failure to recognize the strategic use of DSH is puzzling when one considers that a classic example of signaling involves precisely a gruesome episode of self-harm.[18] It conveys with great clarity exactly how DSH gains its signaling force in a situation of conflict. We owe the story to Livy, the Roman historian. Around 500 BC, when the Etruscans were besieging Rome, a brave man known as Caius Mucius infiltrated the enemy's camp aiming to kill Porsena, the king of the Etruscans.

Afraid to ask which of the two was the king, lest his ignorance should betray him, Mucius struck as fortune directed the blow and killed the secretary instead of the king. . . . He was seized and dragged back by the king's bodyguard to the royal tribunal. Here, alone and helpless, and in the utmost peril, he was still able to inspire more fear than he felt.

Rather than acting cowed, Mucius threatens Porsena, hinting at the fact that many more like him are queuing up to try to kill him.

> The king, furious with anger, and at the same time terrified at the unknown danger, threatened that if [Mucius] did not promptly explain the nature of the plot which he was darkly hinting at he should be roasted alive. "Look," Mucius cried, "and learn how lightly regard their bodies those who have some great glory in view." Then he plunged his right hand into a fire burning on the altar. Whilst he kept it roasting there as if he were devoid of all sensation, the king, astounded at his preternatural conduct, sprang from his seat and ordered the youth to be removed from the altar. "Go," he said, "you have been a worse enemy to yourself than to me. . . . I send you away exempt from all rights of war, unhurt, and safe."[19]

The case of Mucius, who later gained the nickname Scaevola (left hand), has all the key ingredients of a signaling episode clearly laid out. Mucius is the signaler and Porsena the receiver. Mucius' interest is to avoid being roasted alive. Porsena in the story appears to be driven neither by a desire for vengeance nor by sadism, but merely by a strictly instrumental goal: make Mucius reveal everything about the plot to kill him. Porsena does not know and cannot observe Mucius' resistance to pain and degree of loyalty to his Romans compatriots. Mucius knows that he has both these properties to a high degree, but how does he communicate that credibly to Porsena?

He could just say that he will not give in to torture and invite Porsena to burn him alive. But words in a case like this are cheap; they fail to meet the cost condition posited by signaling theory, as they do not differentiate between a truthful and an untruthful claimant. Porsena knows that anyone could say that, and would in the circumstance. The question for Mucius is: Is there a signal that I can afford that is less costly than being tortured to death, but is such as to leave Porsena in no doubt that torturing me is pointless? Is there a signal that someone who merely pretends to have the resilience and loyalty that I have could not afford? Incinerating his hand is just that signal. Mucius pays a high cost, in terms of both pain and of inflicting a permanent handicap on himself, but still much better than death. Mucius keeps his life and honor, while Porsena avoids a useless act.

The high cost endured by Mucius is what persuades Porsena. If Mucius can do that to himself, Porsena infers, then there is little more that I can do to him, for he would die and bear extreme pain rather than betray his countrymen. More precisely, the credibility of the signal is sustained by the difference between the cost borne by Mucius and the cost that a hypothetical mimic could afford to pay. When such a difference cannot be bridged, the signal is perfectly discriminating. No feeble man pretending to be tough could have endured Mucius' feat.[20]

EVIDENCE FROM PRISON ETHNOGRAPHY

Is Mucius the protagonist of a perhaps mythical story conceivable only in a bygone era permeated with martial and manly virtues, or does he have modern incarnations? Is DSH in the modern world ever sustained by signaling reasoning of which the protagonists are aware, or has our civilizing culture made us too enfeebled to engage in such acts?

Ethnographic research on prisons yields some stark episodes that indicate that Mucius lives on. Marek Kaminski, who, as we know, was in prison in Poland in the 1980s, reports the following case:

The guard shoved Prince deeper inside the cell and closed the gate. A few tattooed figures instantly surrounded the new inmate. "Are you ..."—Prince interrupted the ritual question. "No, I am not a grypsman [a member of the prison fraternity]." The natives approached him closely. Prince took a blade out of his cuff and shouted crazily: "I am a sucker [low-ranking prisoner], sucker-madman! ... Leave me alone or—" he looked at the calm faces "I will slice you into pieces, grypsmen." Nobody moved. Prince quickly cut the skin of his left hand. Drops of blood marked the floor red. The grypsmen stepped back slowly. One of them made a decision. "OK, you are a sucker but you are a tough-boy. You are kind, we are kind. Now, clean it up."[21]

Prince, who told the story to Kaminski (who interprets it explicitly as a case of signaling), showed him a few five-centimeter-long scars, evidence that he had used the technique more than once. Prince tried to find out from the guards what kind of cell he was about to enter and resorted to DSH, which he regarded as a means of last resort, only if the cell was expected to be dangerous. Once, when Prince entered Kaminski's hospital cell, he was relaxed and did not cut, further evidence that his decision to inflict DSH was conditional on the level of threat he faced. As a junkie he could not aspire to join the prison fraternity, but DSH ensured that he was at least left alone.

Adrienne Rivlin (who was primed to look for signaling episodes by Heather Hamill and me) did some research for her master's dissertation in Grendon, a British prison housing about 240 of the country's most dangerous violent and sexual offenders, and found some episodes of DSH consciously aimed at deterring attackers.

Outside prison, if [P026] found himself in a fight and somebody was "squaring up to him" he would smash a bottle and cut himself and say "look you can't hurt me any more than I hurt myself." Whilst in a young offender's institute he was being bullied by "four black kids" who repeatedly harassed him, wanting him to "buy them stuff [drugs]." When P026 refused, the youths beat him up leaving him with a broken jaw and a fractured cheek bone. "As soon as I come back on the wing" the prisoner commented "I cut with a razor across the face and from then on they just left me alone. I just done me own thing. The way I see it I should have done this from the off." P026 disclosed that other inmates saw him as a "*bit mad*," someone not to be "messed with." He believed that he "kept constantly doing it so *it didn't matter what they'd done to me 'cause I'd already done it to meself.*"[22]

L007 described to me a similar set of signalling motives behind some acts of self-harm that had been privately disclosed to him at Grendon. An inmate who was a "people pleaser . . . a tea-boy, running round cleaning cells, ironing clothes for people" was being "walked all over, manipulated and used" so the prisoner decided to self-harm, according to the listener because: "if he cut himself—especially if other people knew he'd done it—he could say '*look I can hurt myself, you can't hurt me any more than that.*'" The inmate was seen as "*mad . . . as somebody not to be approached*" whose message, according to L007, was "you can't hurt me . . . you're not going to destroy me . . . you're not going to upset me. I am not being degraded or bullied or picked on."[23]

These episodes suggest that DSH can emit a double message. It signals "madness" or dangerousness and thereby induces *fear* in the receiver: *If I am crazy enough to do this to myself, imagine what I can do to you.* In this sense DSH makes threats credible or simply makes one threatening, exactly in the sense in which Schelling suggested referring to the advantages of "mad" acts generally. But by showing indifference or resilience to pain DSH also signals *fearlessness: If I can do this to myself, there is nothing you can do to me that would break me.* DSH can show that it is pointless to try to control the perpetrator by inflicting pain on him. Some acts of DSH send both messages to the audience, whereas in other cases, such as those in which there is asymmetry of force and the signaler could easily be overpowered by his opponents, the latter message is more relevant while the former is deactivated. In such cases DSH shows that "breaking" the signaler would be very costly or, in Mucius' case, impossible.

The strategic use of DSH, which clearly emerges from these accounts, has gone unrecognized perhaps because it causes revulsion among bystanders. This is conveyed by an episode in Patrick Chamoiseau's novel

Solibo Magnificent, which takes place in Martinique and involves a police-man, Diab-Anba Feuilles, and a "formidable street vendor," Doudou-Ménar, known as the Tigress. The Tigress is threatening both Diab and his chief, Bouaffesse. Diab's response goes as follows:

> Just because I am wearing the police blues of the Law you think: Oh yeah he's probably an auntie! . . . Well, I'm no auntie, I'm no auntie, just see if I'm an auntie . . .—and he brings his fist to his mouth (snap!), bites himself (hramphgrmm!) and shakes his head with rage tearing up his skin. A-ah! Lips open on a set of bloody teeth, he holds his wound out before his prey: Did you see that? He growls, bloody skin between his teeth, you saw that? *aprézan zafè tjou'w* [you should appreciate that forever], from now on it's going to be hell for you: FOR YOU I HAVE BLED! . . . Everyone is fro-zen. The fire-and-rescuemen move back. Those of us standing in line are seized by fright again. Bouaffesse has raised an eyebrow and flutters his eyelids: he is no longer enjoying this. Diab-Anba-Feuilles's freak show slightly lacks official dignity. *The bleeding trick, that's thug behaviour, not that of a police officer.*[24]

What is interesting about this episode is not only that a policeman too, at least in fiction, can defy the "civilizing process" and emulate thugs, but also the response of the crowd and of Diab's boss, who experience both fright and revulsion in equal measure. Diab's act violates a convention, which casts self-inflicted brutality as a mad, abnormal gesture unbefit-ting of an officer of the law. This reaction is germane to that caused by suicide attackers, berated in countless commentaries not so much be-cause they kill others as because they kill others by killing themselves. Killing others at the cost of one's life seems worse than just killing them by "conventional" means. Revulsion if anything adds to the strategic value of DSH, as we fear more what we cannot comprehend. What can be scarier than knowing that some people wish to kill you so badly that they are prepared to die for it?[25] What was once the stuff of heroes is now that of lowlifes and mad terrorists.

TYPES OF DSH

Ethnographic reports tell us that it is conceivable for DSH to be driven by an intent to signal dangerousness and fearlessness, but they do not tell us whether this motive can explain more than a few sporadic cases. Only research designed especially for the purpose of finding this out could provide a clear answer. For the moment, I can only take some preliminary steps and use the existing research to examine whether the styles and patterns of DSH occurrence that one can predict from the signaling hypothesis are compatible with the evidence. My predictions are identical to those concerning the likelihood of fighting that I presented in the previous chapter: namely that the greater the uncertainty over an individual's toughness and resilience, the greater the incentive not only to fight but also to self-harm (below I discuss the differences between the two responses). However, the interpretation of the secondary evidence in the case of DSH presents greater difficulties. For while fighting is by definition a "social" event and an obvious manifestation of conflict, the mere record of a DSH act does not reveal the extent to which it is related to conflict, let alone whether it is meant to signal anything. If we witnessed firsthand a DSH meant to signal, we would easily recognize this intention. Yet the evidence we have, collected by scholars and practitioners oblivious to the signaling possibility, is too lacking in details to allow us to determine the motivations with any degree of certainty. So, before reviewing the evidence related to the predictions, we need to take a few steps, at once logical and empirical.

First, we need to know whether DSH is more likely to occur in situations in which an individual fears being attacked. If DSH occurs independently of conflict with other inmates, then its causes are likely to be either solipsistic—one or another of the several pathological factors mentioned in the psychological literature—or driven by other instrumental motives such as affecting one's trial outcome or obtaining something from the authorities by feigning madness.[26] Either way, cases in which DSH is unrelated to conflict cannot be explained by our hypothesis.

The problem, however, is that even DSH that occurs in conflicts with other inmates does not ipso facto qualify as a signaling act. A conflict could simply cause unbearable stress and anxiety and lead one to harm oneself out of a sense of impotence and despair. To be a candidate for signaling, an act of DSH needs to pass two further tests. It needs to be nonsuicidal, and it needs to be displayed rather than performed in isolation and kept hidden.

Even if it passed both tests, however, rather than signaling toughness, DSH could be driven by the intent of inducing prison authorities to protect one. In this sense DSH could do more than just attract attention. It could still be a form of signaling, but of a different kind. After all, how does one demonstrate that one is in earnest when one pleads with the authorities: *Please transfer me, I'm in fear of my life?* Such a plea by itself may not be enough, as there could be many reasons for wanting a transfer. DSH could thus be a credible signal showing that one is genuinely at risk and seriously distressed. It would signal fearfulness rather than fearlessness. To further identify whether an incident of DSH is a signal of toughness or of desperation, we would need to know something about both the intended audience—inmates or prison authorities—and about the severity of the act. DSH aimed to show toughness and fearlessness needs to be performed in a seriously painful and forceful manner lest it induce the opposite effect and, by showing feebleness and inability to cope, encourage assaults rather than inhibit them.

Let us examine what we know about these features of DSH to check how large the pool of recorded self-harming acts potentially qualifying as signals is. As sources for this and the following sections, I used what I could find in the literature on prisons and other confining institutions, as well as three sets of interviews with a total of eight practitioners who have experience with DSH, one set of interviews in an adult prison and the other two in units for troubled and mentally disturbed adolescents. The interviews were carried out in 1998—I have been entertaining this hypothesis for a number of years—with my colleague James Sandham. We spoke with

- Dr. John Wheeler, senior medical officer, Tom McCulloch, nurse, and two prison guards, in HM Brixton Prison, London

(650 inmates, 550 of whom were on remand or in transit between prisons, about 100 of whom were residential sentenced prisoners, 80 of these with life sentences);

- Dr. John Wallace, consultant psychologist, and Jeremy McDowell, senior nurse manager, at St Andrews Hospital in Northampton–Adolescent Unit (the unit consisted of 36 beds and 29 patients, only 2 of which were males, fourteen to twenty-two years of age, average stay two to three years, communal open ward);
- Dr. Caroline Bradley, Wellcome research registrar, Department of Psychiatry, University of Oxford, and Dr. A.C.D. James, Highfield Adolescent Unit, Warneford Hospital (10–12 occupants, 5 males and 7 females at the time of interview, with an age range of thirteen to eighteen and an average stay of three months).

Conflict

A universally recorded fact is that DSH is far more frequent among the denizens of confining institutions than among those of the outside world. The rate of self-injury among prisoners "is reportedly much higher than the rate reported among the general population. This has been found even when equivalent populations have been studied."[27] "The incidence of self-injurious behaviour in young offenders held with adult prisoners is five times greater than amongst same-age adolescents in the general population."[28]

This difference, however, could be amplified by factors other than the higher frequency of conflict in prison relative to the outside world. It could be due to self-selection—inmates are on average both more mentally disturbed and more violent than the general population, and they could equally turn their violence against themselves as against others. In addition, unlike ordinary people, inmates are closely monitored, so their acts are more likely to be recorded than those which take place in the outside world, which come to light only when they are serious enough to require hospitalization (and even so people may claim that their injuries were the result of an accident rather than of self-harm). This condition, however, could have the reverse effect: precisely because they are "exposed to a restrictive environment and subject to the relevant control measures,"[29] which provide fewer means and opportunities to act freely, inmates could find it harder to self-harm than people in the privacy of their own homes. On balance therefore, although it could be exaggerated to an unknown extent, the difference between civilians' and prisoners' rates suggests that DSH is very likely to concentrate in prisons, where both conflict and aggression are more likely to occur and it is harder to select one's company. It is plausible to expect, in other words, that a fair share of inmates who self-harm in prison do not engage in it when they are free.

The evidence from self-reports and other sources gives support to the idea that DSH is often carried out by individuals who fear being attacked. A variety of studies find that bullying and DSH are correlated.[30] Livingston's survey of prison literature finds that DSH is more likely "when levels of supervision are at their lowest," implying that under weak supervision the opportunities to self-harm are increased.[31] However, when supervision is at its lowest the opportunities for aggression too are increased. Thus, by removing aggression, supervision could indirectly remove not only the opportunities but also the motivation to self-harm. Power and Spencer report that 78 percent of their sample of seventy-six young Scottish offenders who self-injured did it not because of feeling psychologically disturbed, but either for "manipulative reasons" (28 percent) or because they "anticipated friction with other fellow inmates" (50 percent).[32] According to Favazza, who cites an earlier study by Johnson and Britt, in prisons motives included, among others, "efforts to evade pressure from other inmates . . . , to avoid homosexual attack . . . , [and] anxieties over relationships with particular inmates, such as the fear of being killed if one was suspected of informing on other prisoners."[33] However, these statements are ambiguous, as they could refer to cases of DSH aimed at avoiding attacks or bullying by attracting authorities' attention and persuading them to take protective action, as well as cases aimed at signaling dangerousness or fearlessness.

Further circumstantial evidence proves the link between DSH and victimization. Among inmates in Italy, foreign men, whose minority status may put them at a higher risk of victimization, are "twice as likely to self-harm as residents."[34] The association of victimization with DSH also helps to explain a puzzling finding in Grendon: "Rates of suicide and self-injury are remarkably low at Grendon compared with other prison establishments. For example, Grendon's rate of self-harm is approximately 29 incidents per 1000 prisoners per year, compared to a rate in the mainstream prison service of between 130 and 137 incidents per 1000 prisoners per year."[35] Grendon is the only prison for men in the United Kingdom that is run as a therapeutic community. Its 240 inmates engage in a variety of programs including small- and large-group therapy, art therapy, and psychodrama. Grendon is considered a good prison by inmates and, since serious misbehavior can lead to being transferred to worse institutions, this is a strong incentive to behave. According to Rivlin, these prison conditions explain the lower rates of assaults, victimization, and bullying found in Grendon, which in turn could explain the lower rate of self-injury.

The link between DSH and conflict goes beyond prisons and is found among adolescents in schools. Schools share one key feature with prisons: one cannot choose with whom to interact as freely as one can in the wider world. Especially in nonselective state schools or in boarding schools, which even if selective are residential, bullies can be hard to avoid. Among high school students DSH (as distinct from suicide attempts) is much more common than one would think if one considers only hospitalization reports: for example, in the Oxford survey of over 6,000 fifteen- and sixteen-year-old pupils, 11.2 percent of females and 4.4 percent of males had engaged in DSH in the previous year.[36] In a comparative study of high school pupils in six European countries and in Australia, on average 9 percent of females and 2.6 percent of males had engaged in some form of DSH during the previous year.[37] A "systematic review of studies of this kind worldwide" found that the average frequency of self-reported acts of deliberate self-harm (as distinct from suicide attempts) among adolescents was 11.2 percent in the previous six months and 13.2 percent during their lifetime.[38]

Just as among prisoners, among adolescents too DSH is related to conflict situations. In the Oxford study, bullied boys were three times more likely and bullied girls twice as likely as the nonbullied to self-harm,[39] and 21 percent of the study subjects reported doing it also "to frighten someone." In a recent U.S. study, replying to a question that offered predefined multiple answers, 37.4 percent of adolescents who had engaged in "moderate to severe" DSH ticked as a reason for doing it "to get control of the situation"; 23.6 percent ticked "to avoid being with people"; and 22.4 percent "to get other people to act differently or change."[40] The predefined answers in these reports uniformly indicate a strategic use of DSH, but by endorsing these statements teenagers might be referring to blackmailing parents, teachers, or schoolmates into doing something they wanted them to do by proving that they were serious, as well as to signaling a cocktail of madness and dangerousness in order to be left alone.

Nonsuicidal Intent

The link between conflict and DSH indicates that many cases of DSH are not driven by solipsistic psychological processes. The latter should by definition occur in a manner unrelated to the threats of the environment, and should involve people who for one reason or another feel compelled to self-harm. Although it seems clear that conflict leads to DSH, the connection is not simple. Conflict leads to DSH in at least three ways (figure 5.1). Two are instrumental—to get help from prison authorities and to signal toughness—while the third is a response to the stress of a confining environment, which occurs when hopelessness and impotence generate aggressive impulses aimed at the self.

If instrumental, DSH should not be carried out with a *real* suicidal intent, which would of course be self-defeating. Furthermore, if one aims to obtain help by proving how badly one feels, then faking a suicide may work. But if one aims at inspiring fear and loathing, even just stating that one wants to commit suicide before engaging in an act of DSH may produce the opposite effect and reveal weakness and inability to cope, which could increase the chances of victimization. The evidence firmly indicates that, even excluding minimally harmful forms,

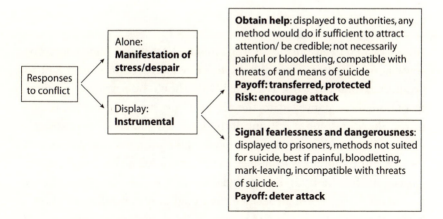

Fig. 5.1. Types of deliberate self-harm

the vast majority of acts of DSH in prisons are nonsuicidal. For example, "Holley and Arboleda-Flórez reported figures from Canada, in which 50% of all prisoners showed [self-injurious behavior], although 'only' 10% were at risk of suicide."[41] Power and Spencer report that in their sample of seventy-six male young offenders the potential for a lethal outcome was minimal in 92 percent of cases of DSH.[42] The least we can infer is that plenty of acts of DSH in prisons pass the nonsuicidal test. It does not follow of course that all nonsuicidal acts of DSH are signals, but only that the pool of acts that might be so is large. (It also does not follow that all acts classified as suicides were intended: acts of DSH that ended in death could be *failed* acts of signaling.)

Also, while a number of studies treat suicidal and nonsuicidal forms of DSH as points on a continuum of distress—"Self-injury may be the first overt symptom of a level of distress only steps away from a final act of despair"[43]—many other studies consider DSH and suicidal attempts as distinct phenomena "because they differ with regard to lethality, the suicidal intent and general clinical characteristics."[44] I suspect that the controversy could be resolved by observing in greater detail the features of the DSH acts and inferring from them the motivation: stress- and anxiety-induced desperate acts may indeed be on a continuum with suicide, but not all DSH acts are of this kind.

Display

An act of DSH can pursue an instrumental goal if and only if it is observable or otherwise knowable by those whose decisions are meant to
be affected. Thus, to work as a signal DSH should be performed in view
of or somehow conveyed to the relevant audience, authorities, or inmates. Short of doing it in front of the intended audience, there are two
other options: one is to rely on some credible source to spread news of
the act, and the other is to display the marks of self-harm (which is less
satisfactory, for the body-borne signal is easier to fake, as one could try
to pass off the results of an accident or a medically controlled act as self-
harm). Regardless, acts of DSH that are both carried out in isolation *and*
not intentionally advertised cannot be motivated by signaling even if
they are a response to conflict situations and even if they become accidentally known.

This requires an important clarification, which I have only hinted at
above. The motive that leads to the *production* of a signal in the form of
an act of DSH need not be signaling. The feature that turns an act into a
signal is whether the act is *displayed* or otherwise advertised to the audience of potential attackers. Production can even be generated by some
psychological urge, but for the signaling hypothesis to be applicable it
suffices that the display be strategically driven. In other words, even those
who deliberately harm themselves because of some psychological syndrome can strategically exploit their acts and display them or their consequences in the knowledge that the audience will be more likely to
leave them alone. The rationality of signaling does not require rationality
in the production of the raw material of the signal itself.[45] One can even
imagine acts of self-harm occurring first for reasons unrelated to signaling and becoming known to the relevant audience without the subject intending this, and still sort out the effect of a deterring sign. Realizing that effect, the subject can learn the strategic value of DSH and
have that in mind in subsequent acts, transforming a sign into a signal.
One can be mad and yet not stupid.

Evidence on the display of DSH is scarce, and since the exact conditions of the acts are rarely recorded—no one, unfortunately, seems to

have thought of display as a relevant feature—the evidence there is, is mixed. Liebling found that DSH in U.K. prisons was more likely to occur when the prisoner was alone, which is consistent with her interpretation of DSH as a desperate response of subjects who cannot cope with the prison environment.[46] However, Rivlin found that all men she interviewed, except one, "had disclosed their [self-injurious] behaviour to at least one other person at Grendon on at least one occasion."[47] Caroline Bradley told us that among her adolescents, "some do it in their rooms and may display later; some do it in view," and that they can "do it because of rage/depression but then display. They display to other patients and staff alike." Dr. James, who worked in the same institution, also mentioned group episodes in which self-cutting was carried out collectively in full view of everyone (more on group episodes in the epilogue below).

Finally, even DSH acts that are carried out when prisoners are alone may have a signaling effect at one remove. A minor offender known to James Sandham when he worked as welfare officer in the Oxford prison had managed to swallow some bedsprings. He was hospitalized, and his wildly extravagant gesture was divulged by the guards to the other inmates, who thought he was raving mad. When Sandham later met this inmate and said, "I hear you have swallowed some bedsprings," the inmate grinned widely, basking in his notoriety for madness.[48]

Means and Manner

Intentional display, whether direct or vicarious, is a key variable that if recorded would neatly separate instrumental and solipsistic motivations, and also help establish how much DSH is nonsuicidal, given that genuinely intended suicides are rarely committed in front of an audience. However, even if a display of DSH reveals an instrumental goal, it does not tell us whether the goal is to obtain assistance from the prison authorities or whether the DSH is a signaling act aimed at deterring attackers. A further clue could be found in the means chosen for self-harm. Suffocating, hanging, or swallowing poisonous substances, for instance, which are methods typical of suicide, do not suggest an intent

to signal toughness or fearlessness; at most, when not intended to be lethal, they could be chosen to prove one's genuine state of despair so as to
be moved or hospitalized. And, unlike swallowing bedsprings, a grue-
somely painful gesture, they would not help one gain a reputation for
"madness" but rather, at most, for inability to cope. To be effective, the
process itself of DSH must be painfully grueling. Mucius would have
been laughed at had he just extinguished a piece of cinder on his arm.
Had Sandham's prisoner swallowed an overdose of painkillers instead of
bedsprings, news of his gesture would not have elicited the same effect
among other inmates, for even though he might have later vomited violently and suffered nasty effects, the initial act would have been painless.

Also, assuming other options are available, for those who harm themselves to signal toughness and fearlessness it is a better "investment" to
pick methods that are not only costly in terms of pain but leave lasting,
observable marks. Again the evidence is not great, but we know that a
large share of DSH in prison consists of smashing or mutilating limbs,
piercing, and above all cutting one's hands, wrists, and especially arms.[49]
Slashing oneself draws blood, leaves scars, and is patently painful. (Considering the sizable presence of prisoners who have or are feared to have
HIV/AIDS, the drawing of blood has gained an extra threatening and
distancing effect.) In Grendon, "the most common methods included
cutting wrists, arms, legs and torso (especially aimed at veins) with glass
or a sharpened object such as a plastic knife, burning arms and legs with
a cigarette or a red-hot melted pen, scalding with hot water, overdosing
with pills, hitting walls and iron bars with one's head or fists, hunger
strikes and self-flagellation. Inmates often reopened existing wounds or
pushed on or picked at existing bruises, sores and scabs."[50]

Many of the above methods give prisoners the opportunity to etch
their CV on their own bodies and display it when needed just as Prince
showed his scars to Kaminski. Once again, it does not follow that self-
cutting is ipso facto meant for display, but it suggests that there is a pool
of DSH open to strategic use.

If inmates are not in a conflict situation or want to commit suicide or
do not display their DSH, then whatever act of self-harm they may commit cannot be motivated by signaling. If, furthermore, they self-harm in

a feeble way or pick means more apt to suicide, then their DSH cannot really work as a signal of dangerousness or fearlessness. However, when all these conditions are absent it is possible for DSH to be intended as just that signal, and more likely that agents will learn its strategic value regardless of why they first engage in it.

Payoff

If they work as effective signals of dangerousness and fearlessness, we should observe that acts of DSH reward perpetrators by making them feared and thus more likely to be left alone. DSH need not succeed all the time but must do so at least some of the time to be worth the price. If perpetrators get no reduction in their chances of being attacked following an act of DSH, this may be because, despite their signaling intent, their act was not convincing enough to deter attackers or even signaled weakness. A superficial cut performed while trembling and with tears in one's eyes is unlikely to impress inmates. Again, as it does not explicitly test this hypothesis, the literature does not record whether this is the case. However, Caroline Bradley told us that "self-cutters are less likely to be attacked. It's a distancing signal. Others are afraid or disgusted to come near self-cutters. Limbs carry proof of self-cutting and can be horrible to look at." According to Preti and Cascio, "adopting a self-harming behaviour creates an atmosphere of diffidence and suspicion that inevitably undermines the whole relationship network in the prison"[51]— and this may be precisely what self-harmers want to achieve. The man who swallowed bedsprings from that moment on was thought to be capable of anything and, according to Sandham, was left well and truly alone by the other inmates, who thought that he might either respond in crazily violent ways or at any rate be immune to coercion by pain.

The Brixton Prison interviewees, when asked about the payoffs of DSH, introduced a revealing distinction. They said that "genuine" self-harmers, namely those who through DSH express their desperation with prison conditions or their suicidal intent, were *more* likely to be bullied, whereas "manipulative" self-harmers were more likely to be left alone. The manipulative self-harmers were seen as stronger people, whose cut-

ting behavior was strategic rather than "genuine." By contrast, the genuine self-harmers, we can surmise, cannot send the two key messages—*if I
can handle this, there is nothing you can do to me that will break me,* or *if I can
do this to me, imagine what I can do to you*—for the fact that they are "poor
copers" is somehow apparent by their demeanor and manner of action.
In fact, unless what they want to signal is precisely that message of being
poor copers in order to be moved or hospitalized, it is rational for them
to harm themselves in isolation and hide it, for if detected by other inmates it may put them in a worse position. (One man whom Rivlin interviewed "admitted never having spoken to anyone about his chronically self-injurious behaviour before. . . . Twice he has tied a plastic bag
around his head in an effort to commit suicide. He had never told anyone of his suicide attempts because 'that sort of thing is personal.'")[52]

The Brixton officers also told us that the manipulative self-harmers
inflict more serious damage to themselves than do the genuine ones.
This could be because the manipulative ones want to emit, in signaling
theory jargon, a more discriminating and thus threatening signal—*this
ain't just a scratch.*

The existence of two types of self-harmers, "poor copers" and "tough
guys," can be inferred also from the inconsistency of the data on the *timing* of DSH, which seems to occur both at times in which prisoners are
alone and at times in which they are with others. Livingston found that
in two studies DSH peaked in the early morning and at night,[53] times at
which inmates in solitary-cell prisons are alone. However, this accounted
for only 50 percent of the instances observed, and other studies have
found that DSH was evenly distributed across times of the day and the
week.[54] The varying distribution may depend on the proportion of "manipulative" acts that are meant to be displayed relative to the "genuine"
ones that are carried out alone and possibly kept secret. Unless one can
somehow control for this distinction, the temporal dimension of DSH
would inevitably oscillate from one study to the next depending on the
relative frequency of the two types.

In conclusion, the evidence indicates that DSH occurs with much
greater frequency when aggression and victimization are more likely to
occur, that most instances of DSH are nonsuicidal, that at least some are

directly or indirectly displayed, and that some yield a payoff of the type that the signaling hypothesis would predict.

UNCERTAINTY

As I explained in the previous chapter, we can expect that wherever there is a risk of aggression and victimization, possible victims will try at first to convey their potential for violence rather than resort to actual violence. If their nonviolent displays succeed in deterring attackers, then there is no need for violence toward others or self. Dr. Wallace of the Adolescent Unit at St Andrews Hospital in Northampton told us that his patients tell each other stories about their contacts with criminals outside and boast about things they did, but clearly their tales if meant to flag their toughness must be too "cheap" to be persuasive, for most of them end up self-harming. With one exception: a young woman who was quieter than most and, unlike most other patients, did not self-harm. "She instilled fear in others by her demeanour." She turned out to be a murderer. (The story came up when he told us that staff are more worried by patients who sit quietly, smile, and observe than by those who self-cut.)

Yet two conditions may constrain this option and make either fighting or DSH more likely to occur: one is environmental and the other concerns the individual's history of violence. The ability to test predictions that DSH is associated with measures of these conditions is weakened by the fact that some of the same factors could increase the likelihood of other types of DSH as well. But before worrying about this let us see what the data reveal.

Limited Knowledge

The environmental condition consists of any factor that limits the knowledge of one's resilience to violence or one's fighting prowess, thus increasing the uncertainty about inmates' traits. One such factor is directly related to the number of new individuals encountered who know nothing about each other's traits. For instance, if there is a high turnover of inmates or prisoners are frequently reallocated to new wings and cells, uncertainty about each other's toughness grows. We saw in the previous chapter that the frequency of fighting grows under such conditions, but what about DSH?

Overcrowding in prisons, a proxy for more encounters, increases the rate of DSH.[55] We also find more DSH in remand prisons or remand sections of prisons, which are a proxy for higher turnover, for inmates remain in this type of institution for shorter periods.[56] The Brixton interviewees confirmed this, telling us that there are "many more cutting and self-harm incidents amongst the remand population than amongst the more settled lifers." "Juniority" in the institution, again a proxy for being both unknown and ignorant of others, has the same effect: "about one-third of self-injury episodes have been found to occur within the first week of imprisonment"[57] or during early periods of custody.[58] According to Dr. Wallace, the longer they stay, the more infrequent and less harming the episodes of DSH become. In his experience length of stay is more important than age. Dr. James told us that a newcomer's arrival can trigger a cycle of DSH in which both the newcomer and the residents are involved, suggesting that the practice is used both to measure the "quality" of newcomers and to show to newcomers the quality of the residents.

Lack of "Violence Capital"

The second condition that makes DSH more likely to occur is when prisoners have little or no experience with violence—when, in other words, potential victims lack a significant "violence capital" to display and thus deter attackers without actually committing violence. Those less versed or less experienced in the use of violence will feel greater pressure to prove their mettle, not only by fighting, as we have seen in the previous chapter, but also by engaging in DSH. Weaker, less violent prisoners should deliberately harm themselves more often.

Most studies find that a majority of self-injurers are in prison for nonviolent crimes, or at most they find no relation between DSH and being in prison for a crime of violence.[59] DSH is also more common among first timers (Brixton interview). Remand prisons, a proxy not only for higher turnover but also for less hardened criminals, have, as we know, the same effect. Women, who are only about 5 percent of the prison population, are universally recorded to engage in DSH more than men.[60] For instance, the study on Italian prisons, which relies on a large number of cases from 1990 to 2002, finds a DSH rate among women of 19 percent and among men of 7.6 percent.[61]

Age too, all else the same, should be inversely correlated with violence capital, as on average a younger individual would have had less time to acquire a reputation for violence. In Brixton the interviewees told us that DSH was more common among young than among adult prisoners. The literature converges in finding an inverse correlation between age and DSH for prisoners under twenty-six. However, when considering adult prisoners the relationship between age and DSH becomes unclear, and different studies have found a negative, a positive, and no relation.[62] In all likelihood one's seniority—the amount of time spent in prison—works as a confounding factor more among adult than among young inmates: among young prisoners age correlates more with being in prison for the first time or with having been in prison for shorter periods, hence the clearer inverse relation between DSH and age; while among adults age and seniority are less likely to be tightly coupled, hence the cacophony of findings.

A majority of studies, mostly from the United States, report a tendency "for black prisoners to be under-represented in the self-injury figures."[63] Haycock conjectures that the difference could be partly explained away by the fact that most prison officers in the United States are white and would be more inclined to record DSH by white inmates. Moreover, he contends, whatever difference remains might be explained by the consequences of the bias: white guards would be more likely to respond helpfully to DSH when performed by white than by black prisoners, and white prisoners, anticipating this, would be more likely to resort to DSH.[64]

However, the correlation was confirmed by our Brixton interviewees ("self-harm is more common among white prisoners"), and in Britain the racial divide is not as marked as in the United States, and among our interviewees there was a Caribbean male nurse.[65] According to some scholars this difference, which they take as genuine, is explained by the fact that blacks, used to ghetto life, are not as easily stressed by prison life as whites are. This account is rejected by Haycock, who points out that it does not square with the fact that, according to several studies, rates of DSH among white and black men in the relevant age category outside prison are either similar or higher among black men.[66] These apparently contradictory findings are consistent with the idea that blacks on average may acquire more violence capital outside prisons or through previous incarcerations, which they can display when in prison and thus have *less* need to self-harm to prove their toughness. In short, race per se would have nothing to do with DSH.

Wright, using multiple indicators of stress and aggressive and self-aggressive behavior in a sample of 942 male inmates drawn randomly from ten prisons in the New York area, found that blacks and whites experience incarceration in very similar terms. More interesting still, he found evidence that the differences in terms of adjustment to prison life depend on (1) prior experience of incarceration regardless of race (in other words, people with more violence capital do better in prison), and (2) level of education: the higher this is, the more likely it is that the prisoner reports "being taken advantage of or hurt. These individuals are less likely to be experienced in institutions or on the 'street,' and are the type of inmates referred to as 'lambs.'"[67] Thus, Wright points out, "past findings of differences among black and white prisoners may be attributable to the fact that blacks have been previously incarcerated"[68] more frequently than whites, and that they are on average likely to be less educated than whites. In a series of multivariate models, Wright found that self-injury and assaults suffered are indeed positively correlated with education, and that race, while having no effect on assaults, still has an independent effect on self-injury, in the sense that blacks are less likely to engage in it.[69] This could be due to the fact that Wright's measures, education and prior incarceration, do not capture the entire differential street experience across race.[70]

CONCLUSIONS

The presence of poor copers who deliberately harm themselves out of desperation or to obtain protection by prison authorities makes it difficult to interpret the regularities in the patterns of DSH occurrence as evidence that prisoners resort to hurting themselves to deter attack: the same factors that could affect the rate of self-harm inflicted because of the former reasons could also affect it when done because of the latter. Because most studies have been done without recording all the key features of DSH episodes, it is hard to say, for example, whether weaker categories of inmates resort to DSH more because of one factor or the other, and the evidence is inconclusive. Still, the fact that DSH follows the same pattern that we found for fighting is a sign that the signaling hypothesis is at the very least a plausible candidate to account for a significant portion of DSH.

A question that remains concerns the relations between fighting and DSH: if the same conditions increase the chances of both fighting and DSH, which further conditions lead prisoners to choose one or the other?

First, the two options are not necessarily alternatives but may form a sequence: one could self-harm first, and if that did not suffice to deter attack one might have to fight anyway.[71] Next, the two options are not always identical, for DSH does not signal exactly the same quality as fighting does: had Mucius been challenged to a fight by one of Porsena's soldiers, he would have accepted perhaps, but then he would have shown his fighting prowess rather than his ability to endure extreme pain, which saved him from torture. Unlike Mucius, Prince was not going to be tortured but attacked, so he could arguably have chosen to fight the grypsmen to prove his toughness. But, especially if an agent fears he is significantly weaker than his opponent, DSH may be a better solution than fighting, as the outcome remains in the perpetrator's control. One can calibrate the degree of pain when it is self-inflicted—whereas in a fight one might be much more severely hurt, perhaps even killed. In addition, demonstrating fearlessness without harming anyone else matters, because harming the other person could provoke subsequent retaliation (by that individual or his mates). If one engages in DSH, by contrast, the tough guys can respect or at least avoid one without feeling that their reputation is being diminished if they choose to do nothing.

The idea that asymmetry of force may encourage DSH gains support from the fact that, in the few detailed stories of signaling DSH that we have, the self-harmers were invariably one against many—Mucius was up against the whole Etruscan camp, Prince entered a cell full of menacing grypsmen, and of the two prisoners in Grendon one was up against "four black kids" and the other was "walked all over, manipulated and used" by an unknown number of coprisoners. Had they chosen to fight their oppressors, they would have been easily overpowered.

The hypothesis can be generalized to argue that the greater the asymmetry of force between the victim and his attackers, the higher is the probability of DSH relative to that of fighting. All else the same, DSH should be more frequent than fighting (1) the more frequent the presence of gangs or clusters of cooperating prisoners ready to collectively "greet" newcomers, and (2) the greater the heterogeneity of violence capital across inmates, which implies a higher number of asymmetrical encounters; for instance, controlling for the level of threat and individuals' levels of violence capital, younger people in adult prisons should self-harm more and fight less, while younger people in young people's institutions should fight more and self-harm less.

EPILOGUE

Deliberate self-harm does not signal only dangerousness and fearlessness, and dangerousness and fearlessness are not signaled by DSH alone. It may be worth elaborating on these two points to give the reader a better sense of the larger family of messages that DSH can convey as well as of the larger set of kindred signaling behaviors to which DSH belongs.

In addition to signaling dangerousness or fearlessness, there are instances in which DSH signals the intensity of one's beliefs or the readiness to sacrifice life and limb for the sake of collective goals.[72] In these cases fearlessness is not the end signal but a means to signal something else, related to the motivation of one's gestures. Martyrs of all persuasions have chained themselves, starved themselves, or burned themselves alive to bear witness, to protest against injustice and oppression, to signal the intensity of their convictions and a determination to fight on, cost what it may.[73] Even a whole class of suicide missions can be interpreted as having a signaling motive.[74]

Reviewing the empirical findings on DSH in confining institutions, I encountered a feature of DSH that suggests it can at times be used as a test of loyalty, of one's willingness and capacity for self-sacrifice within a group, rather than as a signal of dangerousness or fearlessness. This feature lies in the semiorganized form that DSH sometimes takes in confining institutions. Dr. Wallace used the term "queen bee" to refer to a person who initiates a cycle of DSH quite deliberately, organizing others to do it. Another study of disturbed adolescents also identified a few subjects as being at the center of orchestrating collective DSH activities.[75] Group episodes of DSH, usually involving self-cutting, require both complicity in preparation and competition in execution. In cases such as these, the practice reaches an almost ritualistic form, a kind of primitive version of the bloodletting rituals the Aztecs used to establish and reinforce their hierarchy. It is worth mentioning that a milder form of self-harm affecting group hierarchy is reported also among U.S. college sororities in a study titled "Social Contagion of Binge Eating" by Christian Crandall: "Evidence of social pressures to binge eat were found as well. By the end of the academic year, a sorority member's binge eating could be predicted from the binge-eating level of her friends. As friendship groups grew more cohesive, a sorority member's binge eating grew more and more like that of her friends."[76] This kind of episode does not suggest an intent to signal dangerousness or fearlessness; rather it signals a kind of resilience through willingness to engage in a pointless and somewhat painful activity, which precisely because it is pointless cannot be motivated by any other reason than that of conforming to the group norm at a cost to oneself. Kaminski observed similar competitions in Polish prisons over doing push-ups or drinking large quantities of water, which unlike food is an unlimited resource in jail. (Several studies report episodes of "contagion" and "epidemics" concerning more serious forms of DSH.[77] "Contagion" is also the "strongest predictor" of DSH in the Oxford school study: males with a friend who deliberately harmed himself were seven times more likely to do it themselves and females four and a half times more likely.)[78]

The study of binge eating offers evidence also on the interesting question of whether in collective episodes DSH is more likely to escalate in seriousness or conform to certain standards: "in one sorority, the more one binged, the more popular one was. In the other, popularity was associated with bingeing the right amount: those who binged too much or too little were less popular than those who binged at the mean."[79] Since both outcomes occurred, the question remains of why a normative standard evolved in only one case.

Deliberate self-harm, on the other hand, is not, of course, the only type of act that can signal dangerousness and fearlessness. DSH has kindred behaviors, which may convey either of those two messages or both. Fighting or credibly spoiling for a fight, as we have seen in the previous chapter, is one such option. It shows toughness, in the sense of both aggressiveness and fearlessness. Displaying aggressiveness reveals disregard for personal safety, and showing fearlessness can induce fear in an opponent because being fearless means that one would not be afraid of entering into a fight. Fearlessness makes one more threatening, and dangerousness implies fearlessness.

The two messages are not necessarily coextensive, however. Engaging in acts of gratuitous violence, such as hitting innocents, does not show fearlessness; it only induces fear. A treacherous attack, such as shooting someone in the back in cold blood, says nothing of the agent's capacity to bear injuries "like a man." The term *vicious wimp* is not an oxymoron. On the other hand, taking a beating without being broken or ratting can signal resilience and loyalty, but not necessarily aggressiveness. The tough nonaggressive type also exists.

As for dangerousness, as we have seen in chapter 1, demonstration of the ability to kill, including killing innocent people, is a common entry test in criminal or violent illegal organizations generally. It is also used to induce fear. Members of the Aryan Brotherhood, an infamous U.S. prison gang, when entering in a new prison "would often carry out a 'demonstration' killing or stabbing in order to terrorize the inmate population.... 'We wanted people to think we were a little crazy,' Thompson said"[80] (Michael Thompson was a leader of the Aryan Brotherhood who now, while still in prison, collaborates with the authorities against his former gang mates).

Going from fact to fiction, in *The Long Goodbye*, a film by the late Robert Altman based on Chandler's novel, a gangster hits his girlfriend with a soda bottle and then snarls at Philip Marlowe: "Now that's someone I love. Think what could happen to you."[81] Though unlikely to endear oneself to one's girlfriends, this sends the same message as DSH at a lesser cost to oneself.

Harming people one loves—a form of vicarious self-harm—can also signal loyalty. In a gruesome story, reported by the investigating magistrate, Lucrezia Pascale was found dead and headless near Altamura, Apulia, Italy, in 1988. She was the girlfriend of a local mobster, Domenico Manfredi, member of a criminal fraternity known as "La Rosa." According to two members of the group who later turned state's evidence, Lucrezia was killed by Manfredi himself because it had become known that she had carelessly talked about Manfredi's criminal organization to some of her friends. Manfredi was summoned by his bosses and severely reprimanded. Of his own initiative, "in order to demonstrate his loyalty to the clan and remove any possible suspicion Manfredi did not hesitate to sacrifice the person he loved." He took the head to the bosses as proof of the deed.[82]

Another episode of "acting crazy" in order to show dangerousness, this time fictional, was detected by Robert Frank in Elmore Leonard's novel *Glitz*. Vincent Mora, a detective, whose girlfriend, Iris, has been murdered in Atlantic City suspects that Ricky, a mob underling, might know something about her death. But how can he persuade a mobster to reveal all he knows? Mora waits for Ricky, who is in a bar collecting protection money, leaning against Ricky's Eldorado. When the mobster Ricky comes out, the following dialogue occurs:

"Get away from the car."

"Somebody smashed your window," Vincent said.

"Where?" He came in a hurry now. Vincent nodded toward the driver's side and Ricky moved past him, intent. Vincent followed, walked up next to him.

"What're you talking about? The window is okay!"

Vincent looked at it, his expression curious. He brought the chunk of masonry out of his raincoat to slam it in the same motion against the tinted glass and the window shattered in fragments. He turned to Ricky and said, "No, it's broken, see?"

Ricky said, "You crazy?" With amazement. "You fucking crazy?" Vincent liked the question and liked the way Ricky stood there in a state of some kind of shock, those dead eyes showing signs of life for the first time, wondering. What is this? His expression, his pocked faced made him appear vulnerable, sad, the poor guy wanting to know what was going on here, perplexed.

Mora succeeds in making Ricky spill the beans, and as Frank points out, "Mora's ploy with the chunk of masonry works because it is not something just anyone could pull off. Most mild-tempered, dispassionate people simply couldn't have done it. The costly-to-fake principle gives Ricky good reason to suspect Mora really is extremely tough or crazy, or both."[83]

While the acts described in the above episodes signal primarily dangerousness, other acts signal primarily fearlessness. Some such acts are related to DSH, but the harm to self is *risked* rather than invariably incurred. One consists of threatening an opponent by moving closer to him, making it easier for the opponent to strike one and thus signaling that one is not afraid of the opponent's attack. Here there is no immediate cost to self; the cost is merely potential and due to the increased risk of suffering should the opponent choose to attack.[84]

Risk-taking activities can be pushed to extremes and de facto amount to a form of vicarious DSH, namely provoking others so as to induce them to inflict harm on one, and then using the harm suffered as a signal of prowess and daring. In these cases one takes a risk and wants this action to result in some harm. The Hoods, a group of Catholic West Belfast youth who studiously misbehave—joyriding, engaging in drug dealing, and generally causing annoyance to their community—are a remarkable instance of this case recounted by Heather Hamill. While so doing they are well aware that the IRA—who act as local enforcers—will punish them, by kneecapping or by inflicting atrocious beatings. Not only are they aware of the consequences, but most of them once summoned by the IRA show up to receive the punishment at the appointed time and place. Being punished, taking it "like a man," and, once out of hospital, starting to misbehave again become the ultimate signals of status in their group. The value of a beating is manifest also in the fact that in a few occasions some of the Hoods faked having received one.[85]

A partially germane case is the *Mensur*, a highly codified duel common in some German student fraternities or *Corps* since the nineteenth century and still practiced today. In the Mensur, unlike the unilateral provocations of the Hoods, both parties mutually seek to fight. The weapon wielded by the fencers, the *Schläger*, is similar to but heavier than a saber. "[F]encers are protected by a chain mail shirt, chain mail gauntlets, padding on the throat and right arm, and steel goggles with a nose guard. They fence at arm's length and stand more or less in one place, while attempting to hit the unprotected areas of their opponent's face and head. Flinching or dodging is not allowed, the goal being less to avoid injury than to endure it stoically. Two physicians are present (one for each opponent) to attend to injuries and stop the fight if necessary."[86]

As noted by Kevin McAleer in his study of dueling in Germany, "in the Mensur the duel's means and ends were reversed. The duel's design was to terminate a dispute; in student circles, disputes were devised to foster phony duels."[87] The purpose of the Mensur was as much to be wounded as to inflict wounds on the opponent. It was not only a test of courage but "was also the way to acquiring a 'badge' of courage. The duelling scar (Schmiss, often called Rennomierschmiss or 'bragging scar'—and it was not misnamed) was of inestimable value because it was the upscale tattoo, borne by a generation of doctors and jurists and professors and officials, certifying the proprietor's claim to both manly stature and cultivated rank."[88] The value of the scar to the bearers is testified by the deliberately rough way in which the wounds were stitched and often tampered with so as to turn them into gory sights, hence more visible and impressive, and also by two reported cases of students who, having failed to acquire a scar from the *Schläger*, just like some of the Hoods resorted to trickery, one hiring a surgeon and the other using a razor.[89] The Mensur amounts to a sort of cooperatively inflicted self-harm, to the joint production of a signal of courage—*I slash your face, you slash mine.*

A related category of signals of fearlessness draws its cost from defying not an opponent's attack but the risk posed by impersonal forces. Russian roulette, the deadly game of chance par excellence, fits into this category. The standard form consists of inserting a bullet in a six-shot revolver, pointing it to one's head, and pulling the trigger, with one chance in six of being killed. In his autobiography, Malcolm X says that when he was a member of a gang of burglars he played Russian roulette, pulling the trigger three times to convince his partners in crime that he was not afraid to die. In the epilogue to the book, Alex Haley says that Malcolm X revealed to him that, with magician skills, he had hidden the bullet in his palm instead of inserting it in the revolver.[90] Other variants include competitive games of nerve known as "chicken games," which can be staged either against opponents or against "nature"—wave chasing, cliff jumping, red-light crossing. British teenagers have been known to put their heads on railway tracks and compete over who moves away last as the train approaches. Modern technology allows youth to film themselves engaging in such activities, and supplies them with a lasting record that they can display to a wider audience than the witnesses, an incentive bound to increase the attractiveness of these practices.[91]

Taking the risk of being harmed, just like actual self-harm, can even signal the veracity of one's statements, in which case the signaling of courage through risk taking is not the end signal but a means to signaling truthfulness. The stirring story of Zossima's religious conversion in *The Brothers Karamazov* illustrates this point. In his youth, before becoming a monk, Zossima provokes a rival who had married a woman he fancied so as to force him into a duel. The night before the duel, how-

ever, Zossima flies into a rage and, for trivial reasons, punches his innocent orderly hard. Shaken by his behavior, that very night Zossima real-
izes the evil of his ways and without hesitation begins his quest for
self-reform. But the duel had been called. . . .

> So we reached the place and found them there, awaiting us. We
> were placed twelve paces apart; he had the first shot. I stood gaily,
> looking him full in the face; I did not twitch an eyelash, I looked
> lovingly at him, for I knew what I would do. His shot just grazed
> my cheek and ear.
> "Thank God," I cried, "no man has been killed," and I seized my
> pistol, turned back and flung it far away into the wood. "That's the
> place for you," I cried. . . .
> The seconds, especially mine, were shouting too: "Can you dis-
> grace the regiment like this, facing your antagonist and begging his
> forgiveness! If I'd only known this!"
> I stood facing them all, not laughing now. "Gentlemen," I said,
> "is it really so wonderful in these days to find a man who can re-
> pent of his stupidity and publicly confess his wrongdoing?"
> "But not in a duel," cried my second again.
> "That's what's so strange," I said. "For I ought to have owned my
> fault as soon as I got here, before he had fired a shot, before leading
> him into a great and deadly sin; but we have made our life so gro-
> tesque, that to act in that way would have been almost impossible,
> for *only after I had faced his shot at the distance of twelve paces could my
> words have any significance for him, and if I had spoken before, he would
> have said, 'He is a coward, the sight of the pistols has frightened him, no
> use to listen to him.'"* [92]

Even his comrades in arms come eventually to be persuaded that the
way Zossima behaved did not disgrace their regiment and that his newly
found pacifism is genuine—"If he had been afraid of being shot, he
would have shot his own pistol first before asking forgiveness, while he
flung it loaded into the forest. No, there's something else in this, something original." Interestingly, had Zossima chosen to self-harm and, say,

shot himself in a foot to stop the duel, he would not have produced an effective signal, as he might still have been deemed a coward engaging in a damage-limitation stunt. Only by putting himself at the mercy of his opponent and risking his life without "twitching an eyelid" did he prove both his courage and the truthfulness of his conversion.

PART 2   Conventional Signals

CHAPTER 6

Conventional and Iconic Signals

In part 1, I explored a class of signals the basic aim of which is to prove to a receiver that something which could be misrepresented is true, be it a criminal's credentials, trustworthiness, or the toughness of the signaler. These signals typically consist of some "costly" action—killing, fighting, self-harming, taking risks, burning bridges, or disclosing incriminating information about oneself. The signaler, by engaging in such action, tries to persuade the receiver in one of two ways that he is truthful: by showing that he has constraints that would prevent him from being dishonest even if he wanted to be, or by performing actions that an untruthful signaler could not afford. These signals are the hard core of criminal communications.

Criminals, however, have a different set of communicative interests that are not met by this class of signals. They want to communicate cheaply and accurately, and to do so they use, just like anybody else, language or other symbolic means. They face a major hurdle, however, one that we all face when we need to communicate with others privately—when, that is, we want our signal s to be received or understood only by A and not by B. If A receives s and clearly interprets it, we benefit. But if A fails to receive s or misinterprets it, or, worse, if B receives s, we suffer. For ordinary people the cost may be embarrassment; for criminals it may be jail or retribution.

This hurdle of communication-cum-secrecy manifests itself in three different circumstances, namely when criminals want to

1. communicate with known colleagues and do not want rivals or law enforcers to intercept or understand their communications or, if they do understand them, want to make sure that no harm results—this we can call *the communication problem*;

2. identify fellow members of an organization whom they do not yet know personally while not being recognized by a third party—*the identification problem*;
3. advertise their goods and services to attract interested people from a pool of individuals whom they do not know at all— brothel owners, drug dealers, illegal bookies, corruptors and corruptees, and generally all those, whether individuals or groups, who benefit from attracting new customers or suppliers face what we may call *the advertising problem*.

In short, before they can ask themselves whether a signal is credible and resort to the hard-to-fake communicative strategies, criminals need to find secret or at least noncommittal ways to communicate, make themselves identifiable, and flag their wares and interests. In this chapter, I consider some solutions to these problems, which lie largely in the skillful use of conventional and iconic signals. I will first describe the properties of these signals and then illustrate how they are employed in tackling the three problems.

CONVENTIONAL AND ICONIC SIGNALS

A conventional signal can be anything—a name, an expression, a logo, a style, a tune, an item of clothing, a nod, or standing on a particular street corner. It can be as simple as a hand gesture or as a rich as a whole language. Communication can successfully rely on a conventional signal provided that at least two people, the signaler and the receiver, understand it as having a meaning and the meaning is the same for both.

In order to understand how conventional signals convey information it is useful to contrast them with the hard-to-fake signals I discussed in part 1. In the latter the receiver's inference from a signal to a certain property of the signaler appeals to the fact that only someone who has that property can afford to send the signal—only someone not afraid of dying can play Russian roulette. In conventional signals the inference that informs does not work in that way. Instead, the receiver somehow comes to have the belief that the signaler has chosen the strategy *if the property or event* k *is the case, then send signal* s, but not because this choice of the signaler is in any way related to what the signaler can or cannot afford.

The essential property of a conventional signal is to bear an arbitrary link with what it signifies—it is an "arbitrary signifier," a concept first introduced in linguistics by Ferdinand de Saussure. Conventional signals are *contingently* associated with the message they transfer; in other words there is nothing in conventional signals that *causally* connects them to a particular quality or message of the signaler. While signals that work on cost discrimination allow the receiver to deduce that the signaler has a particular quality, conventional signals denote by induction. As such they do not inform us directly about the properties of the signaler. We may know that, say, clapping is a signal of being pleased with a performance, but we know this not because it is too costly for someone who is displeased to clap. We know it because of the widespread social under-standing that arbitrarily posits an association between clapping and satisfaction.

The contingency of the link between signal and message when pri-vately established allows "insiders" to keep "outsiders" in the dark as to what they are communicating to each other. If two people privately agree that *s* means *k*, a third party intercepting *s* would not know what *s* means. If I say "harvest is nigh" having previously agreed that it means *kill that man*, an English speaker who overhears my utterance will under-stand that expression but miss the intended message. If, more prudently still, instead of using words we agree that when I sport a tie with a pat-tern of tiny horseshoes it means *kill that man*, an innocent observer would not even understand that wearing the tie was a signal. Card play-ers who jointly cheat know how to exploit this property of conven-tional signals. Tattoos can flag inmates' "number of kills and criminal specialization,"[1] but if there is nothing in the tattoo design as such to reveal those features to a third party, only observers who have prior knowledge of the meaning of a certain tattoo will be able to grasp its message. Furthermore, even if a third party does suspect that *s* means *k*, the arbitrariness of the link gives the signaler a chance to deny either that he meant what he did or that he meant to signal anything at all—"pace Jeeves, I just like horseshoe ties!" It is one thing to suspect that for a Japanese man having tattoos all over one's chest is a sign he is a yakuza, quite another to treat that as definitive evidence.

A belief linking s to k can emerge in a number of ways. The simplest way is by agreement between two or more agents ("if I scratch the tip of my nose that means . . ."). Another is via an authority's action, which stipulates and informs all those concerned that from now on s means k (plenty of examples below). Unlike agreement, this requires more than two parties and preexisting communicative links between them. A third way is by exploiting a well-known association between s and k that arises from public events or the actions of an innocent third party but has nothing to do with the communication problem of the agents. I discuss the grand example of this—exploiting the verbal, visual, and musical inventions of gangster movies—in chapter 10. Yet another way in which conventional signals emerge is by unplanned progressive diffusion: they may, in other words, emerge "naturally" without an agreement or an authority intervening to establish them.[2] The emergence of nicknames, as we shall see in chapter 9, is a case of this kind. There is no agreement that someone should be called, say, "Big George." It is simply the case that that nickname may have been invented for fun, then used in successive encounters between individuals and spread in that way.

Conventional signals are often understood, as Quine put it in the introduction to David Lewis's book on conventions, as being characterized by "a certain indifference: the syllable 'big' could have meant 'small' for all we care, and the red light could have meant 'go.'"[3] (In *Gulliver's Travels*, Swift made fun of the passions that people feel over issues about which they should be indifferent. He tells the story of the Little-Endians of Lilliput and the Big-Endians of Blefuscu, who go to war over which end of an egg should be broken before eating it—the little end or the big end.[4] This is similar to British people who claim that driving on the left-hand side of the road is, so to say, the right thing to do, or to a youthful view of my wife, who told me that as a child she could not stand the vowel i.)

Indifference among conventions, however, defines only the pure case of a conventional signal. For practical purposes, the design of conventional signals needs to take into account how they will be used and how they could be misused. The features of a good signal's design must reflect the receiver's psychology. As Marion Dawkins and Tim Guilford argue, the receiver needs to be able to

1. *detect s* from the background—in other words, *s* must not be cryptic relative to the environment (when the Chinese Red Guards wanted red to mean go and green to mean stop in traffic lights, Chou-en Lai's driver made him oppose it because green is harder to see in the dark or a fog);
2. *discriminate s1* from *s2*, namely perceive the nonidentity of *s* with competing signals—a village in which many men are nicknamed Ciccio will either face many misunderstandings or develop additional names sufficient to distinguish *Ciccio-1* from *Ciccio-2*;
3. *memorize s* easily so as to be able to reidentify *s* over successive encounters (we may be indifferent as to whether "big" means small, but we would not be so indifferent if we used a thirty-five-letter word with no vowels to mean either small or big).[5]

It is also important in designing signals to make it unlikely that someone will emit *s* by accident, causing confusion. (In Dorothy Sayers' *Murder Must Advertise,* a newspaper reporter accidentally gives a signal that causes the member of a cocaine distribution gang to slip a packet of the powder into his pocket.)[6] This may require an *s* that is unique or at least unlikely to occur "naturally" in the circumstances in which we want to use it. Dark glasses alone cannot denote a mobster, since many ordinary men sport them. Thus, although conventional signals are arbitrary with respect to their message, they are not arbitrary with respect to other features; their design must try to optimize the capacity of *s* to be detected, discriminated, and memorized, and not to be confused with unrelated emission of it.

Conventional signals also have the attractive property of being potentially cheap to think up, learn, recall, and transmit. The cost of producing, displaying, transferring, and memorizing them can be minimal. This, however, can turn into a major disadvantage since it makes conventional signals open to mimics' abuse. They can be imitated and used to deceive.

As we shall see in chapter 7, a key feature of successful signals is that they are protected from mimics, whether by their design or by the policing of their use.

Iconic signals share some of the features of conventional signals, but they have the advantage that they can convey information successfully with no need for agreement, authority, or precedent. Like conventional signals they have no causal relation with their message, but their design is not arbitrary with respect to the message—they are nonarbitrary signifiers. Icons are signals designed or realized in such a way as to allude to or resemble the message the signaler wants a receiver to understand. Whereas the colors of traffic lights and their meaning are conventionally related, a traffic sign with an arrow pointing in one direction is iconic. Icons denote conventionally, but their conventional denoting is supported by the similarity with the message that the signaler wishes to convey. They are easier to memorize because of that, but what makes them interesting is that they can be understood even at the first interaction, when there is nothing to remember yet. They are not as cryptic as pure conventional signals, in which nothing connects a signal to the message conveyed. Since the meaning of an icon can be surmised without previous information by anyone who shares the same symbolic universe as that of the signaler, the drawback of icons is that they can also be understood by those whom the signaler would rather keep in the dark. However, they can be chosen or designed to be ambiguous enough to permit communication without overtly stating one's intentions or identity; they will thus generate suspicions rather than certainty among third-party receivers and so be useless as evidence in court.

Let us now review how these two types of signals, conventional and iconic, are put to work in the underworld.

COMMUNICATION

The problem of maintaining the secrecy of communication between agents who know each other can be solved by making it physically hard to spy on their exchanges. This may explain some criminals' penchant for playing golf or going fishing in a boat: conversations during these activities cannot be easily eavesdropped on. When isolation is not easy or convenient to arrange, environments with a high level of background noise—bars, discotheques, or stadiums—offer an alternative, for the acoustic turbulence makes eavesdropping harder. Both of these options require face-to-face encounters to maximize privacy, which can make them costly and limits their use. Those who want to communicate at a distance can choose media that are difficult to intercept—they may change mobile phones frequently, use public phone boxes, or pick radio frequencies known only to them. However, regardless of the medium of communication used, whenever the risk of detection is not negligible, criminals just like spies or terrorists resort to conventional signals—secret gestures, coded messages, nicknames, and the like.

Agents who know each other personally, whether through an organization or otherwise, can agree on conventional signals to use in special circumstances, just as many of us did as children. When Donnie Brasco was given a contract killing he was told he could enlist the help of a Miami made man, called Maruca. Maruca told Brasco that Brasco could call him up when he needed him and "just say 'I am buying a car and I want you to check it out.'"[7] "For instance," mafia turncoat Tommaso Buscetta explains, "when two mafiosi are stopped [by the police] while carrying a gun in their car, a sign between them, even just a look, is enough and one of them says that he knows nothing of that gun, whereas the other takes responsibility for it."[8]

During the trial of Rocco Zito, a boss of the 'ndrangheta (the mafia of Calabrese origins) in Toronto, Lee Lamothe saw Zito—who was charged in the shooting that killed an extortion victim—while sitting in the dock turning to make eye contact with his brother, Pasquale, a convicted heroin trafficker. Rocco dropped his right hand down to his hip and made a rapid series of hand movements, including a palm-down movement, a few quick circles. Pasquale, in response, nodded and touched his face. Rocco made a few more movements then nodded at Pasquale.[9]

Examples such as the above abound. Virtually every conversation among criminals is laced with conventional signals. In the summer of 1988 Lee Lamothe interviewed a young 'ndranghetista in Toronto. A man associated with his "cell" had gone missing and was presumed dead.

Lamothe asked the young 'ndranghetista what people were saying about the disappearance. The young mobster said that when he had asked his "maestro" about the man's fate, they were sitting at a table in a cafe; "the master lazily stretched his arm out and, without breaking eye contact, brushed invisible crumbs from the table top by flicking his fingertips. This, I was told, indicated 'the mess on the table had been repaired.'"[10] The brilliant TV series *The Wire*, which features Baltimore's drug dealers and police, is replete with true-to-life examples of astute coded messages; in one instance, the police discover that the dealers, in order to arrange meetings with suppliers, send by mobile phone the photograph of a clock, the arms of which are set to indicate the geographical coordinates of the location in East Baltimore in which the meeting is to take place. Read the transcripts of any wiretaps recording criminals in conversation and the ubiquity of conventional signals will be glaringly apparent.

In fact, anyone who has reasons to keep his communications secret resorts to a conventional lexicon. When homosexuality was criminalized, the London gay community employed an argot, called Polari, to "encrypt" their conversation. According to Paul Baker, who researched it, Polari was particularly popular between the 1930s and the early 1970s, when homosexuality began to be progressively decriminalized.[11] Here is an example:

> Polari: "Ooh vada well the omee-palone ajax who just trolled in— she's got nanti taste, dear, cod lally-drags and the naff riah but what a bona eek. Fantabulosa!" Translation: "Have a good look at that homosexual nearby who just came in. He's got no taste—awful trousers and tasteless hair—but what a lovely face. Absolutely fabulous!"[12]

Polari was used to maintain secrecy in the presence of others:

> Chris Monk, a 64 year-old former nurse from Chelmsford, learned it in his late teens. "It's an age when your brain just soaks up information, but the words were generally short and easy to remember

anyway. There was something joyful about it, and it felt very daring. You could say "bona cartes" ("good cock") in a crowded pub without anyone else twigging.[13]

Interestingly, according to Baker, Polari was also used by other illegal or stigmatized groups such as prostitutes and beggars. It probably has its origins in the nineteenth century, a lexicon cocktail, according to Baker, "derived from a variety of sources. Some of the most common include rhyming slang, backslang (saying a word as if it's spelt backwards), Italian, Occitan, French, Lingua Franca, American airforce slang, drug-user slang, Parlyaree (an older form of slang used by tinkers, beggars, and travelling players) and Cant (an even older form of slang used by criminals)." Baker counted five hundred words but says that only a core of about twenty was known by all, and "then there was a much larger fringe lexicon, of which most people would only know a small sample."[14]

Terrorists face much the same problem as anyone else with something to hide. In August 2000 Italian police intercepted some conversations in Arabic between al-Qaeda members, which ex post can be interpreted as referring to the plan for the September 11 attack. A senior Italian intelligence official said to the *New York Times* that a tendency of al-Qaeda cells to communicate in wild imagery made interpretation difficult.

A suspected Al Qaeda member from Yemen tells an Egyptian living in Italy that he is "studying airplanes," and adds: "God willing, I hope that I can bring you a window or piece of airplane the next time we meet." According to the Italian translation of the Arabic, he goes on: "We must only strike them, and hold our heads on high. Remember well: the danger in the airports." Referring to the United States, he says, "We intermarry with Americans, and thus they study the Koran. They have the feeling they are lions, a world power; but we will do them this service, and then the fear will be seen." . . . [In one passage the Yemeni, Mr. Abdulrahman,] says, "There are big clouds in the sky, there in that country the fire has been lit, and awaits only the wind." The official said that such images can often mean the opposite of what they appear to mean.[15]

The dialogue showed "clearly that they were organizing something," but their language made it hard to decipher what exactly was afoot.

> Using a chatroom, Atta [9/11 mastermind] sent messages in German from America, posing as a student, to "Jenny," his fictitious girlfriend. The real recipient was Mr. bin al-Shibh [Ramzi bin al-Shibh]. In al-Qaeda's code the World Trade Centre was "the faculty of town planning" (Atta hated skyscrapers, preferring traditional Islamic architecture), the Pentagon was "the faculty of fine arts" and Congress was the "faculty of law." In a final telephone call Atta told Mr. bin al-Shibh the chosen date for the attacks. "Two sticks, a dash and a cake with a stick down," he said, meaning 11/9.[16]

So far I have considered one-to-one cases of communication. However, there are instances of one-to-many, in which criminals wish to inform many other criminals in their network. In 1982 Pietro Inzerillo, who belonged to a Palermo mafia family, was found dead in New York. Both his mouth and rear end were stuffed with dollars to make clear he had been killed because he stole money that did not belong to him.[17] The singer Pino Marchese was found murdered on a bench in Palermo with his genitalia in his mouth. He had committed "an unforgivable offence of having an affair with the wife of a man of honour."[18] These iconic messages revealed to other mafiosi both that some from their nest had carried out the killings and why, while also giving pause to anyone scheming to defraud the mafia of its money or to elope with a mafioso's wife. The viability of such signs relies on the near certainty that the gruesome details will be leaked to the press and published. If this occurs, they are an extremely efficient way of communicating to lots of people.

In the one-to-many variety iconic signals are also used to inform large groups of people about the transmission of power from one individual to another in a criminal organization. Funerals of important mafiosi take on a particular salience in this regard. They mark in no uncertain terms the passing of a boss, as a result of which new alliances are formed and a new boss is chosen. People's decisions in the network depend on showing and knowing who is siding with whom and who the anointed successor is. Mistakes can be deadly. Thus, both participation in the funeral and the manner of participation are used as public displays aimed at informing an audience of the changes that will follow the boss's death. In 1908 Giuseppe Guercio, the boss of bosses, died in Monreale, Palermo. The body was already decomposing but could not be buried till Calogero Vizzini from Villalba had arrived, for he had to close the eyes of the dead boss and kiss his forehead, as a sign of the transfer of power.[19] And when Vizzini died, fifty years later, Giuseppe Genco Russo, his successor, took part in the funeral and held one of the golden ropes of the black mantle over the coffin.[20] After Carmelo Colletti, boss of Siculiana, was killed in his shop in 1983, a meeting was held in Gennaro Sortino's house to patch up the remains of the "family." At the end of the meeting the participants proceeded to the main bar in the town, in full view, respecting an "ordine di parata" based on members' hierarchical position: at the head marched Sortino, Colletti's brother-in-law, adviser and emissary of the family in the United States. According to investigators, the parade was meant to inform everyone of the position Sortino had now attained within the family and to present his credentials as the new legitimate boss.[21]

Absence can be just as informative as presence. In 1984 the funeral of Leonardo Rimi, the son of Don Filippo (the boss of Alcamo), killed a few days earlier in the surrounding countryside, was oddly followed by about a hundred women in black and only seven men. The local paper commented: "There was a sense that the atmosphere around this funeral was going to be 'cool.' But it was hard to imagine that in order to carry the coffin it would have been necessary to have recourse to the women. . . . People attributed men's desertion to the fear of being seen by the police and the carabinieri, but above all to the will of avoiding, out of prudence, a display of friendship to the Rimis, a family believed to be on the losing side."[22]

While above I mentioned cases in which signaler and receiver(s) communicated with each other within cooperative relations, conventional and especially iconic signals can also shape communication in relations of conflict. In particular, they are useful as threats. In this case the target of the threat can be, but need not be, another criminal. And the threat can be issued by one or by more agents—it can be a many-to-one case.

Iconic signals are useful also because one can avoid direct contact with and explicit intimidation of the victim. A silver heart—of the kind donated to Catholic churches to give thanks for grace received known as ex voto—was employed at least twice in the 1980s: in both cases the heart was perforated by bullet holes. One was placed on the back door of Salvatore Catania, who lived to tell of the threat. Pasquale Gramaglia was less fortunate; he was executed in his shop a few days after receiving the same message.[23] Raimondo Lampo, clearly someone on whom the subtlety of religious items would have been lost, had to be sent an even clearer message: an empty coffin was deposited at his lodgings.[24] Gioacchino Basile, a trade unionist in the Palermo shipbuilding industry, found a dead bird in his (locked) car after trying to organize an antimafia conference.[25] Menacing deliveries have also included postcards with coffins and crosses,[26] tarot cards featuring spade characters (about which more in chapter 10), and the severed heads of domestic animals—the equine rendition of this message was made world famous by *The Godfather.*

Sometime threats are issued not through objects but by verbal *allusions* and *metaphors*, which produce a threatening effect because of the identity of the speaker. Judge Giovanni Falcone, while interrogating mafiosi, was told, for example: "you are working too hard, it's bad for your health, you should take a rest," or "you are in a dangerous profession; I, in your position, would take my bodyguards even to the toilet."[27] Soon after completing my fieldwork in Palermo in 1987 I myself was bizarrely threatened over the phone by means of a riddle of religious inspiration. The anonymous caller, who had a slight Sicilian accent, was able to track down the phone number of my apartment in Rome. Without introducing himself, he first asked me whether he was speaking to such and such telephone number to make sure I understood that he had indeed intended to call *my* number rather than making a mistake. He then asked:

"Am I speaking to the church of La Madonna del Riposo?" After my baffled denial he proceeded by asking the totally incongruous question: "Do you happen to know where it is *located*?" He did not ask me whether I knew the church's correct phone number, which would have been odd, but he asked if I knew *where* it was, which did not make any sense at all. I replied that I had no idea and put down the receiver. After a moment of hesitation pondering over the oddity of what I had just heard, a search in the phone book revealed that the church in question was "located" in the cemetery very near where I lived—the Riposo alluded to being that of the eternal kind.

Issuing threats or signing murders by signals of this kind may seem quaint. Yet they are efficient. The meaning of all these signals can be understood even if one is not explicitly told what they mean before receiving them. So they are used to threaten or inform not merely people who share in the use of an agreed array of signals but also outsiders who share only the same general symbolic universe. Making an uninformed receiver understand comes at the cost that other receivers intercepting the message can guess the meaning too. However, the way these signals work is such that even if a third party understands the meaning, this is of little consequence. A direct threat or an explicit claim, on the other hand, would be compromising and prosecutable.

IDENTIFICATION

Conventional signals are used by organizations to assist in the identification problem, namely to make members who have not met before identifiable to each other. Any criminal organization or network that grows in size beyond the number of people who can know each other personally needs to develop and coordinate identification signals. Conventional signals with this purpose have been applied for specific operations. On May 1990, for instance, "a King Yee triad boss in Kwun Tong succeeded in mobilizing 700 men to try and drive away other prospective buyers from queuing at the sales office to buy new residential flats. . . . To identify the people of theirs who were hired to disrupt the queue, the King

Yee triad leader asked his 700 men to wear a *white glove on their right hand.*"[28]

Such artifices are useful not only for criminals. According to Marek Kaminski, in order to recognize each other

> secret police agents during Solidarity demonstrations in Poland would use "disposable" conventional signals. According to my reconstruction, they were informed shortly before a demonstration what the signal for this particular demonstration was, and next they were given the required accessories and information. In one case, it was a scarf of particular sort, in another case, it was a brown sweater tied around the waist. The secret police was infiltrated by Solidarity sympathizers, and announcing the signal too early would lead to disseminating this information among demonstrators. The signalling devices were becoming obsolete anyway over time as Solidarity radio technicians were decoding critical pieces of information overheard from police airwaves.[29]

(The ease with which conventional signals can be exploited by mimics is revealed by Kaminski's "private strategy" during the May Day demonstrations, which "was to keep a small red flag or a red flower in my pocket, and then use it to cross a police cordon when needed. The flag signaled flawlessly that I was a participant of the *official* May Day parade. The cost was frequent nasty comments from fellow-demonstrators.")[30]

Conventional signals have served to identify members of criminal organizations not only for specific operations but also to allow member recognition generally. Chu Yiu Kong reports:

> Over the years triad members have developed numerous methods, such as passwords, phrases, poems, hand signs, gestures, seals, slang, and jargon, to show their identities. Traditionally, the initiated members were taught those means of identification so that they could easily identify themselves and communicate with each other. In Hong Kong, most means of identification are commonly used throughout the triad community. For instance, the Fung, Lao, Po

and Yan are universal verses, which can be used by all triad members in Hong Kong. Some means of identification, however, are specifically for the identification of a particular society. In Hong Kong, well-organised triad societies normally have their own "title" verse. For example the title verse of the 14K is: "The name of our family rises high as the phoenix dances and the dragon flies, like a bolt from the blue the title of our family rumbles over the land, with K Gold as our mark, China with the righteous 14 guard."[31]

Yakuza too, according to Hiroaki Iwai, displayed

unique forms of greeting and identification. . . . When two yakuza meet for the first time, each of them will take up a pose. Stepping forward slightly, bending his legs, putting his clenched fist on the right femur, and stretching out his left arm each will recite at length his place of origin, present residence, the name of his oyabun, and his own name in stilted archaic language. When he has finished, the same type of greeting is repeated by the other party.[32]

One of the advantages of belonging to an organization with a central authority is that by establishing conventional identification signals it can put criminals who have not met before in touch while reducing the risk of costly mistakes. And not just criminals: any organization that must both identify members and prevent opponents from identifying its members may resort to conventional signals. Here is one example from the peasant anti-Bolshevik insurgent movement that was active in Russia, in Tambov Province, from 1920 to 1921. Erik Landis writes:

One young boy (only sixteen years of age) from Penza province, Semen Samokho, was apprehended [by the Bolsheviks] in Tambov near the border with Saratov. He was found to be a spy working for the Saratov rebel, Popov, and had been travelling throughout the region on the railways, establishing contacts with similar "spies" from Tambov, Ukraine, Penza, and the Don region. He told Soviet investigators that a basic system of designations had been developed to help assist the network. "Spies" could be identified at busy railway stations by what they wore. For instance, one could recognize an agent of Makhno's army by his military service cap that would have a small bundle of black thread attached to the left side; an agent of Antonov's Partisan Army could be identified by his boots, one of which would be cut shorter than the other; a spy from Penza, representing the rebel group led by Marus, would have the bill of his (or her) cap cut in a distinctive way.[33]

ADVERTISING

The examples offered so far have dealt with either communicative or identification problems. What about the advertising problem, though? That is, when the target receiver is unknown and part of a larger crowd of people, how can one maintain secrecy or at least not risk negative repercussions and still reach the target? Few are as fortunate as the yakuza were, until recently. The Japanese mobsters enjoyed a semilegal status and greater freedom to advertise their services without causing negative consequences for themselves. They even had, according to David Kaplan and Alec Dubro, "business cards . . . embossed with the gang's emblem and clearly identifying the bearer's syndicate, rank, and name. Other symbols [were] widely used as well, such as flags and lanterns, and even official songs. Anthropologist Stark's host gang . . . displayed large round sofa pillows emblazoned with the group's gold emblem, stuffed in the rear window of the boss's Lincoln Continental."[34] A 1990 survey of two thousand firms in Japan confirmed that business cards bearing name, address, and telephone and fax numbers were as common among yakuza as among any other Japanese businessmen.[35] After new anti–organized crime laws were introduced in 1992, matters changed somewhat. In anticipation, Wolfgang Herbert writes, "Already in 1991 more than a 1000 Yamaguchi-gumi offices had had their emblems dismantled, while many gangs had also removed their membership lists, their articles of association, photos of former oyabun (bosses) and other such paraphernalia."[36] Yet, only a year later, in 1993, according to Christopher Seymour, the Hara-gumi in Kyoto restored their public sign: "The square piece of heavy pine is then pushed firmly into the plaster. On the plaque is engraved 'HARA-GUMI HEADQUARTERS.' Yoshi [a junior member] steps forward and throws up his arms, leading the group in shouting 'Banzai! Banzai! Banzai!,' and then gleeful applause."[37] And Peter Hill informs me that the yakuza have maintained their cards, though they "now have two sets, one for use within the underworld (which clearly show gang affiliation and position) and one when dealing with those in the upperworld."[38]

Most people who want to purchase or offer criminal goods are not so lucky, and if they are not smart either, advertising can cost them dearly. Paul Clark, thirty-two, an electrical engineer, was arrested on 14 December 1999 after police raided his mother's home in Portsmouth, England, and was tried a year later for making threats to kill. British police were alerted by the FBI after the names, address, and telephone number of Brandy Arnett and of her husband Rick of El Paso, Texas, appeared on the Web with a request that they be "terminated." A wedding photograph was included on the website. The message read:

> I require the persons on this page to be terminated. I am 100 per cent genuine and will honour all promises. To collect payment, all you need to do is erase the persons listed below, take a photograph of the task and then send the picture to me. Once the picture has been verified, I will e-mail you the location of the $25,000 which has already been placed at a pre-determined location.

Jonathan Sharpe, prosecuting, told the jury at Winchester Crown Court that Clark and Brandy Arnett had exchanged photographs and flirtatious e-mails after she had sought his help in building a website to advertise her catering business. The court heard that Clark's response, when he discovered that Brandy Arnett already had a husband, was "explosive." Clark initially sent e-mail messages expressing his love for her and pleading with her to reconsider. But after she rejected his proposal to fly out to Texas to discuss the matter, he turned "nasty" and set up the website advertising for a contract killer, and got the FBI instead.[39]

If information could travel freely in the underworld, the number of fruitful matches would multiply, and crime would soar. The problem for

those who want to advertise what they demand or supply in the criminal domain is essentially that they are involved in a double bind—with
potential kindred spirits, who could help them, and against the law, who
could put them in jail. Striking the right balance between the two is
hard: on the one hand the latter can intercept information meant to
reach only the former; on the other hand, a disguise meant to hide from
the law may prevent one from reaching other criminals and entering
into profitable deals.

The range of tricks devised to overcome that hurdle is large. Polari
was not only a lexicon for secret communications between gays who
knew each other as gays but also a bait to check whether someone was
gay and interested in making contact. John Foster said:

> Everything was illegal in those days and you had to be very careful.
> I always looked straight, I never minced about, so dropping in the
> odd Polari word would be a way of checking the other person out.
> If you liked the look of someone at the theatre, you might say to
> them, "That was a bona scene, wasn't it?" If they were straight they
> wouldn't pick up on it but if they were gay there might be a shriek
> of recognition: "She's camp, this one."[40]

The so-called hanky code is a more elaborate way of advertising dis-
creetly that one is interested in homosexual sex and in what type. Signalers vary the color of a handkerchief that they display, and further vary
it by wearing it on the right or the left of their body. The color denotes
the type of service one is looking for, while the side denotes whether
one wants to have a passive (right) or active role (left). While most colors
used in the hanky code are purely conventionally associated with the
activity they mean to convey, some can be iconic, such as yellow and
brown when an interest in excrement-related sex is meant. I could not
find any research on where the code developed, how it spread, and how
much it is really used. A few variants of it are available on the Internet, a
means of communication that has contributed to spreading knowledge
of the code (just google "hanky code"). The different versions share a
common core but vary with regard to the more outlandish practices.

This suggests that there is no standard version but only local variants. In one version I counted 76 colors, which multiplied by right/left options comes to 152 combinations.[41] At first it seems as if this would make the code hard to use, for such a large lexicon fails the "easy to memorize" test. However, given the large variety of sexual activities that it conveys, it is inconceivable for anyone to be interested in them all or even in a sizable proportion; by memorizing the few combinations of interest, one may still use a subset effectively.

Greggor Mattson, who has done ethnographic research in gay bars in the San Francisco area, wrote to me:

> Many stores in San Francisco sell the handkerchiefs, and they can be had off and on around the world. The "core" colours—red, blue, brown, light blue etc—hankies can be bought easily at department stores, Western clothes stores, etc. so the core colours aren't rare or expensive. . . . I have seen in use, over time, the following: orange (anything anytime), red (fist fucking), dark blue (anal sex), yellow (piss), brown (shit), light blue (oral sex), black (S&M), and purple (which I had known as meaning "safe sex anything," but is listed as various things on the lists I found on the Net). The ones I've seen are relatively easy to interpret in a dark bar and it's relatively easy to find someone around who can interpret them. But the fine shades of yellow and orange would not be distinguishable in a dark bar. . . . Even within the gay community, the hankie code is not really that well known, more within the S&M and dive bar type places, not gay bars in general. I haven't really been in a bar where there were many people with the hankies . . . just one to 3 guys, maybe. I occasionally see guys walking in San Francisco with one. I don't know if there was ever a bar where there would be, say, 50% of the guys with hankies, or if such a thing exists any more in S&M bars or private parties.

An effective signaling code can spare agents from time-wasting, embarrassing conversations and favor encounters between people of compatible preferences, as well as pass unnoticed by all those who ignore the existence of the code. There does seem to be a need for implicit communication of this sort inside gay communities, and "sightings" of analogous codes are reported from around the world. Taste and status seem to influence the use of codes. Mattson wrote:

> The hankie code is regarded as "disgusting" by most young gay men in San Francisco and a majority of the gay community in general. Signalling a willingness to have sex is regarded as unattractive in mainstream gay bars. It's a combination of regarding signals of a willingness to have sex ("sluttiness") as crass, perhaps an AIDS risk, and in general as a mark of "low class" behavior.[42]

Another example of a leaner homosexual signaling ruse is the "lookback." For a man to ogle another man walking toward him could be embarrassing or even dangerous, for if the approaching man turns out to be straight he may be annoyed or even outraged. So one walks past and only then looks back. If the other man is looking back too, then he must also be homosexually interested. If he were straight he would not look back at men but only at women. This convention is—as Michael Biggs, who told me about this case, wrote—"a beautifully efficient signalling system because the 'wrong' person will not receive *any* signal at all." Beautiful too because it does not require complicated arrangements such as direct contact, a preexisting lexicon, or an organization to achieve coordination on the meaning. It could even work with people who did not speak the same language.[43]

The following case, reported by Thomas Schelling, did by contrast rely on an organization: "[a] nice identification game [that] was uncovered in New York suburbs a few years ago. Certain motorists carried identity cards, which identified them to policemen as members in a club; if the motorist with a membership card was arrested, he simply showed the card to the policeman and paid a bribe. The role of these cards was to identify the motorist as a person who, if the bribe was received, would keep quiet. It identified a man whose promise was enforceable."[44] The card acted as a conventional signal: the corrupt policemen, by seeing the card, knew that the driver was offering a bribe.

(Whether the conventional signal did also guarantee that the driver would keep his mouth shut, as Schelling contends, and whether it also guaranteed to the policeman that he was not facing an anticorruption undercover agent, are further matters. If so, this means that the policeman somehow knew that "unreliable" people could not obtain that card. He trusted the selection procedures, just as an employer trusts that only someone with the right competence is given a degree by a reputable university. But in this case, he further trusted that those who did obtain the card kept its meaning secret so that no unreliable individual who had not gone through the selection admitting them to the club had a reason to forge or steal one. I return to the issue of protecting conventional signals in the next chapter.)

Most drivers who when stopped by police would prefer to pay a bribe rather than a fine (provided the former is cheaper) cannot count on such an organized scam. They do not know whether the policeman who stops them is prepared to accept a bribe or, if offered one, may instead arrest them for attempted corruption. Thanks to his uniform and his other customary appurtenances, the policeman looks like he is a noncriminal. But what if he is corruptible? If he is, the policeman too wonders whether the driver is prepared to pay a bribe but may be afraid of revealing it. Both may fail to be better off if they cannot indicate their real preferences to each other.

Not all is lost though. In Italy and in Poland the initiative to signal one's readiness to bribe was at times taken by drivers, who used to "forget" a large banknote kept with their driver's license.[45] If the police stopped them for some irregularity, they would hand their license over to the policeman. A quick-witted and corrupt policeman could choose to pocket the banknote (or bargain for more); if not corrupt, he was unable to treat the display of the ostensibly "forgotten" banknote as sufficient evidence of attempted bribery.

Why should a banknote inside a folded driver's license signal the driver's corrupting intention? The policeman might have known that this was a conventional practice and worked by induction from previous experiences. His belief would be supported by pure conventional association, and the fact that it was a banknote would be merely incidental, as by definition the signal could have been any other item (provided it was equally detectable and easy to discriminate and memorize). But this simply begs the question: why did this work in the first case ever? Even if policemen did not know that the banknote was such a signal to start with, nonetheless it could still denote because it stands as *an icon* of the willingness to pay a bribe. Had the item inserted in the driver's license been a leaf or a photo, the signal could have worked if and only if in some way the policeman had prior knowledge of these other items being used with that meaning, for they do not remind one of a bribe. But a banknote can make it work without prior agreement or precedent—and it is quick. It works by conveying the driver's intention, for it embodies a key aspect of a corrupt transaction: cash. If the policeman has no reason to suspect a trap by the anticorruption police squad, then that signal may suffice to make him respond to the offer as desired by the driver.

In other instances police officers may solicit a bribe by similar means. In Poland, according to Kaminski, policemen were signaling their readiness to take a bribe with a question: "So, are we going to *write* a ticket?" A driver could then declare that he preferred an unwritten ticket and seal the deal, paying usually half or less of the customary fine. A Russian traffic policeman who stopped a Polish professor on holiday with his wife in Kaliningrad, Russia, in 2002, used a different signal, silence. He just stood there looking at the professor for a while, a sign that the professor interpreted as an invitation to offer him a bribe. Given how frequently traffic policemen asked for bribes from motorists in Russia,[46] the policeman must have thought that the message was obvious without any additional signaling effort. Interestingly, however, the professor did not pay, for he did not know how much would be the right sum to offer; too much he did not want to pay, too little and he might offend the policeman. In the end, the policeman reluctantly fined him for the ruble equivalent of one U.S. dollar.[47] In the account of a Chicago professional thief, when a corrupt policeman arrests a thief he signals to the thief that he is ready to set him free in exchange for money in the following way: "Then the copper will look down at his overcoat and say 'My overcoat is getting pretty old. I really should get me a new coat.'

That means he wants $50 or $75, and you say, 'I could arrange to get a new coat for you from a friend who sells me things at wholesale.'"[48]

CONCLUSIONS

In illegal markets the problems of managing effective signaling codes—spreading the knowledge, overcoming variations in meaning, avoiding the difficulties of memorization or ambiguity—are compounded by the need for secrecy. Even if conventions emerge naturally in one group, it may be hard to spread them to other groups or to codify them consistently, even within one large group. The emergence of conventional signals follows patterns and requires conditions that give no rock-solid guarantee of coordination. Mistakes happen in underworld communications, and more so than among ordinary citizens, who are not so often forced to use indirect and coded ways of communicating.

The misinterpretation of a signal can happen in three main ways: the simplest is that s is not recognized as a signal at all. The reluctance of an employee to do his duty and perform a service may be put down by an innocent citizen to laziness or excessive workload, not to its being a covert bargaining ruse. When I arrived in a snowy and empty Prague on New Year's Eve in 1979, I visited three hotels before it dawned on me that the concierges' claim of there being no room available was in fact a request for a bribe. The hotel in which I finally found a room after "greasing the wheels" was in fact empty.

The second mistake occurs because of overinterpretation, namely when something that is not a signal is mistaken for one. In a menacing atmosphere people develop a heightened sensitivity to signs, which transforms mere allusions into intimidating or challenging gestures (sometimes mistakenly so). This, on the one hand, aids the signaler, as it extends the pool of signs from which he can choose to produce a threatening effect with minimum effort—the raising of an eyebrow can become a compelling menace. When Stefano Calzetta, a small-time Palermo crook, was addressed by Carmelo "Nono" Zanca, a big-time mafioso, with the words "Have you seen X, have you seen Y?" Calzetta

knew, he said in his confession, that this was meant as a warning that he
himself had to be careful and change his behavior, for he knew that X
and Y "had met an ugly death 'cause of their behaviour."[49] Salvatore
Cancemi, a mafioso who turned state's evidence in 1993, said that "if
Totò Riina had suspected from just a look, if he had felt from just the
smallest movement of the eyes that those of the Noce [a Palermo mafia
family] were not following him [in his plan to kill judge Giovanni Fal-
cone], he would have had all of us killed."[50] One can understand why
mafiosi develop a stony face; even their eye movement appears exceed-
ingly parsimonious. They are very attentive to many aspects of their demeanor and their appurtenances. Standardizing—everyone doing and
wearing the same things, because everyone is watchful about devia-
tions—is one way of "silencing" the communication effects that could
be accidentally generated by variations. On the other hand, it is easy to
see how receivers' paranoia can lead them to overinterpret certain gestures and attach a meaning to trivially mundane actions. The testimonies
of mafiosi who turned state's evidence show ad nauseam that every sentence they exchange is scrutinized for potential ambiguity and hidden
messages. They are obsessed with details, minute alterations in attire, slips
of the tongue. While the choreography of certain murders leaves little
doubt—stuffing dollars into the mouth of a victim can hardly be interpreted as a meaningless accident—other features associated with murders may be entirely accidental. In Sicily the bodies of many murdered
victims have been found with their hands and legs trussed together (*inca-
prettati*), in the manner in which butchers handle slaughtered lambs.
People believed this gruesome arrangement to be reserved for traitors
(*infami*) and aimed both at revealing the reason of the execution and at
"signing" it as a mafia job. Vincenzo Sinagra, a mafia member turned
informer, however, revealed that no such aim was in the perpetrators'
mind: it was done for stuffing corpses into car trunks more easily.[51] Mafia
executions are carried out so as to maximize efficiency, and some of
their features are wrongly interpreted as signals.[52]

   Finally, misinterpretation occurs when an *s* that means *k* is thought to
mean *j*. Conventional signals require coordination to be viable, and
when iconic they require that signaler and receiver share the same sym-

bolic or behavioral universe. People need to know what exactly a signal means (and need to know that the relevant others have the same knowledge too) before they can emit or receive them without making mistakes. If for whatever reason coordination fails, the same signal can take multiple meanings. Even as well-established a criminal organization as the Sicilian mafia suffer from this problem. The management of information is a serious headache for a mafioso. "The important thing is precise information," says mafia turncoat Antonino Calderone—"Within the mafia there must circulate accurate and exact information. Otherwise no one understands anything anymore, and there is great confusion."[53] Quite, and there often *is* confusion. "If," Buscetta said, "men of honour belonging to the same mafia family are arrested for a crime and one of them tells the others 'ni consumaro' he means that they are taking responsibility for the crime for themselves and the family as well."[54] However, according to another mafia turncoat, Salvatore Contorno, the same sentence has more than one meaning: "[it] may be used for many different occasions: 'cause they are arresting me, 'cause we are killing someone and get caught, 'cause we are loosing money, it may be used in so many ways."[55] None of the meanings that Contorno mentions coincide with a claim of responsibility, so one wonders whether Buscetta and Contorno would have understood each other. The additional information emerging from the context in which the sentence is uttered may suffice to discriminate among the different meanings, but there is no guarantee of that, and even if no one meant to deceive, mafiosi end up misunderstanding each other more often than people appreciate. Buscetta also claimed that even silence can be a clear message, and Marino Mannoia maintained that no words are needed when someone wants to take responsibility for killing someone.[56] However, Salvatore La Barbera was killed because of an unfortunate misunderstanding that followed his "revealing" silence. Everybody thought he was responsible for Calcedonio Di Pisa's murder since he was not making a fuss about it. They were wrong, and the misunderstanding contributed to sparking the internecine war between mafia families in Palermo in the 1960s.

CHAPTER 7

Protecting Easy-to-Fake Signals

> Irwin Schiff, a mob linked businessman, shot to death
> in a Manhattan restaurant in 1987, "committed the sin of
> using the Pagano name without permission."
>
> —*New York Times*, 13 June 1989

"Each group has a signature," Bob Levinson, FBI special agent from 1976 to 1998, said. "Some groups use a sniper rifle to take out their enemies, some use a machine gun, some use a pistol. The group with which Mr. Mogilevich [a Russian mobster] is associated, their signature is the car bomb."[1] Analysts of criminal matters often confidently interpret certain acts as carrying a precise meaning, as does Levinson. In reality, they often risk overinterpretation, for it is never easy to establish to what extent criminals' choices are intended as signals of anything, including of their identity. The choice of weapon, for example, can be driven by considerations other than signing a murder. It may merely reflect availability, efficiency, or expertise.

The more serious problem, however, is another: even if the car bomb is a signature, we cannot easily know whether it is genuine or "forged." As long as there are people who associate certain groups with certain weapons, and provided that this is common knowledge[2] among criminals, group B can choose a weapon *believed* to be associated with group A in order to pin the blame on A. If one wants to blame the mafia for a murder, why not dispose of the victim's body with the mouth stuffed with money or tied up like a slaughtered goat? The risk of mimicry applies to tattoos as well. Hall writes in a comprehensive review of this practice in United States prisons: "Some prison tattoos do symbolize specific crimes, but it is a mistake to read them on that level only and then judge an individual by them. Wanna-bes often wear the same symbols."[3] There is an unavoidable uncertainty surrounding the interpretation of signals that are easy to mimic.

Mimicry threatens not just observers' interpretations but also those of criminals themselves. This was apparent at the funeral of Oleg Vagin, first godfather of the Centralny criminal group in Yekaterinburg. Mourners were waiting for Konstantin Tziganov, boss of the Uralmash gang, to show up and kiss Vagin's embalmed body. Failing to do so was believed to be an admission of guilt. Tziganov arrived at the cemetery minutes before the coffin was to be lowered into the grave and kissed Vagin on the face.[4] Should people thus be sure he did not order Vagin's killing? Although it is probably easier to kiss a corpse if one was a friend of the deceased, the gesture is still perfectly affordable by one who only wants us to believe that he was, especially one like Tziganov, whose occupation is not for the squeamish. An aristocratic "ancestor" to this event occurred at Pushkin's funeral in 1837. Prince Gagarin was suspected of writing the anonymous letters in which Pushkin was mocked for being a cuckold and which eventually led to the duel in which Pushkin was killed by George d'Anthès Heckereen. Serena Vitale, in her book on Pushkin's death, writes: "Turgenev kept an eye on Gagarin at the poet's funeral the next day: if he failed to approach Pushkin's body for the final farewell, it would be indirect confirmation of his guilt. But the young man ... went to the bier and brushed the corpse's ashen forehead with his lips." According to Vitale only Turgenev was naïve enough to be "reassured by this pious gesture."[5]

Unlike cost-discriminating signals many conventional signals, whether pure or iconic, can be cheaply produced and displayed by mimics. If this occurs frequently enough and the ploy is uncovered, either by the honest signalers or by the receivers, the value of the signal becomes corrupted. Ultimately, it will become useless for everyone—honest signalers, receivers, and mimics themselves.[6]

Conventional signals that are cheap to produce or display survive by themselves only to the extent that there are no incentives for signalers to misrepresent them. The case of vocabulary is the paramount example of this happy situation: in most interactions most people want their words to mean what the convention says that they mean, so words by and large do not lose their ability to denote accurately. As Joseph Farrell and Matthew Rabin argue in an article titled "Cheap Talk," the better the alignment between the interests of the two players, the more reliable will be their communications, linguistic or otherwise. So fellow mobsters who have closely parallel interests will be able to rely on each other's signals and assertions, but when their interests conflict, as they often do, a rational mobster should ignore the other's assertions.[7]

When interests conflict, honest signalers who wish to prevent mimics from abusing and corrupting signals, and receivers who do not like to be fooled, need ways to protect themselves from mimicry. Underworld strategies for protecting signals—which reflect in a crude fashion those the legal world employs to protect trademarks and intellectual property rights—consist essentially of imposing constraints of affordability on the mimic. In other words, to make conventional signals work. one has to construct or handle them in such a way as to give them a cost-discriminating component. The strategies are of two broad types: one consists of increasing the cost of *displaying* the signal and the other of increasing the cost of *acquiring* or reproducing the signal.

ACTING ON THE COST OF DISPLAY

A common strategy to defend conventional signals from mimics consists of increasing the cost of their display by policing their use and punishing mimics who, like the businessman Irwin Schiff, use them without permission. In such cases the cost-discrimination component is achieved not by making the signal more expensive to realize but riskier to display.

In the underworld not all mimicry is amenable to sanctioning. During the 1960s in France a gang of vicious criminals began robbing banks while wearing comical "Groucho" masks consisting of a big nose, a mustache, and eyeglasses frames. They became feared and known as the "mustache gang." Soon, throughout France, robbers of all sorts took to wearing the mask to exploit the fear it caused. "Mustache gangs" proliferated, but the disguise, donned by incompetent robbers, eventually lost its potency.[8] Even if they had wanted the mask to retain its value as a signal of viciousness, the original gang had no means by which to find the mimics before they struck and to enforce their "property right" on the mask, or to license it only to equally vicious colleagues who would not have diluted the fear-inducing value of the mask.

Yet a mixture of accident and determination can promote signal policing even in unpromising circumstances. In Los Angeles a group of youths joined many others in wearing fashionable "gangsta" outfits. They eventually strayed into the "wrong" district, and a group of real ganstas shot them. One was killed. To no avail they pleaded their innocence, claiming they did not mean to pass themselves off as the real thing. The shooters were protecting their "property rights" over the use of the outfit in their territory. Indeed, they were making the point that, in that district, even if you are not making a serious claim you must not wear that type of clothes and if you dare to do so you will be punished. Detective St. John, who contributed to catching the killers, Elliot (Chocolate) Singletary and Tommy Lee (Ace Capone) Williams, explained that "with more youths adopting gang clothing and slang, the prospects of deadly confrontations with the gang members rise: 'It's cool to be that way,'" he said. "Many wear that clothing and are challenged a hundred times and nothing happens. But the 101st time, Chocolate and Ace Capone drive by, then what do you do?"[9]

Youth gangs might punish illegitimate bearers of their insignia sporadically, but established, organized criminals try to do it systematically. In his ethnography of the yakuza David Stark describes how the Japanese mobsters go about policing their identifying insignia:

Once expelled or discharged, an ex-member can stay in the gang's territory but he may not claim membership or influence by virtue of past affiliation or current connection to a gang. He loses his badge and name card and cannot derive income from illegal activity. He is banned from joining another gang, is warned against roaming the street aimlessly, and must refrain from the use of mannerisms and styles of a gangster. (These include wearing flashy or garish clothes; walking the street with confidence that the way will

clear before him; a boastful stance; unusual and over-confident behaviour for an ordinary citizen). If caught doing any of the above,
the ex-member would be challenged by the gang. . . . I witnessed
two such challenges. Once in a bar, a customer boasted that he was
affiliated with the Araki gang and knew Noda Boss. He was challenged by the Araki gang member with whom I was drinking. A
brawl ensued. The customer was humiliated and forced to leave.
Another case occurred when walking the streets and a *chimpira*,
hoodlum, came swaggering about acting tough and challenging
pedestrians . . . the impostor ran off barely escaping the violent
kicks of the pursuing *kobun*.[10]

In a third instance reported by Stark, the impostor, who had been making money from illegal activities, was first chased out of the gang's territory; subsequently, fearing that the ostracized man could become an informant, the gang hunted him all over the country and finally murdered
him.

Sicilian mafiosi too worry about impostors who either pass themselves off as mafiosi in order to extort money or use the name of a mafia
boss or family without permission to gain some advantage.[11] The former
pretend to be protectors and steal the reputation; the latter pretend to be
protected by someone when they are not. Although some mimics succeed,[12] the fate of those who are caught can easily be guessed. Salvatore
Buscemi was not a member of the mafia, but he must have aspired to
make a position for himself as a protector.

He was killed because he had taken the liberty of asking for protection money ("il pizzo") in the area of Villabate and Bagheria,
without permission, and from persons who were already paying
Marchese and Greco. Buscemi tried to justify this by claiming that
he did not know to whom the area belonged. The justification was
not very plausible, because we were familiar with the subdivision
of the areas of Palermo and to which mafia organization they were
subject.[13]

Not only did Buscemi pirate protection rights in a territory that "belonged" to someone else; he also had the cheek to subcontract them: he told Antonino Migliore he had received the consent of "an important character," and for acting on Buscemi's instructions Migliore too "was promptly strangled" (I return to this issue in chapter 8).[14]

Entry into the brotherhood of the Russian *vory* was marked by being given a nickname[15] but also by having a tattoo done especially for the occasion. Federico Varese reports: "Gurov writes of a *vory* tattoo picturing the suits of aces inside a cross and symbolizing membership into the society. In his view, criminals had tattoos 'to prove their strength. The tattoo also had a "communicating function." It helped the recidivists to recognise each other.' Accordingly, the *vory* sought to maintain exclusive use of their tattoo designs; non-*vory* found wearing them were punished by death."[16]

The yakuza, rather than discouraging outsiders from having one of their tattoos by threatening punishment as the *vory* did, increased, as we will see below, the cost of the tattoos by making them at once more elaborate and extending them to a larger part of their body. The choice of which strategy to use may be dictated by external conditions that affect the strategy's relative costs. The original *vory*'s environment was the gulag, in which other inmates could be monitored, and anyone abusing the signal could easily be spotted. In U.S. prisons too, gang members have been able to police their tattoos. Hall writes: "Certain tattoos inspire fear and respect and give the wearer an abrasive edge. In prison that edge becomes reason enough for acquiring them. Inmates take risks for security. A few well-chosen motorcycle gang tattoos might make life in tough cellblocks a lot safer and easier. On the other hand a convict caught wearing gang tattoos fraudulently may suffer serious disgrace and even get himself killed."[17]

In the post-Soviet criminal environment, Varese no longer finds tattoos being used as part of the new *vory*'s identity-signaling repertoire.[18] Once the *vory* regrouped out of prisons and moved into the wider world after 1989, it is likely that their tattoos lost their identifying value, for it became much more difficult to police them and thus easier for mimics to use them undetected. Ultimately, once the real *vory* stop bearing them, tattoos will lose their value for mimics too.

Signaling by Breaching Norms

If being caught breaching a norm elicits a high social cost, it can turn the act of breaching itself into a robust conventional signal. In the 1770s Giacomo Casanova was in Spain, a country he detested above all others in Europe for its bigotry and provincialism, and in which the Inquisition's intrusiveness knew no bounds. In his memoirs, Casanova wrote:

> The chief subject of dispute at that time was the fashion of wearing breeches. Those who wore "braguettes" were imprisoned, and all tailors making breeches with "braguettes" were severely punished [trousers with a codpiece, a crotch patch that makes male genitalia stand out]. Nevertheless, people persisted in wearing them, and the priests and monks preached in vain against the indecency of such a habit. A revolution seemed imminent, but the matter was happily settled without effusion of blood. An edict was published and affixed to the doors of all the churches, in which it was declared that breeches with braguettes were only to be worn by the public hangmen. Then the fashion passed away; for no one cared to pass for the public executioner.[19]

(Such effects can be unintended by-products. Avinash Dixit told me that in India in the mid-1970s there was a fashion among young men of carrying portable radios, a kind of early boom box, and playing them very loudly in public. The government, to encourage its policy of slowing population growth, started to give such radios as rewards for getting a vasectomy. The fashion died almost instantaneously!)

There was another potential effect of the cunning edict regarding braguettes. Had hangmen needed a conventional signal to identify one another with certainty, they would have found it. From then on they could count on the fact that no one would want to be seen wearing braguettes. As a by-product, the church's edict created a self-sustaining convention: if everyone believes that only hangmen wear braguettes, only hangmen will. In reality, it is unlikely that anyone, including hangmen, would want or need to be identified as a hangman, but the anecdote captures how the fear of social reproach, of causing revulsion, of breaching a norm, can be exploited to create signals that credibly inform.

People do not want to be confused with people of a type others dislike, unless there is some advantage to flagging their membership in precisely *that* category and they want to be so identified by kindred spirits or interested individuals. The signaler can don precisely those identifiers no one else dares to wear. For instance, advertising prostitution commonly consists of walking the street at a leisurely pace in eye-catching and skimpy attire. By displaying what is on sale, this signal is allusive enough for those who want that sort of business to understand it but vague enough not to warrant an arrest, for anyone is free to walk the street. Above all, the signal prevents confusion, for ordinary women would not walk around like that. This ensures that a woman with that demeanor and outfit is *really* a prostitute. An ordinary woman would not only fail to obtain any benefit from looking like one but would pay some cost.

The driving force behind this effect is a self-enforcing belief, which in the above examples is sustained by social norms but which can work regardless of how the belief comes about. Thomas Schelling offers an entertaining list of such beliefs, for example: "if people believe that only men and women looking for sexual partners will go to singles bars, only men and women looking for sexual partners will go to singles bars."[20] Since no one who does not want a sexual partner would want to go to singles bars, patronizing one is a good signal that one wants a sexual partner.

A Digression

The strategy of policing signals and punishing those who display them "illegitimately" is of course common outside the criminal world—the laws protecting trademarks being the grand example in ordinary business. Historically, the zeal people have put into defending signals and thus their meaning has stretched to extravagant lengths, worthy of a brief digression. So-called sumptuary laws, aimed at banning fashion items or regulating the style of modifiable bodily traits such as beards, are found in a variety of societies and times. These laws usually emerge when a change in the price of the signaling items removes the cost discrimination that gave the items their informative value. Paul Blumberg writes: "A Massachusetts Act of 1651, for example, prohibited status disguises in such matters as dress, and declared 'our utter detestation and dislike that men and women of meane Condition should take upon themselves the garb of gentlemen, by wearing gold and silver, lace or buttons, or points at their knees or to walk in bootes or women of the same rancke to wear silke or tiffany horlles or scarfes, which though allowable to persons of greater estates, or more liberal education, yet we cannot but judge it intollerable in persons of such like condition.'"[21]

It was not only in Massachusetts that those who enjoyed the once exclusive possession of their distinctive items fought by law against their devaluing diffusion: "During the Tokugawa period (1603–1868) in Japan, people of every class were subject to strict sumptuary laws, which extended even to the types of umbrellas different people could use. In the second half of that period (the 18th–19th centuries), the merchant class (chōnin) had grown far wealthier than the aristocratic samurai, and these laws sought to maintain class divisions despite the ability of the merchants to wear far more luxurious clothing and to own far more luxurious items."[22] Misrepresentation of rank, as Richard Saller writes in *The Cambridge Ancient History*, was also a problem in the Roman Empire, and Roman writers satirized the illicit assumption of symbols of rank: "More than once Petronius' *Satyricon* characters manipulated those symbols of social identification. Martial repeatedly poked fun at men who attempted to misrepresent themselves as *equites* by wearing purple and sitting in rows reserved for the second *ordo* at the games. . . . Guards were employed by the emperor at public spectacles, but in general the administrative machinery was inadequate to keep the empire's tens of millions of inhabitants in their proper place, despite the threat of serious penalties."[23]

When the relative cost of certain items declines and more and more people can afford them, they lose their value as signals of status. In contemporary societies this process is allowed to follow its natural course. Think for instance of mobile phones, which were a prized trophy at first but are too common now to retain any status connotation. Or of suntans: ladies of means were supposed to protect their skin from the sun when peasant girls naturally bronzed in the course of their toil. Only when most women started to work indoors did having a tan became a sign of status, of being able to afford expensive holidays in the sun. Attempts to protect signals such as these would be laughable and, in liberal societies, highly controversial. Nowadays, Western societies regard items of personal adornment as fashion and consider it a right to decide freely what to don. Fashion, typically, is a set of volatile signals of status that work for limited periods and then decay. When an item signaling status spreads, the original users switch to some new signal. When in the 1970s youths started wearing T-shirts bearing the insignia of the University of Oxford, the real students simply stopped using them. Some started using their college's insignia, which used to be harder to purchase on the open market. Often, the link between fashion and meaning is loosened to the point of meaninglessness. Umberto Eco provides an amusing description of the meaning of the beard in Italy. Before 1968 the beard was a sign of being a little to the right. In 1968 it became a sign of being a revolutionary Marxist. Since 1968 it has meant nothing at all. Right, left, and center, there are men on every part of the political spectrum wearing one. Displaying a beard conveys no information about one's political preferences, and no group can claim exclusive rights to beards.

And yet, the likes of sumptuary laws still rear their ugly head in religious matters. France introduced a contentious prohibition of Islamic head scarves in public buildings, and in Turkey the military leaders, who are staunch secularists, tried to outlaw beards for men and head scarves for women as a measure against the spreading of the insignia of Islamic fundamentalism.[24] Conversely, in Afghanistan men who trim their beards rather than leave them to grow to their naturally scruffy state, as strict fundamentalist rules dictate, have been jailed,[25] and in Iraq barbers who comply when men want their beards shaved have been threatened and even murdered.[26]

ACTING ON THE COST OF PRODUCTION

Not all conventional signals are ipso facto cheap to produce. Contrary to a common belief, denoting by cost differentials and denoting by convention are not mutually exclusive—even talk is not necessarily cheap. Certain signals come in a cocktail that contains elements of both.

Consider the case when the set of cost-discriminating signals that only genuine possessors of the property being signaled can afford is plural. There are many ways, for instance, to signal that one is not afraid to die.[27] In one family of such signals, known as "games of chicken," one must prove to be as tough as or tougher than others who are simultaneously competing—the toughest is the person who is the last to slam on the brakes before a precipice, to move away from the railroad tracks when a train is approaching, to drive on the wrong side of the road on a highway. Groups opt for one form or another of the game, which may then persist and become their tradition. But a priori they could be indifferent about which game to adopt. The convention in the group consists of playing *that* game rather than another, while the cost discrimination, which separates the tough from the weak, lies in being prepared *to play* any such game and play it well rather than not playing it or playing it badly.

Here is another example of conventionally denoting yet costly signals. Having the upper part of one's body fully tattooed is a signal of belonging to the yakuza. "This elaborate art"—writes Christopher Seymour— "often covering the complete torso and thighs, is traditionally executed with wooden needles and it is an excruciatingly slow and painful process. Even with an electric needle, a full body tattoo can take a year to complete."[28] Also, having a missing little finger—an act of self-punishment among yakuza—is a signal of belonging to the yakuza. Depending on the gang, the proportion of members without at least one little finger ranges from 40 to 70 percent.[29] It takes considerable resilience to have such large surface of one's body tattooed, and a great deal of courage to lop one's little finger off. Tattoos and a missing little finger are therefore cost denoting with respect to not doing them. People who display these features reveal resilience and courage whether they are yakuza or not. These signs however also conventionally denote membership in the yakuza: other forms of equally painful and self-inflicted surgery, like cutting one's ear off, could conceivably be used as alternative identifiers of yakuza. Signals such as those mentioned above show whether someone is tough while at the same time identifying him as a member of a group or criminal organization. It is very important to notice that if the signals were not costly to produce, they would fail not just at conveying the first message but the second too, for impostors could easily perform or don them. So their being signals of toughness sustains their robustness as signal of identity too.

Sometimes nature (and the technological innovations that allow us to exploit it) offers us signals that, while conventionally associated with a trait, are very hard to reproduce. The face or the fingerprints we are born with may be considered conventional to the extent that we could have been born with other faces or fingerprints, which could just as well identify us. But these are also naturally protected. The near uniqueness of these features makes confusion unlikely. Above all, the fact that no one else can easily choose to don our face or fingerprints makes them reliable signatures, costless for us and impossible for others to replicate. If replacing one's face with a different one were as easy as switching names, the face would no longer identify anyone with the same certainty (there are many anecdotes about the mischief that identical twins enjoy by exploiting their near-identical faces). One can modify soft features of the face—the hairdo, the beard, the eye color (with contact lenses). But we are essentially stuck with the face we have. While this may be a hindrance when one wants to avoid identification, it also makes our face a very safe identifier. At most one can undergo plastic surgery—many criminals have done so—and acquire a new face that did not exist before, but one will never be able to look precisely like someone else in particular. Besides, with the limits of today's surgical techniques, facial alterations are both very costly and irreversible. Friends and foes alike can identify each of us by our face because they reidentify that face as the same one we displayed in previous encounters, as they do when they reidentify us by name. Unlike names, which are easy to change, the face or fingerprints are much safer identifiers, for the cost of someone else's "wearing" them in order to pass as us is infinitely high.

If nature does not help, signals that conventionally denote may also be made more costly for mimics, by making them more costly to produce for the real possessors. The extra cost is worth it if it is outweighed by the benefit (and if alternative signals would be even more costly).

The ability of conventional signals to remain reliable can be sustained by policing them not at the level of their use but at that of their knowledge, in short by keeping them secret. The cost of mimicking the signal here is increased simply because secrecy arrangements make it harder for mimics to find out what the signal is. This strategy applies in particular to symbolic signs. Computer passwords are conventional, and their legitimate possessors can coin them at little cost. Once known they would be costless to mimic, yet thanks to a number of technological and organizational arrangements, they can be made expensive for hackers to get hold of. Similarly, code names serve their purpose by conventionally identifying individuals to those in the know while making their real identity mysterious to strangers, insofar as the other names of the bearers remain a secret.[30] The receiver will be more likely to believe that signals are "honest" if he believes that the costs for a mimic to discover the signal are high. For instance, the IRA devised a secret code—known only to the British police—that they used when they issued ex ante warnings about bombs they had placed or when they claimed the paternity for them ex post. Not only did the code make the information credible because it reidentified a group that had acquired a reputation for planting bombs but also (so long as it was believed to remain secret) because it created an obstacle for would-be IRA impersonators who might like either to play nasty pranks or to plant a real bomb to discredit the IRA.[31]

A strategy often used to keep signals secret consists of changing them frequently—we are all asked to change our passwords regularly—to keep one step ahead of the mimics who may learn them in some way. Kaminski[32] provides a good example that he collected during his unplanned stay in Polish prisons in 1985. The grypsmen, a group of veteran prisoners whom we have already encountered, used a secret argot, which they taught to novices in nocturnal courses, to be able to identify each other when moving from prison to prison. This language, when used by prisoners belonging to the lesser caste known as suckers, "contains frequent mistakes that a grypsman is strictly and explicitly forbidden to commit." These mistakes give away the suckers who try to pass themselves off as initiated grypsmen. "Though there exist dictionaries of prison argot, they become slightly inadequate just in the moment of, or a short while after, publication." To counter the weakening of secrecy, "With an amazing degree of coordination among grypsmen in various prisons, every several years some key elements of prison language or symbolic tattoos are exchanged or transformed."[33]

Another way of keeping mimics at bay consists of realizing the signals in such a way as to make them costly to reproduce. Introducing special paper or watermarks on banknotes or bar codes on personal documents are methods of this kind that prevent mimics' forgeries at a cost for the real signaler. An underworld equivalent, for instance, involves making a signal more painful to acquire, such as extending the part of the body that needs to be covered by a tattoo. The strategy of increasing the cost of reproduction of an otherwise conventional signal is feasible if the signal has some tangible aspect to it, an object or body part for instance. If there is learning involved, however, one still can make the code more elaborate, so as to be more difficult to be learned. "In pre-war *yakuza* society"—Peter Hill writes—"an important aspect of training was the learning of *jingi*. Literally *jingi* translates as humanity and justice though it later came to be used by *yakuza* to refer to correct *yakuza* conduct and in particular to the formal greetings, given in a half-crouch, half-bow posture, peculiar to this world. *Jingi* takes three distinct forms, *ait-suki-mentsu*, *mawari-mentsu* and *goro-mentsu*, which are used as a form of *yakuza* self-introduction in one-to-one, group and threatening situations respectively. Trainees who failed to correctly recite *jingi* greetings in public could be beaten without impunity by *yakuza* from other groups."[34] The nature and use of *jingi* made it hard for mimics to reproduce it and worked well as an "authentic" signature. Even if one saw it performed once, one could not memorize and imitate it faultlessly. While purely conventional, in that one can think of an infinite number of alternative configurations that the ritual could take, it was so costly to learn for mimics that it was well protected. One could only learn it the hard way, and be taught by those who knew it. Furthermore, additional elaboration and new variants could be introduced to make *jingi* increasingly costly to learn.

Interestingly, the use of both *jingi* and its equivalent in the Chinese triads have now faded, and "nowadays, secret hand signs, poems and passwords are seldom used."[35] There are two explanations for this decline: either yakuza found cheaper yet safe ways to identify each other, or the cost of producing *jingi* increased beyond its value. If mimics kept up with yet more elaborate versions, and the versions used became indeed very elaborate, there would come a point at which increasing the cost of learning them could no longer be sustained by the genuine signalers as it eventually outgrew the benefit.

The most elaborate (and unbearably gruesome) case I know in which costly and conventional signals have been coupled occurred in London in the summer of 2001, when police discovered by the side of the river Thames the torso of a six-year-old boy of African origins. Timothy Taylor, a forensic archaeologist who was asked by police to study the case, wrote: "His head, arms and legs had been severed in a practiced five-point dismemberment that left short sections of protruding bone, terminating in neatly sawn and snapped ends."[36] Although Taylor's immediate impression was that a lone psychopath had performed this ritual killing, he noticed odd details. The missing parts of the body of Adam, the name the police gave to this unfortunate child, were never found, so why not hide the torso too? Why dispose of it in a way that would make it easy to discover? In addition, the torso had been dressed postmortem in orange shorts, and the autopsy established that the boy was administered a drink, made from a poisonous African bean, to paralyze him.[37] Taylor's conclusion was that the perpetrators of this heinous crime wanted it to be discovered. A similar case had occurred in Cape Town in 1994 and had been linked to the trade in body parts, which in some parts of Africa are believed to have healing powers. This trade of ritual medicine, practiced by witch doctors called *isangoma*, is known as *muti*. It includes plants and animals, but "the most sought after kind of human muti is made from children's body parts and its production follows strict rules," two of which are that the parts delivered for healing "must be wrapped in different coloured cloths" and "the torso left in water."[38] The police investigation concluded that Adam too was the victim of a ritual killing linked to muti.

Even more than in other criminal trades, in the case of muti the buyers, who must be paying vast sums of money, need to trust that what they are getting is the genuine article; they "want to know that what they are getting did not come from a dead animal, a dodgy undertaker or a hospital morgue with lax security."[39] Taylor's interpretation was that "the orange colour of the boy's shorts served not simply to attract attention to his dismembered torso, but put out a specific signal to those for whose benefit the ritual was being conducted. In retrospect, it is easy to see that releasing details to the media aided the transmission of this signal. The perpetrators wanted the torso to be found quickly and described publicly so that they could complete the process of ritual validation, demonstrating that this was not any torso, but one that had been shorn of body parts in traditional fashion."[40] The color of the shorts was a signal that identified conventionally a muti ritual killing, but it did that only because it was coupled with an actual child's torso in those conditions of dismemberment, something that only a trained isangoma could carry out. It was a fiendishly elaborate signal, which did not require any contact with the intended receiver and which, at first, only the receiver must have understood. While the practice continues in South Africa,[41] Adam's killers remain unknown.

Avoiding Easy-to-Fake Signals

In some cases the only way to protect a signal from mimics is to avoid its use altogether: *people like us never use s to mean k*. This is the first step before further establishing alternative ways to convey *k*, usually by coupling different conventional signals with some costly-to-fake arrangements. A mafioso, for instance, cannot introduce himself directly to another mafioso whom he does not yet know by saying "Hi, I am a mafioso." First, real mafiosi do not use the term *mafioso*. Next, they have established that a third mafioso, a guarantor who knows both parties in their capacity as mafiosi, is always required to certify membership. The third mafioso knows that the other two are too, either by having witnessed their initiation ritual or by having been introduced to one of them in the past by yet another mafioso. The introduction is then conventionally phrased in one of the following ways: "this is our friend" or "this is the same thing," "this is like you and me," "this is the same thing, this is our thing." By using the plural they ensure that in the first person those sentences would sound ungrammatical and awkward —"I am a friend of ours" or "I am like you and me"—and they avoid the confusion with the phrase "this is a friend of *mine*" when meant literally. When misused, these utterances would not only be disbelieved but reveal that one was facing a fraud. While breaching an external norm or convention, as I discussed above, can signal authenticity, in this case breaching the (internal) norm is a sign of mendacity.

A case reported by Antonino Calderone, a prominent mafioso who turned state's evidence, indicates that this ritual is scrupulously observed: in the 1950s Indelicato "Al" Amedeo, son of Giuseppe, a member of the Catania family, migrated to Philadelphia, where he was subsequently initiated into the local family. When Al returned to Sicily a few years later he could not introduce himself as a man of honor to his own father: they had to wait for the return of Calogero Sinatra, who knew about Al's membership.[42]

This strategy, which reduces the likelihood that a mimic will succeed in passing himself off as a mafioso by simply saying that he is one, comes however at a considerable cost. The following story illustrates just how many intermediaries are required for two "made guys" belonging to two mafia families, one in New York and the other in Milwaukee, to set up a meeting. Lefty Ruggiero wanted to meet Frank Balistrieri to obtain the latter's permission for Donnie Brasco and Tony Conte to get into the business of vending machines in Milwaukee. In order to do that Lefty first had to meet with Tony Riela, an eighty-year-old capo of the Bonanno family in Newark, New Jersey. Tony Riela was the only guy whom Lefty knew who had contacts in Chicago. "The understanding was, Riela would make the calls to Chicago to set up a meeting. The

Chicago people would call people in Rockford. And those people would make the introductions to Balistrieri in Milwaukee."[43] "More than a month had gone by so far in arranging for the meet." Lefty said to Donnie, "I got me [*sic*] a sitdown with the two main guys in that town where you are now [Rockford]. I can't get no names until I get out there. When I get there, I gotta make a phone call back to New York at six o'clock, tell them where I am, what room number. They call the Chicago guy. He is gonna come and pick me up. They are gonna take me away. They're gonna talk to me. And they are gonna check this guy [Tony Conte] out completely."[44]

When the preliminaries were sorted out, "Lefty flew out. We went to our room at the Midway Motor Lodge. Lefty called New York and told them what room he was in. New York was to call the Chicago-Rockford people and tell them what room Lefty was in. Then somebody would call and say they were on the way to pick us up. We just had to sit and wait for the phone call."[45] In the end they had to wait for several days. And that was just to be introduced by the Chicago-Rockford mob, which had good connections with both New York and Milwaukee, to the wiseguys in Milwaukee. The same operation in the world of ordinary business would have taken minutes and one or two phone calls.

There are, however, other circuitous identification strategies that are cheap for honest signalers and impossibly expensive for impostors. To issue a credible request for protection money, for instance, some criminals do not mention their names or that of their organization but instruct the victim to find out about their credentials in a very astute way. A request for protection money made to a building contractor came over the telephone and was phrased as follows: "You are well-advised to get in touch with *the friends* of Palizzi" (Palizzi is a small hill town of about one thousand families in southern Calabria, Italy). The contractor's reply must have been something like "who the heck are they and where am I supposed to find them?" The counterreply, of which we have a record, was simple: "ask around and you'll find out."[46]

This seems unnecessarily tortuous: why not just say there and then who these "friends" are and where they can be found? The fact is that a mere verbal claim would be easy to mimic. Anybody could ring up, claim to be the "*friends* of Palizzi," and "fraudulently" get protection money. Alternatively, if the "real" friends of Palizzi chose to be direct, they might not be taken seriously and might be refused protection money, forcing them to send more costly signals, such as the proverbial warning bomb placed on the construction site. By contrast, here the signaler makes a deliberate generic claim, attracts the attention of the contractor, and encourages him to check the identity of the caller by asking around. If by asking people at random the contractor finds that everybody provides the name of the *same* man or men, he receives the implicit guarantee that the caller must be one of the right "friends," those whose permission he must obtain if he wants to work in Palizzi without trouble. No impostor could persuade such an assortment of his fellow citizens to speak in unison and provide the same answer. This outcome can only be effortlessly achieved by the real thing.

This form of verification also happens naturally, without any special effort being made by the signaler. The following account, recorded in court proceedings, captures Peppino Settecasi—the most prominent mafia man in Agrigento, Sicily, until he was shot dead in 1981—trying to sell protection. The targeted entrepreneur was asked by the prosecutor to describe the exact nature of his relationship with Zu' Peppino:

> I met [Settecasi] at the building site. The foreman told me he [Settecasi] was a very amenable man who knew just about everybody in town and that by coming to the building site he [Settecasi] was making himself available to sort things out for the firm as well as its employees. I was told that he [Settecasi] had been involved in trying to house some of the workers, that he used to take workers in need to see the doctor [who happened to be his son-in-law], and to make bargain purchases [presumably protecting the sellers from competition]. I myself remember that once I opened a bank account at the Banco di Sicilia and that I went there accompanied by my accountant. There I met Settecasi who intervened on my behalf to speed up the paperwork. I believe his son worked there. I realized that Settecasi was a well known and respected man when at the feast of the "almond tree in blossom" I was near the Bar Patti

with my family for about an hour looking at the floats. Settecasi was nearby and *I noticed that everybody who went by stopped to greet him and addressed him with deference.*"[47]

This process, which has the form *if everyone treats X as the top man, then X must be the top man*, works in many settings for legitimizing the authority of individuals, not just organized-crime characters.[48]

Sometimes this process is understood as purely self-fulfilling rather than as conveying preexisting information about the standing of a certain individual, as if the *only* reason why X becomes the top man is that people believe that he is. Although conceivable in theory, I do not think that this elegant state of affairs is the case among mafiosi. To be and to remain the top man, a mafioso has to do bad things to establish his reputation. Once his deeds become known, people believe in his power. Even if this can become a self-sustaining mechanism—in the sense that just the collective belief in his power can sustain a top man in his position of authority even after the memory of the deeds from which the belief originated has faded—it can continue only so long as his position is not challenged by competitors. In the tough mafia world, that period tends to be short, as rivals suspecting weakness tend to test the incumbent, and the incumbent has to either resort to violence again or succumb.

CONCLUSIONS

There is a general feature of communication that can support the strategy of coupling conventional signals with cost-discriminating ones. When people make a purely conventional claim, by means of words for instance, they do not do so in a void. Whenever we send a signal, we use a medium that carries other signs with it whether we like it or not. Even in relatively simple cases, signalers cannot easily avoid conveying other information about their identity. When signed, even a name, this most conventional of signs, carries further information—as a *signature*—that is harder to mimic than just the name, such as the handwriting of the signatory. If a claim is made through the telephone, the speaker reveals his accent and voice; and if the claim is made face-to-face, he will have to reveal his looks and bodily features. If it is known that a certain claim can only come paired with other features that are costly to acquire unless one truly has them, that claim is screened by those other features also. Any absence or inconsistent variation induces suspicion in the receiver. Mimics have to work hard both to veil any incongruous feature and to acquire those additional signs necessary to make their total presentation consistent with their lie. We will see, in the next chapter, how being Sicilian or, more generally, how signs of ethnicity can fulfill that function and protect the mafia against mimics.

CHAPTER 8

Criminal Trademarks

> "Listen, the word Mafia no one can touch it, no one!
> They can destroy mafiosi but not the Mafia, understand?"[1]

"We miss something, Charlie"—Meyer Lansky once told Charlie "Lucky" Luciano, who was starting a new gang—"You've got to give the new setup a name; after all, what the fuck is any business or company without a name? A guy don't walk into an automobile showroom and say, 'I'll take the car over there, the one without a name.'"[2] Renowned for his shrewdness, Lansky understood that criminals need names to advertise themselves as buyers or suppliers in their illegal trade.

One of the most important functions that names and other conventional signs fulfill is to help reputations travel through time and from person to person. Once we come into contact with producers or with their products, we gain experience of their quality. If they are identifiable by some sign, we can then establish an association between the quality and their signs. When we encounter these signs again, they will evoke the quality in our minds. The cluster of signs that conveys the reputation of well-established firms is known as a *trademark*. Trademarks can include names and symbolic insignia, such as a logo, as well as other features—color scheme, shape of a product, packaging design, advertising slogans, and jingles—that enable consumers, after a first encounter, to reidentify a producer or his products and distinguish them from others. Trademarks are a form of signaling quality by signaling identity.[3]

There is a problem, however. Most economic studies of reputation consider the accurate reidentification of the signs associated with a product or a producer as unproblematic. All it takes—economists assume—is to achieve a good reputation by doing the right things and to continue behaving well to maintain it. This assumption, however, skips a crucial step. The reidentification of a trademark is not straightforward, and producing high-quality goods does not suffice. First, people make identification mistakes. In order to avoid them the signs used to identify a firm must be easy to memorize and to distinguish from other signs.[4] They must also be capable of drawing the attention of consumers, and be attractive in themselves. If the world of trademarks becomes crowded— as is now the case of domain names on the Internet—signalers will also compete on design grounds, and latecomers will find it increasingly difficult to think of signs that satisfy those requirements. The design of trademarks is an essential part of maintaining a reputation.

The serious threat to correct trademark identification, however, comes from mimics who deliberately copy the signs of a successful firm in order to exploit its reputation. Copying conventional signs can, as we know, be relatively cheap. If a dealer relies on his personal presence to convey reputation, then he will have little to fear from mimics, for faces cannot be reproduced. But most firms need to advertise far and wide without requiring the presence of key personnel, which is the point of having a trademark. If the sign conveying the reputation is, for instance, some pictorial rendition of the founder's face inscribed in a logo, its reproduction becomes easier. Ideally, firms need to design trademarks that are not just memorable and distinctive but also difficult for mimics to reproduce. The more successful a firm is, the more its trademark is in danger of being fraudulently reproduced, and the higher the risk that its value will be destroyed. If mimics supply lower-quality goods under the signs of the higher-quality ones, not only do they ride on the original producer's reputation, but they can tarnish it by confusing consumers. Design alone, however, is often insufficient to prevent mimicry, and firms also need to protect their trademarks by policing and punishing abuses.[5] In the world of legal business the law assists firms in this endeavor, but in the underworld people cannot rely on the law. Can criminals still develop trademarks and protect them from mimics? This is the topic of this chapter.

THE LIMITS OF UNDERWORLD REPUTATIONS

When we consider how we assess the quality of the goods we purchase, we find two extremes. At one extreme there are goods whose qualities are transparent and which are traded in a medium that allows for assessing their quality at low cost, such as fruit or cheese bought at the market. These goods need no reputation, as their quality can be assessed by looking at them and by tasting a morsel. At the other extreme there are goods that are "inscrutable," such as religious services: insofar as they are attended for eternal salvation, only after death will we be able to find out their quality.[6] The closer a good is to inscrutability, the higher the value of reputation to those who sell it. The vast majority of goods, however, fall between these extremes; they are not inscrutable, yet their quality is not immediately perceivable. The quality of these goods— called "experience goods"[7]—is not assessed by simply examining the product. People who buy them have no clear knowledge of their quality—a knowledge that they gain only by experiencing the good over a period of time. Lenders, for instance, "buy" a promise from borrowers that they will get their money back plus interest. How do they know whether someone is a good debtor before getting their money back? Even goods the quality of which is apparent at close range—such as clothes—become harder to assess if traded at a distance. If a potential buyer does not trust a supplier's reputation, if he fears getting stuck with a "lemon," he may not buy, and if that supplier is actually honest, the lack of trust prevents a beneficial exchange to the detriment of both parties.

Those who sell goods whose quality is not apparent fare much better if they can rely on a good reputation. At times, prospective buyers can test the quality of a product by sampling it, as with a wine, a fabric, or a car one can test-drive. A dealer can thus establish a good reputation with first-time customers and live off it in subsequent exchanges with those customers and their friends. But when options such as these are not readily available and testing a product's quality before purchase is too costly, reputation becomes even more important.

Criminal firms are no exception. They too trade in experience goods, such as bets, drugs, or prostitution. The trouble for them, however, is that while the secrecy and instability that characterize the underworld increase the demand for reliability, they also make it harder to both reassure and feel reassured by others. There are no certifying institutions assisting illegal markets. "There is no equivalent in the marijuana mar-

ket"—Peter Reuter writes—"to the Department of Agriculture's grad-
ing of meat. The marijuana purchaser must resort to self-testing";[8] and it
is expensive to test the quality of marijuana, especially in retail transactions that involve small quantities. Typically, there are no enforcing institutions either, which could make guarantees credible or to which one
could resort when cheated. In the case of goods or situations in which
testing is either physically impossible or uneconomical, firms in the legal
world still have other means to signal their qualities, for instance by
costly advertisements that show one trusts one's own business to do well,
or by pledging to replace items or give money back in case of customer
dissatisfaction. These strategies, however, are not open to criminals. Not
only can they not advertise, but the lack of an enforcement agency in
the underworld makes guarantees void, for nothing, no independent
agency such as the law, backs them up.

Other things being equal, the value of a good reputation should therefore be even higher in the underworld than in the world of legal business. So, for instance, as Reuter points out, "Bookmakers place a high
value on reputation since the nature of their business requires frequent
extensions of credits to customers; the only alternative is joint escrow
accounts, which create risk of legal exposure and have significant transaction costs."[9] In most criminal markets, however, other things are not
equal. The restrictions under which people operate in the underworld
make it harder to develop and divulge a reputation. Reuter, for instance,
says that in the heroin market the risks are so high that traders are not
likely to share information with other traders, thereby hampering the
spread of reputations, good and bad alike.[10] Furthermore, the uncertainty
besetting the underworld makes it essential that the reputation bearer be
an individual and hinders the reputation's extension to supraindividual
entities, as would happen in the normal business world. In the underworld, people find it harder to assess the trustworthiness of abstract entities or groups. First, they cannot if cheated retaliate against them as easily
as they can retaliate against a specific person. Next, they cannot as easily
generalize from the qualities of an individual to the qualities of supraindividual entities. This is because corporate reasoning here hardly applies,
for why should other individuals carry forward the pledges of someone

else? There is no mechanism for transmitting obligations that criminals can develop and on which their customers can rely.

As a result, the time horizon of a criminal enterprise tends to coincide with the life expectancy of the individuals at its core, which given the nature of the business is shorter than that of individuals in ordinary business. In fact the time horizon is shorter than individual life expectancies, for criminals can go to jail or into hiding, and become unable to live up to their promises. Also, reputation assets cannot be easily transferred to others by selling or bequeathing them. The names that count in the underworld are those of individuals. At best, reputation extends only to family members.[11] These limitations imply that the value of building a long-lasting reputation is generally lower for illegal business than for legal business, as the expected returns are lower over time and more uncertain. So while criminals may still be eager to establish personal reputations, they will be less likely to try to establish metaindividual trademarks like those which populate the business world. Even if they wanted to do so, they could not easily succeed.

This prediction is largely borne out in practice. Still, there are two exceptions in which trademarks of a sort have emerged: the heroin market in some cities of the United States and the illegal protection market in various parts of the world. How was this possible? The rest of this chapter is devoted to investigating these exceptions.

HEROIN STAMPS

Over the past thirty years in some U.S. cities, heroin has been sold to consumers in bags carrying marks, such as colored strips of tape or, more often, stamps containing a name and a logo. Two ethnographies of the phenomenon in New York City, where the practice seems to have emerged first, identified hundreds of stamp names, ranging from the threatening (DEAD MAN WALKING, FINAL NIGHTMARE, REST IN PEACE) to the boastful (MAGIC TOUCH, DYNAMITE, RED HOT), drawing from pop culture and movies (TERMINATOR, GODZILLA, BLACK SUNDAY), or mimicking designer brands (MERCEDES, GUCCI, DOM PERIGNON).[12] The protagonists of the heroin market interviewed by the ethnographers provide a few explanations of the emergence of stamps, one of which stands out above all others: dealers believe that stamps are good both to reassure buyers and to make the reputation of their heroin travel from consumer to consumer. As many dealers themselves said, customers who experience a good bag come back for more and tell others about it, a view confirmed by customers themselves. The stamps, by allowing reidentification, make both steps possible even if the street dealer changes.

The reason why this is important is that consumers fret about quality: heroin comes to the retail market in varying qualities, for, in order to make more money, unscrupulous dealers, often other addicts themselves, cut the heroin with various inert substances.[13] Heroin can thus be diluted and sold at various levels of purity to the point that some bags, known as "beat bags" or "dummies,"[14] contain no heroin at all. Although a few temperate consumers look for lower levels of purity aiming to reach only a controlled experience,[15] most look for the purest heroin because it enhances the high they achieve—so much so that a death by overdose, when it becomes known, is a sign of high quality rather than a warning to stay away, and when a stamp is associated with a death, sales of the relevant heroin are boosted.[16]

There are no easy ways to establish heroin purity on the street. As a customer said, "Anybody can say 'I got good dope.' Nobody will say, 'Try this and if you don't like it, you'll get your ten dollars back.'"[17] Also, "usually price does not vary within a local market,"[18] and every dealer sells bags of the same size at the same price—for instance in New York in the early 1980s "dope was universally sold in stamped $10 bags."[19] Clinton Taylor suggests that price invariance is due to the pressure for speedy transactions, which leaves little time for bargaining on the streets. Whatever the reason, buyers cannot use price as a guide to quality, and dealers compete on purity.[20]

There is also more than anecdotal evidence that stamps are intended to signal quality. First, on the basis of the Office of National Drug Control Policy yearly reports, Taylor established that, remarkably, in cities in the American West the phenomenon has *not* emerged; it is found only in cities east of the Mississippi River. This is because in western cities the dealers sell "Mexican brown or black tar heroin, which cannot be improved or diluted,"[21] thus making heroin a standardized commodity and removing uncertainty about quality. Next, evidence that uncertainty about quality was crucial in the emergence of stamps can be induced from the period in which they appeared. First spotted in the early 1970s in New York, the use of stamps increased massively toward the end of that decade. According to Richard Curtis and Travis Wendel, the heroin market in New York City began to fragment in 1957 when "the mafia 'officially' withdrew from the heroin market."[22] Even though some individual mafiosi continued to be involved, the weakened monopolistic control allowed new distributors to enter, and quality started to vary.

At first, the new players were few and well established, and since "distribution was tightly controlled within a given neighbourhood customers knew whose heroin they were buying."[23] Three events in the 1970s, however, led to further fragmentation. First, at the beginning of the decade an "influx of new users, including many returning Vietnam veterans introduced to heroin while serving overseas, led the markets to increase in size and volume of sales,"[24] and this attracted new dealers. Next, in 1973 there was a "dope panic," a shortage that led to a 150 percent price increase, which, the demand being rather inelastic because of addiction, attracted yet more dealers. The expansion had, however, a weakening effect on quality assurance: heroin became easier to buy, but the market became anonymous, and one did not know whose heroin one was buying. It was around that time that identifying marks began to appear.[25] At first they were colored strips of tape; however, since these "proved too easy to counterfeit"[26] and, one can further suppose, too limited in number to offer sufficient options for differentiation, they were quickly replaced by stamps with names and logos. These first appeared in Harlem in the mid-1970s.

There is a further cause to consider. Law enforcement was rather absent from the retail (street) level during most of the 1970s paradoxically because, following the Knapp Commission hearings of 1968–72, which had revealed widespread corruption among police officers who were taking bribes from dealers, the New York Police Department had removed officers from the street to remove opportunities for corruption.

At the same time, however, the police started targeting bigger fish until, in 1979, they arrested Harlem's kingpin, Nicky Barnes. "In destroying the Barnes monopoly, law enforcement practices created . . . an opening in the market that was filled by new distributors, who literally wanted to make a name for themselves in order to increase their share in a burgeoning market. The usefulness of stamps was reinforced by the entry of freelancers and small businesses who rushed in to fill the vacuum. . . . Even if they [are] outnumbered by sellers of high-quality heroin, a few 'beat artists' can serve to create enough uncertainty among buyers that they ultimately set the tone of the market."[27]

Wendel and Curtis report a decline in stamps in New York since 1995,[28] confirmed by Taylor's data for 2001 and 2002.[29] They explain it by the decline of street sales caused at once by more aggressive law enforcement and by the growth of "beeper dealers" who deliver at home. The decline, however, is not universal. In 2001 and 2002 there was a marked increase in the presence of stamps in Philadelphia. In early 2001 several federal agencies dismantled an "elaborate syndicate" of drug traffickers in the city: "The number of brands in Philadelphia skyrocketed in the months following Operation White Horse," and even though "there is no way to confirm the increase in brands had not already began before the arrests,"[30] this evidence strengthens the hypothesis that brands tend to emerge when hegemonic dealers are removed from the market, which as a result becomes more uncertain and fragmented.

Taylor points out that the existence of stamps poses two puzzles: "first, competitors could adulterate or counterfeit a successful brand, and no court exists to enforce a drug dealer's trademark. Second, brands offer a clear chain of evidence that could lead law enforcement right back to the seller."[31]

Consider the latter question first. Relative to anonymous bags, branded heroin may indeed be more traceable to the seller. On the other hand, as the carriers of reputation, stamps are much better than personal names: they are the product equivalent of nicknames, distancing the given name of the dealer from the name of his wares.[32] So it is not obvious that they provide such a clear chain of evidence. They may provide evidence that bags sold under the same stamp come from the same source, and they may allow law enforcement to have an idea of the number of dealers and their relative market share; but they say nothing about who the source is. At worst, they may offer proof that a bag with a certain stamp bought by an undercover agent was provided by a dealer who sells bags with that stamp, or constitute evidence that buyer A found in possession of a stamped bag is linked to seller B who sells them. But, by themselves, they do not reveal much of the dealer's identity. Ultimately dealers have a choice, as a customer said: "depending on how much risk they're willing to take when they have a stable product [same stamp and same good quality], they attract more customers, and then they get more police attention."[33]

The first puzzle is more serious: how could heroin stamps survive the threat of mimicry? We know that "a few stamps acquired long-term reputations (like POISON, NO JOKE, and 9½ PLUS) and lasted for years" offering quality that was "consistently good," but very few stamps have been in circulation for more than two or three months, and "many stamps last only a few days before being replaced."[34] So this question has two horns: first, why do only a few stamps manage to be stable and reliable over long periods of time despite the threat of counterfeiting, and why do dealers of all sorts continue to put stamps on bags even though the longevity of most of them is so short?

The answer to the first question seems to be that "a major deterrent to counterfeiting labels was that counterfeiters would be, and have been, threatened, assaulted or killed by the real dealers of that particular label."[35] Sometimes the punishment was carried out impromptu by angry customers; at other times, the customers would alert the real dealers; for instance, if the mimicry was badly executed, savvy customers would detect some imprecision in the features of the stamps or in the way bags were folded and taped; or they would become suspicious when the street dealer appeared "sick from heroin withdrawal," a sign that he was an addict in a state that made him ready "to rip anyone off."[36] However, the key element is probably that the handful of stamps that managed to survive over long periods of time "were issued by large organisations with outlets throughout the city,"[37] for only large, well-organized outfits could muster the power to police and deter counterfeiters.

What about the smaller dealers, however, the so-called freelancers, who continued putting stamps on their bags even though they expected their brands to be short-lived, and who kept changing them frequently? This defeats the purpose of branding, as the association between signs and quality is disrupted, making it impossible for a reputation to develop; it implies that the explanation we gave of the emergence of stamps cannot explain why they spread to involve dealers who could not really protect them and were forced to change them frequently. To understand the possible logic of their choice, we have to consider the alternative they faced, namely selling *anonymous* heroin bags. It seems likely that in a market in which some stamps begin to appear, it becomes marginally better to have a stamp, however fleeting, than no stamp at all. Customers would be more suspicious of anonymity than of even a weak stamp. A stamp signals at least an intention to develop a reputation by making one's product minimally identifiable. Also, if it has a catchy name (and there is good evidence that dealers chose their stamp names with a view to making them salient[38]), even an unfamiliar stamp may attract customers in one-off encounters. This may be an underworld instance of a tendency we find in markets dominated by established brands, be they brands of watches or perfumes: even the smaller and less established producers give their products names and logos, even if these are unlikely to develop into widely recognizable brands. It is only where everyone is anonymous that anonymity is not conspicuous.

PROTECTION AND REPUTATION

Mafia-like groups need to have certain properties, which I have amply discussed elsewhere,[39] to succeed in business. The property that concerns us here is the special value that reputation has in the protection business. First, not only do protection firms benefit enormously from reputation; they do so in a very distinctive way. Reputation does not just save on signaling and testing costs for them and their customers. It saves on production costs directly. Building a reputation is *the* main production cost. Once one has a reputation as a reliable protector, one can cash in on it and does not need to do much else. Car manufacturers benefit from a good reputation, but they still have to produce cars. By contrast a reputation for providing high-quality protection and the production of protection itself largely overlap. The more robust the reputation, the lower the chances that anyone will challenge a mafioso's rulings and that he will need to back up his threats by actual force. The crucial element that makes the supply of protection viable is that the mafioso's threats be credible, which he established by his reputation. A mafioso could not run his business if he had to take action to establish his credentials at every transaction. People will gladly buy protection from and comply with protectors' decisions if they fear them and believe others fear them too. This is why mafiosi are so famously jealous of their professional reputation, as any loss might be fatal for them.

Next, protection agencies benefit enormously from developing as organizations, much more so than many other businesses. There are several "military" and economic reasons for this, but that which concerns us here is that an organization can become independent of the fate of its individual members. Insofar as the costs of starting a business and gaining the initial reputation are very high (as is true in the protection business), an organization that succeeds in embodying the reputation makes sure that one does not need to start again every time an individual dies or goes to jail. For this to happen, the organization must have clear and credible rules and practices capable of uncoupling the reputation of the organization from that of any particular individual. This permits the reputation to be transferred to subsequent generations of incumbents.

The more established a protection agency is, the less its reputation resides with a specific individual or even his gang. Criminal outfits that rely on individuals or at most on families of kin rather than on organizational rules and practices, such as the Neapolitan Camorra, may be less likely to produce turncoats, but as organizations they are not as effective as mafia-like agencies that succeed in growing out of those limitations. While for most illegal markets reputation is individually based, in the protection market the pressures to grow and to attach the reputation to a whole organization are particularly strong. The strength of the Sicilian mafia in the 150 years of its history is due largely to its success in this

regard. Judge Fabio Salamone captured with great accuracy the quintes-
sence of the Sicilian mafia as follows: "every associate can use [the
strength of intimidation] as an incorporeal good . . . an asset common to
all associates and therefore belonging pro indiviso to every single one of
them. . . . It is . . . a 'capital' which represents the result of a process of
'collective accumulation' and which can provide a 'rent' to the individual member even if he did not take part in the process. . . . Only because
he is known as such can a mafioso fulfill his aims."[40] Individuals and subgroups benefit from and contribute to the reputation of the organization as a whole, and the reputation is itself their common asset. To become a "made member" means being authorized to exploit the collective
reputational asset by those who "own" it. It amounts to being recognized as a legitimate bearer of that reputation by other members.

   Mafia-like groups thus have a paramount interest in carefully guard-
ing entry, thereby regulating the number and the quality of members
who can benefit from the collective reputation. According to Abadinsky,
for instance, in 1957 the American mafia families chose to stop admitting new members until 1976, and Frank Scalice, who "was selling membership to persons who wanted to have the status of being a member of
the mob . . . was shot to death in 1957."[41] Mafia families have a collective
interest in making sure that all families and members respect certain
rules in handling their business, so that their reputation and indirectly
the reputation of the industry remains solidly attached to the whole and
as detached as possible from individual vagaries. There have been conflicts among mafiosi on the best ways to uphold the collective interest,
especially in matters of which field of activity they should or should not
get involved. The protection of prostitution and drug trade has caused
controversy, for example, which was largely due to the risk these posed
to their collective reputation. However, at a fundamental level, the collective interest and that of each member have been aligned in sustaining
the common asset.

   A key feature of successful mafia-like groups, pace *The Godfather*, is
that their membership goes beyond kin. Mafiosi, contrary to a widely
held view, actively choose to initiate people who are not from the same
family. Kinship does not automatically qualify one for membership: Sal-

vatore Umina, a member of the Vicari mafia family, "was willing to let his brother Giuseppe in the family, whereas he was firmly opposed to the entry of his other brother, Gioacchino, since he thought he was not clever enough."[42] Members of the same biological family can be initiated in different mafioso families: Pietro Lo Iacono belongs to the Santa Maria del Gesu' family, whereas "Andrea Lo Iacono ... belongs to the Brancaccio family."[43] According to small-time criminal Stefano Calzetta, Carmelo Zanca was "in charge of the area," and his brothers, cousins, and brothers-in-law were his staff.[44] None of these, however, was a made member. Only two of the many Grado brothers were members of the family of Santa Maria del Gesu'.[45] Stefano Bontade agreed to "make" Salvatore but refused Gaetano, on the grounds that he was unreliable in sentimental matters. The same selection is reported with regard to the Vernengos. Pietro had been a member for some time, Nino was made in 1979, but Cosimo, despite Mannoia's backing, was rejected. "It suffices to make Nino," Bontade said.[46]

Succession also is not a family affair. In the early 1960s, the young Stefano Bontade replaced his father Paolino, who had diabetes,[47] and John Gotti appointed John Jr. to succeed him at the helm of the Gambino family in New York. But the cases in which the new boss was not related to the old one are many more. In 1943 Michele Navarra replaced Calogero Lo Bue as the boss of Corleone.[48] In 1963 Pippo Calò replaced "Filippone" as the head of Porta Nuova, a Palermo district, although the latter had a son of his own.[49] In 1974 in Ribera, near Agrigento, Carmelo Colletti replaced Paolo Campo, who had had a stroke,[50] and in the same year Mariano Marsala took over from Biagio Macaluso as boss of Vicari, near Palermo, because the latter could no longer walk properly.[51] The list could go on.

There is also evidence of an effort aimed at separating kinship from hierarchical positions: "After my brother's death, I knew that in some provinces it had been established that those two positions [*capo mandamento* and *rappresentante*] could not be held either by brothers or father and son at the same time."[52] In 1975 the "Commission" (or "Cupola," as the body formed by the dozen or so top mafiosi in Sicily is called), laid down the rule that "fathers and sons or brothers cannot be part of any

collective body at the same time, apart from those cases already in existence."[53] These rules are also applied by other mafia-like groups, such as
the triads[54] or the yakuza, and bosses' sons, for instance, do not normally
inherit the title.[55] In recent years, Peter Hill informs me, "The most no-
table exception to this pattern is the case of the Inagawa-kai. The current head of this group is Inagawa Chihiro son of the founder Inagawa
Kakuji. There was however a brief inter-regnum of Ishii Susumu."[56]

These practices are perhaps the mafia's most striking feature, those
which have given it its unique strength. They give "families" an organizational strength that goes well beyond the necessarily limited ties of a
family of kin. They guard the organization against the creation of internal factions, thus maintaining solidarity, and the meritocratic rather than
hereditary selection criteria ensure that the quality of membership remains high regardless of who is in power at any one moment. These are
the rules that can make an institution's reputation and thus its longevity
independent of the fate of its individual members. Michele Greco, the
grand boss in the 1970s, was elated when he found out that, unbeknownst to him, his son and nephew had been initiated in a different
family. Rather than taking it as a slight, he thought it was a sign that his
son had what it took to be recognized by other mafiosi and was particularly pleased to know that everything had been done "according to the
rules."[57] He took pride in seeing that his offspring succeeded without
his support. Far from being driven by a feudal or monarchic mentality,
mafiosi display a surprisingly modern mind-set in managing their organization, at odds with much of the Italian nepotistic and corrupt style.

THE NAME MAFIA

The question we need to address now is: by means of which signs does
the reputation of the mafia subsist? How does one make sure one is
dealing with the people who deserve the reputation rather than with
someone who just pretends to be a mafioso?

The name mafia itself seems to carry a powerful message. In the protection market, those believed to be members of the entity connoted by that name have a tremendous advantage over those who cannot induce that belief. They are capable of effective intimidation or reassurance, depending on whether one is their victim or protégé. The first to believe in the power of the name seem to be the mafiosi themselves. On 18 November 1993 Italian police recorded a conversation between two mafiosi discussing their current predicaments in view of the action of Italian law enforcement against them, which became much tougher during the 1990s. Many mafiosi, including nearly all prominent bosses, were captured and jailed. In the recorded conversation, one of the two mafiosi, whose identify was not disclosed, says: "The mafia was ruined by Totò Riina [the boss of bosses in the 1980s] in the last few years. He was too heavy handed [this refers to the murder of prominent judges, which induced a vigorous law-enforcement response]." The other, Salvatore "Robertino" Enea, who was arrested a few months later, replies: "Listen, the *word* Mafia no one can touch it, no one! They can destroy mafiosi but not the Mafia, understand?"[58]

Perhaps the most striking feature of the mafia is that its name has reached an almost mythical status independent of the individuals "incarnating" it at any one time. Only powerful entities such as nation-states, organized churches, corporations, or ancient academic institutions can achieve as lofty a status as that Robertino claims "the Mafia" has achieved. Before discussing whether Robertino's belief is warranted, we must consider where that name came from and how it gained its force.

Most trademarks in the legal world are invented and designed by their rightful owners. However, mafiosi did not choose the name that embodies their collective reputation. As in the cases in which mobsters have taken inspiration from movies and the media generally,[59] even in the case of the name they simply adopted the word that was used by outsiders to identify them. Its first appearance in an official document occurs in 1865, in a letter from the *delegato di Pubblica Sicurezza* in Carini (a town near Palermo), who justifies an arrest by referring to a "delitto di mafia." The prefect of Palermo, Gualterio, does likewise in a report to the minister of the interior later that year.[60] The hypotheses concerning the etymology of the word are no fewer than nineteen:[61] apart from two ludicrous exceptions, not a single one of them suggests that the word originated inside the mafia.

The most likely origin of the current meaning of *mafioso* and of its derivative *mafia*[62]—as suggested by the nineteenth-century Sicilian ethnographer Giuseppe Pitré—is a play by Placido Rizzotto, *I Mafiusi della Vicaria*, first performed in 1863 in Palermo. In Palermo dialect the word *mafiusu* means arrogant, cocky, and bold. Apparently the idea of using such a term arose by chance when Rizzotto overheard the irritated question "Chi vurrissi fari u mafiusu cu mia?" (Are you trying to be arrogant with me?) in a Palermo street.[63] The play describes the lives of a group of prisoners in the Palermo jail who command particular respect: although individualistic and quarrelsome, they are members of an association with definite behavioral rules, including an initiation ritual and a hierarchical structure, that claims it can influence the political and administrative system of the island. The reader may wonder how a single play could be responsible for the spread of such pervasive a word as *mafia*. The answer lies partly in its enormous success:[64] it was performed fifty-five times in 1863 alone and staged at least two thousand times over twenty-one years of touring in Southern Italian and Roman theaters. Few other plays can boast such a record.

It seems that the very word *mafia* was therefore coined externally, by a fictional source loosely inspired by the real thing, and was taken up by law enforcers. The fact that outsiders invented the word does not imply that those who identified with it could not adopt it as their own. Identities are reinforced by reference to outsiders, and no social or psychological law decrees that insiders should necessarily provide the linguistic tool kit upon which a self-conscious identity can be constructed. (Even insults can become names: "Tory," which refers to Conservatives in Britain and Canada, and "Whig," which refers to liberals, were both terms of abuse, meaning highway robber and yokel respectively, which progressively lost their pejorative meaning.)[65] The word *mafia* supplied outsiders with a label to identify a blurred conglomerate, thereby making it possible to speak and think of it as a whole. And the word provided the opportunity for individuals to associate themselves with an entity that carried a threatening reputation. In 1876, the same year in which the word appeared in the *Times* for the first time, Leopoldo Franchetti, an early and insightful scholar of the mafia, wrote: "Thus the term mafia found a class of violent criminals ready and waiting for a name to define them, and, given the special character and importance they have in Sicilian society, they had the right to a different name from that defining vulgar criminals in other countries."[66]

"Cosa Nostra," a more recent designation of the mafia common in the United States, also derives from an external interpretation and its subsequent internal reappropriation. First mentioned in the late 1950s by Joe Valachi—a mafioso turned state's evidence—during the hearings of the McClellan Senate Commission, it was interpreted as a proper name to be written with capital letters: Cosa Nostra. That interpretation was mistaken. Joe Bonanno wrote: "I often used to hear this expression from Vincent Mangano. He used it idiomatically, as I use the phrase 'in my world.'" Bonanno adds that what he calls "My Tradition" was referred to in several ways: "some prefer the word Mafia others like Cosa Nostra. These are all metaphors," he concludes.[67] Three mafiosi, whose conversation was secretly recorded by Canadian police in Paul Violi's bar in Montreal, use the term "la nostra cosa."[68] It is clear from the context that—even in 1973, ten years after the press adopted it as a proper name—it is being used metaphorically to mean our world, tradition, affairs. According to Buscetta, the mafioso officiating at an initiation rite says: "And now you know the secrets of this thing." *Thing*, transcribed in the court files with a capital T, is assumed to refer to an entity rather than simply to indicate a lack of vocabulary.[69]

Still, this misinterpretation was self-fulfilling. Fostered by a conspiracy-minded FBI and disseminated by the media, this designation gained wide currency, and, according to several mafiosi who turned state's evidence, "Cosa Nostra" is now a term sanctioned by mafiosi themselves. Since Bonanno's day it increasingly became the name they prefer: "The word 'Mafia' is a literary creation"—said Buscetta with unwitting irony— "as a whole this organization is called 'Cosa Nostra' as in the United States."[70] Contorno and Calderone confirm this.[71] Yet all three of them in their testimonies frequently resort to the word mafia. Vincenzo Marsala, on the other hand, a mafioso from the countryside—in 1985, a year after Buscetta's statement—asserted the opposite: "the organization of which my father was part was and still is called the Mafia, and its members are called mafiosi. I have come across the term Cosa Nostra only with reference to the organizations which operate in America."[72] Before his initiation ritual, Melchiorre Allegra, an Italian army medical doctor initiated in 1916 and turned state's evidence in 1937, was informed that he was about to become part of what "only outsiders" called the mafia, whereas members called themselves "men of honor" or "brothers."[73]

In 1987 Calderone said that the novices were informed at the ritual, first of all, that "what is called 'Mafia' is, in reality, called Cosa Nostra."[74] Subsequently, in his interview with Pino Arlacchi, Calderone added further details. The officiating boss said to the new recruits:

> "Do you know the Mafia? Have you ever heard it mentioned, do you have any idea of what this Mafia which everybody talks about is?"
>
> "Yes, yes, of course," some said.
>
> "Well, then tonight...." The rappresentante stopped. He was going too fast. "Mind you, the true Mafia is not the same Mafia which others talk about. This is Cosa Nostra. It is called Cosa Nostra!"
>
> He said this raising his voice, as if it was an official announcement. It was as if he was getting rid of a burden. I was surprised. That was the first time I heard that name. Or rather, I had heard it before, at the time of Valachi, the American pentito. I had read it in the paper, but I thought Cosa Nostra was the American one. "Ours is called Mafia," I had said to myself.
>
> Yet the rappresentante went on repeating, stressing the words to impress them in our minds: "This is Cosa Nostra. Co-sa-No-stra! Do you understand? It is Cosa Nostra not Mafia. Only cops and newspapers call it Mafia."[75]

And yet, Robertino Enea, many years later, still enthused about "the Mafia."[76]

Here we have a crystal clear example of how difficult it is to coordinate the meaning of conventional signs in the underworld. Advertising in illegal business must rely to some extent on accidental and externally generated symbols; this inevitably causes some confusion and instability in the symbols themselves, as there is no centralized control over what the correct term is. Sometimes the preferred name depends on where the users stand in relation to each other. The police and establishment media in Japan prefer to use the term *boryokudan* (violent groups) instead of the word *yakuza*, which has "positive, romanticised and emotional connotations," according to Peter Hill. Yakuza themselves prefer to use terms such as *ninkyo* (chivalry) or *gokudo* (extreme way).[77]

Searching for the real and only name of the Thing is a fruitless effort; there is just no such thing for all times and places. Depending on the context, one claim is as good as any other: Buscetta may simply have heard his associates use the expression Cosa Nostra more frequently than others, whereas Robertino and Marsala heard mafia, and Bonanno continued to speak of My Tradition. In Calderone's story as well as in Allegra's there is an illuminating inconsistency: it reveals that insiders have had to rely on the term coined by outsiders, even if only to deny it. To inform their audience of their fame and status in the world, they have to use an "untrue" name. The true trademark is simply that which "others talk about"; even if one wants to be distinguished and adopts a new name, the discarded name must still be referred to—formerly Prince, or Cassius Clay, or Cat Stevens. Insofar as people are aware of the synonyms, there is no confusion.

The Immortality of the Word *Mafia*

Regardless of the uncertainty over what to call the Thing, are Robertino's expectations as to the impregnability of the name well founded? To some considerable extent they are, especially insofar as the expectations of the public with regard to the resilience of the mafia are themselves resilient. Whether or not these expectations are in fact accurate is irrelevant, for they have a self-fulfilling effect. If everyone believes that there is something threatening out there called "the mafia," the incentive for new generations of gangsters to claim to be the rightful bearer of that name is tremendous. A trademark value is predicated on those beliefs. One that remains momentarily without an owner is up for grabs. If *mafia* maintains the reputation of a dangerous entity, to be able to claim "we are the true mafia" carries a powerful, effective economic value.

Two mechanisms fuel such beliefs in the immortality of "the mafia." First, there are organizations and individuals who make a career as anti-mafia fighters. In order to reproduce themselves and defend their identity, they have an interest in sustaining the belief in the resilience of the Thing. In this regard law-enforcement agencies, academics, and nongovernmental organizations that define themselves as antimafia form a common front, since the resources they receive also depend on the strength of those beliefs. Next, and less trivially, it is particularly hard to prove that the mafia has lost its battle against the state and that it has been disbanded once and for all. The suspicion that it might be out there, duly camouflaged, lingers on, and individual crimes, like a case of extortion or an unsolved murder, are seen as proof of the existence of the whole. In the past twenty years, the Sicilian mafia has received the toughest blows of its entire existence. Thanks first to a handful of courageous judges and next to the outrage caused by their assassination, the Italian state became more determined and cohesive in its fight against it. Virtually all the important mafiosi of the postwar period are now in jail or dead. Yet, when Pino Arlacchi, a student of mafia affairs, claimed in December 2000 that the Sicilian mafiosi were nearly defeated, scores of people were up in arms, many of them earnestly entertaining the same beliefs as Robertino's. Don Luigi Ciotti, a very active priest who funded Il Gruppo Abele e Libera for the care of drug addicts, was worried: "The Mafias [*sic*] do not die, unless both politics and the economy change. And so the mafia is now forcefully lifting itself up. It shoots less, but it is reshaping its future in silence."[78] Well, maybe. The trouble is that it is hard to know. Does the silence mean that the dog is not barking or that there is no dog? How does one detect the disappearance of an entity supposed to be secret and whose main product—protection by intimidation—is intangible? If God died, how would we know? No one has enough authority to stand up and proclaim convincingly that the mafia is gone forever.

The God parallel is less far-fetched than it may seem. The mafia has some godlike properties. It is invisible, and can thus be ubiquitous. It metes out punishments, and it protects. It instills fear as well as reassurance. And it is believed to be near omnipotent in doing so. All those who turned state's evidence believe fatalistically that the Thing will eventually catch them and kill them, though many have died of natural causes in their beds. We even find quasi-magical powers associated with mobsters, as in Sumatra for instance, where there are two main gangs, the Ikatan Pemuda Karya (Association of Working Youth) and the Pemuda Pancasila (Pancasila Youth). "Both Mr. Olo Pangabean, the Batak who heads the IPK, and Mr. Azwanni Wan, a senior figure in the PP, are regarded as magicians; rumour has it that, when Mr. Azwanni Wan was beaten in captivity by a soldier, the soldier went home to find his wife inflicted with identical injuries."[79] Even in Sicily the persistent beliefs in the enduring vitality of the mafia float in murky waters where self-interest, cognitive traps, and superstition blend.

MIMICS

Still, we are left with a fundamental question. If a name has such power, what do agents claiming to be the legitimate bearer of it have to do to persuade others of that? Can anyone just stand up and say "We are the mafia" and be believed? If that claim were sufficient, we would expect mimicry to be rife, and then would not the power of the name be corrupted to the point of irrelevance?

The danger of mimicry is there. It comes from infiltrators, low-quality protection groups, and impostors. There is growing evidence that this previously disregarded aspect of organized crime groups does affect the industry and explains some of their communication strategies and "weird" rules.[80] Protectors have to fight hard to prove their authenticity, and the problem of accurate identification reaches obsessive proportions.

However, since mimicry does not seem to be fatal to the trademarks of this business, as it was for the "Groucho" mask donned by French robbers, we need to understand why, for in theory the same features that make for the success of mafia-like groups are at the same time incentives for mimics.

First, since reputation is nearly everything in the protection business, mimicking its trademarks is all one needs to do to reap the benefits. If one wants to sell fake Rolex watches, one still needs to produce look-alike watches. Not so to fake being a mafioso; just the belief that someone is a member can do the trick. This feature of the business helps not only those who falsely claim to be members but also those who falsely claim to be protected by a real member. The former is an instance of counterfeiting, namely selling low-quality goods packaged as high quality. The latter is an instance of consuming a commodity without paying for it. Spending a reputation for protection amounts to "spending a name," and it is therefore difficult to prevent, all the more so in a secretive world: "You just do me favors," explains Tony Plate to a prospective customer, "and you'll be with me and nobody will ever bother you. If you ever have any problems, somebody wants to cause you harm, you just tell them that you are with me—use my name Tony Plate."[81]

Next, the reason why reputation is so effective in this business has to do with what it is a reputation for. It refers to the ability to intimidate, ultimately to use violence effectively. If one believes that someone is a real mafioso, one is not likely to be willing to probe whether that person is bluffing. The mafioso reputation puts those at the receiving end in a situation similar to Pascal's wager: If I believe that someone is a real mafioso and I am wrong, I will waste my protection money and end up cheated. But if I doubt whether someone is a real mafioso and I am wrong, I may save my money but end up dead. If I decide to challenge, I have to be prepared to resort to violence myself—a prospect not many people easily entertain. It follows that even if one believes that someone is a mafioso with a *small* probability, one may decide to comply. The mimic may thus succeed by simply instilling the suspicion that he is a real mafioso.[82]

Third, although specific individuals are exposed to mimicry, groups are more at risk. There are countless episodes in which impostors have successfully mimicked, by forging, impersonating, stealing, or otherwise copying, the personal identifiers of specific individuals. Credit card fraud, for example, is a major instance of what now goes under the name of identity theft. However, individuals have a relatively easy life, for the number of identifiers that they carry naturally and can display if needed are many, and some of them, such as the face or the voice, are hard to reproduce. The reidentifying problem becomes more serious for membership in corporate entities or groups. It is generally easier to pretend to be a member of a group than it is to pretend to be a particular person. Thus, if on the one hand developing a collective trademark called "the mafia" represents a great asset for those who can claim convincingly to be the legitimate "owners" of it, on the other hand it exposes them to mimics.

Opportunities for mimics are also positively affected by other circumstances. First, the higher the secrecy that a criminal organization is forced to use in its transactions, the harder it is to check somebody's claims to be a real mafioso. In Japan, where the yakuza have traditionally had greater freedom than mafiosi in either Sicily or the United States to display their identifying markers, mimics have a harder time. In situations like that of Japan, more people will know or be able to find out who the real mobsters are and thus avoid confusing them with impostors. Impostors will also be more exposed to the peril of being detected by the genuine article and, as we saw in the previous chapter, to be duly punished. Second, the probability that one can pass oneself off as a mafioso increases as the size of the protection market increases. If, on the other hand, all parties to such transactions are relatives, or if the community is so small that everyone can be monitored, the problem evaporates. If Palizzi were a large city rather than a little Calabrian village, no matter how much you asked around to check, not many people would know who the "friends of Palizzi" were. Once again, practices valued by mobsters, being secretive and expanding their reach, turn out to be a disadvantage in terms of the risk of mimicry.

To understand how mobsters protect their trademark entails focusing in more detail on the elements that make it up.

ELEMENTS OF THE *MAFIA* TRADEMARK

The onus of protecting legal trademarks falls largely on the law. Coca-Cola, for instance, now one of the most famous trademarks in the world, was first produced in 1886, but by 1906 there were already about fifty beverages labeled with the same or similar words—cola, coke, koke, ola in various combinations. The original firm fought in court until 1942 to protect its name, even to protect the vocalism Coke, and to make sure that "if the word is enunciated in an order, only Coca-Cola must be served."[83] In the criminal world, however, mafiosi have to take care of trademark protection themselves. I illustrated some of their strategies in chapter 7, as instances of the more general case of protecting conventional signals; here I shall review them in greater depth.

Mafiosi decided early on that the name *mafia* should never be pronounced, except in the most secret and sacred meetings. As we shall see in chapter 10, they worked hard to ensure that the name was not mentioned in *The Godfather*. Ostensibly meant to foster the belief in the nonexistence of the organization, this rule has the effect of making mimicry based on the use of the name *mafia* harder. The result is not only that mimics cannot say "we are the mafia" to those who know the rule but also that if they do, they are detected as impostors. As we know, mafiosi also have a rule that prevents one, even the genuine article, from introducing oneself directly to another mafioso. A third mafioso, who knows both parties as bona fide mafiosi, is required for introducing them to each other. (Ultimately, the only certain way to know whether someone is a made member is to have witnessed his ritual initiation.) The third-party introduction rule ensures that members who have not met before can recognize each other as such without mistake. The existence of this rule indicates that the scale of mafia membership has exceeded that critical point at which kinship, friendship, and local intelligence or some combination thereof suffice to identify who is who.

Salvatore Contorno indicates that the rule is intentionally conceived as a way to guard against impostors:

In our world we use [this rule concerning introduction] because if I, for example, want to conduct a robbery outside Palermo and in that town there is, say, Peppino or Iachino, I can go to him and obtain protection because he is a man of honor. And [if] I do not need an introduction [from someone else], I [can just] show up and say I am a friend of Stefano Bontade and manage to sneak in.[84]

Interestingly, the same method was used by Polish prisoners, among whom there existed a high-status category of old and initiated inmates known as grypsmen. The first question facing a newcomer entering a cell was: "Are you a grypsman?" A member of the caste could not answer simply yes. "His line should be: 'ask other grypsmen.' This appeal to reputation indicates that the inmate's caste membership is widely known and that it can be easily verified."[85] This method of authenticating one's identity is, as we saw in chapter 7, the same as that used by the "friends of Palizzi" when asking for protection money. "Who are these friends?" a victim inquires. "Ask around," comes the reply. The ban on using the names *mafia* and *mafioso* as identifiers effectively protects them by making them unusable by outsiders and by shifting the burden of proof to more robust identifiers.

On the whole mimics are not likely to try to pass themselves off as made members to real mafiosi. It is too easy to get caught. Members of groups in general and of the mafia in particular have an advantage over nonmembers in recognizing whether they are dealing with an impostor. Members have a greater armory of information to cross-check each other's claims—friends in common, shared experiences and language, and in the case of Polish grypsmen an argot deliberately designed for that purpose. And they have in-depth knowledge of the "natural" features that characterize the demeanor and appurtenances of a real mafioso as opposed to an impostor. Infiltrators, like Donnie Brasco, can at best persuade mafiosi that they are bona fide plain criminals, but they would not go far if they tried to persuade them to be made members.

Smart mimics try to fool nonmembers. Not only are they easier to dupe; if discovered, the mimics are at less immediate risk of violent reprisal. The more distant the intended dupe is from the world of the real mafia, the easier it is for a mimic to persuade him of the mimic's "mafioso" identity. In Sicily people approached by "mafiosi" may often know how to check whether the claim is truthful, and are encouraged to do so by mafiosi themselves, for in this way they can detect impostors and punish them. By contrast, in some of the examples of successful mafioso mimicry in Sicily, the victims were firms from the North that did not know how to operate in that environment; in particular they did not know how to verify the identity of those asking for protection money.

Ethnic Markers

Mafia membership comes with a series of other attributes that taken together restrict the chances of mimicry even with respect to nonmembers. The expectation is that, for instance, a real mafioso will be of Sicilian origin, at least in Italy. In a multiethnic society ethnic features, for instance, can be effective against phony mafiosi. If a tall blond guy with freckles and a Norwegian accent tells you that he is a mafioso, you are not likely to be convinced. Mafiosi are strictly Sicilians and want it to be that way: if they admitted Norwegian or Piedmontese men, those constraints would evaporate. By keeping their membership limited to an ethnic type with its distinctive features, they reduce the pool of potential impostors and guarantee that misrepresentation by one signal alone cannot succeed. When making a threatening phone call, saying for instance "the coffin is ready for you," mafiosi, according to Judge Giovanni Falcone, accentuate the Sicilian accent.[86] Tommaso Buscetta claims that to be Sicilian is a crucial feature in drug dealing for instance:"Colombians, Bolivians, Turks, or who else deals in drugs have to show the money to the drug carriers ... whereas the Sicilians do not have to. A Sicilian arrives [at the meeting], he knows where to bring the bag or the luggage to ... and he goes away without receiving any money since that will be delivered later on without doubt"[87] "Sicilianness" seems to have a strong reputational value attached to it. An unwelcome stigma for the countless honest denizens of the island, it is a bonus for the local underworld.

Ethnic groups with a long common history are usually very robust because the constellation of signs that identify them is extensive. Art Spiegelman reports that, during the German occupation of Poland, his father used to travel to town by the tram. It had two cars, neither likely to welcome a Jew: "One was only Germans and officials. The second, it was only the Poles. He always went straight to the official car," where a simple salute, "Heil Hitler," was enough not to call attention, whereas "in the Polish car they could smell if a Polish Jew came in." It was harder for a Polish Jew to mimic the nuanced multiple signs of a Polish gentile than the fewer superficial gestures of a pro-Nazi.[88] Oblivious to the ethnic constraint that only Chinese people are members of organized crime gangs in Hong Kong, "in December 1991 two Nigerian men appeared on the construction site of a hotel in Tsimshatsui [a Hong Kong district]. When they met the manager of the site they claimed, in English, that they were 'triads' and demanded protection money."[89] The manager called the police, who arrested the impostors.

The presence or lack of the expected ethnic origin assists mafiosi in discriminating the truthfulness of claims. A gangster called Francis "Turatello was boasting to the whole world about his close friendship with Frank Coppola, we suspected that the latter, member of Cosa Nostra in the US, had made Turatello a member in Italy, against all rules."[90] A reason why Tommaso Buscetta, the mafioso who reports this episode, and his associates suspect Turatello's claim was that Turatello was Neapolitan, not Sicilian, a trait that would disqualify him from membership in Sicily (though not in the United States, where the matter has, however, been the source of controversy[91]).

Ethnic origin also helps mafiosi to distinguish themselves from organized crime groups of other Southern Italian regions, such as Neapolitan Camorristi or Calabrian 'ndranghetisti. But in Sicily itself the advantages of ethnic distinctiveness are annulled by the fact that everybody enjoys the same ethnic features. To maintain the mafia distinction is especially important since, contrary to the belief that the mafia in Sicily has an absolute monopoly on illegal protection, there are not just local impostors to guard against but also several lesser gangs with which members of the mafia do not want to be confused. In Carini there is a "nonrecognized" gang that must not be confused with the mafia family of Villagrazia di Carini.[92] In Barrafranca there is a group known as "Stiddari," which was established by former members of the mafia expelled from the organization.[93] This group has branches in the Agrigento and

Caltanissetta areas. In Catania the mafia family is only a group among others, which are designated by their founders' nicknames, such as Mussu di ficurindia, Carcagnusi, Puntina, and Malpassoti. No wonder that Antonino Calderone sternly stated: "It is important to make a distinction between the true mafiosi, those who belong to Cosa Nostra, and the others."[94] Where "Sicilianness" does not suffice, other means must be used.

Style

Much has been made of a supposed mafioso style that would be instrumental in identifying made members. As Alongi, an early student of the mafia, eloquently warned in the nineteenth century, this must be taken with caution:

> Those who have studied the mafiosi only through fiction and newspapers believe that they can identify them by the way they dress. The tradition of wearing corduroy jackets and bonnets with a large silk tassel led police officers who came from elsewhere in Italy to believe that all those who wear those garments are dangerous subjects, and caused them to make mistakes of a comical nature, painful at times for their consequences. It must be stressed that the dominant feature of mafiosi character is their suspiciousness and dissimulation, especially after they realized that the new government was not joking and was truly persecuting them. They promptly stopped dressing in that fashion, which was instead taken up by naïve and innocuous characters, who believed they were making themselves look important that way, and whom the true mafiosi disparagingly call percia pagliaru [straw barn piercers]. . . . The real mafioso's style of dress is modest, his language displays a friar-like bonhomie, naïve, stupidly attentive, he patiently puts up with insults and slaps in the face, but at night . . . he shoots you.[95]

Style refers to "soft" features, which can easily be donned or removed; so the presence or absence of such features does not mean much. For

example, "To appreciate how much the organization valued secrecy"—
Antonino Calderone said to the prosecuting judge—"I remember that
in 1979–80, Nitto [Santapaola] told me that it was no longer advisable
for us to kiss and embrace in public to prevent law-enforcement agents
from seeing us, and inferring from that our common belonging to the
same organization."[96] Also, while the majority of Sicilian mafiosi still
today dress modestly, with dark (not black) jackets, white shirt, and no
tie, which blends them with the general middle-aged male population
of the island, the sartorial range varies enough to make it impossible to
use style of dress as a positive identifier. While some bosses were renowned for their shabbiness and for looking like "goat shepherds,"[97]
others like Nino Badalamenti, the Vernengo brothers, Tommaso Spadaro,
Lorenzo Ferro, and Salvatore Inzerillo used to spend millions of lire to
buy clothes. Inzerillo "used to buy garments for himself and his family
and friends who were with him."[98] The same heterogeneity is found
among the American cousins. While the clothing style of many fictional
characters in The Sopranos leaves much to be desired, accurately reflecting that of their real counterparts, there is evidence, in particular from
the autobiographies of a couple of ex-wives, that several mafiosi wore
expensive clothes.[99] Still, an extravagant elegance or the wearing of garish clothes, just like the driving of flashy cars or any other attempt to
impress, are frowned on—not just in Sicily, according to Bonanno,
whose only touch of flamboyance was by his own admission to wear a
"pinky ring"; otherwise he liked and approved of those who did not
dress to impress.[100] Even John Gotti, the late boss of bosses, whose origins, as the Sicilian American members liked to point out with disdain,
were Neapolitan, was disapproved for his sartorial excesses.

While style of dress is not a signal of mafia membership, there are
more robust and subtler aspects to style that are harder to fake. Some of
the prosecution judges themselves, such as Giovanni Falcone, who was
not easy to impress, noticed that the bosses they interrogated had a special air of self-assurance and command about them, and were intimidating just by their presence and demeanor. These features are hard to describe, but easy to perceive once one sees them.

OTHER NAMES

If one looks closely at the mafia world, it is not just the name *mafia* or the "Sicilianness" of its members that convey membership. Individuals become mafia members by becoming members of a "family." There is no centralized hierarchical organization to which an individual can belong, but rather a federation of families. They are held together by a shared initiation ritual, by shared norms of behavior, and by their mutual acknowledgment of being the legitimate bearers of their collective reputation asset. Being part of that federation is of great importance. All else equal, a family of organized criminals is much more likely to carry weight if it is known as belonging to that federation. Reputation in the mafia world is thus conveyed by a web of personal, kin, and mafia family names, which serve as identification signs and act as a potent filter against impostors and members of other petty, local mafia-like groups.

This kind of filtering applies to other groups such as the yakuza. As Peter Hill pointed out to me, "People who do not come into contact with yakuza may find the word in itself frightening, but those who are closer would require to know more. Members are not barred from using the term as in the mafia, still when doing business yakuza do not say they are yakuza—they specify the group and sub-group to which they belong."[101] This may also be because there is not a strict parallel between the mafia and the yakuza in terms of their basic organizational structure. On the one hand, "The yakuza have shared norms and rituals and generally recognise this commonality—though they are quick to disparage groups which indulge in businesses or practices (e.g. drug dealing) which fall short of the supposed yakuza standards. They do therefore share a common identity."[102] On the other hand, much of the organizational weight falls on very large families rather than on their federation. Groups like the Yamaguchi-gumi, which unlike the mafia is not a federation of families but has a pyramidal structure, are much larger than mafia families and carry a reputation of their own. "A closer comparison"—Peter Hill suggests—"could be made with the Kanto Hatsuka-kai, which is a sort of 'commission' or 'cupola.' The Kanto Hatsuka-kai does not however have a recognised collective brand as such—it is more like a trade association."[103]

In Japan the family names used by organized crime groups are not necessarily determined by the name of the current boss. Some groups, "which started off with some sort of ultra-right wing motivation or a boss with such political leanings, have a name reflecting that—kokusui-kai (national essence society), shinwa-kai (pro-harmony/Japan society—'wa' can refer to either harmony or Japan)."[104] Other groups take composite names: a "reorganised gang was now called Aizu Kotetsu-kai. Aizu, for the region where the gang originated, and Kotetsu, after Senbachi's [the current boss] favourite brand of sword."[105] Yet others "incorporate boss family names into the gang name. The Yamaguchi-gumi's founder was Yamaguchi. Many of the subgroups within the Yamaguchi-gumi are also named after their founders—Takumigumi, Yamaken-gumi, Konishi-ikka"[106]—even though the founders are no longer around. On the whole, the groups do maintain a pragmatic attitude in assessing whether or not the maintenance of the boss's name is reputation-effective. David Stark writes: "When Okada joined the city assembly in 1952, he retired from the gang and Araki became the new boss. Often, if a group is powerful, the subsequent bosses keep the founder's name and add onto that name the generations they represent. . . . Because the Okada group was a local group comprised of a small following bound by personal ties to a boss and lacked a significant organisation, distant ancestral roots, and national ties, there was no benefit deriving from keeping the name Okada. Therefore, the gang was renamed for its new and powerful boss, Araki."[107]

The names of the five New York mafia families—Bonanno, Gambino, Genovese, Colombo, and Lucchese—have followed a similar pattern. These names have become famous and seem to be preserved, even though the founders or their relatives of the same name are no longer in charge. While the families themselves have been unable to advertise efficiently, the media and the law-enforcement agencies have done the job for them: no matter how horrific, publicity has conferred on those names a near-mythical status. Just as the names Ferrari or Jaguar elicit immediate reactions among lovers of sports cars, names such as Gambino or Bonanno evoke an equally immediate response, if of a different

nature. An interesting name change following a change in who was boss
did occur however: Joe Profaci was in charge of a crime family for thirty
years, but he was not popular with his men, who apparently deemed
him to be stingy, and did not leave fond memories. After he died of
natural causes in 1962 they dropped the Profaci name and took that of
Colombo, the new boss.

In western Sicily, where the mafia is territorially organized, a family
can at times be identified by the name of the area over which that family
rules. This usage seems, however, more common in the media and law
enforcement than in the island underworld, where personal names carry
more weight than those of the territory. Most mafia families are identified by the name of their boss. When a boss dies, goes to jail, or resigns
because of ill health, his former mafia family takes the name of the new
boss, even though the territory and the members remain the same. The
reputation of a mafia family resides in the name of its head, even though
its reputation qua *mafia* family survives across different names. "The
Inzerillo family"—Buscetta explained in court—"still exists, it changed
its name, it is no longer Inzerillo but the head of the family is now Buscemi."[108] The names Inzerillo and later Buscemi refer not so much to
the individual or his relatives with the same name but to the whole
membership in the Passo di Rigano area near Palermo. The lack of sepa-
ration between the name of a family and that of the boss is revealed by a
misunderstanding that occurred during the interrogation of Salvatore
Contorno, a mafioso who turned state's evidence. The judge asked
whether he could tell the court the names of the Palermo families. "In
Corso dei Mille," Contorno replied, "there is Filippo Marchese . . . in
the lower part [of the same *corso*] there was Pinuzzo Abbate and his cronies, while in via Messina Marine. . . ." "I would like to know the names
of the families, not those of the members," complained the judge. But
Contorno replied, "if I do not name one [particular individual] we cannot understand each other . . . in a family one must put a person."[109]

Using the boss's name to identify a family provides a protection of
sorts against mimicry. In order to claim to be a member of the mafia, an
impostor may be naturally expected to mention the family to which he
belongs. The mimic needs to show that he knows more than just the

area name, which is easy to know. He needs to know the name of the boss, which is harder to know for someone who is not connected. By mentioning the name of the boss he also gives the intended dupe an opportunity to check.

Moreover, despite the mafia's attempts to distance the bonds within the "families" from the bonds of kinship, which we discussed above, kinship still intersects the mafia world. There are several dynasties, which have more than one member involved in the mafia and endure across several generations. The Greco family, the Bontade family in Sicily, and the Gambino family in the United States are well-known examples.[110] Mafia families at times take on the name of their leading natural family, but unlike the yakuza or the U.S. Cosa Nostra, only insofar as some members of the kin group are heading them. The family based on the territory of Ciaculli (a district on the outskirts of Palermo) is named after the Greco family, which is made up mostly of three subsets of relatives. In the history of Cosa Nostra there are also plenty of reference to sets of brothers, such as the Cillaris, the Grados, the Fidanzatis, the Mafaras, and so forth. It suffices that a single relative be a member of Cosa Nostra to turn his surname into a reputational asset for his kin. The Enea brothers are all called Robertino, the nickname of Salvatore. Buscetta claims that he cannot even specify their real names, and usually Robertino suffices to identify the whole lot.[111] And kin members pay for the privilege of having a reputable name by being held collectively responsible for each other's behavior. In the Vernengo family each brother has his own specialization, since "the most important things have to be done within the family itself, because they know that in case one is arrested he would not say anything; if one talks 'their reputation is gone.'"[112] When Leonardo Vitale made a wide-ranging confession to the police following a "mystical crisis," he threw the mafia into disarray, and particularly his mafia family. He belonged to the Altarello di Badia family, which since at least the 1920s had been led by the Vitales. His uncle, then boss of the family, was deposed because of Leonardo's confession and the family entrusted to Rosario Riccobono, and it was never again established under the Vitale name. In the meantime other members of Vitale's mafia family went into hiding fearing for their lives.[113]

The structure of the mafia is an extraordinary array of nested reputations, ranging from the whole to the individual member, via the mafia "family" and natural kin. This provides a close-knit network of names but also shared features, experiences, and knowledge that make that world very hard for nonmembers to penetrate. While mafiosi benefit from the power associated with the Thing as such, they have maintained a close local control, sustaining capillary networks that ease the task of accurate identification by monitoring and filtering out impostors.

A SPECIAL KIND OF MIMIC

When Don Mariano Marsala was replaced as the boss of the small mountain town of Vicari, following the modifications caused by the mafia war in the late 1970s and early 1980s, he was not killed immediately. This caused confusion among his clients, especially those who were both loyal to Don Mariano and ill informed about the change. These people continued to ask for Don Mariano's protection when he was no longer in a position to supply it "legitimately." Since his being ousted, any attempt he might make to use his mafia authority would be considered an imposture. Don Mariano could not quite bear that idea and went on as before. In a particularly poignant case, he himself, out of his own pocket, secretly paid the protection money the new boss expected from a client: he did so without informing the client to prevent the latter from realizing that he was no longer in charge.[114]

This ambiguous situation continued until early 1983, when a man returned from abroad to find that someone to whom he had leased a piece of land before migrating was now refusing to comply with the original agreement and return it. To settle the dispute this man went to Don Mariano. As the land and the leaseholder did not belong to the mafia territory of Vicari but were under the "jurisdiction" of neighboring Caccamo, Don Mariano had to come out into the open in order to contact the Caccamo family and settle the dispute, and thus he revealed that he was still in business. Four days later he disappeared.

According to the sentence of the Palermo Corte di Assise, Francesco

Paolo Montalto, from the nearby town of Lercara Friddi, was murdered for the same reason: "It is clear that many people did not know that there had been a change at the head of the cosca mafiosa of Lercara, so they continued to ask for protection from the victim; and it is furthermore clear that the latter had not given up taking an interest and acting as a mediator on their behalf . . . this fact represents—as in the case of Marsala—a more than adequate motive for the execution of the old Montalto, whose death was necessary for the new delinquents to assert their power."[115]

In a world where information is imperfect, reputation has a strong inertial force and may be difficult to shake off when no longer "legitimate." Thus the new boss chose to inform customers who had not caught up with the change that their old supplier of protection services was no longer in business for the very good reason that he was now dead.

CHAPTER 9

Nicknames

> Real names did not mean anything to these guys. They didn't
> introduce by last names. I knew guys that had been hanging out
> together for five or ten years and did not know each other's last
> names. Nobody cares. You were introduced by a first name or a
> nickname. If you don't volunteer somebody's last name,
> nobody'll ask you. That's just the code. The feeling is, if you
> wanted me to know a name, you would have told me.
>
> —Joe Pistone[1]

From school yards to professional sports, from politics to intimate relationships, nicknaming is practiced virtually worldwide.[2] The evidence,
however, suggest that nicknames are more widespread among criminals
than they are among ordinary citizens. Even in societies where nicknames have disappeared in other professions and are in decline among
the general population, they are still used by criminals. "The criminal
moniker," wrote Maurer and Futrell, "is an international phenomenon
and has been prevalent in Europe since the growth of professional crime
during the early fifteenth century."[3]

Proper names are conventional signs associated with persons that are
expressed orally through specific sounds and in writing through strings
of letters. Unless we believe in some esoteric theory of the power of
names, there is no causal connection between one's proper name and
one's character's traits. Neither does a name create a trait, nor does a trait
require that one end up with a certain name. Although often colored by
family or ethnic traditions, well-wishing, or religious inspiration, the
connection between person and name is arbitrary: one known as Peter
could just as easily have been known as Paul. Any associations between
names and properties follow rather than precede naming—once someone is named Peter, the mention of his name to those who know him

will evoke by association those of Peter's traits that they have experienced, in short Peter's reputation.

There are, however, interesting limits to pure conventionality. First, associations between certain names and persons can become so strong in people's minds as to either enhance or tarnish the names themselves. They come, for instance, to embody certain properties through the behavior of a widely known individual who carried that name, especially if the name is distinctive. Adolf does not have the same connotations as Peter, not since the 1930s that is. Neither Attila nor Judah ever made it into the top one thousand names in the United States throughout the twentieth century.[4] Next, some names, especially nicknames, which are bestowed when people have grown up sufficiently to display some of their physical or psychological traits, are chosen to reflect these traits—a profession, a behavioral quirk, or a bodily feature for instance. So a word that denotes a trait or property is used as a nickname: "Nose" (Jackie D'Amico) could not have been nicknamed equally well "Fat Tony" (Anthony Salerno). This process extends to exploiting strong associations between names and properties. Thus Peter could be mockingly nicknamed "Adolf" if he shared some of Hitler's traits.

In spite of these constraints the number of names that remain interchangeable is vast, and a person can be indifferently known under many alternative names or nicknames. Nobody *owns* exclusive rights to use a name or a nickname; unlike the names of corporations or brand names of products, there is no property law protecting the use of proper names. Switching names can be an inexpensive act. In domains that are fragmented enough and in which people move freely from place to place and group to group, one can be known to some by his birth-certificate name and to others by his nickname. What Jackie D'Amico does in group A will not be associated with the person known as "Nose" by group B, even if Jackie and Nose are one and the same person. By having two disconnected identifiers "Jackie-Nose" will be able to preserve cross-secrecy about his doings insofar as the connection is not made. This strategy is not of course watertight. It is impossible to make sure that people will never work out that Jackie and Nose are one and the same. "By the way, did you tell Gwendolen the truth about your being

Ernest in town and Jack in the country?" Algernon asks in Wilde's *The Importance of Being Ernest.*

A sign that such connections are actively sought and often made is that in police files criminals are commonly identified not just by their birth-certificate name but by their nickname as well. Furthermore, when misrepresentation can have serious negative consequences for those who are duped, people will not be satisfied by being told only one's name, but typically will search or ask for further proof of one's identity. Thus, if one wishes to maintain a new identity, one will typically have to forge or otherwise misrepresent not just the name but supporting identifiers as well. Still, using different names with different people is not useless. It makes cross-identification laborious, and can delay it for the time necessary to gather additional identifiers that establish the match between a person's nickname and his birth-certificate name. As the epigraph at the start of this chapter indicates, the need to preserve secrecy could be the main reason for the popularity of nicknames among criminals.

THE ATTRIBUTION OF NICKNAMES

To understand more about the use and frequency of nicknames in the underworld, I use the judicial files of the so-called maxi trial, which was held in Palermo in 1986–87. The trial involved 459 individuals who were, allegedly, either mafiosi or associates of mafiosi. Among the defendants, 31.6 per cent are mentioned in the files as having more than one name, including many nicknames. These data confirm that the higher frequency of nicknames found in criminal circles generally applies to Sicilian mafiosi too, even though in Sicily the use of nicknames is declining.[5] The same seems to apply also to the ordinary Sicilian petty criminals who, while not among the trial defendants, are mentioned in the files.[6] There is no record of any other profession in contemporary Italy in which so many individuals bear a nickname.

Among the names listed in the trial records, especially in phone calls recorded by police, I found twenty-four ordinary first names or diminutives of first names, such as Pinuzzo, Giorgio, Roberto, used instead of the first name on the person's birth certificate. Several of these additional names correspond to the name of the father of the person the speaker meant to identify. There is a convention in Southern Italy of naming individuals after their fathers. So even if the person has a different name, provided the listener knows both the convention and the name of someone's father, he would understand to whom the speaker is referring (if the father is dead there is no ambiguity). These are effectively used as *code names* of the kind adopted, for instance, by spies, which are coined and used to prevent strangers from understanding whom the speaker means to identify. They have the advantage that the key to decode whom they identify exploits a local tradition and thus requires no prior agreement.

Insofar as a nickname is generically defined as being "not derivative from a person's given name or a diminutive of it" and as a name "which is substituted for, or used alternatively with a person's given name,"[7] code names and nicknames cannot be distinguished conceptually.[8] Code names, however, differ from nicknames proper in three ways.

First, they can be their bearer's creation in a way in which nicknames cannot. Code names are bestowed mainly for the purpose of veiling the true identity of the bearer. They are usually given by or with the agreement or at least the knowledge of the bearer. And they can be created for specific operations. "Nakaho, Yoshida and the other two hit men assigned to the squad were assigned nicknames—"North," "South," "East" and "West"—because their real names "didn't need to be known" for the plan."[9] Nicknames, by contrast, are *bestowed* on individuals regardless of their intervention, whether they like them or not: "they called me *Coriolano*"—Salvatore Contorno, a mafioso who turned state's evidence, said—"have I ever been able to figure out when they gave it to me?"[10] Friends and acquaintances of the bearer coin his nickname, often behind the latter's back. And, unlike a code name, the nickname is not bestowed for any instrumental purpose.

Next, assuming one discovers one's nickname, one can promote it by choosing to use it when referring to oneself. There is however no easy way for the bearer to prevent others from using it behind his back, just as there is no easy way to prevent others from gossiping about one. Nicknames are a collective property that sticks regardless of the bearer's wishes.[11] For example, "Stop calling me *Bruto!*" is an injunction with little hope of success; it may even backfire, for it reminds the audience of the nickname as well as informing them how they can annoy "Bruto." Mothers in Kalymnos, Greece, know that a nickname bestowed once for fun can become a curse for life, and they advise their children "not to resist being given a nickname. They tell them that resisting only creates fun for others at their own expense."[12]

The third difference between nicknames and code names concerns their *semantics.* Code names tend to be neutral, carrying neither positive nor negative connotations, like "North" or "South." When code names suggest undesirable associations, objections may be raised—as they are, memorably, in Quentin Tarantino's film *Reservoir Dogs,* in which two gangsters complain about being code-named "Mr. Pink" and "Mr. Brown," colors that in their minds carry disagreeable associations (one with femininity and the other with excrement). Noms de guerre too are chosen by their bearers, but they tend to be positive, or at least so the bearers hope. They choose a name to highlight favorable qualities, often by picking a name borne by a real or fictional heroic character with whom they wish to be identified ("Che," "Tarzan"). The monikers of Russian mobsters, which are chosen by the bearers (see below), are far more positive than those of mafiosi.[13] Noms de guerre (and noms de plume) may be bestowed for keeping identities secret too—unlike code names, however, their semantics are not purely functional but are also shaped by reputational ambitions.

Nicknames, by contrast, carry negative connotations more often than either code names or noms de guerre. Only a small share of mafiosi nicknames that we collected refer to positive features of the bearer. Some relate to skills or accomplishments. "L'Ingegnere" (Engineer) acquired his name "because he was in charge of fixing radios used by smugglers at sea"[14]; "u'Dutturi" (Doctor) had a golden touch refining heroin.[15] "Il Senatore" (Senator) never stood for election but "was involved with politicians, he could rely on all sort of favors."[16] "U'Tratturi" (Tractor) refers to its bearer's skill "in murdering people. . . . He flattened everything and wherever he went the grass stopped growing."[17] Many other seemingly positive nicknames such as "Re della Kalsa" (King of Kalsa), "Principe di Villagrazia" (Prince of Villagrazia), "Principe della Cocaina,""Papa"(Pope),"Generale"(General),and"Cavaliere"(Knight)— including some derived from famous individuals—"Pinuzzu Garibaldi," "L'Agnelli del Contrabbando" (Agnelli of Smuggling), and "Onassis-sino" (little Onassis)—are so grand as to be mocking.

Although this is not the case in every profession—in sports for instance fans often attribute laudatory nicknames to their favorite athletes—among mafiosi mockery rather than admiration, ridicule rather than appreciation, seem the predominant triggers of nicknaming (nicknames are here reminiscent of gossip, and they could be deemed the shortest form of gossip[18]). The very word 'nciuri, Sicilian for nickname, means abuse. Insulting epithets in ordinary language are turned into nicknames—such as "Il cornuto di Buffalo" (Cuckold of Buffalo) and "u'Scemu" (Fool).[19] Also, nicknames can be derogatory not because of their literal meaning but because of how they are meant. "Gioielliere" (Jeweler) was a fishmonger whose merchandise was said to be as expensive as diamonds.[20] Alfio Ferlito "was scornfully nicknamed *Filippo* by Mangion Francesco." Ferlito was a smuggler, and Filippo was the name of a coastguardsman who had given him lots of trouble.[21]

Most nicknames of Sicilian mafiosi pick on the person's oddities; they are metonymies. The most popular genre is inspired by physical features (twenty-seven cases)—"u'Beddu" (Handsome), "Il Grosso" (Fat), "u'Riccio" (Curly Haired), "Turchiceddu" (Little Turk, because of the dark color of his skin), "u'Buttigghiuni" (Large Bottle), "Faccia di Pala" (Shovel Face, "because of the wide shape of his face"). There is even an intriguing "Cosce Affumate" (Smoked Thighs, apparently because of the visual effect of his hairy legs.[22] "Pietro u'Zappuni" owed his nickname to his "two horsey front teeth"[23] or, rather, "hoe-like."[24] He worked in team with "Il Vampiro," who was tall, slim, and spooky.[25] Another man was dubbed "Scillone" (Pendulum) because "he swings when he walks."[26] Sebastiano Laudani earned the name "Mussu di Ficurindia" (Prickly Pear Mouth) because of the shape of his mouth.[27] Stefano Giaconia, a man with a talent for minting monikers, nicknamed Salvatore Federico

"Pinzetta" (Tweezers) because of his habit of plucking his eyebrows and cheeks."[28]

Psychological or behavioral features occur in twenty-three cases, such as "u'Tranquillu" (Quiet), "u'Guappo" (Braggart), "Abbruciamontagna" (Burn Mountain, because of his hot temper), "u'Cori Granni" (Big Heart), "u'Facchinu" (Ill-bred), "Parrapicca" (Few Words), "Piluseddu" (Hairy, also Stingy), "Farfagnedda" (Stammer), and "Tempesta" (Storm, "because for him it's always stormy").[29] While we found no nickname derived from minerals, both animals and vegetables occur. The animal herd (thirteen cases) makes up an undistinguished zoo, which, among others, contains "Il Cane" (Dog), "Il Lupo" (Wolf), "Capretto" (Kid), "Pecora Bianca" (White Sheep, because of his white curly hair), "Cavadduzzu" (Little Horse), "Conigghiu" (Rabbit), "Musca" (Fly), "Farfalla" (Butterfly), and "Salamandra" (Salamander). Two nicknames are inspired by cooking vegetables, "Milinciana" (Eggplant) and "Cipudda" (Onion). Nicknames derive also from objects (seven cases): "Alfio Lupara" (Sawed-off Shotgun) is self-explanatory for a mafioso, but for others we found no explanation of their origin: "Scagghidda" (Little Scale), "Pinnaredda" (Little Feather), "Puntina" (Little Nail). We also found a couple of pun-based aliases: Francesco Di Noto becomes "Franco Noto" (Renowned), and Gaetano Galatolo becomes "Tanu Alatu" (Winged). Hobbies and inclinations are also a common inspiration of nicknames: "Turi Karaté" (Turi Karate), "Scarpapulita" (Clean Shoe), "Pupo" (Dapper), "Cacciatore" (Hunter), "Studente" ("because he went to University," though never graduated),[30] and "u'Masculiddu" (Little Male). The least flattering nickname in this category we found was "Il Bruto" (The Brute), who "went on trial for the rape of a little girl."[31]

I also found several cases in which different turncoats refer to the same individual by a different nickname, an indication that an individual may be known under different monikers by different groups of people. "Mario Aglialoro" appears also as "Salamandra," "Il Falco" is also "Il Principe di Villagrazia," "Lucchiceddu" is "u'Picciriddu," "Fifu Tistuni" is "Milinciana," "u'Viddanu" is "u'Tratturi," "Il Ragioniere" is "Il Corto," "Ninu il Babbo" is "Il Cacciatore," and "Tistuni" is "Farfalla."

Nicknames do not seem a necessary mark of leadership: only a quarter of the mafia bosses involved in the trial are reported as having an additional name. The range of their meanings is as wide as in the case of lesser mafiosi. Some bosses just have code names. Others have nicknames derived from famous characters. Others still—contrary to Skipper's claim that bosses enjoy only resounding aliases[32]—are saddled with derogatory epithets: "Ninu u'Babbu" (Nino the Fool), "Fifu Tistuni" (Thick Head), "Saru u'Bau" (Ogre), and "Calò Tabarano" (Downhearted). Giuseppe Madonia was nicknamed "Piddu Chiacchiera" (Joe Baloney) because of his inclination to exaggerate events.[33] Even Totò Riina—the mafia top man in the 1990s—is known as "Il Corto" (The Short); and Bernardo Provenzano, Riina's closest acolyte and successor, as "u'Viddanu" (The Uncouth). (These two men enjoyed a joint nickname, "Le Belve" (The Beasts), because each was thought to be responsible, counting only up to 1978, for at least forty murders.)[34]

Contrary to what Marco Jacquemet found among Neapolitan racketeers,[35] I found no evidence that nickname givers are powerful individuals within the group, or that the giving of nicknames confers particular power on them. And, contrary to the stereotype, some mafiosi do have a sense of humor. Stefano Giaconia "stuck upon me the name *Mozzarella*," Marino Mannoia reveals in his testimony, "since I like mozzarellas so much and when I was in Naples . . . I used to buy them in great quantity. Once I found a rotten one and since then he began to call me *Mozzarella*." Nickname givers can be peers, and the power that devolves on them from that practice is no greater than the power gained by those who know how to tell a joke. Minting clever nicknames confers popularity rather than power.

The imaginative variety of meanings found in mafioso nicknames, and the stories of how they were first bestowed, suggest that expressive rather than instrumental reasons primarily motivate their attribution, because of the mischievous *fun* we seem to derive from finding a biting and concise way to capture a person's salient feature—a fun way to make fun of others. Mafiosi, Rosenberg wrote, "size each other up, and then, put their findings in pithy nicknames—names which explain the man in a word—his weakness, his racket, how he works, or some peculiarity about him."[36]

THE USE OF NICKNAMES

People invent nicknames for each other all the time, but only some of them stick, and only some of those that stick spread beyond small circles. What makes some resilient and others perishable?

Like gossip, nicknames have attracted shoddy functionalist explanations.[37] An array of functions has been attributed to them such as reinforcing social norms and strengthening social control: "[Nicknames] verify and constantly remind their bearers of their own socially unacceptable characteristics. By making such things as stinginess, rumour mongering, the persistent use of vulgar language and other anti-social characteristics the butt of constant joking, *society continuously reminds itself* of what it considers good and bad behavioural traits."[38] Other authors have by contrast pointed out how nicknames fuel aggression and competition.[39] Some deem them to provide a sense of community, others to maintain social boundaries.[40] They are said to be a function of tradition, but they may survive in modern contexts.[41]

These explanations fail to tell us which are the individual motives that sustain these hypothetical processes. Societies do not act with a purpose; only individuals do. And it seems far-fetched to suggest that when we create or use nicknames we think of fulfilling such grand functions. "[I]ndeed, nicknames rarely if ever serve a singular function, but instead simultaneously play a variety of roles within the social environment in which they occur"[42]—none of which, we should add, are particularly strong, unambiguous, or always intended.

So why do certain nicknames survive? Some may survive for the same expressive reasons that make people invent them in the first place— just as happens with jokes, it is simply fun to repeat nicknames. The reasons why nicknames appear, however, do not necessarily coincide with the reasons why they survive and spread. Whether nicknames are used for instrumental purposes also, and whether they turn out to be useful or detrimental, are further questions, which we shall now consider. It must be stressed, however, that above a certain threshold of use the survival of a nickname (or of any name for that matter) requires no special explanation: people use it simply *because* it is used. Once a nickname comes to refer to a certain individual who is known to others by *that* nickname, then to identify that person the nickname will do. A nickname can thus spread regardless of any particular motive, much as no motive is required to call people by their proper name other than that it *is* their name. "We call him Michele and I have always called him Michele, I know him as Michele."[43] Salvatore Contorno refers to someone who was baptized Orazio but renamed Michele after his dead father. Similarly, Contorno says, "I know *Pietro u'Zappuni*, I don't know if his name is Franco or Giovanni." Users can forget or never know why a certain nickname was bestowed, and still use it. Filippo Marchese, the boss of the family of Corso dei Mille in Palermo, was known as "Milinciana" (Eggplant). "Perhaps"—Buscetta, a mafioso who turned state's evidence, says—"because he was short, dark, chubby. I don't really know, I know that instead of saying 'Marchese' we said 'Milinciana.'"[44]

The use of nicknames requires an explanation only at those junctures in which people have a real choice between using either the nickname or another name to identify themselves or others. After a nickname is minted, it can die out unless there is some motive for people to prefer using it instead of alternative names. To understand whether the motives that keep nicknames alive and spread them into the mafia world are more than just fun, we must explore how they are used.

Favoring Identification

The hypothesis I want to pursue is that nicknames are useful in circumstances in which, had they not been available, code names would have had to be coined. In other words, I will try to find out whether they are employed not because of their meaning, but merely because of the properties they share with code names.

Insofar as the same proper name is borne by more than one person within a network of people who know or speak about each other, that name, unlike a social security number, will not uniquely identify that person. Nicknames can help to differentiate individuals with the same proper name and thus to *identify* them accurately. In Sicily the frequency of individuals bearing the same first name is high because of the practice of christening people with the names of a handful of patron saints.[45] And since often several members of large families of kin are involved in mafia activities, the surname alone may not suffice to differentiate among them.[46]

At the same time, among mafiosi the pressure for accurate identification is higher than among ordinary Sicilians. Mafiosi need to monitor the activities of many people and refer to them accurately. Mistaken identities can be a cause of conflict and even cost people's lives. Because of both of these constraints—the abundance of identical names and the pressure for accuracy—it is plausible to expect that mafiosi will have a higher than average incentive to use nicknames for identification.

In the files I examined there is much evidence that nicknames help mafiosi in this regard. Picking just one of many examples, Carlo Teresi, the oldest of three cousins all named Carlo, was nicknamed "Numero Uno" (Number One). The distribution of nicknames on either side of the urban-rural divide in Sicily lends indirect support to this hypothesis. Among ordinary people living in small towns nicknames are still common, while Sicilian cities constitute no exception to the trend of diminishing use of nicknames detected in urban settings in the rest of Italy and around the world.[47] By contrast, Sicily's underworld follows the reverse pattern. In the mafia family of Vicari, a village near Palermo, and in the families of a cluster of small towns in the province of Agrigento, both rural areas for which we have very good information, nicknames are much rarer than they are among mafiosi in Palermo or Catania.[48] In an urban context, in which it is harder but equally important to identify one another accurately, nicknames have a greater chance of surviving. This effect may also explain why in the American Cosa Nostra, which is an entirely urban phenomenon, the use of nicknames is even *more* common than in its Sicilian counterpart. Nicknaming is not a relic of a rustic mafia.

Hampering Identification

While mafiosi have an interest in identifying each other accurately, they also have an even keener interest in preventing being identified by the authorities or rival mafiosi. The evidence strongly indicates that nicknames are used deliberately for this purpose (which is different from saying that they are invented for this purpose). Pasquale Sciortino, a member of Salvatore Giuliano's gang,[49] was accused of having taken part in the massacre of a group of peaceful protesters at Portella della Ginestra on 1 May 1947. Taking advantage of the different name by which he was known to the other bandits and his covillagers, he walked free.[50] In a different case, "Gambino Giuseppe Giacomo ... was very proud, because"—when he was accused of various crimes by Leonardo Vitale, a mafia turncoat, in his 1974 testimony[51]—"he saved himself from being identified by saying that he was called Giacomo and not Giuseppe."[52] Leonardo Vitale mentioned also two characters he knew only by their nicknames, "u'Pacchiuni" and "u'Tranquillu," in connection with certain crimes, but until ten years later, when Tommaso Buscetta, another major mafia turncoat, matched those nicknames with pictures of their bearers, Vitale's confession did not harm them.[53] Several mafiosi, who were not among the defendants, are mentioned in the trial *only* by their nicknames—"Jachinu u'Spurpatu" (Scrawny),[54] boss of Rocca; "Taninu Babbuneddu" (Thick-Headed), boss of Barrafranca;[55] "Cipudda" (Onion), boss of Vallelunga;[56] and "Ciccio Occhialino" (Small Glasses), boss of Giardino Inglese. They were never identified. No match could be made between their nicknames and their birth-certificate names, and of course no legal action could be taken against them.

Having a nickname can help equally well in reverse. In order to disclaim actions carried out under one's nickname, one can retreat to one's birth-certificate name. Vincenzo Sinagra, yet another mafioso who turned state's evidence, declared in court that "everybody knew [that man] as *Pietro u Zappuni*." "My name," the accused retorted, "is Paolo Alfano. Who told [Sinagra] that my name is Pietro?"[57] Before becoming a state witness, Francesco Marino Mannoia denied for similar reasons that his nickname was "Mozzarella."[58] Shifting from one name to another makes it possible to rely on a second identity and escape trouble— Pietro in the country and Paolo in court.

When one's nickname becomes associated with one's proper name and loses its secrecy value, there is an incentive to resort to yet new

aliases. Every mafioso knew Giuseppe Greco as a ferocious killer, and
every mafioso would associate him with his odd nickname, "Scarpuzzedda" (Little Shoe), "because newspapers spread it, and his fame was
well known within Cosa Nostra ... , in 1978 he was not yet 30 but already he was food for chatter."[59] When Scarpuzzedda met Vincenzo Sinagra—who was considered to be unreliable (rightly as it turned out)—
he was introduced as "Giovannello Greco," which ironically was the
name of one of Scarpuzzedda's worst enemies.[60] Francesco Marino Mannoia confirms Sinagra's version that Scarpuzzedda was introduced to
Vincenzo Sinagra under a false name "in order to prevent Sinagra from
knowing too much."[61]

Records from the maxi trial of 1986–87, mentioned above, allow us
to make an indirect test of whether nicknames survive better when
keeping one's identity secret is a greater concern. When one observes
the frequency of nicknames sorted by the position of their bearers
(bosses, "soldiers," hit men, and external associates—according to how
the bearers were classified by mafiosi who turned state's evidence), the
distribution (table 9.1) shows that only one in twelve mafia associates
involved in the trial, namely dealers (who are protected rather than dis-
pensing protection to others[62]), bore a nickname, whereas one out of
four bosses and one out of three ordinary made members (known as
soldiers) had a nickname. The highest frequency, however, is found
among hit men: among them, two out of three bore a nickname. (Oddly,
killers seem to enjoy nicknames that are deprived of threatening connotations or are even endearing—"Scarpuzzedda" [Little Shoe], "u'Picciriddu" [the Kid], "Anatreddu" [Duckling], "Il Ragioniere" [The Ac-
countant]).[63] The correlation between rank and having a nickname is
statistically highly significant, and consistent with the hypothesis that the
more a mafioso needs to avoid identification and to lead a secretive life,
the more likely a nickname sticks to him. Both associates and bosses are
less exposed to law enforcement because they are less likely, for different
reasons, to be involved in manifestly criminal actions. "Soldiers" and,
above all, those among them who specialize in killing, have a greater
need to hide their identities.

TABLE 9.1
Mafiosi with and without nickname, by rank (chi-square = 13.049;
p-value = 0.005)

	With nickname		Without nickname		Total	
	N	%	N	%	N	%
Associates	1	9.0	12	91.0	13	100
Bosses	29	26.3	85	73.7	114	100
Soldiers	108	34.1	210	66.0	318	100
Hit men	9	64.3	5	35.7	14	100
Total	147	31.6	312	68.4	459	100

SOURCES: OSPA; AC; TB; SC; VS; TC.

Unintended Consequences

Matters are not so straightforward, however. There are plenty of examples that show that while mafiosi try, by manipulating nicknames, both to enhance their identification and to prevent people from identifying them, the effects can be unpredictable.

For instance Carlo Teresi, known as Numero Uno, a mafioso we already met, wished he had no nickname when he found himself in court:[64] "The Teresis are as many as drops in the sea," said Mannoia to the judge, who was listing them according to their fathers' names. "If you list them telling me 'Carlo Teresi Numero Uno' I can answer 'yes he is,' but if you mention his father's name, I don't recognize him."[65] So the "Numero Uno" nickname helped the mobsters to identify the right Carlo Teresi, but it ultimately helped prosecutors to do the same thing. In another case in which there were multiple people with the same name and surname, it was *the absence* of nicknames that proved an advantage: Tommaso Buscetta revealed that Francesco Maiorana was a member of the mafia, but no one could be charged, since "there were two men [with that name] . . . both alleged mafia members,"[66] and it proved impossible to decide which of the two Buscetta meant. In cases such as these other identifying marks, such as a job, must be resorted to. "I don't want to make any confusion"—Contorno says—"I want to be more

precise instead . . . [are we talking about] Giovanni Prestifilippo's son, the
one who works in the garbage collection agency?"[67] Contorno was in
doubt because there were eight Prestifilippos among the defendants. On
one occasion the judge himself chose to impose a nickname: "The way
they call him is absurd"—complained Michele Greco to the court—"I
called him Totò. . . . Neither Cicchiteddu nor Ciaschiteddu [small bird]
suits him, since he has an athletic physique. Where did Cicchiteddu or
Ciaschiteddu come from then?"[68] The judge, however, decided not to
discard that nickname: "Let us call him [Cicchiteddu] . . . unfortunately
there are too many of you bearing the same name and surname [Salva-
tore Greco] . . . therefore this Cicchiteddu, whether true or false, will do
to identify this individual."

As there is no monopoly on nicknames, the same moniker may occur
more than once and cause confusion, keeping guilty mafiosi out of
trouble while landing innocent ones in jail. In the trial files I found
three "Tignusi," a couple of "Ragionieri," "Ingegneri," and "Pugili" (Bo-
xers), several "Pacchiuni," "Pacchiuneddi," "Corti," "Lunghi," "Grossi,"
and "Siddiati" (Grumpys). "I'd like to make a statement"—said Buscetta—"there is a *Tignusu* (Hairless) in this court who must not be confused with another *Tignusu*."[69] Vincenzo Sinagra confessed that among
his accomplices there was one called "u'Siddiato." Detectives failed to
match this nickname with a birth-certificate name and ended up putting three others also nicknamed Siddiato in jail. In the end none of
them turned out to be Sinagra's mate, and were all released. The "real"
Siddiatu got away.[70] But in a trial against organized crime in Naples the
same type of confusion arising from a multiplicity of individuals with
the same nickname led to miscarriages of justice.[71]

Why Not All Criminals Use Aliases

Only a *third* of the defendants in the trial did have a nickname. This is
probably an underestimate, for some names may have been either not
known or not revealed by witnesses. Even so we are far from a universal
phenomenon. Pace Maurer and Futrell, nicknames are not "an ineluc-ta-
ble trait anchored deep in the criminal psyche, the most permanent pos-

session of an individual who lives in an insecure and ever-changing world."[72] Such a dramatic conclusion does not seem warranted. Whatever their purpose, nicknames do not appear to be an essential tool of the mafioso trade.

This does not, however, imply that criminals do not need something that serves the same purpose. Mafiosi have other means at their disposal for hampering and favoring identification when referring to each other. As Lamothe and Nicaso report in their book on the Caruana and Cuntrera crime family, few actual names or even nicknames are spoken in the thousands of wiretaps they analyzed.[73] The mobsters say "this guy there . . . ," "that old fellow, who's older than us . . . ," "that nephew, the fat one . . . ," "the Moustache . . . ," "the tall one . . . ," "the short one . . . ," "that cousin from where the children are . . . ," "the uncle from over there. . . ." Being such a tightly knit network, mafiosi can exploit a wide range of shared information to identify uniquely a person without naming names. So they make do even if no nickname is available by using paraphrases that point to a feature of the person (as a nickname does) or to kin and other relations. Unlike nicknames, these terms are fleetingly associated with persons, something that probably makes it even harder for snooping strangers to match them with the identity of the person.

A sign that when nicknames or network-based paraphrases are not available alternative aliases are still needed is that in other criminal groups members deliberately coin them. Jacquemet found that Neapolitan gangsters give themselves noms de guerre.[74] The Russian *vory* choose a new name as a formal entry requirement into the organization. The mentor discusses names with the novice, and they agree on one. Sometimes the new name is simply the nickname the man already had. "At his crowning, the officiating *vor* [ends] the ceremony by saying: 'we shall call you *such-and-such*' stating the agreed nickname."[75] The practice is reminiscent of that found in some orders of the Catholic and the Russian Orthodox churches and in some secret societies. When a novice is accepted into the ranks of the organization, he is given a new name. Monks and nuns bear two names, the worldly name and the faith name. Nothing of the sort happens at the initiation rituals of the mafia or of any other major organized crime group, such as the yakuza or the triads.

The most plausible explanation of these different practices is that both the Russian and the Neapolitan groups lack the rich community ties that other mafia groups enjoy. That kind of background is essential to provide people naturally with a nickname that has a chance to travel and with the kind of information from which to construct other identifiers. The Neapolitan gangs are many and fragmented, while the Russian *vory* form a national network and operate at great distances from each other, disconnected from local realities and kin networks. Neither, in other words, can rely on the natural emergence of alternative names.

OTHER MOTIVES FOR THE USE OF NICKNAMES

The motives for using nicknames may not be limited to managing identification. Nicknames are likely to satisfy other purposes, which are harder to prove but plausible enough to be discussed. David Gilmore writes: "[N]icknames in the Mediterranean area are a form of verbal aggression, a displacement for competitive envy, especially among men. This envy derives from sexual, economic and status competition among individuals and families where personal autonomy, honour and reputation are paramount concerns. Thus the onomastic distortions of injurious sobriquets in these communities should be seen as manifestations of aggressive, controlling impulses, as partially unconscious attempts to gain dominance over others by attacking their sense of self-identity, family honour and masculine self-esteem."[76] The semantics of mafioso nicknames does suggest that nicknames relate to some extent to mocking others. The special importance of envy and honor in sustaining negative nicknaming, however, is unconvincing. This explanation is at odds with the large presence of derogative nicknames in cultures in which macho values or envy are not especially relevant.[77] The taxonomy of nicknames seems stable across cultures. They allude to oddities and disabilities, draw comparisons between features of the person and animals or objects, signal unusual personal features and peculiar habits:[78] "nobody is spared a name, if he is in any way unusual."[79] And Gilmore's explanation seems also in contrast with the fact that in other groups in which envy and amour propre are present—academia for instance—nicknames are not common; they may be minted, but they do not spread. Finally, within Mediterranean peoples we find not only mocking but also appreciative or neutral nicknames,[80] a fact that suggests a broader spectrum of motives for minting and repeating nicknames.

The greater proportion of derogative or jocular over positive nicknames could simply be due to the fact that they provide more fun, much as negative gossip, which is also predominant over positive gossip, does. Humans everywhere seem to take pleasure in mocking others or cutting them down to size. As in the case of gossip, in which the listener searches not for truths but for plausible, juicy stories, the linguistic brilliance and humorous content of nicknames must be part of their success. Nicknames may survive even if they serve no particular purpose. Still, there is something to be said for Gilmore's interpretation in that the presence of creeping *interpersonal tensions* may enhance the pleasures of mocking allusions and of sharing humor at others' expense. Think for instance of the nicknames that pupils routinely assign to their teachers. The fun and the relief that nicknames provide may suffice to motivate their repetition. The brittle bonds permeating mafiosi lives as well as the high risk of making these tensions explicit could thus partly account for the use of nicknames.

There is a further fact to be considered. Outside traditional societies, nicknames are found mostly among groups of men and mostly among men engaged in team activities. Nicknames were common, for example, among miners in Virginia[81] and among workers at the Great Western Train factory in Swindon, England.[82] Nicknames are also common among surfers, and players of baseball and American football.[83] According to Skipper, who wrote about miners, the presence of shared risk would encourage the use of nicknames.[84] Mafiosi too are quintessentially a society of men. They spend much time together, engaging in both vernacular activities—cooking, hunting, loitering—and nerve-racking actions, like killing people, including sometimes one another. How exactly nicknames would assist the lives they lead is not, however, clear.

They may perhaps provide a facetious easing of the tension connected to risky actions and treacherous circumstances. There is however a different hypothesis, which is in contrast with the purely psychological idea that they help release tension. Nicknames that are manifestly derogatory are likely to cause irritation if used in the presence of the bearers. There is evidence that bearers generally allow only close friends to use them.[85] Since among mafiosi the mere hint of an insult suffices to unleash a violent reaction, it might seem unlikely that derogatory nicknames would be used to address the bearer (unless there was an intention to offend). And yet mafiosi know their own nicknames, and this suggests that at least some of the time their peers or superiors must address them by their nickname, and not just use it in their absence. The value of revealing such nicknames may lie precisely in their dangerousness. It is not uncommon to greet male friends with terms of abuse—this is frequently witnessed in Southern Italy. Friends, young men especially, often salute one another by resorting to abusive epithets—they do so when they meet rather than when they part. To engage in such greetings, one needs to feel confident that the target will not be offended. When used in the presence of or to address the bearer, nicknames may well be part of the same practice—"*look who's here, u Curtu, ya old bastard, how're ya?*"

This sort of usage seems a jocular custom, a form of bantering, and it would be a stretch to attribute such uses to an instrumental motive. Unintentionally, though, the ritual tests the solidity of friendship, for if the target bore a grudge, such lighthearted abuse could not be delivered without causing a reaction. It is the failure of playful informality to be accepted or reciprocated that reveals its social value. When it engenders a negative response, this brings about a switch from innocent banter to strategic interaction. We have evidence that mafiosi become worried if someone who previously addressed them in a familiar way suddenly resorts to formality. Referring to Luciano Liggio, a prominent mafioso from Corleone, Antonio Calderone said: "I noticed something odd in his behaviour, although in the past he addressed me with 'you' now he was calling me 'sir.' I asked him the reason for this change and he replied that I had disobeyed his orders." Similarly, Antonio Ferro from Canicattì began to call Calderone *vossia* (sir) after Calderone's brother's death, "forcing me [Calderone] to reciprocate and call him vossia in return," and causing him to become suspicious.[86] Men who work in teams in risky or demanding jobs do need to be able to trust one another, and to feel reassured that their trust and loyalty are well placed.

CONCLUSIONS

Many of the motives and conditions conducive to the use of nick-names—helping and hindering identification, diffusing interpersonal tensions, reinforcing risky collective undertakings—are present in the mafia. One would therefore expect that the use of nicknames extends to other criminal groups that operate in similar conditions. This expectation is met in the case of Italian American mobsters. We also know that members of the triads in Hong Kong use nicknames to identify each other,[87] a circumstance that suggests that ethnic differences are irrelevant.

Yet there is an exception. The Japanese yakuza is the only significant organized crime group in which members do not use nicknames or code names. It offers a contrary case by which to test our hypotheses, which indicates that the set of causes we have discussed so far, while necessary for the use of nicknames, is not sufficient. In the yakuza it is common to address fellow members with affectionate shortened names—Yamamoto Kenichi, for instance, turns into "Yamaken." This diminutive is called *aisho*, and can be found quite commonly among Japanese males who want to demonstrate their closeness to each other. Or, similarly, one finds the ironic use of the childish/feminine suffix *chan* after a man's name, a sort of linguistic inversion ritual. But there is no trace of full-blown nicknames or even of code names.

The absence of nicknames among the yakuza is consistent with the lower secrecy requirements that they enjoy, which also is rather unique. Less exposed to the perils of law enforcement, they do not need to make a special effort to hamper identification. Members have given interviews to journalists even in very recent times, and used their real names for that. Furthermore, within groups the highly structured hierarchy "means that big/little brother, father/son, gashira (literally head) and kumi-/kai-cho[88] is the prevalent type of address."[89] Wolfgang Herbert wrote to me:

In a small kumi underlings of the same rank would address each other either by an affectionate form of their name or, more commonly, the younger one (not necessarily of age but of date of joining the group) would call his immediate older brother(s) aniki meaning "older brother." In return he would call the younger one

by his (shortened) name. The boss can be addressed as "oyabun"
(parent or father) or in the affectionate form (very common) as
"oyaji." In bigger societies the boss can be addressed/referred to as
"kumicho"—which is sort of a formal title, used particularly when
everyday interaction is scarce due to differences in hierarchy both
personal and organisational (the underling belonging to some affiliated group with little direct contact with the mother organisation). All the other members can be called by their titles mostly
being the terms for the fictive kinship or the position in the
hierarchy.[90]

The availability of hierarchical terms offers an alternative way of identifying members and fulfills one of the functions of nicknames. As I mentioned above, mafiosi too sometimes resort to such terms, though not as
universally as yakuza do, as they tend to mix their use with that of other
aliases. What may prevent the yakuza from doing the same might well be
their strong sense of hierarchical deference and their stress on politeness,
traits typical of Japanese society at large that become obsessively important among mobsters. The Japanese language provides only a limited vocabulary for swearing or calling somebody names. The use of nicknames
would be indicative of disrespect and a breach those codes. When referring to, or addressing, a subordinate, this constraint would not necessarily apply; even so, I found only two nicknames, "Jumbo"[91] and "Rambo,"[92]
both of which referred to junior gang members. Within this normative
constraint, the titles indicating status are efficient in that they can be
used to refer to a person but also to address him directly without causing
offense, and they offer a range of variations from the formal to the affectionate. Japanese practices thus seem to offer both alternatives to and
constraints on the use of nicknames.

CHAPTER 10

Why (Low) Life Imitates Art

Conventional signs and codes can evolve naturally, just as nicknames do, from within the underworld without any effort or explicit agreement on the part of the criminals. Other signs and codes arise by common consent from within groups of criminals, especially small ones in which members can interact face-to-face often enough to agree on their meanings. Yet others emerge from interaction between criminals and the outside world: signs that carry a clear meaning and are spread by institutions capable of reaching large audiences—such as religion, literature, or folk stories—are sometimes recycled by criminals for their own purposes even though in their origins and normal usage the signs have nothing to do with crime.[1] In this chapter I focus on a particular aspect of that type of interaction—that is, on whether fictional portrayals of criminals feed back on the practices of criminals themselves. I will show some evidence of this effect and discuss why it occurs, with particular reference to the influence of cinema, which has had a special relation with the underworld since the medium's earliest days.

THE CASE OF JUZO ITAMI

On a mild Friday night in May 1992 at about 8.45 p.m. three young men dressed in black approached Japanese film director Juzo Itami as he was parking his car near his apartment in Tokyo. Two held him down while the third pulled out a knife and slashed his face and neck. "They cut very slowly; they took their time," Itami later said. They left him bleeding on the sidewalk and sped off in a black car.

A few days before, *Minbo no Onna* (translated as either "Mob Woman" or "The Gentle Art of Japanese Extortion") had opened to rave reviews in Japan. In the film yakuza gangsters are depicted "as crude bullies who are outsmarted and eventually beaten by a female lawyer." "The lawyer is played by Itami's wife, Nobuko Miyamoto, who stars in all his movies," including *Tampopo*, the cult film for which Itami is best known in the West. In *Mob Woman*, a young yakuza member stabs the lawyer in an attack that soon "was imitated in real life." Thus victimized, Itami dragged himself to his apartment. "He was covered with blood," Miyamoto said. "But he told me to calm down and call an ambulance." He eventually recovered: "Thank God he didn't die," she said. "The God of moviemaking stepped in to save him." Five yakuza were later sentenced to jail for this crime.[2]

Tolerated by Japanese society and enjoying a near-legal status, yakuza once were also the pampered darlings of the Japanese B-movie industry. Yakuza films became a genre in their own right in postwar Japan. They were mostly low budget—each film was shot and packaged in less than a month—and yet they became so popular that around 1974 studios were producing a stunning hundred of these films a year. In an insightful essay director and scriptwriter Paul Schrader traces the first fully developed Yakuza film to 1964.[3] Yakuza movies (the most detailed and engaging description of which in English is offered by Ian Buruma[4]) can be compared in some respects with Western films. Like cowboys, these outlaws define their own code of morality, and help the weak and the oppressed, but unlike cowboy movies Yakuza films do not contain the essential theme of social mobility but rather stress the immutability of the social order, and they are driven, like many other Japanese films, by nostalgia for a preindustrial past. Also, the characters, conflicts, and themes are preset, drawing from traditional samurai stories and from Kabuki theater: "Yakuza films are litanies of private argot, subtle body language, obscure codes, elaborate rites, iconographic costumes and tattoos."[5] They tell similar stories and feature the same ritual scenes, so much so that they are sometimes hard to tell apart.[6]

Buruma writes that "real mobsters in Japan are among the greatest fans of this cinematic genre, often imitating the style of movie *yakuza*"[7] but gives no evidence to support the claim. Still, judging by the evidence of how movies have influenced mobsters elsewhere, which I discuss below, it is plausible that they did have an effect in spreading and standardizing style and rituals among different yakuza families. Certainly, for almost thirty years, countless ordinary Japanese watched and loved these films. So broad was their audience that they appealed to far right activists and far left radicals alike.[8] Even though the yakuza movies are now in decline[9] and made largely for the video market rather than for general release, they have not altogether vanished.[10]

Itami's *Mob Woman* must thus have come as a nasty shock to yakuza. It was the first (and possibly the last) Japanese movie to poke stinging fun at the yakuza. Spoiled as they were by these films, they were not amused at being portrayed as bumbling, violent idiots. They particularly resented being shown as unable to live up to their threats and as committing un-dignified acts more suitable to incompetent delinquents. Tokutaro Takayama, "the imposing boss of the Aizu Kotetsu, a yakuza group based in Kyoto with more than 2000 members," was interviewed by the *New York Times* a few weeks after the attack on Itami. He complained of a scene in the movie in which yakuza plant a large insect in the food served by a hotel they are targeting and then ask for money to compen-sate for the alleged contamination. "Nobody would put a cockroach in a restaurant's food like that," Takayama complained. Itami paid a personal price for these portrayals. Not only did low life imitate art. It also took revenge on the author of that art.

There is no record of anyone else ever having been punished by ma-fia-like organizations for an unflattering fictional portrayal. There are all sorts of subgenres in mob movies—light comedies (*Mickey Blue Eyes*, *Bullets over Broadway*, *Married to the Mob*, and many Italian films), realistic accounts (*Salvatore Giuliano*, *Donnie Brasco*), romanticized stories (*The Godfather*), dark meditations (*The Funeral*), and near-sociological studies (*Casino*). There are also comedies that poke fun at mobsters on the side (*Some Like It Hot, The Sting*). The only conspicuously absent genre is that of pointed satire. No film other than Itami's has ever annoyed its mob-ster models to the point of vengeance for the simple reason that there has been little for them to be annoyed about.[11]

Movies that make mobsters look vicious are actually good publicity, not just because all publicity is good but because they advertise mobsters' threatening image, which is their greatest asset. Adrian Wootton, director of the London Film Festival, missed this point when he tried to defend the movie industry, which was being criticized by John Abbott, director general of the National Criminal Intelligence Service, for making organized crime attractive. "There is no sense I feel that gangsters are being overtly glamorized," Wootton said. "They are shown as pretty repulsive and an extremely unpleasant bunch." But this is just how they like to be regarded.[12] Itami's film is unique in displaying mobsters' faults *in their own professional terms.* What they worry about is not being thought of as bad, quite the opposite. They resent being seen to be bad at being bad.

Around the time that Itami's movie appeared, the yakuza were grappling with troubles not limited simply to their tarnished image. In early 1992 the authorities began to crack down on them. The new Violent Groups Control Law gave greater powers to police. Once bold enough to display openly the insignia of their gangs, yakuza were now forced underground.[13] The core yakuza membership, which stood at 63,800 in 1991—much larger than that of the mafia in either Sicily or the United States—had declined to 48,000 by 1994.[14]

Not only was *Mob Woman* special but so were the conditions in which it appeared. Yakuza were at once under pressure from law enforcement but still strong enough to regard themselves not as local racketeers but as a business with a national image to protect. Roberta Torre's farcical musical (*Tano to Die For*), a parody of Sicilian mafiosi, which came out in 1998 in Italy, is the only other film I know of that might similarly have offended its models. In one scene a group of fat dons sing "Noi simmo a Mafia" (We Are the Mafia) and dance while stroking each other's noses, a heavy allusion to homosexuality—enough to make any self-respecting don go ballistic. Yet nothing happened to Roberta Torre. It may have helped that her film also makes fun of the antimafia people, or that the production company, according to Salvatore Zanca and Marcello Fava, two mafiosi who turned state's evidence, paid 15,000 euros to the boss of La Vucciria, a Palermo neighborhood, to be able to shoot without problems.[15] In any case, even if the content of the movie was thought to be offensive, when the movie came out the most important Sicilian mafiosi were in jail, and the rest had very strong reasons to keep a low profile.

A brave, quietly charismatic man, Itami remained unbowed and carried the scars that the attack left on his face as marks of honor. He committed suicide in rather strange circumstances in December 1997. He was sixty-four. This time the god of movie making remained impassive.

EXTORTION AND PROTECTION

For nearly a century movies and mobsters have maintained a symbiotic embrace, one feeding on the other. Their relationships, however, have not always been peaceful, and have at times been as much about culture as they have been about business—the business, that is, of extortion and protection. In order to shoot in peace and enjoy the collaboration of the locals, for example, crews in various parts of the world have been asked by mobsters to pay up or else face the consequences. Chu Yiu Kong documents this practice extensively in Hong Kong, which spread when outdoor filming became more common in the 1980s, exposing the industry more to extortion.[16] Tullio Kezich, a veteran Italian film critic—who worked with Francesco Rosi on the set of *Salvatore Giuliano* in 1961 in Sicily—said that the crew came under pressure from locals as well as from jailed mobsters working through their lawyers. The message was, "You are taking pictures of my windows and you must pay me, or else I'll lean out of the window and ruin your take."[17] Back in 1986 in Rome I interviewed a film director who worked extensively in Sicily (and claimed to have taught the art of movie making to the son of Michele Greco, then the boss of bosses). He told me: "if [the local mafia boss] comes out to have a coffee with you at the bar, as if by a miracle, the crowd gets out of the camera's way and everybody becomes cooperative. Sometimes the Carabinieri themselves point out to you the right man to turn to."[18] Crews in Sicily eventually learned to move first and ask for "protection" without waiting to be prompted. British director Anthony Waller, when filming *Mute Witness* in 1993 in Moscow, said: "we were told by our Russian co-producers that we had to pay off three different mafia groups to allow us to shoot in peace. They were quoting prices more expensive than Hollywood. Contracts meant nothing—it was a question of bargaining on a daily basis—I could speak Russian fluently by the end of the four months."[19] When several gangs are trying to squeeze the producers, having to deal with just one mafia can seem like a blessing.

Shooting movies is a vulnerable activity. Crews work to a tight schedule. They book actors for limited amounts of time. They rely on the full cooperation of the people who live where they shoot. They need submissive extras. Any minor incident can have large costs. Movie making is easy prey to extortion for reasons similar to those that make the construction industry a favorite target.

Mobsters, however, have not just been parasitic on the movie industry. The industry itself has often used "muscle" to control its labor force or stifle the competition. Hugh Grant, talking about shooting *Mickey Blue Eyes* in New York in 1999, "observed that Mr. [Rocco] Musacchia's presence seemed to help head off location problems: 'Anywhere we wanted to shoot, we could shoot,' Mr. Grant said. 'We had no teamsters problems whatsoever.'" "Mr. Musacchia was identified in an F.B.I. affidavit as the partner of a ranking member of the Genovese crime family."[20]

Mobsters, on behalf of producers, have also forced well-known actors to accept lower than market fees or to act in movies against their will. This activity has been documented, for instance, in Bollywood, the Bombay film industry.[21] Chu Yiu Kong gives many examples in Hong Kong, where, in the 1980s and 1990s, there were several vicious attacks on recalcitrant stars.[22] Since such episodes become known mostly when someone rebels or gets hurt, we are probably observing just the tip of an iceberg. Although some actors have been at the rough end of organized criminals, others have enjoyed their protection and professional advice. Dressed in an off-white double-breasted suit and wearing a ponytail, Mickey Rourke went to the late John Gotti's trial in New York together with Anthony Quinn in a show of solidarity with the Gambino family boss. Rourke said that he and "Mr. Gotti were friends. I do roles that are urban-type roles, and he knows about them," Mr. Rourke said. "He's very intelligent, he's very generous with his time."[23]

There are, however, few cases of mobsters turning into producers. Toei, the studio that shot hundreds of yakuza movies, "owed much of its success to its general producer, Kouji Shundo," who was an expert in the matter, being himself an ex-yakuza.[24] He is an exception though. "When the Hong Kong film industry boomed from 1985 to 1993, some triad bosses set up their film companies. Their major job was to use their reputation to 'force' famous stars to make films for them. But they would let film professionals undertake the actual production. These film companies went bankrupt one by one when the film industry started to decline in 1995."[25]

Movie production and organized crime do not really merge. At most they are linked by a limited business partnership, sometimes forced on producers and sometimes sought by them. Mobsters may be popularly depicted as shrewd businessmen when in fact they only know how to run *their* business—enforcement, protection, and bullying—while if they stray into other businesses they tend to go bankrupt and make fools of themselves. There is a peculiar incompetence among mobsters, which I discussed in chapter 2, and the smart ones let the professionals do the work. The main business of a well-functioning mafia is protection, and when it engages in other activities that do need protection, it does so by what economists call "vertical integration" rather than by taking over the business altogether.[26]

Mobsters' attraction to movies in this respect is similar to that which they feel for other sectors of the economy, such as construction, garbage collection, street hawking, and wholesale markets. Peter Reuter and I showed that the sectors that attract (or often ask for) mobsters' protection have certain features in common—firms are small, there are low entry costs, they are unionized, they have lots of unskilled labor, and they need low technology.[27] B movie making is work of this kind. And much of mobsters' involvement in it has been low key—nasty maybe, but unremarkable.[28]

ART IMITATES LOW LIFE

Once we shift from the economics of making films to their content, the links between movies and mobsters become more peculiar, and more interesting. Both sides seem irresistibly attracted to each other.

Scriptwriters have ransacked the underworld for stories. Nick Pileggi, who wrote *Wiseguys* and *Casino*, both made into films by Martin Scorsese, is one of the most successful examples. Mike Newell, who directed *Donnie Brasco*, based the movie on the experience of FBI agent Joseph Pistone, who as we know infiltrated the New York mafia in the late 1970s. Other scriptwriters have drawn on fragments of mobsters' lives rather than on entire stories. Sicilian mafioso Cesare Manzella traveled through the United States hidden in a large cargo crate. The same trick was used in *Il Mafioso*, where comic actor Alberto Sordi is shipped to the United States to commit a murder as payment for the protection he received from the mafia in the past.[29] Mario Puzo, who scripted the most famous mafia movie of all, *The Godfather*, "read his way through a mountain of Senate hearings about the mafia, garnering a mass of authentic details to use in the story of the Corleone family."[30] "Readers of *The Godfather* assumed Puzo had an insider's knowledge of the people and practices he portrayed but in fact, when Puzo came to write the novel in his mid-forties, he knew no more about the mafia than any of his fellow Americans whose surnames didn't terminate with a vowel. 'I wrote *The Godfather* entirely from research,' he admitted in an interview. 'I never met a real honest-to-god gangster.'"[31]

Film writers' attraction to mob stories makes good sense, given the commodity they produce. The terror and violence of the underworld provide ideal fuel for the dramatic and gripping stories that successful movies require. Gangster movies and real gangsters have something special in common: they thrive on making people afraid. In movies the effect is temporary and safely mediated, and one can console oneself munching popcorn, but the fabric and details of the stories most apt to stir emotions in the movie audience are similar to those actually experienced by gangsters and their victims. It is thus unsurprising that films should take inspiration from real life.

Mobsters have not just passively inspired the film industry; they have actively meddled in movie making. Capone is said to have showed Howard Hawks how to shoot a tommy gun.[32] American mafiosi took a keen interest in *The Godfather* before and during production. "I still vividly recall," Peter Maas wrote, "listening to an undercover FBI tape recording of a sombre gathering of mafiosi. The subject under prolonged discussion was the casting of *The Godfather*. Everyone's favorite (to play himself, naturally) appeared to be Paul Newman."[33] During a criminal investigation in the late 1990s, the FBI tapped the phones of some New Jersey mafiosi. A large part of their conversation was taken up with discussing on whom the characters in *The Sopranos* television show were based. "Yeah," said David Chase, the series creator, "very odd. It makes you wonder what are we doing here. In truth, mobsters' lives are pretty prescribed. And the things we've come up with, which have been gotten from ex–wise guys and cops, of course it sounds like their lives because that's where we get the information from."[34]

The crew of *The Godfather* and its actors happily communed with the "boys." James Caan was seen in the company of Carmine "The Snake" Persico so often that the FBI thought he was part of *that* crew. Sicilian mafioso Antonino Calderone used to hang around the set of a movie called *The Godson of the Godfather*, a parody of *The Godfather* by a lowbrow comedian. "I was there every evening. I always loved the movies. I was a friend of an important actor, I chatted with the crew, watched them shoot. My presence was very welcome, they even asked me whether a certain scene was OK, and if it was funny."[35] Mobsters have even provided critical feedback. Meyer Lansky, a longtime Jewish associate of Italian American mafiosi, telephoned Lee Strasberg, the actor who played "him" in the Godfather: "He said, 'you did good.'" But he also added, somewhat more ominously: "Now, why couldn't you have made me more sympathetic? After all, I am a grandfather."[36]

A whole demimonde has grown around the industry of mob movies, and nowhere more so than in New York. There is an Italian-American hangout, Rao's in East Harlem, where "a network of would-be wise guys, celebrities, prosecutors and crime reporters" meet and "form a kind of pseudo-commission ruling on the mob's narrative mythology."[37] Rocco Musacchia, who made a job out of assisting producers and actors to shoot mob movies, mingles with that crowd. He advised John Huston's *Prizzi's Honor* and several lesser films. The *New York Times* says that Huston hired him "despite the bad publicity generated by the F.B.I. affidavit" that implicated him in the Genovese family. But that publicity was exactly what Musacchia needed to be credible with the filmmakers. Liz Hurley, the British actress who produced *Mickey Blue Eyes*, "lavishes praise on Musacchia, whom she refers to as the link between the likes of Al Pacino, Johnny Depp and Barry Levinson and the kind of men who could be on F.B.I. surveillance lists." On CNN Hugh Grant said that Mr. Musacchia "introduced us to another guy called Jimmy Seven Heads, who then introduced us to another guy called Tony Mussolini and, one by one, we got deeper and deeper into that world."[38]

"There's actors that want to be wise guys and wise guys that want to be actors," Musacchia said.[39] Such desires to switch roles remain, however, largely unfulfilled. There are a "tiny" number of men with a criminal past "who are getting parts as wise guys in mob-themed movies and television shows because of the tough-guy demeanors they have cultivated since they were kids."[40] Bobby "Blue" Martana is one example. He "moonlighted as a bodyguard to Robert de Niro's Al Capone in the *Untouchables*, then returned to his day job"—described as "busting heads across Brooklyn and Staten Island for the Gambino family."[41] Other mobsters appeared as extras in the crowd scenes in *The Godfather* in Little Italy. But they tend to be small-time crooks who in most cases have given up crime.

Joe Bonanno took acting classes in his youth,[42] but there is no record of serious actors becoming mobsters.[43] Besotted by the mob, Frank Sinatra loved to congregate with and sing for such mobsters as Lucky Luciano and Sam Giancana, but he was not initiated, even though he sometimes liked to play the part. (Mia Farrow, who was married to Sinatra before her marriage to Woody Allen, admitted in court that one of her ex-husbands had offered to break both of Woody Allen's legs but added that he had been joking).[44] And there is no record of mobsters becoming actors, with one exception, which is found, once again, in Japan. Noboru Ando, once the boss of a Tokyo crime family, the Ando-gumi, became an actor after the fall of his gang. He was a handsome man, and one can easily guess what role he played in the movies: himself. He appeared in fifty-one films in the 1960s and 1970s, several of which told the story of his crime family.[45] The almost sacred treatment that yakuza enjoyed in Japanese movies may explain this exception.

Mobsters may in fact be exceptional actors in their own world—as Noburo Ando once told Mark Schilling, "All yakuza have to be actors to survive"[46]—but the act they perform requires them never to reveal that it is one. They gain much from their fearsome reputation, and the more they can advertise it by a sheer display of menace and self-assurance rather than by actual acts of violence, the better it is for them. Mobsters would lose their repute if they went into acting. Acting is, quintessentially, about make-believe. So while mobsters may be attracted by actors' ability to scare and impress the public while being fakes, and while they like being seen in the company of celebrities, the last thing they want is to be seen as impostors. Some actors, on the other hand, while lacking what it takes when it comes to shooting things other than movies, may be fascinated by the fact that mobsters cannot easily afford a second take and keep acting even when the camera is off. Mobsters and actors flirt with each other but ultimately stick to their own roles. "Back when I was working with Marlon Brando in 'The Freshman,'" Musacchia said, "John Gotti happened to be at a restaurant across the street." "Brando was like a kid: 'Oh, I got to go meet Gotti!' So I introduced them. But who kissed whose ring?" he wonders.[47] Who indeed! Let us now look at how low life imitates art.

LOW LIFE IMITATES ART

Criminals imitate art for diverse reasons. Some imitations are trivial affectations, such as when fictional characters inspire criminals' choice of code names.

As the Nigerian government combed the world in pursuit of more than $4bn (£2.76bn) that disappeared under the rule of General Sani Abacha, one trail led to Switzerland where the late dictator's sons had opened a series of bank accounts. To the investigators' surprise, they found many of the Swiss accounts used one of two code names—Kaiser for those opened by Ibrahim Abacha and Soze for his brother Mohammed. There could be no more apt names: Keyser Soze was the name of a shadowy Turkish Mafia leader in *The Usual Suspects*, the 1995 film starring Kevin Spacey.[48]

If rationally motivated, imitation can be one of two main types.[49] In the first, the imitator copies something particularly novel or efficient that had not occurred to him before. For instance, "In the early 70s the Argentine Montoneros "kidnapped" the corpse of General Pedro Aramburu from his grave and demanded in exchange for the body that the body of Eva Peron be returned from Spain. Within weeks Burmese terrorists removed the body of UN Secretary U Thant from its crypt and used it for coercive bargaining with the Burmese government."[50] Observing others doing something effectively, whether in fiction or in reality, gives one new ideas: "Toto' Di Cristina had just finished reading *The Godfather*"—said Antonino Calderone—"and he had the idea of doing like in the book.... They disguised themselves as doctors and killed [Candido Ciuni, a hotel manager] in his [hospital] bed."[51] The practice has spread to other cultures too: Wong Long Wai, a gangster turned movie producer, was stabbed in Wanchai, hospitalized, and later murdered in his hospital bed in the dead of night.[52] Mario Moretti, one of the leaders of the Red Brigades, an Italian terrorist group, said that when they started to rob banks to finance their activities they followed "the same technique we saw in films."[53] An observation of effectiveness in fiction may inspire imitation in any profession, but it is likely to inspire criminals disproportionately, for criminals can rarely observe their seniors at work.

In *The Godfather*, a mafioso who is about to testify against the Corleone family takes his life to make sure his relatives will not suffer from his behavior. Suicide is rare among mafiosi. Yet Antonino Gioé, arrested in connection with the killing of Judge Giovanni Falcone, did exactly that. He was moved to a jail in Rome apparently as a prelude to becoming a state witness. In all likelihood he took his life because that was his only way to signal that he was not about to betray.[54] We shall never know whether the film inspired him or whether he independently decided that that was his optimal choice in the circumstances. The late director Robert Altman suggested the grandest and most tragic example of this dynamic. He believed that a Hollywood genre he calls the "comedy of apocalypse" may have been a contributory factor in the staging of the 9/11 terrorist attacks on the World Trade Center and the Pentagon: "The movies set the pattern, and these people have copied the movies. Nobody would have thought to commit an atrocity like that unless they'd seen it in a movie. How dare we continue to show this kind of mass destruction in movies? I just believe we created this atmosphere and taught them how to do it."[55] I thought that was an exaggeration till I read that "the CIA has found evidence in seized Al Qaeda documents that Bin Laden's operatives watch action-adventure movies for ideas."[56]

Movies also help to expand one's armory of arguments. Frankie Locasio was John Gotti's codefendant and was convicted of murder and racketeering. At the trial his son Salvatore was "one of a sleek-suited crew who populate[d] the public benches. 'This is America!' shouted Mr. Locasio after the judge dismissed one of his father's lawyers. 'Haven't they ever heard of the Bill of Rights? Tell them to go over there and read it.' In 1959, when Rod Steiger played Al Capone, he used the same line."[57]

All these actions could of course come to mind without one's seeing them in a movie. Optimal solutions are spread by imitation, but the optimal solution exists independently of it. And mobsters tend to know what is best for them without much need to be taught by movies.

The second type of imitation, however, is more important. It occurs when the optimal course of action is not independently defined but becomes optimal (or at least a good thing to do) *because* the model adopts it first. There is nothing intrinsically optimal in, say, wearing a certain hat one has seen in a movie other than the fact that it is used in *that* movie and that one wants to be seen to be doing as *in* the movie. "One of the most astounding exhibitions of popular devotion came in the wake of Mr. Disney's films about Davy Crockett. In a matter of months, youngsters all over the country who would balk at wearing a hat in winter, were adorned in 'coonskin caps in midsummer."[58]

Among mobsters, this type of imitation is not merely the result of expressive emulation. To appreciate its value we must remember that mobsters cannot communicate as easily as we can. This constrains their

ability to identify and transmit efficient conventional signals and to advertise a desirable image. Can imitating movies carry them over these
hurdles?

CONVENTIONS

How a real mobster should behave, dress, and speak are questions for
which there is no optimal technical solution that presents itself independently of what others do and perceive as the meaning of their action.
While criminals need conventional signals to communicate with each
other and with the outside world, they are also hard put to agree on
what these signals are and how to establish them credibly. They lack a
coordinating and standardizing authority, and have to operate in secrecy.
They cannot for instance devise a company jingle and make it known to
everyone without getting caught.

Movies can accidentally offer some solutions to those problems. What
they offer is "common knowledge," the foundation of coordination in
the absence of a central authority: coordination occurs when everyone
knows that everyone else knows that *s means k* or that *people like us always do j*.[59] When I was in Palermo, I learned that in the late 1970s a Sicilian aristocrat lent a country villa to a mafia boss for his daughter's
wedding reception. About five hundred people took part in the festivi-
ties, to the tunes on the soundtrack of *The Godfather*. Consider now a
scene at CaSa Bella, on Mulberry Street in New York City, at about the
same time. Lefty Ruggiero, his partner Louise, and "Donnie Brasco" (Joseph Pistone) were having dinner together. "The restaurant's strolling
guitarist came by our table," Pistone wrote. "Louise requested the theme
from *The Godfather*. The guy sang it in Italian and then in English."[60]
Consider now a scene at a different restaurant in the same area, a few
years earlier. Bob Delaney, an FBI agent who infiltrated the mafia in the
mid-1970s by setting up a fake business, Alamo Transportation, in his
testimony to a U.S. Senate committee said that on one occasion Joe
Adonis Jr. "gave the waiter a pocketful of quarters and told him to keep
playing the same song on the juke box—the theme song from *The God-*

father. All through dinner, we listened to the same song, over and over."[61] The soundtrack acts as an icon that gives a clear meaning without constituting evidence of affiliation.

In May 1991 three building contractors from Palermo found the severed head of a horse in the company car.[62] Ten years later the same "cadeau," with a knife between its eyes, was left in the car of Carmelo Di Caro, forty-nine, foreman at the Palermo shipyard,[63] a sign that the tradition is not dying out. In *The Godfather* the head is deposited on the victim's bed and does not have a knife stuck between the eyes—but the dissimilarities did not obscure the meaning of the message to the receivers. (Who imitated whom is uncertain in this case, though. In 1956, in a turf war that raged over Palermo funeral homes and street flower sellers, Carmelo Napoli was killed. Sometime before the shoot-out he was delivered the severed head of his German shepherd, kidnapped a few days earlier.)[64]

Movies, or fiction more generally, can create styles and signs that previously did not exist or carried a different meaning. "[Eddie Mars'] voice"—Chandler wrote in *The Big Sleep*—"was the elaborately casual voice of the tough guy in pictures. Pictures have made them all like that."[65] Shifting from talk to looks, Giuseppe Pellegriti, a Sicilian mafioso who turned state's evidence, describes the late Pino "Scarpuzzedda" Greco, a vicious mafia murderer, as "a slick and gloomy guy, he looked like a killer in the movies."[66] The benefits of dressing up like the gang of thugs in *A Clockwork Orange,* a style that several youth gangs adopted in the wake of this violent film,[67] appeared not because of any intrinsic reason but because the style was a reference to *that* film. Without the movie, the style would have been meaningless.

William Everson, a film historian, argues that gangster lore was invented in a 1912 silent film called *Musketeers of Pig Alley*, in which all the protagonists wear suits and hats, and that Al Capone and the Chicago mob adopted the movie tradition.[68] I have shown elsewhere how the use of dark glasses as an identifying item of "gangsterhood" was probably created by the pictures.[69] Everson himself told me that *Gun Crazy*[70] was possibly the first film in which a gangster sported dark glasses.

This view of the creative interplay between fiction and reality should not be mistaken for postmodernist blabber. Without movies we would still have gangsters. We did have them. But without films, mobsters would need different sources for their conventional signals. Mobsters' approach to communication would exploit other sources, such as religion, superstitions, or literature, which, like films, make stories widely known. I, for instance, received a tarot card with a jack of spades under my apartment door when I was in Palermo doing research in 1987. The senders counted on the fact that the meaning of tarot cards is well known, especially in Southern Italy. They did not expect an ignorant receiver. Since I knew nothing about tarots, however, my first thought was that some kid had accidentally dropped it. Later, after more explicit communications had occurred, I reconsidered the episode and discovered that the jack of spades conventionally signals that "a nosy man should watch out for he may be in for punishment." Had that same card been used in a well-known movie or book to threaten someone, even I might have understood more quickly what it meant. The efficiency of conventional signals is predicated on common knowledge, such as that so effectively spread by movies and other forms of fiction.[71]

Knowing how to behave has been a serious headache for the many new gangs that have sprouted in Russia since 1989. They have no history, no agreed-upon codes, and they plunder anything that plausibly can be plundered. Russian mobsters are said to mimic "the clothing and swagger of American gangsters in 1930's movies."[72]

> When the leaders of the Soviet mob wanted to see how to bribe, blackmail, embezzle, hijack and smuggle more efficiently, they found ready-made lessons available. They watched American crime movies. "I have seen [the movies]. They are rather detailed" said Lt. Col. Alexander Gurov, one of the leaders of the Soviet government's fight against organized crime. "Our criminals don't need trial-and-error methods. They have models that are tried and true."[73]

Others in Russia have looked to Sicily, as mediated by fiction, as a source of inspiration. In a restaurant called Diomga in Komsomolsk in the Rus-

sian Far East in 1993 there was a wedding feast that was secretly video-
taped by an anti–organized crime unit. The scene resembles the wedding in *The Godfather.* The boss makes a speech in which he refers to his
city as "our little Palermo." He repeats "Palermo" four or five times, a
city that while lying nine thousand miles away is peculiarly close to his
heart. He blesses "our fraternity" and displays a terminology he must
have picked up watching *The Octopus*, an Italian soap opera about the
mafia that was also broadcast by Russian television. Lacking homegrown
styles and codes, the Russians resorted to importing foreign models.[74]
Although they surely know without much help how to carry out their
crimes, they are uncertain about which codes and emblems can contribute to a more effective "packaging" of their endeavors.

The effectiveness of movies is particularly relevant for transmitting
conventional codes to younger generations. Newcomers and would-be
mobsters cannot easily learn how a mobster is supposed to behave. Movies help not just to create but to spread the codes of behavior. "Young
gangsters or triad members," Chu Yiu Kong wrote, "like to watch gang
movies to learn how to behave as a triad. It should be noted that triad
membership is a criminal offence in Hong Kong and the gang movie is
one of the major sources for youngsters to learn how to behave to be a
triad."[75]

Fiction seems to affect other professions in which secrecy is equally
crucial—John Le Carré said that young spies have looked at his books as
a source on which to tailor their demeanor and vocabulary.[76] Ordinary
professions too, possibly those in which manners and codes play an important role but are not formally codified, seem to be influenced. Rakesh
Kurana told me that a friend of his "went to work on a college intern-
ship for an investment bank in New York. When he asked what he
should wear at the office he was told to go watch the movie *Wall Street.*"
In his biography of Kipling, "David Gilmour makes a similar point about
Kipling's 'Departmental Ditties' and 'Barrack-Room Ballads'; they
taught the British soldiers in India to talk and act like Danny Deever
and Tommy Atkins."[77] And the practice is not even new: "The Medieval
European aristocrats, from the 13th century on, emulated the actions
they admired in books. The so-called rules of chivalry, whether they

governed combat (real warfare or jousting) or courtesy (elegant speech and good manners), were largely self-conscious borrowings from the fictional world of romance."[78]

Two conditions jointly foster the generation of conventional codes through fiction. First, there must be a value in having commonly shared and stable conventions. Next, there must be obstacles to creating and spreading them by means of an overarching authoritative forum—because of a need for secrecy, perhaps, or because of poor means of communication or coordination (both certainly problems for medieval knights). Groups under such conditions find it useful to imitate one or a few widely known texts or images, which lay out the basic rules via the stories they tell. If all members of the group know the piece of fiction, and they all know that they know it, then they all know what doing or donning X means, even without a concerted effort to agree on X's meaning.

ADVERTISING

Mobsters cannot easily project the image they want to project to the outside world. They cannot hire Saatchi & Saatchi to run an advertising campaign, and this, arguably, is where movies come in most handy. Mobsters benefit from and revel in the publicity they vicariously get from movies about them. This gives them an additional reason to do as they see done in the movies. To inform their own audience that they are those whom the movie really talks about—*that guy on the screen is me!*— they need to sport those signs that permit the cross identification—the voice, the vocabulary, the songs, the looks, the clothes, and many other appurtenances. The more movies imitate real mobsters, the less of course real mobsters have a need to imitate them. But art often improves on and spreads widely the sparse and accidental quirks of real mob lives.

In the 1950s Lucky Luciano returned to Lercara Friddi, his hometown in Sicily. His contribution to local culture was to provide financial backing for the opening of the first cinema in the village. The first film showed there was *Little Caesar*, a gangster classic with Edward G. Robinson. "The people was comin' up to me," Luciano writes in his autobiography, "and practically kissing my hand—not only because I brought them the pictures but because they wanted to show me that I was a bigger shot than Little Caesar."[79]

The absolute winner of the contest to supply the best free mafia advertising is undoubtedly *The Godfather*. That film had for the mafia the same effect that Marilyn Monroe's famous quip about her nocturnal dress had for boosting sales of Chanel no. 5. Mobsters loved it, and still do. "The Godfather is everything to these people," says David Chase, creator of *The Sopranos*. "It's their Bible, their Koran. Their Mona Lisa, their Eiffel Tower."[80] Sammy "The Bull" Gravano, John Gotti's lieutenant, whose testimony was crucial in sending his former boss to jail, saw *The Godfather* in 1972, and later acknowledged that "[Puzo] influenced the life, absolutely." "I would use lines in real life like 'I'm gonna make an offer you can't refuse,' and I always tell people, just like from 'The Godfather,' 'If you have an enemy, that enemy becomes my enemy.'"[81] Gravano also stressed that seeing "his" life on the big screen gave him a new sense of legitimacy that helped him to carry out his many hits. "It made our life seem honorable."[82] "It was a validation of everything we believed in. I left that movie stunned. I mean I floated out of the theatre. Maybe it was fiction, but for me, then, that was our life. It was incredible. I remember talking to a multitude of guys, made guys, everybody, who felt exactly the same way."[83] More evidence of the same effects is provided by Louise Milito, the wife of Louie, a member of the Gambino family, in her autobiography:

> Louie watched it like six thousand times. It was like a searchlight had lit up on something he had always believed in but never seen the proof before. . . . All our friends were watching it . . . the guys who came to the house were all acting like *Godfather* actors, kissing and hugging even more than they did before and coming out with lines from the movie. . . . Louie and Frank [de Cicco] watched it in the den and Frankie came upstairs looking like he's just seen God . . . Louie thought it was close to reality, but I didn't. Back then I laughed at all that, like it was a farce.[84]

The "advertising" persuaded the mobsters first of all of the value of their deeds; it boosted their sense of their own legitimacy. It boosted—as an FBI agent responsible for the successful bugging of Paul Castellano's home revealed—their social self-confidence:

> *The Godfather* ... had also given thugs a whole range of ready-made things to say when they wanted to sound tough, sincere, righteous or even wise. The scripts—which a fair number of wise-guys seemed to have memorised—made them less disinclined to talk. It is a general truth that, outside their own circle, many wise-guys are painfully insecure and even shy ... they are acutely aware of their lack of education and afraid of sounding stupid. Being able to say something that Al Pacino or Robert de Niro already said helps them get started in a conversation.[85]

John Abbott, director general of the British National Criminal Intelligence Service, has openly blamed films, such as *Lock Stock and Two Smoking Barrels* and *Snatch*, both by director Guy Ritchie, for glamorizing and thus encouraging organized crime. He said that filmmakers have made a concerted effort to show organized crime as a "bit of a laugh" carried out by colorful personalities and "cheeky chappies." Abbott said he recognized that filmmakers were "anxious to make money," but a "sense of balance" was needed.[86] Muzzling the film industry would no doubt be a cure worse than the problem. Still, if the feelings *The Godfather* induced in Gravano are representative of the effects that mobster films can instigate, Abbott had a point.

The Godfather is often accurate in details. For example Sammy "The Bull" Gravano said:

> Remember that scene when Michael [Corleone] goes to whack that drug dealer and the police captain? ... Remember how Michael couldn't hear anything as he's walking up on them? Remember how his eyes went glassy, and there was just the noise of the train in the background, and how he couldn't hear them talk? That's just like I felt when I killed Joe Colucci.[87]

The film as a whole, however, is romanticized and offers an unrealistic portrayal of the mafia—as Puzo himself said many times. The role of the blood family is, for one, exaggerated. The mafia is a society of men who are more often than not unrelated by kin (see chapter 8). Novices take an oath of loyalty, which explicitly includes undertaking to serve the "family" first and their own family next. The lack of realism, however, simply made *The Godfather* more attractive to its models. "Never mind—said Gravano—that loyalty and honor played no part in the actual Cosa Nostra. Perceived reality was what mattered. *The Godfather* saga contained everything that concerned and excited us: family, romance, betrayal, power, lust, greed, legitimacy, even salvation. And all played out on a grand stage, with death, inevitable and often violent, waiting in the wings."[88]

The Godfather transfixed not just the Italian American mobsters or their Sicilian cousins. Denizens of the underworld loved it in Hong Kong, in Japan, and in Russia—for all of whom the film was even less realistic. According to Nikolai Modestov, the mobsters of Sergei Frolov's Balashikhino gang could recite parts of the *Godfather* films by heart.[89] It was a truly global movie, whose transcultural success shows how organized criminals are not inanely trapped within the ethnic boundaries of their local subcultures. If foreign sources are more gripping, more widely known, more forceful in conveying a powerful image of their industry, they gladly adopt them. They are perfectly capable of recognizing their foreign counterparts; they know who is in the same business they are, and copy whatever practices or symbols seem to them most effective. Even in Japan, where homegrown influences on mobsters' mannerisms were strong and close to all-encompassing, the film's success was so great that it rocked the ritual solidity of yakuza movies, some of which redrafted their story lines as a result amidst a heated controversy between "innovators" and "traditionalists."[90]

Not only did mobsters like *The Godfather*, they intervened in its production. The producers were energetically encouraged by Joe Colombo not to use the word *mafia* or the name "Cosa Nostra" in the film, which were duly deleted from the script. This effort at language control was presented as a reasonable insistence on ethnic correctness, as it were, for officially it was the Italian American Civil Rights League that demanded that the good name of Italian Americans not be soiled. Also, at that time, doubts about the existence of the Cosa Nostra were widespread. Most scholars writing on the mafia were going to great lengths to demonstrate that it did not exist[91]—and the mobsters wanted to keep their brotherhood secret. Rather than requiring protection money, the mobsters exerted control over the film's message in return for their assistance—just as any firm commissioning its advertising does to protect its image. After a plenary meeting in a New York theater of six hundred members of the Italian American League with one of the producers, a deal was struck, and as a result the film crew got all the collaboration they wanted when shooting in Little Italy.[92]

In 1999, discussing the movie with Jeffrey Goldberg, Steven Kaplan, allegedly John Gotti Jr.'s bodyguard, revealed how much the film is valued by its models to this day:

> One evening earlier this month, while debating the strengths of various mob movies, Kaplan lavishly praised "The Godfather." I [Goldberg] countered that "The Godfather," while hugely entertaining, kept alive destructive myths, and suggested "Donnie Brasco" as a compelling depiction of hard-luck mob life. It is for this reason that "Donnie Brasco" is not popular in certain circles. Kaplan's eyes grew beady, and he said, very slowly, in a manner meant to preclude further dissent, "The Godfather" is a better movie.[93]

Goodfellas, by Pileggi and Scorsese, is a much more realistic movie also, which, as film critic Jim Shepard said, is "littered with the corpses of guys who thought they were in a movie called *The Godfather*."[94] Yet the status of the latter as a cult movie is unsurpassed in the eyes of those concerned. *Donnie Brasco* is arguably one of the best mob movies ever made on the subject (it took a British director who went to public school to portray effectively this society of men, their weaknesses and quirks, the mutual intimidation, the paranoia, the subjugation, the displays of power). But precisely because of its realism, because it portrays a case in which mobsters were conned by an astute undercover agent, it is unpopular with gangsters. Advertising is not supposed to dwell on shortcomings.

CONCLUSIONS

In *The Sopranos*, a long-running and highly successful television series (now concluded) on the lives of a group of New Jersey mafiosi, the effects of cinema on mobsters are built into the story itself. The men of fictional family boss Tony Soprano model themselves on movie mobsters of *real* films. One has a car horn that blares out the first bars of *The Godfather* theme; another routinely impersonates Al Pacino as Michael Corleone. Tony's nephew Christopher tries to write a screenplay about his mob experiences. He even takes acting classes, as the very real Joe Bonanno did before him,[95] and like Bonanno he eventually decides to stick to a criminal career. When Tony Soprano goes with a neighbor to play golf at a country club in which he would like to become a member, he is bombarded with questions: "How real was *The Godfather?*" and "Did you ever meet John Gotti?" Tony's daughter, Meadow, reveals to her younger brother, Anthony, the truth about their father's business by showing him a website that features pictures of mob bosses. "There's Uncle Jackie!" says Anthony as he spots one of his father's best friends."[96]

We have come full circle: now art imitates low life imitating art. According to James Gandolfini, the actor who played Tony Soprano, the series was closely monitored by mobsters, who did not hesitate to pass their verdicts on the show and let the actors know if their behavior did not ring true. "I talk to some gentlemen who have friends who are these people and most of them enjoy the show," said Gandolfini. "They get a good laugh out of it, although once when I wore shorts in a barbecue scene it was relayed to me that it was not something these gentlemen would do, even at a barbecue."[97] And, sure enough, in the following series this message is related to Tony.

Whether, following *The Sopranos*, mobsters will now feel so relaxed about their neuroses as to start patronizing shrinks, as Tony Soprano did, remains to be seen. Only once in the history of the Italian American

mafia was a member rumored to be seeing a psychiatrist. In the 1950s
Vito Genovese spread the story that Frank Costello was doing so "to
overcome 'his terrible feelings of inferiority' touched off by his lack of
education and breeding when among the people of high finance and
society" (with whom Costello mingled more than any other mafioso,
before or after). Costello's reputation suffered, and after a botched attempt on his life in 1957, he went into early retirement. He died in his
bed twenty years later.[98]

Notes

Introduction

1. An inspiring early study that uses an approach germane to that of this book, but in a different field, is Robert Jervis's *The Logic of Images in International Relations*.

2. Pistone 1989: 159.

3. Gambetta 1993 and 1994a.

4. Bacharach and Gambetta 2001; Gambetta 2005a, 2009; Gambetta and Hamill 2005.

5. For a collection of general definitions see Hauser 1996: 7.

6. Schelling 1960: 147.

7. Hauser 1996: ch. 1.

8. Robert Jervis uses a different terminology, defining *signals* as "promissory notes," which "do not contain inherent credibility" (1970: 18), while he calls *indices* "statements or actions that carry some inherent evidence that the image projected is correct" (1970: 18). Michael Spence, one of signaling theory's founders, defines an *index* as "an observable but unalterable characteristic" and a *signal* as "an observable alterable characteristic" (1974: 10).

9. On signaling theory generally see Spence 1974; Zahavi 1975; Zahavi and Zahavi 1997; Gambetta 2009.

10. See, respectively, Zahavi and Zahavi 1997 and Frank 1988.

11. On the theory of common knowledge and applications germane to those in this book see Chwe 2001.

12. Schelling 1960: 20.

13. Stiglitz 2000: 1441.

14. From a letter by Steve Coombes and Dave Robinson, *New Yorker*, 29 September 1997.

CHAPTER 1. Criminal Credentials

1. Schelling 1960: 140.

2. *Independent*, 24 April and 11 March 2003.

3. *L'Espresso* 48, November 2000.

4. *La Repubblica*, 8 November 2001.

5. Initially unbeknownst to the Italian authorities, the bars were also eagerly sought by the CIA and the FBI. *La Repubblica*, 8 November 2001.

6. Blumstein et al. 1986: 139.

7. Sutherland 1957: 27.

8. Avinash Dixit, personal communication. See also Dixit 2003.

9. *Phoenix New Times*, 15 May 1991.

10. See Varese 2000 and "Comparative Characteristics of Bribery of the Russian Representatives of Power," *Zvezda*, 5 July 1995. I am grateful to Federico Varese for letting me know of and translating this article.

11. Åkerström 1983: 129. Also taxi drivers in dangerous cities claim to be able to identify potential attackers mimicking a passenger by gut feelings or a sixth sense (Gambetta and Hamill 2005).

12. Pistone 1989: 39.

13. Sutherland 1957: 20, my emphasis.

14. Blumstein et al. 1986: 139.

15. Sutherland 1957: 20.

16. Åkerström 1983: 147, my emphasis.

17. Sullivan 1989: 171. In the George V. Higgins novel *Cogan's Trade* Cogan establishes his bona fides by invoking common acquaintances. The dialogue goes something like this: "Who are you? I've never seen you before and now you are telling me all these things." "I am just a guy. Very few people know me. Oh, yes. China Tanzi knows me." I am grateful to Avinash Dixit for pointing this out to me.

18. See for instance John Irwin (1985), who provides an ample portrait of prisons as places where conventional sensibilities are lost, rabble mentality is acquired, prisoner are acculturated into deviant subcultures, and where networking takes place. See also Kolstad (1996); in the sample of forty prisoners he interviewed, nine out of ten agreed partly or completely that prisons were universities where they learned how to offend as well as learned deviant behavior and ways of thinking. No one disagreed with the above, and two-thirds definitely agreed. According to a priest who works with delinquent youths in Palermo, there is also a hardening effect. The first time they go to prison, they are terrified, but they then get used to it and, once released, they do not fear ending up in it as much as they did before, a sort of declining marginal disutility.

19. Shaw 1966: 109–10.

20. Åkerström 1983: 33.

21. Åkerström 1983: 38–39.

22. Blumstein et al. 1986: 27.

23. Boyle 1977: 73.

24. Boyle 1977: 128.

25. Quoted in Irwin 1985: 98. Being in prison could be seen as a sign of bad luck, a result of professional hazard that affects everyone in the underworld, but it could also be read as a sign of greater incompetence. But I have no evidence suggesting the latter to be relevant.

26. Varese 2001: 156.

27. Kaminski, personal communication.

28. Seymour 1996: 75.

29. Kaminski, personal communication.

30. Varese 2001: 156.

31. Varese 2001: 249, fn. 21.

32. Servizio Centrale Operativo, *Rapporto operativo. Esin et alii*, 3 vols. (Rome: Polizia di Stato, 1997), vol. 1, pp. 97–98. I am grateful to Federico Varese for bringing this story to my attention.

33. Chen and Shapiro 2006: 4.

34. Chen and Shapiro 2006: 3.

35. Chen and Shapiro 2006: 9.

36. Chen and Shapiro 2006: 2.

37. *Washington Post*, 3 September 1998.

38. *New York Times*, 21 January 1998.

39. See Gambetta 1993: ch. 3.

40. Valentine 2000: 4.

41. Valentine 2000: 11.

42. See "Medellín: La legge delle bande (reportage dalla Colombia)," *La Repubblica delle Donne*, 2003, n. 331, pp. 80–88.

43. See Hamoumou 1993. I am grateful to Jon Elster for telling me about this case.

44. Pistone 1989.

45. Pistone 1989: 48.

46. Pistone 1989: 112.

47. Pistone 1989: 111.

48. Pistone 1989: 66.

49. Pistone 1989: 66.

50. Pistone 1989: 41.

51. Pistone 1989: 113, my emphasis.

52. Pistone 1989: 47.

53. Pistone 1989: 47.

54. Pistone 1989: 64, my emphasis.

55. Pistone 1989: 60, my emphasis.

56. Pistone 1989: 158.

57. Pistone 1989: 52.

58. Pistone 1989: 52.

59. Pistone 1989: 50.

60. Pistone 1989: 56–57.

61. Pistone 1989: 57.

62. Pistone 1989: 205.

63. Pistone 1989: 209.

64. Pistone 1989: 211, my emphasis.

65. Pistone 1989: 234.

66. Pistone 1989: 52, my emphasis.

67. Pistone 1989: 408.

68. Pistone 1989: 408, my emphasis.

69. Pistone 1989: 265.

70. Pistone 1989: 228.

71. Pistone 1989: 403.

72. Pistone 1989: 406.

73. Pistone 1998: 405, my emphasis.

74. "The Counterterrorist Myth," *Atlantic Monthly*, July/August 2001, www.theatlantic.com/issues/2001/07/gerecht.htm, accessed September 2008.

75. Aleksenko 2003: 73.

76. K. V. Guzev, *The SR Party from Petit Bourgeois Revolutionarism to Counter-revolution* (Moscow, 1995), p. 75, quoted in Aleksenko 2003: fn. 10. I am grateful to Marek Kaminski for alerting me to this case.

77. *Toronto Sun*, 20 June 1996.

78. *Toronto Sun*, 20 October 1995, my emphasis.

79. Security Intelligence Review Committee, Annual Report 1994–95, p. 10, http://www.sirc-csars.gc.ca/pdfs/ar_1994-1995-eng.pdf, accessed November 2008.

80. See Sanders 2005.

81. Wright and Decker 1997: 62ff.

CHAPTER 2. The Power of Limits

1. "In a succession of experimental studies exploring the circumstances surrounding cooperation in n-person prisoner's dilemmas, we have collected data about subjects' expectations of others' behavior. One of our most consistent findings throughout these studies—a finding replicated by others' work—is that *cooperators expect significantly more cooperation than do defectors....* [there are further] findings consistent with expectations' being dependent on the actor's own behaviour" (Orbell and Dawes 1991: 519, my emphasis).

2. Åkerström 1983: 144.

3. Chandler [1939] 1993: 120.

4. Hammett 1969: 347.

5. Klerks 2000: 9.

6. See Hobbs 1995: 15–7, 20–21, 25, 26, 34, 39.

7. Plato 1942: 30–31. I am grateful to Ernesto dal Bò for bringing this passage to my attention.

8. *La Repubblica,* 25 June 1998.

9. He was prosecuted only on corruption charges and for making threats against the *rettore.* He was finally acquitted of the former charge but sentenced to one year and eight months in jail for the latter (*Ansa,* 6 June 2005).

10. Varese 2001: 155.

11. Sullivan 1989: 170.

12. Williams 1988: 8.

13. Williamson 1993; 1999: 245–46.

14. Bacharach and Gambetta 2001.

15. *Katmandu Post,* 3 March 1998, reported in *Private Eye,* 12 June 1998, my emphasis.

16. Åkerström 1983: 55.

17. Williamson 1965: 111.

18. *Guardian,* 28 April 2001.

19. Phelan and Hunt 1998: 283.

20. Quoted by Phelan and Hunt 1998: 283.

21. See Simone (1993: esp. pp. 49–90); Froio 1996; and Perotti (2002, 2008). Roberto Perotti (2002) concludes as follows: "Among OECD countries, [Italy's] relative position is almost uniformly at the bottom of research output in virtually all disciplines, hence it is unlikely to have improved much in the last twenty or thirty years; the exceptions to this statement, like organic chemistry, were star disciplines even in the past. Accusations—and evidence—of cronyism

and favouritism are as rampant today as they were in the past" (p. 55). Perotti
also monitored the academic competitions for positions in economics in Italy
from 2002 through to 2006, recording the academic qualifications of the members of the selection panels and of the candidates. He found that among the
former academic qualifications are low or nonexistent, and that those of selected candidates are almost invariably weaker than those of rejected ones. The
bulletins with the results can be seen at www.igier.unibocconi.it/whos.
php?vedi=1653andtbn=alberoandid_doc=177, accessed October 2008. For data
on medicine see M. Panara, "Concorsopoli, polveriera dell'universita,'" *La Repubblica*, 11 and 15 July 1995.

22. For a general account of how it works see Gambetta 1998.

23. The same seems to apply to institutions of scientific research as distinct
from universities. See F. Prattico, "I travet della ricerca," *La Repubblica*, 25 February 1993.

24. Matters worsened because in the early 1970s many temporary university
teachers were given tenure by law without any competition as a means to select
among them. Low-quality people who are still around today were thereby in-
jected into the system (Simone 1993: 50–51).

25. A spoof cyclical model of this case in academia was once jokingly suggested to me by Massimo Egidi, an Italian economist. There comes a point at
which the incompetence will be such that those who appoint the next generation will not even realize that they are appointing somebody smart. The snag is,
however, that this happens at random, so that there may be occasional lapses
into excellence, but never the simultaneous promotion of talents such as to
change the system as a whole.

26. Machiavelli 1976: 163, my translation. A friend of mine, let's call him L.,
got this wrong and was punished for that. He was promoted to the Italian
equivalent of an associate professorship. He thought he deserved it. He therefore did not bother showing any special gratitude to the baron who was instrumental to his promotion. In terms of that system L. was insolvent. At the competition for a full chair some years later he was failed while less deserving
candidates got through. The baron in question frankly explained to a dejected
L. that this was to teach him a lesson never to assume that promotion and merit
have anything to do with each other.

27. Pietro Corsi heard a well-known Italian philosopher say that pushing
forward able candidates was far too easy, and boast that he had been able to "put
on a chair" five incompetent ones (personal communication).

28. Licandro and Varano 1993: 16–17.

29. Strayer 1970: 102. For both this quote and Machiavelli's quote above I am indebted to Stephen Holmes.

30. Williamson 1983: 522, fn. 11.

31. Schelling 1956: 282.

32. Cf. Gambetta (1993: 160) for evidence of this.

33. In 1988 Joseph D. Pistone testified before the U.S. Senate Permanent Subcommittee on Investigations of the Committee on Governmental Affairs. The full text of his testimony can be seen at www.americanmafia.com/Pistone_Testimony.html, accessed October 2008.

34. J. Pistone's testimony before the U.S. Senate Permanent Subcommittee on Investigations of the Committee on Governmental Affairs, www.americanmafia.com/Pistone_Testimony.html, accessed October 2008.

35. Gambetta 1993: 159–60.

36. Arlacchi 1992: 29.

37. Pistone 1989: 275–76.

38. Seymour 1996: 83.

39. Tzvetkova 2008: 295.

40. Seymour 1996: 81.

41. Varese 2001: 154.

42. Cf. Pizzini-Gambetta 1999: 263–68; Pizzini-Gambetta 1996.

43. AC: 185.

44. Quoted by Hess 1973: 52.

45. TB: I, 49.

46. TC: 31.

47. *New Yorker*, 17 and 24 June 2002.

48. Pizzini-Gambetta 1999: 267.

49. Quoted in Pizzini-Gambetta 1999: 267.

50. Englund 1989.

51. Mousnier 1979–84: 109–11.

52. Popkin 1979: 261.

CHAPTER 3. Information as Hostage

1. Here I am not referring to the conditions for the success of blackmail in any one instance, but only to the general conditions that make it worthwhile considering it as a plausible option. The former depend on payoffs, which in turn depend on certain beliefs. The damage incurred by the victim if he rejects

the blackmail and the compromising information is revealed must be greater than the damage incurred by the victim's modifying his actions according to the blackmailer's wishes. This will depend on whether the victim believes that the blackmailer (1) will truly reveal the information if his blackmail is rejected and (2) will not continue to blackmail ad infinitum. If the blackmailer is not "trusted" to stop, the victim expects that the stream of "payments" will eventually exceed the cost of rejecting the blackmail and may choose to risk the revelation. The best signal that a blackmailer can give that he intends to stop blackmailing is by giving up or destroying the damaging information he has for good. To arrange for this to be done in a way that the victim can verify is often hard.

2. See Ledeneva 2002: ch. 2 and 2006: ch. 3.

3. Ledeneva 2006: 58.

4. Some postcommunist countries—Bulgaria, Romania, the Czech Republic, Slovakia, Lithuania, and Poland—resorted to the practice known as "lustration," whereby "proven collaborators are either explicitly banned from running for office or their past is revealed to the electorate, who are likely to judge them harshly" (Kaminski and Nalepa 2006: 2). One of many arguments in favor of lustration was that politicians from the countries named above feared that without it Russian politicians could have a dangerous weapon in their hands in the form of copies of secret police archives from the formerly vassal countries (Marek Kaminski and Monika Nalepa, personal communication).

5. *Times*, 20 October 1999.

6. *Sunday Times,* 24 October 1999.

7. Travaglio and Veltri 2001.

8. *International Herald Tribune*, 14 July 1998.

9. *Moscow Times*, 30 January 2002.

10. See Schelling 1960 and Laver 1982.

11. Schelling 1960: 43–44.

12. Written by Christian Forte and directed by Kevin Spacey, USA, 1996.

13. Hiaasen 1995: 234.

14. See Licandro and Varano 1993: 77–83, also ch. 4.

15. In Agatha Christie's *Murder on the Orient Express*, twelve people commit a murder all at once, and although Hercule Poirot discovers the truth they walk free.

16. Falcone and Padovani 1991: 31.

17. *Daily Telegraph*, 14 February 2001.

18. *Times*, 14 February 2001.

19. *Washington Post*, 3 September 1998.

20. *Boston Globe*, 3 July 2002.

21. *Ottawa Citizen*, 3 July 2002.

22. *New Yorker*, 17 August 1998, my emphasis.

23. Another prostitute said: "We were all sitting down in the lounge and this man walked through and he was actually a friend of my cousin. He picked me and I just froze. I knew his wife and everything and I said 'don't tell my cousin, don't tell my cousin.' He didn't and I just gave him a massage. He said he had chosen me because he could never choose someone else in front of me because I know his wife. He said he would never say anything because I come here for my needs and you come here for your needs and he has been fine with me" (Debbie, sauna). Both quotations come from Teela Sanders' fieldwork in Birmingham, U.K. (2002), and am grateful to her for letting me use them.

24. Plutarch 1992: 71, my emphasis.

25. On the use of hostages to support exchange in ordinary business see Williamson 1983.

26. Pizzini-Gambetta 1996.

27. Pistone 1989: 373.

28. *Guardian*, 10 July 2002.

29. I am grateful to Ernesto dal Bò for his comments on this point.

30. See for instance *Mondo Economico*, 17 July 1993; *La Stampa*, 4 March 1993; and *Il Sole 24 Ore*, 5 January 1996.

31. Ernesto dal Bò, personal communication.

32. See Travaglio and Veltri 2001 and Gomez and Travaglio 2001.

33. Bacharach and Gambetta 2001. See also chapter 2, pp. 37–40.

34. The ultimate test of which game one was playing may come, partially, expost: if the truster destroys or loses the evidence and the trustee, knowing that, continues to comply the truster will know that it was a case of signaling and that the trustee was a good type. If by contrast the trustee defects the truster will not know for sure which game it was: it was either a case of binding in which the binding force was misjudged and was in fact too weak to work, or it was one of signaling in which the bad type successfully mimicked the good type.

35. *Ottawa Citizen*, 3 July 2002, my emphasis.

36. In *The Last Seduction* the heroine played by Linda Fiorentino persuades her lover that she earned a rich honorarium for killing another woman's infidel

husband. A few clever tricks help her to authenticate this claim in the lover's eyes. Then she convinces the lover to kill her own husband. In the end Fiorentino's husband is dead, the lover is turned in by her and is in prison, and when he tries to use his "dirt" of last resort, it turns out that the man supposedly murdered by Fiorentino is alive and well. I am grateful to Marek Kaminski for bringing this plot to my attention.

CHAPTER 4. Why Prisoners Fight (and Signal)

1. On the nature of prison deprivation see Sykes' classic 1958 study, pp. 65–78.

2. Poole and Regoli 1983: 213.

3. Kaminski 2003: 190.

4. Edgar and Martin 2001.

5. McCorkle 1992: 166, my emphasis.

6. See Krebs and Davies 1993: ch. 7.

7. This hypothesis, in a general form, was put forward by the late Roger Gould in his excellent book *Collision of Wills*, in which he presented a theory of interpersonal violence: "I contend that conflict is harder to resolve, and thus violent conflict more likely to occur, when cues concerning which person outranks the other are absent or mixed" (2003: 70). This would happen mostly in "ill-defined or symmetrical relations," such as those which can be found among peers rather than in institutions such as armies in which ranks are clearly defined. Gould did not, however, pursue the communication aspect of that statement, implicit in the importance he assigns to cues and their clarity. A further difference is that Gould assumed that the key source of conflict does not come so much from competition over material resources as from an overarching desire to maintain one's honor and position in the social hierarchy even if these have a mere "symbolic" value, while here the value of fighting when material resources are not at stake (e.g., simply responding to insults and provocations) is understood as real indeed (i.e., as aiming at creating a reputation that the prisoner can spend in future conflict situations); so fighting still concerns material resources, but in the future. Although the latter reason for conflict, according to inmates themselves, seems to be frequently the case in prisons, Gould may be right in describing the general human inclination to respond to insults as being driven more by a prerational emotional response than by a cool rational calculation of the consequences of losing one's reputation.

8. Bowker 1980: 38. See also Polsky 1962.

9. McCorkle 1992: 166.

10. "When an individual enters the presence of others, they commonly seek to acquire information about him or to bring into play information about him already possessed. They will be interested in his general socio-economic status, his conception of self, his attitude towards them, his competence, his trustworthiness etc. Although some of this information seems to be sought almost as an end in itself, there are usually quite practical reasons for acquiring it. Information about the individual helps to define the situation, enabling others to know in advance what he will expect of them and what they may expect of him. Informed in these ways, the others will know how best to act in order to call forth a desired response from him" (Goffman [1959] 1990: 13).

11. Shields and Simourd 1991: 189.

12. Kaminski, personal communication.

13. Toch 1977: 151.

14. *New Yorker*, 3 April 2000.

15. Toch 1977: 153.

16. Baroin 2002: 37–38. Interestingly, Romans displayed their battle scars only when circumstances clearly justified it. They would have considered showing scars all the time as undignified, improper, and ugly—the marble bodies of heroes were unblemished. The scar was "un événement, non un monument" (Baroin 2002: 45). I am grateful to Giulia Sissa for bringing this to my attention.

17. Toch 1977: 153.

18. Phelan and Hunt 1998: 280.

19. Phelan and Hunt 1998: 280.

20. Connell and Farrington 1996: 83; see also Kaminski 2004: 38ff.

21. See Sparks, Bottoms, and Hay 1996.

22. Toch 1977: 154–55.

23. Toch 1977: 151.

24. McCorkle 1992: 166.

25. Toch 1977: 157.

26. Toch 1977: 153.

27. Kaminski, personal communication.

28. Toch 1977: 156.

29. Toch 1977: 150.

30. Bottoms 1999: 213.

31. These and other germane studies are reviewed in Bottoms 1999: 216ff.

32. Edgar and O'Donnell 1998: 636.

33. Edgar and Martin 2001: 3.

34. Edgar and O'Donnell 1998.

35. Edgar and Martin 2001: 12.

36. Edgar and Martin 2001: 12, my emphasis.

37. Edgar and Martin 2001: 13.

38. McCorkle 1992: 166.

39. Edgar and Martin 2001: 16.

40. See Shields and Simourd 1991: 181 for an overview.

41. Walters 1998; see also Gottfredson and Hirschi 1990.

42. One could speculate that younger prisoners have a longer time horizon ahead, and thus benefit or suffer more from the reputation they gain in jail once they are released, so they are particularly sensitive to being challenged. However, the prison ethnographies strongly suggest that the calculations that drive fighting behavior are driven far more by immediate circumstances and consequences.

43. Hunt et al. 1993: 403.

44. Cited in Bottoms 1999: 234.

45. For the United States see for instance the Bureau of Justice Statistics Bulletin, Women in Prison, U.S. Department of Justice, Office of Justice Programs, NCJ-145321, March 1994. This is available online at www.ojp.usdoj.gov/bjs/pub/ascii/wopris.txt, accessed October 2008.

46. Zedner 1992.

47. Zedner, personal communication.

48. In 1991 in the United States "about 54% of the women had used drugs in the month before the current offense, compared to 50% of the men. Female inmates were also more likely than male inmates to have used drugs regularly (65% versus 62%), to have used drugs daily in the month preceding their offense (41% versus 36%), and to have been under the influence at the time of the offense (36% versus 31%). Nearly 1 in 4 female inmates reported committing their offense to get money to buy drugs, compared to 1 in 6 males." Bureau of Justice Statistics Bulletin, Women in Prison, U.S. Department of Justice, Office of Justice Programs, NCJ-145321, March 1994. This is available online at www.ojp.usdoj.gov/bjs/pub/ascii/wopris.txt, accessed October 2008.

49. Edgar and Martin 2001: 20.

50. Edgar and Martin 2001: 20.

51. See Berk and de Leeuw 1999.

52. Sparks, Bottoms, and Hay do make such a hypothesis (1996: 113).

53. Sparks, Bottoms, and Hay 1996: 242.

54. Sparks, Bottoms, and Hay 1996: 107–12; 273.

55. Bottoms 1999: 232.

56. Kaminski 2003: 191.

57. Kaminski 2003: 189.

58. Bottoms 1999: 233.

59. Bottoms 1999: 233.

60. Toch 1977: 150.

61. Kaminski 2003: 200.

62. Kaminski 2003: 189.

63. Kaminski 2003: 202.

64. Toch 1977: 159.

65. Edgar and Martin 2001: addendum VI, p. xiii.

66. Toch 1977: 155.

67. Krebs and Davies 1993: 155.

68. Zahavi 1980: 79; see also Zahavi and Zahavi 1997, ch. 2.

69. Zahavi and Zahavi 1997: 19.

70. Schelling 1960: 199–200; also Dixit and Nalebuff 1991: 156.

71. See Kaminski 2003 and 2004.

72. Toch 1977: 158.

73. Sparks, Bottoms, and Hay 1996: 185.

74. Sparks, Bottoms, and Hay 1996: 181.

75. Krebs and Davies 1993; also Gould 2003.

76. Sparks, Bottoms, and Hay 1996: 177.

77. Sparks, Bottoms, and Hay 1996: 122, 185.

78. Edgar and Martin, personal communication.

79. Sparks, Bottom, and Hay 1996: 178.

80. Kaminski 2003, 2004.

81. Kaminski 2003: 193.

82. Kaminski 2003: 196.

83. Kaminski 2003: 193.

84. Kaminski 2003: 197.

85. Kaminski 2003: 189.

86. Kaminski 2003: 198.

87. Kaminski and Gibbons 1994.

88. Kaminski, personal communication.

89. Abadinsky 1983: 24.
90. Braly 1976: 51.
91. McVicar 1974: 173.
92. McVicar 1974: 179.

CHAPTER 5. Self-harm as a Signal

1. See Klein 1987 and 2001.
2. Favazza 1996.
3. Klein 1987: 358. An attempt to explain traumatic and painful rites with a signaling perspective is in Sosis et al. (2007). While the theory they use is the same, the difference is that in their case the signal refers to commitment to group activities, especially warfare, and is not aimed at deterring attackers as in this case.
4. Shea 1993.
5. Rivlin 2006: 10, 41.
6. Preti and Cascio 2006.
7. Kaminski, personal communication.
8. Liebling 1999: 286.
9. Liebling 1999: 304.
10. Favazza 1996: 261.
11. A vivid reminder of how this cultural transformation is far from being universal emerged from a TV interview with a Taliban who had been badly treated while in custody of the U.S./Northern Alliance: "I didn't mind the physical beating [fairly serious, judging by his visible scars]," he approximately said, "but the sexual humiliation [which was something like being naked in front of a female soldier] means that I will have to fight them to the death." The reaction of most Westerners, as Michael Biggs, who brought this story to my attention, suggests, would be exactly the opposite.
12. Lloyd-Richardson et al. 2007.
13. Favazza 1996: 286.
14. There is a cursory mention in Favazza, in an appendix following a discussion of self-harm in other animals: "Redirection of aggression is an evolutionary expedient for neutralising aggression. . . . By demonstrating their wounds and vulnerability, self-mutilators may hope to forestall further attacks against themselves." But the underlying force of the act is interpreted differently, as pity-inducing rather than as fear-inducing: "In some cases repetitive self-mutilation may represent an attempt to form a social bond with a perceived attacker

such as a vicious cell-mate in a prison. On an unconscious level, it may even represent an attempt to obtain a loving relationship with a parent" (1996: 79).

15. Kimball 2005.

16. Schelling 1960: 17.

17. If we adopt Jon Elster's distinction between threats and warnings, a threat by a "madman" is transformed into a warning—it does not have the form *if you do X then I will punish you by doing Y*, but rather the form *if you do X you will bring about Y*. Y becomes something ineluctably triggered by doing X: *I will not be able to stop myself from doing Y, Y is not under my control*. Threats that come in the form of a warning are credible and thus effective if the warning itself rests on a casual mechanism that is believable (Elster 1998: 103–4; 2000: 38–39).

18. Austen Smith and Banks 1998.

19. Livy 1912: 2.12.

20. I discuss this case at greater length in Gambetta 2009.

21. Kaminski 2004: 102.

22. Rivlin 2006: 81, my emphasis.

23. Rivlin 2006: 82, my emphasis.

24. Chamoiseau 1999: 57, my emphasis. I am grateful to Adrienne LeBas and Jennifer Tobin for the translation of the Creole sentence.

25. Gambetta 2005b.

26. Kaminski 2004.

27. Ireland 2000: 605.

28. Livingston 1997: 23.

29. Preti and Cascio 2006: 127.

30. Livingston and Beck 1997.

31. Livingston 1997.

32. Power and Spencer 1987: 231.

33. Favazza 1996: 169–70.

34. Preti and Cascio 2006: 131.

35. Rivlin 2006: 41.

36. Hawton and Rodham 2006.

37. Hawton and Rodham 2006: 45.

38. Hawton and Rodham 2006: 14. Also, among 633 high school students (grades 9–12) in the southern and midwestern United States a staggering 46.5% reported injuring themselves in the past year on multiple occasions; this study however surveyed a broader set of behaviors including some acts of modest severity, that is, not only "cutting/carving, burning" but also self-tattooing, scrap-

ing, and erasing skin (i.e., using an eraser to rub skin to the point of burning and bleeding) (Lloyd-Richardson et al. 2007).

39. Hawton and Rodham 2006: 79–80.

40. Lloyd-Richardson et al. 2007: 1189.

41. See Lohner and Konrad 2006: 371.

42. Power and Spencer 1987: 230.

43. Liebling 1999: 304.

44. Lohner and Konrad 2006: 372.

45. Gambetta 2009.

46. Liebling 1993.

47. Rivlin 2006: 49.

48. Sandham, personal communication.

49. Favazza 1996: 166.

50. Rivlin 2006: 41.

51. Preti and Cascio 2006: 132.

52. Rivlin 2006: 49.

53. Livingston 1997: 2.

54. For example, Kerkhof and Bernasco, quoted by Livingston 1997: 24; Rivlin 2006: 40.

55. Livingston 1997: 24; Favazza 1996: 167.

56. Liebling and Krarup 1993.

57. Livingston 1997: 24.

58. Loucks 1998.

59. Livingston 1997: 30.

60. Livingston 1997: 22; Powis 2002: 39.

61. Preti and Cascio 2006: 131.

62. Livingston 1997: 23; Powis 2002: 39.

63. Livingston 1997: 23.

64. See Haycock 1989.

65. According to Dr. Wheeler, borderline personality disorder is more common in white inmates than black ones, and this may explain the former group's greater amount of self-cutting behavior. This view was challenged by the Caribbean nurse who was present at the discussion.

66. Haycock 1989.

67. Wright 1989: 85.

68. Wright 1989: 81.

69. Wright 1989: 86, table 7.

70. An alternative explanation might be that if whites are in a minority among the prison population they will have the added fear of being victimized because of their color. Where the above has been true one would therefore expect to find a higher frequency of DSH among minority groups, as found by Preti and Cascio among foreigners in Italian prisons. Another explanation is that blacks may be incarcerated more often because of gang-related crimes and may be placed with other members of their gang, thus being less likely than white prisoners to be isolated.

71. In this chapter I do not discuss the possible use of DSH in situations in which two gangs or armies confront one another. There is however one battle in which collective self-harm, suicide in fact, was used purely as a threatening signal, and coexisted with fighting. In 496 BC the army of Gou Jian, king of Yue, was confronting the king's enemies from the state of Wu. The king organized "three parties" of criminals, who "went to the Wu lines and with a great shout cut their own throats." Eric Henry—a specialist in ancient Chinese literature and philosophy at the University of North Carolina, who translated this passage (from *Shiji* 41, chapter 11, on "Hereditary Houses," titled "Gou Jian, King of Yue") and kindly wrote to me about it—also wrote: "suicide as an act of bravado may have been strongly enough implanted in the culture that a group of men may actually have been capable of cutting their own throats to shock and disorient an enemy. Perhaps they could anticipate some posthumous restoration of honour, or some favour done to their families. But I know of no other reference to this practice. I know only of a few passages describing the men of Yue as being wild, volatile, and unpredictable." Gou Jian won the battle.

72. Sosis et al. 2007.

73. See Biggs 2003 for an overview.

74. Gambetta 2005b: 264–67.

75. Rosen and Walsh 1989.

76. Crandall 1988: 588. I am grateful to Laura Stoker for bringing this case to my attention.

77. Favazza 1996: 167; Rosen and Walsh 1989.

78. Hawton and Rodham 2006: 84. Kaminski conjectures that seemingly contagious episodes of DSH could be manifestations of learning. "In the grypsmen subculture"—he wrote to me—"there is a subfield of secret knowledge related to self-injury: what to do and how to do that in the least painful and most successful way. It is not taught as widely as the more basic skills since few inmates become competent enough to teach it. Nevertheless, a large number of

self-harming techniques is common knowledge among more experienced in-mates, both grypsmen and suckers." DSH feasibility and hence frequency could thus depend on whether the know-how is available and transmissible, either by imitation or by teaching, within an institution.

79. Crandall 1988: 588.

80. David Grann, "The Brand," *New Yorker*, 16–23 February 2004, p. 161.

81. I am grateful to Dan Sperber for telling me about this. In *The Usual Suspects*, there are two brutal events of the same species. "Rival smugglers working for the Hungarian mob invade Kayser Söze's house while he is away, raping his wife and holding his children hostage. When Söze arrives they kill one of the children to show him their resolve. They then threaten to kill his wife and re-maining children if he does not surrender his business to them. Rather than give in to their demands ... he murders his family and all but one of the Hun-garians, whom he spares knowing that the survivor would tell the mafia what has transpired" ("Keyser Söze," *Wikipedia*, accessed online July 2008).

82. Rinella 2006: 96–97.

83. Frank 1988: 99–101.

84. See Gambetta 2009.

85. Hamill 2009.

86. http://en.wikipedia.org/wiki/Academic_fencing, accessed October 2008.

87. McAleer 1994: 135.

88. McAleer 1994: 145.

89. McAleer 1994: 147–48.

90. The origins are uncertain, and it is not clear whether the game was in-vented by Russian officers and how widespread it ever really was. In *Wikipedia* under "Russian roulette" one finds that "the only reference to anything like Russian roulette in Russian literature is in a book entitled *A Hero of Our Time* by Mikhail Lermontov (1840, translated by Vladimir Nabokov in 1958)." Epi-sodes involving this game have been used in countless films. Ian Malcolm tells me that in Boris Akunin's *The Winter Queen* (a Russian detective novel) the characters call it "American roulette."

91. One such case ended up, briefly, on You-tube and was reported in the British press in January 2008: www.dailymail.co.uk/pages/live/articles/news/news.html?in_article_id=507592&in_page_id=1770, accessed October 2008. A similar example is train surfing, popular for a while among South African youth. See http://news.bbc.co.uk/2/hi/africa/5117318.stm, accessed October 2008.

92. My emphasis, from F. Dostoevsky, *The Brothers Karamazov*, part 2, book 6, "The Russian Monk," ch. 2, "Recollections of Father Zossima's Youth before he became a Monk. The Duel," online edition, The Literature Network, www.on-line-literature.com/view.php/brothers_karamazov/40?term=first%20shot, accessed October 2008.

CHAPTER 6. Conventional and Iconic Signals

1. Phelan and Hunt 1998: 282.

2. See Lewis 1969; Schelling 1960; Skyrms 1996.

3. Lewis 1969: 12.

4. Swift 1990: 44–45. I am grateful to Adam Thirlwell for telling me about this.

5. Guilford and Dawkins 1991.

6. I am grateful to Avinash Dixit for this example.

7. Pistone 1989: 376.

8. TB, I, 117.

9. Lee Lamothe, personal communication.

10. Lee Lamothe, personal communication.

11. Paul Baker, who published a book on Polari (2002), provides some basic information in his website, www.ling.lancs.ac.uk/staff/paulb/polari/home.htm, accessed September 2008.

12. *Guardian*, 14 July 2003.

13. *Guardian*, 14 July 2003.

14. www.ling.lancs.ac.uk/staff/paulb/polari/home.htm, accessed September 2008.

15. *New York Times*, 30 May 2002.

16. *Times Online*, 9 September 2002.

17. OSPA, XII, 2438.

18. Falcone and Padovani 1991: 27.

19. Poma and Pirrone 1972: 212.

20. Roma and Pirrone 1972: 213.

21. OSAG Arnone: 123–24.

22. *Il Giornale di Sicilia*, 9 October 1984.

23. OSAG: 128.

24. OSAG: 42.

25. *Il Manifesto*, 4 July 1990.

26. Falcone and Padovani 1991: 40.

27. Falcone and Padovani 1991: 56.

28. Chu 1999: 29, my emphasis. The Sicilian mafia man Francesco Di Carlo, who turned state's evidence, revealed a similar episode to Palermo prosecutors. In 1970 the fascist Prince Junio Valerio Borghese was planning a coup d'état in Italy. He enlisted Cosa Nostra help in Sicily in return for leniency after power was seized. "The Prince wanted a list of all Sicilian mafiosi before the day of the coup," a request that understandably caused controversy among "the men of honour." Furthermore "he proposed that during the coup in order to be recognised mafiosi should wear an arm band" (*La Repubblica*, 25 January 2001). The coup failed, the band was never worn, and mafiosi remained safely anonymous.

29. Kaminski, personal communication.

30. Kaminski, personal communication.

31. Chu 1999: 35.

32. Iwai 1986: 223.

33. Landis 2004: 225.

34. Kaplan and Dubro 1986: 142–46.

35. *La Repubblica*, 22 November 1990.

36. Herbert 2000: 153.

37. Seymour 1996: 109.

38. Peter Hill, personal communication.

39. *Daily Telegraph*, 15 December 1999 and 1 December 2000.

40. *Guardian*, 14 July 2003.

41. http://www.the-px.com/flagging.htm, accessed September 2008.

42. Mattson, personal communication.

43. A slightly more sophisticated version, "the double look back," can be found at http://gaylife.about.com/od/gaysexadvice/a/howtoflirt.htm, accessed October 2008.

44. Schelling 1960: 141.

45. I am grateful to Valeria Pizzini-Gambetta and Marek Kaminski for telling me about these cases.

46. "To gauge corruption among traffic police, Interior Minister Anatolii Kulikov sent a truck loaded with vodka on a 700 km trip across southern Russia, Reuters reported on 22 August. Police stopped the truck 24 times and asked for bribes on 22 of those occasions" (*Komri Daily Digest*, no. 164, part 1, 23 August 1995).

47. I am grateful to Zofia Stemplowska for this story.

48. Sutherland 1957: 84–85.

49. SC: IV, 69.

50. *La Repubblica*, 14 November 1993.

51.VS: I, 45.

52. Falcone and Padovani 1991: 26–27.

53.Arlacchi 1992: 24.

54.TB: I, 117.

55.TC, 26/4/1986.

56. FMM: 15.

CHAPTER 7. Protecting Easy-to-Fake Signals

1. "The Billion Dollar Don," BBC1 Panorama, 7 December 1999.

2. Chwe 2001.

3. Hall 1997: 10.

4.Varese 2001: 254, fn. 124.

5.Vitale 1999: 155.

6. Gambetta 2005a.

7. I am grateful to Avinash Dixit for suggesting this reference. He also pointed out that one cannot interpret cheap talk as meaning the opposite of what it says, because that too is manipulable; you have to ignore it altogether.

8. Gambetta 1993: 141.

9. *Herald Tribune*, 19 June 1995.

10. Stark 1981: 109–10.

11. Gambetta 1993: ch. 6. See also Smith and Varese 2001.

12. Gambetta 1993: 34; Smith and Varese 350–52.

13.VS: I, 40–44.

14.VS: I, 48.

15. See chapter 9.

16.Varese 2001: 238, fn. 4; see also Varese 1998: 516.

17. Hall 1997: 10.

18.Varese, personal communication.

19. Casanova (1894 English edition, online version) tells this story in his *Memoirs*, in the part titled "Spanish Passions—Spain," ch. 3.

20. Schelling 1998: 39.

21. Blumberg 1974: 491.

22. In "Sumptuary law," *Wikipedia*, accessed August 2008.

23. Saller 2000: 822; see also p. 820.

24. *Guardian*, 2 March 1998.

25. *New York Times*, 13 October 1998.

26. *Independent,* 13 June 2005.

27. See chapter 5.

28. Seymour 1996: 25–26.

29. Stark 1981: 109.

30. See chapter 9.

31. Bacharach and Gambetta 2001.

32. See Kaminski 2003; also Kaminski and Gibbons 1994.

33. Kaminski 2003: 209.

34. Hill 2003: ch. 4

35. Chu 1999: 36.

36. Taylor 2002: 7.

37. *Times*, 17 October 2003.

38. Taylor 2002: 8.

39. Taylor 2002: 11.

40. Taylor 2002: 10.

41. *Times*, 17 October 2008.

42. AC: II, 512.

43. Pistone 1989: 193.

44. Pistone 1989: 193.

45. Pistone 1989: 194.

46. Gambetta 1993: 125.

47. OSAG Arnone: 264–65, my emphasis.

48. See Chwe 2001: ch. 2.

CHAPTER 8. Criminal Trademarks

1. Salvatore "Robertino" Enea, Palermo mafia member, speaking on the telephone with another anonymous mafioso. *La Repubblica*, 11 February 1994.

2. Gosch and Hammer 1975: 146.

3. Bacharach and Gambetta 2001.

4. See chapter 6.

5. There is a peril of a quite different nature to which trademarks are exposed, as the extraordinary case of Procter & Gamble indicates. In its logo, which has been around since 1851, at some point thirteen stars were added, symbolizing the original American colonies. Around the 1980s a rumor began to circulate among religious-right fanatics linking the stars to Satan and his "brand number," 666. "The accusation is based on a particular passage in the

Bible, specifically Revelation 12:1, which states: 'And there appeared a great wonder in heaven; a woman clothed with the sun, and the moon under her feet, and upon her head a crown of twelve stars.' Since P&G's logo consists of a man's face on a moon surrounded by thirteen stars, some have claimed that the logo is a mockery of the heavenly symbol alluded to in the aforementioned verse, and hence the logo is satanic. Where the beard meets the surrounding circle, a mirror image of 666 can be seen when viewed from inside the logo, and this has been interpreted as the reflected number of the beast, again linked to satanism. Also, there are two horns like a lamb that are said to represent the false prophet" (http://en.wikipedia.org/wiki/Procter_ &_Gamble#Logo_controversy, accessed October 2008). Procter & Gamble received many letters of complaint and, more significantly, was ostracized by a distributor of that persuasion, and competitors allegedly contributed to spreading the rumor. The company has since been engaged in several successful lawsuits, which however have not killed the rumor.

6. Gambetta 1994b.

7. Nelson 1970.

8. Reuter 1983: 152.

9. Reuter 1983: 152–53.

10. Reuter 1983: 153.

11. In some legal sectors too reputation is limited to specific individuals. Artists' reputations, for instance, die with them. Only Martin Scorsese can make *Scorsese's* films. "Scorsese" is an inalienable trademark. Scorsese's kin may get a head start because of the name they carry, but would still have to prove their skills. Wally Toscanini used to say with a laugh: "I have only the name of Toscanini, not his genius" (*Independent*, 10 May 1991). Had Donatella Versace not been known by both the same surname *and* the same creative qualities as her brother was, the Versace fashion firm might have collapsed after Gianni's murder. Firms in which the creative input of the founders is the essential ingredient in producing high-quality products seldom outlast their founders' demise. Only in those sectors of the lawful economy in which goods are standardized can reputations take on a life of their own, which goes beyond that of their originators. People assume that the properties of the original goods are transmitted to subsequent generations of goods that appear under the same trademark, even if these are physically produced and managed by others. Among criminals this assumption is much harder to make.

12. Goldstein et al. 1984; Wendel and Curtis 2000.

13. Goldstein et al. 1984: 557.

14. Wendel and Curtis 2000: 230.

15. Wendel and Curtis 2000: 16. Goldstein et al. 1984: 556; Wendel and Curtis 2000: 239.

17. Goldstein et al. 1984: 558.

18. Taylor 2007: 7.

19. Wendel and Curtis 2000: 231.

20. Taylor 2007: 7.

21. Taylor 2007: 15.

22. Wendel and Curtis 2000: 228.

23. Wendel and Curtis 2000: 228.

24. Wendel and Curtis 2000: 229.

25. Goldstein et al. 1984.

26. Wendel and Curtis 2000: 230; Goldstein et al. 1984: 565.

27. Wendel and Curtis 2000: 230.

28. See Wendel and Curtis 2000.

29. See Taylor 2007: 14.

30. Taylor 2007: 18.

31. Taylor 2007: 3.

32. Goldstein et al. 1984: 565; Wendel and Curtis 2000: 14; see chapter 9 on nicknames.

33. Wendel and Curtis 2000: 11.

34. Wendel and Curtis 2000: 10–11.

35. Goldstein et al. 1984: 562.

36. Goldstein et. al. 1984: 563.

37. Wendel and Curtis 2000: 10.

38. Wendel and Curtis 2000: 14–5.

39. Gambetta 1993 and 1994b.

40. OSAG: 280, 287.

41. Abadinsky 1983: 117–18.

42. VM: 34.

43. TB: III, 19.

44. OSPA Calzetta: IV, 65–66.

45. OSPA: VI, 1209.

46. FMM: 180.

47. Calvi 1986: 90.

48. Hess 1973: 58.

49. TB: I, 11.

50. OSAG: 279; OSAG Arnone: 280.

51. VM–GdS.

52. AC I, 122.

53. AC I, 122.

54. Chu 1999.

55. Iwai 1986.

56. Peter Hill, personal communication.

57. AC: II, 573.

58. See *La Repubblica*, 11 February 1994. This belief is shared by Harold "Kayo" Konisberg, a Jewish gangster who worked as a contract killer for the mafia in New York. In an interview he said, "'This thing won't die.' (This Thing the Mafia)," *New Yorker*, 6 August 2001: 49.

59. See chapter 10.

60. Hess 1973: 2.

61. See Gambetta 1993, appendix 6.1.

62. In the most authoritative article on this topic, Lo Monaco (1990) argues that the noun *mafia* derives from the adjective *mafioso*. The etymology of the former must be sought through that of the latter.

63. Gambetta 1993.

64. Novacco 1959: 208–9.

65. There is also the odd case, which Ian Malcolm brought to my attention, of the "Old Contemptibles," British troops who embraced an alleged insult from the kaiser.

66. Franchetti [1876] 1974: 93.

67. Bonanno 1983: 164.

68. OSPA Stajano: 57; OSPA: V.

69. The origin of "al-Qaeda" (the Base) as a name that identifies the worldwide terrorist organization led by Osama bin Laden is strikingly similar to that of Cosa Nostra. It was founded in 1987–88 in Peshawar by bin Laden and his spiritual mentor, Abdullah Azzam, a Palestinian-Jordanian ideologue who preached global jihad. As is clear in the following passage, Azzam did not use the term as a proper name: "Every principle needs a vanguard to carry it forward and put up with heavy tasks and enormous sacrifices. . . . It carries the flag along the sheer, endless and difficult path until it reaches its destination in the reality of life, since Allah has destined that it should make itself manifest. This vanguard constitutes the strong foundation (Al-Qa'ida al-Sulbah) for the ex-

pected society" (Gunaratna 2003: 4–5). Scott Atran, who helped me with this case, wrote to me that "Bin Laden seems to have used the term primarily to refer to an organizational database for keeping track of personnel (and provisions) recruited for the war against the Soviets in Afghanistan. Only after the FBI began investigating the U.S. embassy bombings in Kenya and Tanzania did U.S. officials begin referring to 'Al Qaeda,' as the noun of an organisation. The FBI's principal source on Al Qaeda as a global network under Bin Laden was gleaned from testimony by Jamal al-Fadl [an associate of bin Laden who defected after being found embezzling the organization's funds, and became one of the prosecution witnesses in the trial for the embassy bombings in 2001]. It is entirely possible that in his testimony Fadl was hyping Al Qaeda to hype his own importance." Not only the origins of the name but also the creative consequences of its use are closely reminiscent of the effects of the terms *mafia* and "Cosa Nostra." Atran again: "The increasing interconnection (though not unification) of regional Jihadi groups into an 'Al Qaeda network' may be, in part, the result of the U.S. over-attributing to Bin Laden and Al Qaeda a global concentration of power and organization. This public targeting and talking up of Al Qaeda has encouraged home-grown groups only tenuously connected with Bin Laden—if at all—to claim responsibility for attacks in Al Qaeda's name in order to be taken more seriously by friend and foe alike."

70. TB: I, 4–5.
71. TC: 1–2, 8; AC: III, 735.
72. VM: 3.
73. MA-L'Ora, 22 January 1962; also Bonanno 1983: 19.
74. AC: I, 3.
75. Arlacchi 1992: 55–56.
76. *La Repubblica,* 11 February 1994.
77. Peter Hill, personal communication.
78. *La Stampa,* 14 December 2000.
79. *Financial Times,* 17 May 1994.
80. See Gambetta 1993; Chu 1999; Smith and Varese 2001. Also, in the course of the fieldwork we carried out for a research project on taxi drivers in Belfast (Gambetta and Hamill 2005), one of the Protestant interviewees referred to a mimicry case that occurred there, at the expense of a Loyalist paramilitary gang that acts as racketeers. But the mimic was caught, and one interviewee told us: "one guy was looking for protection money and when he went to pick it up the guys who actually ran the area were sitting waiting on him coming in—it

was brought out that 'you aren't even linked up with us. You ever use our name again they will be picking you out of the Lagan [the river in Belfast].'"

81. Abadinsky 1983: 132.

82. This case shares some features with the case (identified by Gerry Mackie) of "belief traps," situations that make one retain a false belief, or at least behave as if one does because, even if one knows that the probability that the belief is true is minuscule, the costs of testing it are too high (Mackie 1996: 1009).

83. Tamony 1969: 279; also 282; cf. also Room 1987: 15.

84. TC-GdS, 24/4/1986.

85. Kaminski 2003: 209.

86. Falcone and Padovani 1991: 56.

87. TB, 7/4/86.

88. Bacharach and Gambetta 2001: 172.

89. Chu 1999: 49.

90. TB: II, 77.

91. See Bonanno 1983: 86–87.

92. TB: II, 18.

93. AC: I, 64.

94. Arlacchi 1992: 4.

95. Alongi [1886] 1977: 54.

96. AC: II, 585.

97. AC: II, 395, 399, 410, 417; TC: 153; Anonimo 1988: 208.

98. OSPA: VII, 1322.

99. Milito 2003: 127; Giovino 2004: 77, 85.

100. Bonanno 1983: 176, also on style 44, 71, 174, 190.

101. Peter Hill, personal communication.

102. Peter Hill, personal communication.

103. Peter Hill, personal communication; also Hill 2003: 70–72.

104. Peter Hill, personal communication.

105. Seymour 1996: 72.

106. Peter Hill, personal communication.

107. Stark 1981: 43.

108. TB-GdS, 6/4/1986.

109. TC-GdS, 25/4/1986.

110. See respectively Lupo 1988; Galante 1986: 96; Calvi 1986: 90.

111. TB-GdS, 8/4/1986.

112. SC: I, 44–45.

113. AC: II, 411.

114. VM: 40.

115. OSPA 1985.

CHAPTER 9. Nicknames

This chapter is a reelaboration of an unpublished essay written with Valeria Pizzini-Gambetta, who also carried out the data collection.

1. Pistone 1989:146.

2. Nicknames are found from Iceland to Africa from China to Central America. See Hale 1981; Nwachukwu-Agbada 1991; Eberhard 1970; Collier and Bricker 1970; Ryan 1958.

3. Maurer and Futrell 1982:248.

4. Adolf (or Adolph) is too rare a name anyway to escape the poisonous aura cast on it by Hitler; in the United States it was already in decline throughout the twentieth century and has now disappeared; by contrast, Stalin does not seem to have affected the frequency of Joseph, in part because Joseph is a more common name and in part perhaps because Stalin did not achieve the same dictatorial reputation in the West that Hitler achieved; see www.babyname wizard.com/namevoyager/lnv0105.html, accessed October 2008.

5. Marrale 1990.

6. Vincenzo Sinagra and Stefano Calzetta, in their testimonies to judge Giovanni Falcone, mention, among the colorful crowd of small-time criminals controlled by the mafia in Palermo, many monikers such as "l'Americano," "Piripicchio," "Pacchiuneddu," "u'Tignusu," "Occhiolino," and "Piluseddu."

7. Skipper 1986:134.

8. A narrower definition reads as follows: "nicknames are unwritten and unsystematically derived names which are given by the community to the individual, the household or the family, usually independent of their stated choice" (Pina-Cabral 1984). Contrary to this definition, nicknames are not always unwritten: Bernard (1968–69) tells of nicknames used in contracts; Manning (1974) reports nicknames written on license plates in the West Indies; Ennew (1980) mentions a telephone directory listing people by nickname in Ness on Lewis. The word *nickname* derives from Middle English *eken*, Old English *eacen*, meaning "to increase, add to" (Skipper and Leslie 1990:253). The Italian word for nickname, *soprannome*, comes from Latin *supra nomen*. Also associations and objects may bear monikers (Murray 1992; Marrale 1990).

9. *Mainichi Daily News*, 17 November 1999.

10. TC-GdS, 21/4/86. "Coriolano della foresta" is the name of a fictional Sicilian Robin Hood, the protagonist of a feuilleton written at the end of the nineteenth century by Luigi Natoli.

11. Brandes 1975: 141.

12. Bernard 1968–69: 69. The use of nicknames is often seen as rude and so is often repressed among children (Bernard 1968–69; Morgan et al. 1979: 120). In this respect too they are akin to gossip.

13. Varese 2001: 150, 195.

14. AC: I, 67.

15. OSPA: 7492.

16. TC-GdS, 19/4/86.

17. AC: II, 394.

18. See Gambetta 1994a.

19. OSPA: 5465.

20. AC: I, 273.

21. AC: I, 21.

22. TC: 153.

23. SC-GdS, 10/7/86.

24. VS-GdS, 25/6/86.

25. SC-GdS, 10/7/86.

26. AC: I, 161.

27. AC: I, 234.

28. FMM: 386.

29. VS-GdS, 5/7/86.

30. TC: 202.

31. TC: 4; TC-GdS, 21/4/86.

32. See Skipper 1985.

33. AC: I, 253.

34. Testimony of Francesco Di Cristina as contained in OSPA.

35. Jacquemet 1992: 11.

36. Rosenberg 1945: 98.

37. For a discussion of the functionalist fallacy concerning gossip see Gambetta 1994a.

38. Bernard 1968–69: 74, my emphasis; also Pitt-Rivers 1954.

39. Gilmore 1982; Hoyer 1976.

40. Brandes 1975; Cohen 1977.

41. Barrett 1978.

42. Holland 1990: 258.

43. TC–GdS, 20/4/86.

44. TB–GdS, 7/4/86.

45. For a case of limited name supply, which promotes nicknames, see Hale 1981.

46. "Investigations dug out at least three La Barbera families, corresponding to three mafia groups, unconnected to one another," *La Repubblica*, 8 August 1993.

47. Rohlfs 1984; Marrale 1990: 46.

48. There are virtually no nicknames in the confession of Vincenzo Marsala from Vicari, a small village in the Palermo countryside; nor are there any in the "trial against Ferro+55," called the Agrigento "maxi trial," which involved a large number of mafia families from the Sicilian countryside (VM; VM-GdS; SSPA 26/1/85, 17/1/86; OSAG).

49. Salvatore Giuliano was a bandit involved in the separatist movement in Sicily in the aftermath of War World II.

50. Another member of the Giuliano gang referred to him as "Pasquale Sciortino from S. Cipirrello, [Salvatore] Giuliano's brother-in-law," but Sciortino claimed that he was known under his dead father's name, Pino. He also said that he was "from S. Giuseppe Jato; [the witness] should have said Nené Micciché's nephew, in that case it certainly would have been me since everybody knows me by that name." Sciortino used to work in his grandfather's estate in S. Giuseppe Jato, and it was true that people there knew him as "Nene' Micciche's nephew." Among the bandits, however, he was known as Giuliano's brother-in-law from S. Cipirrello, since he married Giuliano's sister and was born in S. Cipirrello, a small village next to S. Giuseppe Jato. (CPM-v, 2 *sixies*, *Dichiarazioni di Pasquale Sciortino*, p. 593, 2/7/1970).

51. Leonardo Vitale, a member of the mafia family of Altarello di Baida, turned state's evidence in 1974. Because of a catch-22 belief, which holds that if a mafioso speaks he must be mad, and if he is mad he is not reliable, Vitale was not believed. He was confined to a hospital for the criminally insane for ten years, freed in 1984, and soon murdered while returning from Sunday Mass with his mother.

52. AC: I, 115.

53. OSPA-ii: 143.

54. TB: I, 9.

55. AC: I, 67.

56. AC: I, 12.

57. VS-GdS, 25/6/86.

58. OSPA: 6129. Eventually he turned state's evidence and acknowledged his nickname in court (FMM, 4.1.90, t.3: 24).

59. AC: II, 482–83.

60. VS: I, 26–27.

61. FMM: 257.

62. These are mostly entrepreneurs who are not themselves mafiosi: according to the prosecutors, "beside entrepreneurs who surely are mafiosi, many others have been extremely reticent when questioned. . . . Both turned to a *protettore mafioso* whenever they wished to carry out their business untroubled" (OSPA: V, 722–23). In this sense they are customers of mafiosi. For a discussion of these distinctions see Gambetta 1993.

63. We cannot be absolutely sure that this distribution is not biased, since a greater effort on the part of the authorities to try to identify dangerous mafiosi may lead to their search for more identifying clues, including their nicknames. Still, there are two reasons to feel confident in the quality of the data. One is that the differences in the frequencies of nicknames by category are too large to be explained only by a bias. The other is that reading the testimonies of mafiosi who turned state's evidence and who represent the main source for the knowledge of mafia nicknames, one can see that the pattern of revelation is constant. When the witness mentions a new mafioso he reveals some distinctive features of his, such as the mafia family to which he belongs, his job (if any), and his rank in the family. When the nickname is known by the turncoat, it comes at the top of this list of identifying attributes and seems mentioned naturally rather than being prompted by questions of the prosecutors.

64. OSPA: 7195.

65. FMM-A, 5/1/90, tape 8: 26–27.

66. OSPA: 6066. Although judges in Sicily used nicknames to identify defendants, they never used nicknames to prove that a defendant was a member of the mafia. By contrast, according to Jacquemet (1992: 733–34), the judges in Naples considered nicknames as evidence of belonging to local criminal gangs. With respect to the Sicilian mafia, belonging was established thanks to the collaboration of *pentiti*—mafiosi turned state's evidence.

67. TC-GdS, 28/4/86. The same happened to Francesco Marino Mannoia, who could not find a way to identify someone called La Rosa: "because there are several La Rosa, I am getting confused" (FMM-A, 5/1/90, tape 7:11).

68. Here, Michele Greco overlooks, probably intentionally, that nicknames often ironically stress an abnormality by attributing the opposite feature. The transcripts of Michele Greco's testimony at the maxi trial were published in *Il Giornale di Sicilia*, 12 June 1986.

69. TB–GdS, 8/4/86.

70. OSPA: 5156.

71. Jacquemet 1992: 14.

72. Maurer and Futrell 1982: 248.

73. Lamothe and Nicaso 2001.

74. Jacquemet 1992: 11.

75. Varese 2001: 195.

76. Gilmore 1982: 687.

77. Skipper 1986.

78. Occasionally, events in a person's life or literary references become nicknames.

79. Morgan et al. 1979: 123; Pitt-Rivers 1954: 3.

80. Smith 1962; Wilson 1969; Hoyer 1976.

81. Skipper 1986.

82. Information found at the Great Western Train museum in Swindon, England.

83. See www.legendarysurfers.com/surf/legends/ls10.shtml, accessed October 2008. Also www.answers.com/topic/list-of-north-american-football-nick names and www.op.net/~lmk/baseball/berman.htm, accessed October 2008.

84. Skipper 1986.

85. See Smith 1962; Brandes 1975; Loizos 1975; Jacquemet 1992; Nwachukwu-Agbada 1991. Also Pitt-Rivers 1954; Foster 1964; Bernard 1968–69; Wilson 1969; Cutileiro 1971; Cohen 1977; Barrett 1978; Morgan et al. 1979; Hale 1981; McDowell 1981; Skipper 1986; Marrale 1990.

86. AC: I, 218.

87. Chu Yiu Kong, personal communication.

88. *Kumi* means gang or group. *Kai* refers to association or meeting. *Cho* means senior or top. *Kai-cho* therefore means boss (whether referring to a business, an association, or a gang), while *kumi-cho* is more specifically gang boss.

89. Peter Hill, personal communication.

90. Wolf Herbert, personal communication.

91. Stark 1981.

92. Seymour 1996: 75.

CHAPTER 10. Why (Low) Life Imitates Art

1. Gambetta 1993: ch. 6.

2. This reconstruction and the quotes are taken from the *Washington Post*, 25 May 1992.

3. Schrader 1974; also Kaplan and Dubro 1986: 153–54.

4. Buruma 1985, ch. 10.

5. Schrader 1974: 13.

6. Schrader compiled a "master list of the set pieces," which includes a total of eighteen scenes. Here are some of them: "The protagonist comes out of prison." "The evil Oyabun plots the takeover of the clan." "The gambling scene ... [which] ends in a minor unresolved confrontation." "A Yakuza introduces himself to a fellow gangster ... these ritual introductions can go on for several minutes." "The revealing of the tattoos. Most Yakuza wear a full upper body tattoo." "The finger cutting. To atone for great offence or injustice a Yakuza is sometimes required to cut off his left little finger and present it to the one he has offended." "The good Oyabun [is] slain by the heavies." "The duel scene. Two honorable Yakuza are forced to fight each other out of duty to their Oyabuns." "The final march. The protagonist and his one or two closest friends walk down darkened empty streets toward the enemy compound." "The final battle. A tour de force fight scene where all the accumulated obligations are expiated in a grand finale of bloodletting" (1974: 14–15).

7. Buruma 1985: 167.

8. Schrader 1974: 12; Buruma 1985: 178.

9. *Washington Post*, 14 January 1994.

10. See Schilling 2003.

11. An exception is reported by Jimmy "The Weasel" Fratianno, who claims that Sam Giancana and other mobsters were unhappy with the TV show *The Untouchables*, aired on ABC in 1959–63, for it portrayed, in John "Johnny" Rosselli's words, "a bunch of Italian lunatics running around with machine guns, talking out of the corner of their mouths, slopping up spaghetti, like a bunch of fucking pigs." They were more than just annoyed: "The top guys have voted a hit. I've already talked to Bomp about it. We are going to clip Desi Arnaz, the producer of this show" (Demaris 1981: 150–51). Even if this story is true, nothing came of it, as Arnaz died of natural cause in 1986. "*The Untouchables* also drew controversy for its stereotyped ethnic characters. The Italian-American community protested the series' use of Italian names for criminal characters.

The Capone family also brought a million-dollar lawsuit against producer Desi Arnaz for using the Capone likeness for profit. This was particularly upsetting for Arnaz, a classmate and friend of Al Capone's son" (Michael B. Kassel, www.museum.tv/archives/etv/u/htmlu/untouchables/untouchables.htm, accessed October 2008).

12. *The Press Association*, 8 September 2000.

13. See chapter 2.

14. This is counting only kosei-in, or fully initiated members, and not associate members. See Hill 2003: 206.

15. *Corriere della Sera*, 1 July 1998.

16. Chu 1999: 71ff.

17. *Corriere della Sera*, 1 July 1998.

18. Gambetta 1993: ch. 7.

19. *Independent*, 2 November 1995.

20. *New York Times*, 29 August 1999.

21. *Times*, 30 December 1997, and *Guardian*, 15 January 2001.

22. Chu 1999: 71ff.

23. *New York Times*, 17 March 1992.

24. Kaplan and Dubro 1986: 154.

25. Chu Yiu Kong, personal communication.

26. Gambetta 1993.

27. Gambetta and Reuter 1995: 127–28.

28. There is probably more to the relationship than that. Rumors of mob involvement have been rife not just in fly-by-night production companies of low-quality movies but in several big Hollywood studios. Sam Goldwyn and Harry Cohn played cards with John Rosselli in the locker room of the Friars Club in Chicago. Cohn and Jack Warner donned "friendship rings," a gift of crime bosses (*Guardian*, 27 February 1999). Movie making is a risky business, and large productions need lots of money. Raising money for risky business is something mobsters can be good at, for investors trust their ability to exact repayment. Some of them also have large quantities of money and are willing to risk it in potentially rewarding business. "Everyone in Bollywood knows that films have been used by Bombay's Mafia as a way of laundering dirty money—with the prospect of huge profits if the film is a success rather than a turkey" (*Guardian*, 15 January 2001). This is, however, speculation.

29. Poma and Pirrone 1972: 192.

30. *Times*, 5 July 1999.

31. See *Independent*, 5 July 1999. In an interview with David Chase, the *Daily Telegraph* reported a similar story: "This is probably not going to be the answer anyone likes to hear, but I don't know any real mobsters," David Chase, creator of the acclaimed HBO series *The Sopranos*, admits over breakfast in a Manhattan hotel. "You would never know if you knew a real mobster anyway. I've met some people who had been involved, and I've met some who claim to have been tangentially involved. And I've met people who never said anything about it but I thought probably were. But I can't say I have a huge pool of mobster acquaintances to draw on to get any of this data" (*Daily Telegraph*, 21 February 2000).

32. *Guardian*, 27 February 1999.

33. *New York Times*, 9 September 1990.

34. *Daily Telegraph*, 30 September 2000.

35. Arlacchi 1992: 110–11. The film was released in 1973 in Italy, directed by Mariano Laurenti and written by Leo Chiosso and Gustavo Palazio. The late Franco Franchi was the main comedian.

36. Lacey 1992: 10.

37. *New York Times*, 29 August 1999.

38. *New York Times*, 29 August 1999.

39. *New York Times*, 29 August 1999.

40. *New York Times*, 27 December 2000.

41. *Guardian*, 27 February 1999.

42. Bonanno 1983: 69.

43. Occasionally, people who acted as minor characters in mafia movies have been suspected of real-life involvement, such as "Big Mike" Squicciarini, who played a part in *The Sopranos* and in *Mickey Blue Eyes*, and was posthumously implicated by prosecutors in the homicide of a drug dealer (*Observer*, 17 November 2002).

44. *Independent*, 27 March 1993.

45. Itsuko Doherty, personal communication. See also *Japan Times*, 17 April 2002.

46. *Japan Times*, 17 April 2002.

47. *New York Times*, 29 August 1999.

48. *Financial Times*, 19 October 2000.

49. For a review of the evidence and of the theories regarding the imitation of violence seen in media see Huesmann 2005, and Susan Hurley's discussion of this paper in the same volume.

50. Schmid and de Graaf 1982: 128. The same authors offer several other examples from the worlds of terrorism or political crime.

51. Arlacchi 1992: 161.

52. *Singapore Business Times*, 13 February 1993.

53. Moretti 1998: 24.

54. There was an unusual spate of suicides in 2005, when three mafiosi killed themselves in jail—Francesco Pastoia in January, Giuseppe Balsano in July, and Michelangelo Pravatà in December. They were members of three mafia families in Palermo's surroundings—Belmonte Mezzagno, Monreale, and Vicari respectively—that are geographically close to one another. At least two of them had close links to Bernardo Provenzano, the grand boss captured in 2006 after a quarter century on the run. Balsano killed himself three days after he was arrested, after he (and fifty other people indicted at the same time) found out that his phone had been tapped by police, revealing various "violations" he had committed, directly or indirectly, at the expense of Provenzano, including an unauthorized killing and creaming off protection money meant for the boss. He may thus have killed himself to avoid retaliation against his family (*La Stampa*, 29 January 2005). His tomb was vandalized two months after his death. No information has emerged about the circumstances surrounding the two other suicides, and there is no evidence that these deaths are connected.

55. *Guardian*, 18 October 2001.

56. *Time*, 8 July 2002.

57. *Times*, 24 February 1992.

58. *New York Times*, 16 December 1966, obituary of Walt Disney.

59. Chwe 2001.

60. Pistone 1989: 219.

61. United States Senate, Permanent Subcommittee on Investigations 1984: 75.

62. *La Repubblica*, 31 May 1991.

63. *La Repubblica*, 4 May 2001.

64. Poma and Pirrone 1972: 204.

65. Chandler [1939] 1993: 56.

66. *L'Espresso*, 3 June 1990.

67. Schmid and de Graaf 1982: 129.

68. *Times*, 24 February 1992.

69. See Gambetta 1993.

70. Joseph Lewis, director, 1949.

71. The process is closely reminiscent of that leading to the identification of "focal points," a concept first introduced by Thomas Schelling (1960), which is a solution to games of coordination. See also Chwe 2001.

72. *New York Times*, 26 November 1995.

73. *Chicago Tribune*, 26 December 1988.

74. *La Stampa*, 3 June 1993.

75. Personal communication.

76. See Timothy Garton Ash, "The Real Le Carré," *New Yorker*, 15 March 1999.

77. Charles McGrath, *New York Times*, 10 November 2002.

78. Joan Haahr, in a letter to the *New York Times*, 24 November 2002. As Dr. Haahr kindly informed me, her major source on the matter is Roger Sherman Loomis, "Arthurian Influence on Sport and Spectacle," in *Arthurian Literature in the Middle Ages*, pp. 553–59 (Oxford: Clarendon Press, 1959).

79. Gosch and Hammer 1975: 300.

80. *Daily Telegraph*, 21 February 2000.

81. *New York Times Magazine*, 2 January 2000.

82. *New York Times Magazine*, 2 January 2000.

83. Maas 1997: 72.

84. Milito 2003: 126–27.

85. O'Brien 1991: 47.

86. *The Press Association*, 8 September 2000.

87. *New York Times Magazine*, 2 January 2000.

88. Maas 1997: 213.

89. Nikolai Modestov, *Moskva banditskaia: Dokumental'naia khronika kriminal'nogo bespredela 1980–90kh godov* (Moscow: Tsentropoligraf, 1997), p. 131. I am grateful to Federico Varese for telling me about this.

90. See Schrader 1974. Yakuza seem coy, however, about their liking of *The Godfather*. The late Makoto Endo, a lawyer who once represented the Yamaguchi-gumi, Japan's largest crime syndicate, was having dinner with Yoshinori Watanabe, the head of the syndicate, in a private room at a restaurant in the Tokyo geisha district of Mukojima. According to Endo's recollections, after dinner a group of musicians entered to accompany Watanabe, Endo, and the other diners as they sang. Watanabe chose a Japanese ballad set to the theme music for *The Godfather*. In his memoir Endo described Watanabe singing the ballad, but when he heard about this, Watanabe persuaded Endo to suspend the book's print run. In later copies the two pages recounting Watanabe's fondness for the

Godfather theme song are left blank. I am grateful to Velisarios Kattoulas for this story.

91. Gambetta 1993: ch. 4.

92. The definitive story of the events surrounding the shooting of *The Godfather* is told by Harlan Lebo (1997).

93. *New York Times*, 31 January 1999.

94. *Sunday Times*, 4 July 1999.

95. Bonanno 1983: 69.

96. *New York Times*, 25 March 1999.

97. *Daily Telegraph*, 23 April 2001.

98. Cummings and Volkman 1990: 42–43.

Bibliography

Abadinsky, H. 1983. *The criminal élite*. Westport, Conn.: Greenwood Press.

Akerlof, G. 1970. The market for "lemons": Qualitative uncertainty and the market mechanism. *Quarterly Journal of Economics* 84, 488–500.

Åkerström, M. 1983. *Crooks and squares. Lifestyle of thieves and addicts in comparison to conventional people*. Lund, Sweden: Studentlitteratur (also published in 1985 in the United States, New Brunswick, N.J.: Transaction Books).

Aleksenko, D. M. 2003. From the experience of the intelligence services of the Russian Empire in combating terrorists. In *High-impact terrorism: Proceedings of a Russian-American workshop*. Washington, D.C.: National Academy Press.

Alongi, G. [1886] 1977. *La maffia*. Palermo: Sellerio.

Anonymous. 1988. *Uomo di rispetto*. Milan: Mondadori.

Arlacchi, P. 1992. *Gli uomini del disonore. La mafia siciliana nella vita del grande pentito Antonino Calderone*. Milan: Mondadori.

Arrow, K. 1974. *The limits of organization*. New York: Norton.

Austen Smith, D., and J. F. Banks. 1998. Cheap talk and burnt money. *Journal of Economic Theory* 91, 1–16.

Bacharach, M., and D. Gambetta. 2001. Trust in signs. In K. Cook (ed.), *Trust and society*. New York: Russell Sage Foundation.

Baker, P. 2002. *Polari. The lost language of gay men*. London: Routledge.

Baroin, C. 2002. Les cicatrices: La memoire du corps. In P. Moreau (ed.), *Corps romains*. Grenoble: Éditions Jérome Millon.

Barrett, R. 1978. Village modernization and changing nicknaming practises in Northern Spain. *Journal of Anthropological Research* 34 (1), 92–108.

Berk, R. A., and J. de Leeuw. 1999. Evaluation of California's inmate classification system using a generalized discontinuity design. *Journal of the American Statistical Association* 94 (448), 1045–52.

Bernard, R. H. 1968–69. Paratsoukli: Institutionalised nicknaming in rural Greece. *Ethnologia Europaea* 2–3, 65–74.

Biggs, M. 2003. When costs are beneficial. Protest as communicative suffering.

Department of Sociology, University of Oxford, Working Paper 2003–04 (www.sociology.ox.ac.uk/research/workingpapers/2003-04.pdf).

Blumberg, P. 1974. The decline and fall of the status symbol: Some thoughts on status in a post-industrial society. *Social Problems* 21, 480–98.

Blumstein, A., J. Cohen, J. A. Roth, and C. A. Visher (eds.). 1986. *Criminal careers and "career criminals."* Washington, D.C.: National Academy Press.

Bok, S. 1981. *Secrets.* Cambridge: Cambridge University Press.

Bonanno, J. 1983. *A man of honour. The autobiography of a Godfather.* London: Unwin Paperbacks.

Bottoms, A. E. 1999. Interpersonal violence and social order in prisons. In "Prisons," special issue edited by M. Tonry and J. Petersilia. *Crime and Justice* 26, 205–81.

Bowker, L. H. 1980. *Prison victimization.* New York: Elsevier.

Boyle, J. 1977. *A sense of freedom.* London: Pan Books.

Braly, M. 1976. *False starts.* London: Penguin.

Brandes, S. H. 1975. The structural and demographic implications of nicknames in Navonagal, Spain. *American Ethnologist* 2 (1), 139–48.

Buruma, I. 1985. *A Japanese mirror. Heroes and villains of Japanese culture.* London: Penguin.

Calvi, F. 1986. *La vita quotidiana della mafia dal 1950 a oggi.* Milan: Rizzoli.

Casanova, G. 1894. *The memoirs of Jacques Casanova de Seingalt. The rare unabridged London edition of 1894 translated by Arthur Machen.* eBooks @ Adelaide (http://ebooks.adelaide.edu.au/c/casanova/c33m/chapter124.html).

Chamoiseau, P. 1999. *Solibo magnificent.* London: Granta Books.

Chandler, D. L. 1976. *The criminal brotherhoods.* London: Constable.

Chandler, R. [1939] 1993. *The big sleep.* London: Penguin.

Chen, M. K., and J. M. Shapiro. 2006. Does prison harden inmates? A discontinuity-based approach. University of Chicago working paper, 4 December 2006 (http://home.uchicago.edu/~jmshapir/prison120406.pdf).

Chu, Y. K. 1999. *Triads as business.* London: Routledge.

Chwe, M.S.Y. 2001. *Rational ritual: Culture, coordination and common knowledge.* Princeton, N.J.: Princeton University Press.

Cohen, E. N. 1977. Nicknames, social boundaries and community in an Italian village. *International Journal of Contemporary Sociology* 14, 102–12.

Collier, G. A., and V. R. Bricker. 1970. Nicknames and social structure in Zinacantan. *American Anthropologist* 72 (2), 289–302.

Connell, A., and D. P. Farrington. 1996. Bullying among incarcerated young offenders: Developing an interview schedule and some preliminary results. *Journal of Adolescence* 19, 75–93.

Crandall, C. S. 1988. Social contagion of binge eating. *Journal of Personality & Social Psychology* 55 (4), 588–98.

Cummings, J., and E. Volkman. 1990. *Goombata: The improbable rise and fall of John Gotti and his gang*. New York: Avon.

Cutileiro, J. 1971. *A Portuguese rural society*. Oxford: Clarendon Press.

Dalla Chiesa, C. A. 1990. *Michele Navarra e la mafia del corleonese*. Palermo: La Zisa.

Demaris, O. 1981. *The last Mafioso*. New York: Bantam Books.

Dixit, A. K. 2003. On modes of economic governance. *Econometrica* 71 (2), 449–81.

Dixit, A. K., and B. J. Nalebuff. 1991. *Thinking strategically*. New York: Norton.

Eberhard, W. 1970. *Studies in Chinese folklore and related essays*. Indiana University Folklore Institute Monograph Series n. 23. Indiana University Center for Language Studies, Bloomington.

Edgar, K., and C. Martin. 2001. Conflicts and violence in prison. Report for the Economic and Social Research Council, January.

Edgar, K., and I. O'Donnell. 1998. Assault in prison. The 'victim's' contribution. *British Journal of Criminology* 38 (4), 635–50.

Elster, J. 1998. Deliberation and constitution making. In J. Elster (ed.), *Deliberative democracy*. Cambridge: Cambridge University Press.

Elster, J. 2000. *Ulysses unbound*. Cambridge: Cambridge University Press.

Englund, P. 1989. *Det hotade huset: Adliga föreställningar om samhället under stormaktstiden*. Stockholm: Atlantis.

Ennew, J. 1980. *The Western isles today*. Cambridge: Cambridge University Press.

Falcone, G., and M. Padovani. 1991. *Cose di Cosa Nostra*. Milano: Rizzoli.

Farrell, J., and M. Rabin. 1996. Cheap talk. *Journal of Economic Perspectives* 10 (3), 103–18.

Favazza, A .R. 1996. *Bodies under siege: Self-mutilation and body modification in culture and psychiatry*. Baltimore: John Hopkins University Press.

Foster, G. M. 1964. Speech forms and the perception of social distance in a Spanish-Speaking Mexican village. *Southwestern Journal of Anthropology* 20 (2), 107–22.

Franchetti, L. [1876] 1974. Condizioni politiche ed amministrative della Sicilia. Vol. 1 in L. Franchetti and S. Sonnino, *Inchiesta in Sicilia*. Florence: Vallecchi.

Frank, R. 1988. *Passions within reasons*. New York: Norton.

Froio, F. 1996. *Le mani sull'università*. Roma: Editori Riuniti.

Galante, G. 1986. Cent'anni di mafia. In D. Breschi et al. (eds.), *L'immaginario mafioso. La rappresentazione sociale della mafia*. Bari: Edizioni Dedalo.

Gambetta, D. 1993. *The Sicilian Mafia: The business of private protection*. Cambridge, Mass.: Harvard University Press.

Gambetta, D. 1994a. Godfather's gossip. *Archive Europeenne de Sociologie* 35, 1–26.

Gambetta, D. 1994b. Inscrutable markets. *Rationality and Society* 6, 353–68.

Gambetta, D. 1998. Concatenations of mechanisms. In P. Hedstrom and R. Swedberg (eds.), *Social mechanisms. An analytical approach to social theory*. Cambridge: Cambridge University Press.

Gambetta, D. 2005a. Deceptive mimicry in humans. Vol. 2 in S. Hurley and N. Chater (eds.), *Perspectives on imitation: From cognitive neuroscience to social science*. Cambridge, Mass.: MIT Press.

Gambetta, D. (ed.). 2005b. *Making sense of suicide missions*. Oxford: Oxford University Press.

Gambetta, D. 2009. Signalling theory. In P. Bearman and P. Hedstrom (eds.), *Oxford handbook of analytical sociology*. Oxford: Oxford University Press.

Gambetta, D., and H. Hamill. 2005. *Streetwise: How taxi drivers establish their customers' trustworthiness*. New York: Russell Sage Foundation.

Gambetta, D., and P. Reuter. 1995. Conspiracy among the many: The mafia in legitimate industries. In G. Fiorentini and S. Peltzman (eds.), *The economics of organized crime*. Cambridge: Cambridge University Press.

Gilmore, D. D. 1982. Some notes on community nicknaming in Northern Spain. *Man* 17, 686–700.

Giovino, A., with G. Brozek. 2004. *Divorced from the mob: My journey from organized crime to independent woman*. New York: Carroll & Graf.

Goffman, E. [1959] 1990. *The presentation of self in everyday life*. London: Penguin.

Goldstein, P., D. Lipton, E. Preble, I. Sobel, T. Miller, W. Abbott, W. Paige, and F. Soto. 1984. The marketing of street heroin in New York City. *Journal of Drug Issues* 14, 553–66.

Gomez, P., and M. Travaglio. 2001. *La repubblica delle banane*. Roma: Editori Riuniti.

Gosch, M. A., and R. Hammer. 1975. *The last testament of Lucky Luciano*. London: Macmillan.

Gottfredson, M. R., and T. Hirschi. 1990. *A general theory of crime*. Stanford, Calif.: Stanford University Press.

Gould, R.R.V. 2003. *Collision of wills: How ambiguity about social rank breeds conflict.* Chicago: University of Chicago Press.

Gower Chapman, C. 1973. *Milocca: A Sicilian village.* London: Allen & Unwin.

Guilford, T., and M. S. Dawkins. 1991. Receiver psychology and the evolution of animal signals. *Animal Behaviour* 42, 1–14.

Gunaratna, R. 2003. *Inside Al Qaeda: Global network of terror.* New York: Columbia University Press.

Hale, C. 1981. Modern Icelandic personal bynames. *Scandinavian Studies* 53 (4), 397–404.

Hall, D. K. 1997. *Prison tattoos.* New York: St. Martin's Griffin.

Hamill, H. 2009. *The hoods: Crime and punishment in West Belfast.* Princeton, N.J.: Princeton University Press.

Hammett, D. 1969. *The big knockover.* London: Penguin.

Hamoumou, M. 1993. *Et ils sont devenus harkis.* Paris: Fayard.

Hauser, M. D. 1996. *The evolution of communication.* Cambridge Mass.: MIT Press.

Haycock, J. 1989. Race and suicide in jails and prisons. *Journal of the National Medical Association* 81, 405–11.

Hawton, K., and K. Rodham, with E. Davis. 2006. *By their own young hand. Deliberate self-harm and suicidal ideas in adolescents.* London: Jessica Kingsley.

Herbert, W. 2000. The *yakuza* and the law. In J. S. Eades, T. Gill, and H. Befu (eds.), *Globalization and social change in contemporary Japan.* Melbourne: Transatlantic Press.

Hess, H. 1973. *Mafia and mafiosi: The structure of power.* Lexington, Mass.: Lexington.

Hiaasen, C. 1995. *Stormy weather.* New York: Alfred A. Knopf.

Hill, P. 2003. *The Japanese mafia. Yakuza, law and the state.* Oxford: Oxford University Press.

Hobbs, D. 1995. *Bad business. Professional crime in modern Britain.* Oxford: Oxford University Press.

Holland, T. J., Jr. 1990. The many faces of nicknames. *Names* 38, 255–72.

Hoyer, E. 1976. Nicknames in Northern Spain. *Folk Copenhagen* 18, 103–11.

Huesmann, L. R. 2005. Imitation and the effects of observing media violence. Vol. 2 in S. Hurley and N. Chater (eds.), *Perspective on imitation: From neuroscience to social science.* Cambridge, Mass.: MIT Press.

Hunt, G., S. Riegel, T. Morales, and D. Waldorf. 1993. Changes in prison culture—prison gangs and the case of Pepsi generation. *Social problems* 40 (3), 398–409.

Ireland, J. L. 2000. A descriptive analysis of self-harm reports among a sample of incarcerated adolescent males. *Journal of Adolescence* 23, 605–13.

Irwin, J. 1985. *The jail: Managing the underclass in American society.* Berkeley and Los Angeles: University of California Press.

Ivanoff, A., S. J. Jang, and N. J. Smyth. 1996. Clinical risk factors associated with parasuicide in prison. *International Journal of Offender Therapy and Comparative Criminology* 40 (2), 135–46.

Iwai, H. 1986. Organized crime in Japan. In R. J. Kelly (ed.), *Organized crime: A global perspective.* Totowa, N.J.: Rowman and Littlefield.

Jacquemet, M. 1992. Namechasers. *American Ethnologist* 19 (4), 733–48.

Jervis, R. 1970. *The logic of images in international relations.* New York: Columbia University Press.

Jones, J. P. 1986. *What's a name? Advertising and the concept of brands.* Aldershot: Gower.

Jones, M. (ed.). 1990. *Fake? The art of deception.* London: British Museum Publications.

Kaminski, M. 2003. Games prisoners play. Allocation of social roles in a total institution. *Rationality and Society* 15 (2), 188–217.

Kaminski, M. 2004. *Games prisoners play: The tragicomic worlds of Polish prison.* Princeton, N.J.: Princeton University Press.

Kaminski, M., and D. C. Gibbons. 1994. Prison subculture in Poland. *Crime and Delinquency* 40 (1), 105–19.

Kaminski, M., and M. Nalepa. 2006. Why do post-communist parties in new democracies hurt themselves? A Model of Strategic Pre-emption. Working paper (www.ruf.rice.edu/ ~nalepa/web-pages/A%20Model%20of%20 Strategic%20Preemption.pdf).

Kaplan, D., and A. Dubro. 1986. *Yakuza: The explosive account of Japan's criminal underworld.* New York: MacMillan.

Kimball, J. 2005. Did Thomas C. Schelling invent the madman theory? Posted 24 October on *History News Network*, George Mason University (http:// hnn.us/articles/17183.html).

King, R. D., and K. McDermott. 1995. *The state of our prisons.* Oxford: Clarendon Press.

Klein, C. 1987. The ideology of autosacrifice at the Templo Mayor. In E. H. Boone (ed.), *The Aztec Templo Mayor.* Washington, D.C.: Dumbarton Oaks.

Klein, C. 2001. Autosacrifice and bloodletting. Vol. 1 in D. Carrasco (ed.), *Oxford encyclopaedia of Mesoamerican cultures.* New York: Oxford University Press.

Klerks, P. 2000. Motives and lifestyle of drug millionaires. Paper presented at the Annual Meeting of the American Society of Criminology, San Francisco, 14–18 November.

Kolstad, A. 1996. Imprisonment as rehabilitation: Offenders' assessment of why it does not work. *Journal of Criminal Justice* 24 (4), 323–25.

Krebs, J. R., and N. B. Davies. 1993. *An introduction to behavioural ecology.* Oxford: Blackwell.

Kreps, D., and R. Wilson. 1982. Reputation and imperfect information. *Journal of Economic Theory* 27, 253–79.

Lacey, R. 1992. *Little man: Meyer Lansky and the gangster life.* London: Arrow.

Lamothe, L., and A. Nicaso. 2001. *Bloodlines: The rise and fall of the Mafia's royal family.* New York: HarperCollins.

Landis, E. 2004. Waiting for Makhno: Legitimacy and context in a Russian peasant war. *Past and Present* 183 (1), 199–236.

Laver, M. 1982. *Crime game.* Oxford: Robertson.

Lebo, H. 1997. *The Godfather legacy.* New York: Fireside.

Ledeneva, A. V. 2002. How Russia really works. Book manuscript, London.

Ledeneva, A. V. 2006. *How Russia really works: The informal practices that shaped post-soviet politics and business.* Ithaca, N.Y.: Cornell University Press.

Lewis, D. 1969. *Convention.* Cambridge, Mass.: Harvard University Press.

Licandro, A., and A. Varano. 1993. *La città dolente. Le confessioni di un sindaco corrotto.* Turin: Einaudi.

Liebling, A. 1993. Suicide attempts in male prisons. *New Law Journal* 143 (6599), 649–650.

Liebling, A. 1999. Prison suicide and prisoner coping. *Crime and Justice* 26, 283–359.

Liebling, A., and H. Krarup. 1993. *Suicide attempts in male prisons.* London: Home Office.

Livingston, M. 1997. A review of the literature on self-injurious behaviour amongst prisoners. In G. J. Towl (ed.), Suicide and self-injury in prisons: Research directions in the 1990s. *Issues in Criminological and Legal Psychology* 28, 21–35.

Livingston, M. S., and G. Beck. 1997. A cognitive-behavioural model of self-injury and bullying among imprisoned young offenders. *Issues in Criminological and Legal Psychology* 28, 45–49.

Livy. 1912. *History of Rome.* English translation by Rev. Canon Roberts. New York: E. P. Dutton & Co (www.perseus.tufts.edu/cgi-bin/ptext?lookup=Liv.++2.+12).

Lloyd-Richardson, E. E., N. Perrine, L. Dierker, and M. L. Kelley. 2007. Characteristics and functions of non-suicidal self-injury in a community sample of adolescents. *Psychological Medicine* 37 (8), 1183–92.

Lohner, J., and N. Konrad. 2006. Deliberate self-harm and suicide attempt in custody: Distinguishing features in male inmates' self-injurious behavior. *International Journal of Law and Psychiatry* 29, 370–85.

Loizos, P. 1975. *The Greek gift: Politics in a Greek village*. Oxford: Basil Blackwell.

Lo Monaco, C. 1990. A proposito della etimologia di Mafia e mafioso. *Lingua Nostra* 51 (1), 1–8

Loucks, N. 1998. HMPI Cornton Vale: Research into drugs and alcohol, violence and bullying, suicides and self-injury, and background of abuse. Occasional paper 1/98, Scottish Prison Service, Edinburgh.

Lundahl, M. 1997. Inside the predatory state. *Political economy* 24 (1), 31–50.

Lupo, S. 1988. "Il tenebroso sodalizio." Un rapporto sulla mafia Palermitana di fine ottocento. *Studi Sorici* 2, 463–89.

Maas, P. 1970. *The Valachi papers*. London: Panther.

Maas, P. 1997. *Underboss. Sammy the Bull Gravano's story of life in the Mafia*. New York: Harper Collins.

Machiavelli, N. 1976. Discorsi sopra la prima decade di Tito Livio. Libro primo. In E. Raimondi (ed.), *Opere di Niccolò Machiavelli*. Milan: Mursia Editore.

MacKenzie, N. 1967. *Secret societies*. London: Aldus Books.

Mackie, G. 1996. Ending footbinding and infibulation: A convention account. *American Sociological Review* 61, 999–1017.

Malafarina, L. 1978. *Il codice della 'ndrangheta*. N.p.: Edizioni Parallelo.

Manning, F. G. 1974. Nicknames and number plates in the British West Indies. *Journal of American Folklore* 87 (344), 123–32.

Marrale, A. 1990. *L'infamia del nome. I modi e le forme della soprannominazione a Licata*. Palermo: Gelka Edizioni.

Maurer, D. W., and A. W. Futrell. 1982. Criminal monickers. *American Speech* 57 (4), 243–55.

McAleer, K. 1994. *Dueling: The cult of honor in fin-de-siecle Germany*. Princeton, N.J.: Princeton University Press.

McCorkle, C. 1992. Personal precautions to violence in prisons. *Criminal Justice and Behavior* 19 (2), 60–173.

McDowell, J. H. 1981. Toward a semiotic of nicknaming: The Kamsa example. *Journal of American Folklore* 94 (371), 1–18.

McKitrick, E. L. 1968. The study of corruption. In S. M. Lipset and R. Hofstadter (eds.), *Sociology and history: Methods*. New York: Basic Books.

McVicar, J. 1974. *McVicar by himself.* London: Arrow Books.

Milito, L., with G. Potterton. 2003. *Mafia wife.* New York: HarperCollins.

Moretti, M. 1998. *Brigate Rosse. Intervista a cura di Carla Mosca e Rossana Rossanda.* Milan: Baldini & Castoldi.

Morgan, J., C. O'Neill, and R. Harré. 1979. *Nicknames: Their origins and social consequences.* London: Routledge and Kegan Paul.

Morgan, W. P. 1960. *Triad societies in Hong Kong.* Hong Kong: Government Press.

Mousnier, R. 1979–84. *The institutions of France under the absolute monarchy, 1598– 1789.* 2 vols. Chicago: University of Chicago Press.

Murray, T. 1992. The nicknames of American Greek-letter organizations. *Names* 40 (3), 173–94.

Natoli, L. [1909–10] 1972. *I Beati Paoli.* Introduction by Umberto Eco. Palermo: Flaccovio.

Nelson, P. 1970. Information and consumer behavior. *Journal of Political Economy* 78, 311–29.

Noonan, J. T., Jr. 1984. *Bribes.* Berkeley: University of California Press.

Novacco, D. 1959. Considerazioni sulla fortuna del termine mafia. *Belfagor* 14, 206–12.

Nozick, R. 1974. *Anarchy, state, and utopia.* Oxford: Basil Backwell.

Nwachukwu-Agbada, J.O.J. 1991. Aliases among the Anamba-Igbo: The proverbial dimension. *Names* 39 (2), 81–94.

O'Brien, J. F. 1991. *Boss of bosses: The fall of the Godfather: The FBI and Paul Castellano.* New York, London: Simon & Schuster.

Orbell, J., and R. M. Dawes. 1991. A "cognitive miser" theory of cooperators' advantage. *American Political Science Review* 85 (2), 516–28.

Perotti, R. 2002. The Italian university system: Rules vs. incentives. Paper presented at the first conference on *Monitoring Italy*, ISAE, Rome, January, (www.igier.uni-bocconi.it/whos.php?vedi=1653&tbn=albero&id_doc=177).

Perotti, R. 2008. *L' università truccata.* Torino: Einaudi.

Phelan, M. P., and S. A. Hunt. 1998. Prison gang members' tattoos as identity work: The visual communication of moral career. *Symbolic Interaction* 21 (3), 277–98.

Pina-Cabral, J. 1984. Nicknames and the experience of community. *Man* 19 (1), 148–50.

Pistone, D. J. With Richard Woodley. 1989. *Donnie Brasco.* New York: Signet.

Pitt-Rivers, J. 1954. *The people of the Sierra.* London: Weidenfeld and Nicolson.

Pizzini-Gambetta, V. 1996. I mafiosi e le donne. Doctoral thesis, Rome.

Pizzini-Gambetta, V. 1999. Gender norms in the Sicilian Mafia. In M. L. Anrnot and C. Usborne (eds.), *Gender and crime in modern Europe*. London: UCL Press.

Plato. 1942. *Republic*. London: Everyman's Library.

Plutarch. 1992. *Essays*. London: Penguin.

Polsky, H. W. 1962. *Cottage six: The social system of delinquent boys in residential treatment*. New York: Russell Sage Foundation.

Poma, R., and E. Pirrone. 1972. *La mafia. Nonni e nipoti*. Firenze: Vallecchi.

Poole, E. D., and R. M. Regoli. 1983. Violence in juvenile institutions. *Criminology* 21 (2), 213–32.

Popkin, S. L. 1979. *The rational peasant: The political economy of rural society in Vietnam*. Berkeley: University of California Press.

Power, K., and A. Spencer. 1987. Parasuicidal behaviour of detained Scottish young offenders. *International Journal of Offender Therapy and Comparative Criminology* 31 (3), 227–35.

Powis, B. 2002. Offenders' risk of serious harm: A literature review. RDS Occasional Paper No. 81 (www.homeoffice.gov.uk/rds/pdfs2/occ81risk .pdf).

Preti, A., and M. T. Cascio. 2006. Prison suicides and self-harming behaviours in Italy, 1990–2002. *Medicine, Science and Law* 46 (2), 127–34.

Puglia, G. M. 1930. Il mafioso non e' un associato per delinquere. *La Scuola Positiva*, n.s., 10, 452–57.

Rasmusen, E. 1989. *Games and information*. Oxford: Basil Blackwell.

Renda, F. 1988. *I Beati Paoli*. Palermo: Sellerio.

Reuter, P. 1983. *Disorganized crime. The economics of the visible hand*. Cambridge, Mass.: MIT Press.

Reuter, P. 1987. *Racketeering in legitimate industries: A study in the economics of intimidation*. Santa Monica, Calif.: RAND Corporation.

Reuter, P., J. Rubinstein, and S. Wynn. 1982. *Racketeering in legitimate industries: Two case studies*. Washington, D.C.: National Institute of Justice.

Rinella, L. 2006. *Dieci anni di mafia a Bari e dintorni. Dal Conte Ugolino al Canto del Cigno*. Progedit: Cassano Murge.

Rivlin, A. 2006. *Suicide and parasuicide at a therapeutic community prison for men*. M.Phil. diss., University of Oxford.

Rohlfs, G. 1984. *Soprannomi Siciliani*. Palermo: Centro di Studi Filologici e Linguistici Siciliani.

Room, A. 1987. History of branding. In J. M. Murphy (ed.), *Branding: A key marketing tool*. London: Macmillan.

Rose-Ackerman, S. 1978. *Corruption: A study in political economy*. New York: Academic Press.

Rose-Ackerman, S. 1997. Corruption and development. In B. Pleakovic and J. Stiglitz (eds.), *Annual World Bank Conference on Development Economics 1997*. World Bank.

Rosen, P. M., and B. W. Walsh. 1989. Patterns of contagion in self-mutilation epidemics. *American Journal of Psychiatry* 146 (5), 656–58.

Rosenberg, B. 1945. Meet the gang. *Journal of Criminal Law and Criminology* 36 (2), 98–103.

Russo, N. (ed.). 1964. *Antologia della mafia*. Palermo: Il Punto Edizioni.

Ryan, D. 1958. Names and naming in Mendi. *Oceania* 29, 109–17.

Sabini, J., and M. Silver. 1982. *Moralities of everyday life*. Oxford: Oxford University Press.

Saller, R. 2000. Status and patronage. In A. K. Bowman, P. Garnsey, and D. Rathbone (eds.), *The Cambridge ancient history. The high empire, AD 70–192*, vol. 11. Cambridge: Cambridge University Press.

Sanders, T. 2005. *Sex work. A risky business*. Cullompton: Willan.

Schelling, C. T. 1956. An essay on bargaining. *American Economic Review* 46 (3), 281–306.

Schelling, T. 1960. *The strategy of conflict*. Cambridge, Mass.: Harvard University Press.

Schelling, T. 1984. *Choice and consequence*. Cambridge, Mass.: Harvard University Press.

Schelling, T. 1998. Social mechanisms and social dynamics. In P. Hedstrom and R. Swedberg (eds.), *Social mechanisms. An analytical approach to social theory*. Cambridge: Cambridge University Press.

Schilcht, E. 1991. Economic analysis and organized religion. Paper prepared for the fourth Workshop on Demography, Economics and Organized Religion, 14–15 June, Linacre College, Oxford.

Schilling, M. 2003. *The yakuza movie guide: A guide to Japanese gangster films*. Berkeley: Stone Bridge Press.

Schmid, A. P., and J. de Graaf. 1982. *Violence as communication. Insurgent terrorism and the Western news media*. London: Sage.

Schrader, P. 1974. Yakuza-Eiga: A primer. *Film Comment* 10 (1), 9–17.

Severi, C. 1980. Le nom de lignée: Les sobriquets dans un village d'Emilie. *Homme* 20 (4), 105–18.

Seymour, C. 1996. *Yakuza diary: Doing time in the Japanese underworld*. New York: Atlantic Monthly Press.

Shaw, C. R. 1966. *The jack-roller: A delinquent boy's own story*. Chicago: University of Chicago Press.

Shea, S. 1993. Personality characteristics of self-mutilating male prisoners. *Journal of Clinical Psychology* 49 (4), 576–85.

Shields, I. W., and D. J. Simourd. 1991. Predicting predatory behavior in a population of incarcerated young offenders. *Criminal Justice and Behavior* 18 (2), 180–94.

Shleifer, A., and R. W. Vishny. 1993. Corruption. *Quarterly Journal of Economics* 108 (3), 599–617.

Simmel, G. [1908] 1991. *Secret et sociétés secrètes*. Strasbourg: Circ.

Simone, R. 1993. *L'università dei tre tradimenti*. Bari: Laterza.

Skipper, J. K. 1985. Nicknames of notorious twentieth-century American deviants. *Deviant Behavior* 6 (1), 99–114.

Skipper, J. K. 1986. Coal miners and group solidarity. *Names* 34 (2): 134–45.

Skipper, J. K., and P. L. Leslie. 1990. The systematic study of personal nicknames: A small step forward. *Names* 38 (4), 253–54.

Skyrms, B. 1996. *Evolution of the social contract*. Cambridge: Cambridge University Press.

Smith, A., and F. Varese. 2001. Payment, protection and punishment: The role of information and reputation in the Mafia. *Rationality and Society* 13 (3), 349–93.

Smith, D. C. 1975. *The mafia mystique*. London: Hutchinson.

Smith, M. G. 1962. *Kinship and community in Carriacou*. New Haven, Conn.: Yale University Press.

Sosis, R. H., C. Kress, and J. S. Bosterb. 2007. Scars for war: Evaluating alternative signalling explanations for cross-cultural variance in ritual costs. *Evolution and Human Behavior* 28, 234–247.

Sparks, R., A. E. Bottoms, and W. Hay. 1996. *Prisons and the problem of order*. Oxford: Clarendon Press.

Spence, A. M. 1974. *Market signalling: Informational transfer in hiring and related screening processes*. Cambridge, Mass.: Harvard University Press.

Stark, D. 1981. The yakuza: Japanese crime incorporated. Ph.D. diss., Michigan University.

Stiglitz, J. E. 2000. The contributions of the economics of information to twentieth century economics. *Quarterly Journal of Economics* 115 (4), 1441–78.

Strayer, J. 1970. *On the medieval origins of the modern state*. Princeton, N.J.: Princeton University Press.

Sullivan, M. L. 1989. *"Getting paid": Youth crime and work in the inner city.* Ithaca, N.Y.: Cornell University Press.

Sutherland, E. H. (ed.). 1957. *The professional thief. By a professional thief.* Chicago: University of Chicago Press.

Swift, J. 1990. *Gulliver's travels.* London: Nonesuch Press.

Sykes, G. 1958. *The society of captives.* Princeton, N.J.: Princeton University Press.

Tamony, P. 1969. Coca-Cola: The most-lawed name. *Names* 17, 278–83.

Taylor, C. W. 2007. "The lawless merchant": Heroin branding and order in spite of law. Draft diss. chapter, Department of Political Science, Stanford University.

Taylor, T. 2002. *The buried soul. How humans invented death.* London: Fourth Estate.

Teresa, V. 1973. *My life in the mafia.* London: Mac Gibbon.

Toch, H. 1977. *Living in prison: The ecology of survival.* New York: Free Press.

Travaglio, M., and E. Veltri. 2001. *L' odore dei soldi. Origini e misteri delle fortune di Silvio Berlusconi.* Roma: Editori Riuniti.

Travis, W., and R. Curtis. 2000. The heraldry of heroin: "Dope stamps" and the dynamics of drug markets in New York City. *Journal of Drug Issues* 30, 225–60.

Tzvetkova, M. 2008. Wrestling for supremacy. The evolution of extra-legal protection in Bulgaria, 1989–1999. D.Phil. diss., University of Oxford.

United States Senate, Permanent Subcommittee on Investigations. 1984. Waterfront corruption. Report, 27 March. Washington, D.C.: U.S. Government Printing Office.

Valentine, B. 2000. *Gangs and their tattoos: Identifying gangbangers on the street and in prison.* Boulder, Colo.: Paladin Press.

Varese, F. 1991. Ethnic groups as strategic coalitions. M.Phil. diss., Cambridge University.

Varese, F. 1998. The society of the *Vory-v-Zakone*, 1930s–1950s. *Cahiers du Monde Russe* 39, 515–38.

Varese, F. 2000. Pervasive corruption. In A. Ledeneva and M. Kurkchiyan (eds.), *Economic crime in Russia.* The Hague: Kluwer Law International.

Varese, F. 2001. *The Russian mafia.* Oxford: Oxford University Press.

Vitale, S. 1999. *Pushkin's button.* London: Fourth Estate.

Walters, G. D. 1998. Time series and correlational analyses of inmate-initiated assaultive incidents in a large correctional system. *International Journal of Offender Therapy and Comparative Criminology* 42 (2), 124–32.

Watson, H. 1992. *Women in the city of the dead*. London: Hurst.

Wendel, T., and R. Curtis. 2000. Heraldry of heroin: "Dope stamps" and the dynamics of drug markets in New York City. *Journal of Drug Issues* 30, 225–59.

Williams, B. 1988. Formal structures and social reality. In D. Gambetta (ed.), *Trust: Making and breaking cooperative relations*. Oxford: Basil Blackwell.

Williamson, H. 1965. *Hustler!* New York: Avon.

Williamson, O. 1983. Credible commitments: Using hostages to support exchange. *American Economic Review* 73, 519–40.

Williamson, O. 1993. Calculativeness, trust and economic organisations. *Journal of Law and Economics* 36, 453–86.

Williamson, O. 1999. *The mechanisms of governance*. New York: Oxford University Press.

Wilson, P. J. 1969. Reputation and respectability: A suggestion for Caribbean ethnology. *Man* 4 (1), 70–84.

Wright, K. 1989. Race and economic marginality in explaining prison adjustment. *Journal of Research in Crime and Delinquency* 26, 67–89.

Wright, T. R., and S. H. Decker. 1997. *Armed robbers in action*. Boston: Northeastern University Press.

Zahavi, A. 1980. Ritualization and the evolution of movement signals. *Behaviour* 72 (1–2), 77–81.

Zahavi, A. 1975. Mate selection: A selection for a handicap. *Journal of Theoretical Biology* 53, 205–14.

Zahavi, A., and A. Zahavi. 1997. *The handicap principle*. Oxford: Oxford University Press.

Zedner, L. 1992. *Women, crime, and custody in Victorian England*. Oxford: Oxford University Press.

Index

Marrale, Antonino, 302n8

Marsala, Mariano, 207, 228

Marsala, Vincenzo, 211–12

Martana, Bobby "Blue," 260

Martin, Carol, 80, 89–90, 91, 94, 100, 104

martyrs, 139

Maruca, Steve, 67

Mattson, Greggor, 167–68

Maurer, D. W., 230, 244–45

maxi trial, 232, 242–43

McAleer, Kevin, 143–44

McCorkle, C., 88, 91, 285n9

McCulloch, Tom, 122

McDowell, Jeremy, 123

McVicar, John, 110

Mensur, 143–44

Mickey Blue Eyes, 256

Migliore, Antonino, 179

Milito, Louie, 269

Milito, Louise, 269

mimicry: criminal communications and,
    xvi–xvii; mafia and, 215–17; protec-
    tion and, 215–17; signals and, 175–76;
    toughness and, 87–88; trademarks and,
    215–17, 300n80; yakuza and, 217

Minbo no Onna, 251–55

Miyamoto, Nobuko, 252

Mob Woman. See Minbo no Onna

Modestov, Nikolai, 271

Monk, Chris, 156–57

Montalto, Francesco Paolo, 228–29

Moretti, Mario, 262

Morgan, J. C., 303n12, 306n79

moustache gang, 176–77

movies, mobsters and: advertising and,
    268–73; conventions and, 264–68;
    imitation and, 261–64; publicity and,
    253–54; Russian gangsters and, 266;
    story content and, 257–61; symbiotic
    relationship of, 255–57, 308n28; yakuza

and, 252, 307n6. See also *Godfather;
    Minbo no Onna*; other film titles

Mucius, Caius "Scaevola," 115–17

Murder Must Advertise (Sayers), 153

Murder on the Orient Express (Christie),
    282n15

Murray, T., 302n8

Musacchia, Rocco, 256, 259–60, 261

Musketeers of Pig Alley, 265

Mute Witness, 255

muti, 188–89

Mutolo, Gaspare, 52

Nalepa, Monika, 282n4

Napolitano, Dominick "Sonny Black," 24,
    49, 67

National Prison Survey of 1991, 89

Natoli, Luigi: "Coriolano della foresta,"
    303n10

Navarra, Michele, 207

'ndranghetista, 155–56

Newell, Mike, 258

New York City: criminal recruitment and,
    9–10; heroin stamps and, 201–2; mafia
    families in, 225–26

Nicaso, Antonio, 245

nicknames: attribution of, 232–37; code
    names and, 233–35; as conventional
    signals, 230–31; definition of, 233,
    302n8; functionalist explanations and,
    238; hit men and, 242; identification
    problem and, 239–43; mafia and, 235–
    37, 304n48; male team activities and,
    247–48; as marks of leadership, 236–37;
    mockery and, 246–47; personal oddities
    and, 235–36; rank and, 242, 305n63;
    survival of, 238–39; traits and, 231;
    unintended consequences and, 243–44;
    uses of, 238–46; vory and, 245–46;
    yakuza and, 249–50, 306n88